ARCHAEOLOGY
An Introduction

The History, Principles and
Methods of Modern Archaeology

Third Edition Fully Revised

Kevin Greene

University of Pennsylvania Press
Philadelphia

Copyright © 1983 by Kevin Greene.

First published 1983 by B.T. Batsford, Ltd.; revised 1991, 1995.

First published in the United States 1995
by the University of Pennsylvania Press.

U.S. Library of Congress Cataloging-in-Publication Data

Greene, Kevin.
Archaeology, an introduction: the history, principles, and
methods of modern archaeology / Kevin Greene. – Rev. ed.
    p. cm.
Includes bibliographical reference (p.) and index.
ISBN 0-8122-1570-2
1. Archaeology. I. Title
CC165.G694 1995
930. 1–dc20   95–6800 CIP

Printed in Great Britain

ISBN 0-8122-1570-2

Contents

List of illustrations

Acknowledgements

The content of this book includes aspects of the subject that I have always found interesting, supplemented by issues raised by Adult Education students when I first began teaching in higher education. I remain grateful for the intellectual stimulation that I gained from these students on a variety of courses in Hexham, Ponteland, Rothbury, Wallsend and Newcastle upon Tyne. The book also reflects the content of a first-year lecture course, 'Introduction to Archaeology', that I have taught in the University of Newcastle upon Tyne since 1978. It is taken by many students who wish to include archaeology in a broader Arts and Science degree, in addition to those specializing in Single Honours Archaeology. Other students follow the course as a subsidiary part of degrees such as History, Geography, Psychology or Music. The book has been influenced by what I felt this mix of students might usefully learn about archaeology. I appreciate their many comments (positive and negative) over the years.

Several individual archaeologists have influenced this book. Among my formative influences were Richard Atkinson and other members of his Department of Archaeology at University College, Cardiff, notably Bill Manning and Leslie Alcock. My debt to the writings of Glyn Daniel and Stuart Piggott on the history of archaeology will be apparent throughout this book. Graham Webster provided a 'role-model' both as archaeology's leading 'adult educator' and as a writer of high-quality books for general readers. I also gained much from working in adult education with Colin Burgess during my early years in Newcastle. Sadly, the most influential of the colleagues I joined in the Department of Archaeology in 1977 – George Jobey, Martin Harrison and John Gillam – have all died in recent years. Fortunately, my current colleagues Chris Tolan-Smith and John Chapman continually enhance my awareness of developments in archaeological method and theory. I am also indebted to Newcastle University's library facilities, in both the main Robinson Library and the departmental Cowen Library, where Pat Southern provides outstanding resources and the empathy of a fellow Batsford author.

Finally, I thank my wife Julia and my children Danny, Liam and Eva for help, support and forbearance at all stages of the Great Rewriting that took place in 1993 and early 1994. I also thank my parents, John and Betty Greene, for stimulating and nurturing my early childhood passion for archaeology, and maintaining their interest ever since. My mother's scientific training in biology opened my eyes to the natural setting of archaeological sites, and she has acted as a useful proofreader and scrutineer of my written style recently. My father's career in the Health Service acted as a useful reminder that compassion for the living should not be overlooked in the pursuit of the distant past, while his research and publications since retirement show that there is nothing indispensable about secondary and higher education. I have also learnt a lot from my brother, Patrick, who followed a very different path through archaeology that eventually led to the directorship of the Greater Manchester Museum of Science and Industry.

Advice and illustrations

I have received help from a large number of individuals in Britain and abroad, some contributing ideas about this new edition, many in providing illustrations. Most of the latter are mentioned in the captions, but others include: Martin Aitken; Lindsay Allason-Jones; Martin Carver; Andy Chopping; Mike Corbishley; J G B Haigh; Heinrich Härke; Robert Hedges; Dr S Ipson; Catherine Johns; Andrew Jones; Mick Jones; Catherine Lavier; David Mattingly; Samantha Middleton; Martin Millett; Barbara Ottaway; Ian Oxley; Georgina Plowright; Julian Richards; Bob Rutland; Chris Saunders; Eleanor Scott; Celia Sterne; Liz Watson; Humphrey Welfare; Felicity Wild; John Peter Wild.

Kevin Greene, May, 1994

UNIVERSITY OF
NEWCASTLE UPON TYNE

Note on references

References to publications made in the text are given in author/year form (e.g. Evans 1860) and are listed in the alphabetical order of their authors' names in the consolidated bibliography at the end of the book. Wherever possible, *books* (rather than articles in periodicals) have been cited in section headings within chapters. These may either be the principal publication on the subject or a particularly good example of the subject that is being explained. References made within the text also include articles in journals (notably *Antiquity*). The extensive 'Guide to further reading' that begins on p.185 includes many further works related to the themes of the individual chapters; details of these are not repeated in the consolidated bibliography.

Preface

Who is this book aimed at?

I have tried to provide a readable and informative book suitable for just about any interested reader from mid-teens upwards. I envisage it as a first point of contact with the subject, and hope that it may lead on to wider reading. It is certainly *not* designed as a textbook, for I lack the comprehensive range of knowledge that this term implies. The book reflects *my* interests, and it does not claim to venture very far beyond my own expertise in the archaeology of Roman and early medieval western Europe. Since introductions to archaeology tend to be written by prehistorians, readers will probably find more examples drawn from historical periods in this book than in most others.

The back cover of the first edition carried an apparently warm recommendation – 'this book scores a 'bull's-eye' – that had actually concluded a rather unenthusiastic review:

Kevin Greene's book is written for the dominant market of the 1980s, that is the first year undergraduate aiming to become a professional archaeologist. Indeed any general reader picking up this new book would be overawed by the massive scale of everything, and the complexity of all the operations, to say nothing of the jargon of the 'new' archaeology. But though one might regret that university teaching is so biassed in favour of large-scale, rather than small scale operations, that's the way it is, and for the market that actually exists, this book scores a 'bull's-eye'. (*Current Archaeology* January 1984, 221)

In reality, a book aimed solely at archaeology undergraduates in Britain would sell very few copies. The North American tradition of 'blockbuster' textbooks has never found favour in Britain; despite its British origins, Renfrew and Bahn's *Archaeology: Theories, methods, and practice* (1991) clearly targets an American market. My own experience, reinforced by reports from colleagues in other universities, is that students read all or parts of my book to gain a *general* understanding of a topic, and then turn to Renfrew and Bahn (or specialist books and articles) for further details and examples.

'Blurbs' dreamed up by copy-writers for book-club brochures captured my intentions more perceptively (and concisely) than most reviewers. My favourite examples of this genre remain 'No other survey says so much that's new about so much that's old' and 'Shows you how fieldwork is done; explains how to interpret remains to get a vivid picture of the past'. I also appreciated the unintentional irony of 'The perfect initiation, clearly written for students and armchair archaeologists' and 'Even if you never take a trowel in hand, this is a totally absorbing look at the practices and methods of the people who spend a lifetime digging up the past'.

Why is a new edition needed, and how does it differ from its predecessor?

Archaeology has moved forward since 1983. Technical advances are most visible in chapters 2, 4 and 5 (fieldwork, dating and science). Existing methods have improved in range and accuracy, and new methods have been developed. Relatively minor changes in emphasis and interpretation appear in chapters 1 ('origins and growth') and 3 (excavation), but chapter 6 (theoretical archaeology) is substantially new, and reveals how much a subject may change in ten years. It now contains discussions of matters that were only just getting on to the archaeological agenda in the early 1980s, such as 'heritage', gender, or the rights of indigenous peoples. Even where the content has changed relatively little I hope that the style has improved, for this edition has been prepared with the help of a microcomputer; I do not think that a single sentence has survived intact. There are now entire books devoted to topics that in 1983 appeared only in specialist journals. However, the proliferation of books on *individual* archaeological techniques or scientific methods has not been matched by new *general* books (with a few honourable exceptions, such as Aitken's *Science-based Dating in Archaeology*, 1990). Thus, guidance on further reading remains an important part of my book, but I have gathered it into a single section this time to allow it to be updated more easily whenever the book is reprinted.

1 The Idea of the Past

One cannot see archaeology emerging as a recognizable discipline until the later nineteenth century; before this we have an amorphous antiquarianism. (Piggott 1989, 8)

The history of archaeology is the history of the ideas that have prevailed, the ideas that have been right in the long term, and it is proper to see the past from the present. The necessary qualification is some real understanding of context, some real respect for the potentials and possibilities that were available, and a decent humility about our ancestors' accomplishments. (Chippindale 1989, 33)

Our knowledge of archaeology is founded upon many basic assumptions that are far from secure and unchanging. Theories produced by scholars may be modified by discussion and criticism, only to be overthrown by a single new idea or piece of evidence; equally, they may simply go out of fashion for no particular reason. The vision of a subject suddenly reversing its ideas can be disconcerting to people who are not directly involved, especially if they have received a traditional education based upon the learning of 'facts' that lead to 'correct' answers. People tend either to reject new ideas or to embrace them enthusiastically, for reasons that may be emotional as much as rational. It is easy to understand why theories from outside the academic world (frequently involving extraterrestrial influences) are so popular, particularly when they dismiss academic 'experts' as rea-c-tionary snobs unwilling to consider ideas proposed by anyone outside their ivory towers.

The most sensible approach to archaeological evidence in the closing years of the twentieth century is not to attempt to keep up with every shift in opinions, but to understand how they were arrived at in the first place. It takes a certain amount of courage to accept that there are no 'right' answers, and that all interpretations are based upon assumptions of varying probability, never certainty. It is very stimulating to approach archaeology without necessarily deciding whether a new interpretation is 'right', but by analysing it in a straightforward manner. How did the archaeologist reach that conclusion? What kind of evidence was involved? What are the assumptions upon which it is based? Several chapters of this book attempt to explain the sources of information on which the assumptions and interpretations are based, and they also aim to show how the basic evidence is actually recovered and studied.

The aim of this first chapter is to give an impression of the slow emergence of archaeology by looking at how some of the principal concerns of modern archaeologists developed in the past. Four issues will be examined: the idea of early human origins; the recognition and interpretation of human tools; the observation and recording of ancient sites; and, finally, the investigation (with the help of excavation) of early civilizations. These issues are not entirely separate, and they will not be looked at in strict chronological order. They reflect my personal judgement of the importance of the concepts involved; I will discuss some aspects further in later chapters.

At first sight, the assumptions early antiquaries made about the past, and the concepts within which they framed their writings, may seem naive today. However, it is important that the benefit of hindsight does not make us forget the constraints of the social and intellectual context in which antiquarians lived and worked. For example, in the early nineteenth century, Danish scholars first organized prehistoric objects into three successive 'Ages' (Stone, Bronze and Iron), but they were content to set these Ages into a time-span that began in 4004 BC, the date of the creation of the Earth calculated from the Book of Genesis by seventeenth-century theologians. The much longer time scale demanded by geology and evolution did not finally displace the biblical scheme until the 1860s. However, such momentous reorientations did not end in the nineteenth century; the dating of prehistory has undergone two significant revisions since the Second World War, first as the radiocarbon dating technique was introduced and accepted, and later as further research demanded a revision and recalibration of its results. Some of today's most convincing interpretations of the past will undoubtedly require comparable re-examination as more sites are excavated, dating techniques are improved and new ideas are devised.

The lesson to be learned from the history of archaeology is clear. We work within the limitations of the best available assumptions, but these are subject to unpredictable changes. Little is gained from treating older research as simply redundant and sometimes humorous; we may learn a great deal of value by examining how early antiquaries and archaeologists tackled the formidable problem of making sense of the human past, without most of the libraries, museums, travel and technical facilities available today. From this point of view, a study of their work will result in admiration, not amusement. At the same time, it is important to avoid the tendency to reduce early scholars to 'textbook cardboard' by giving them credit for inklings of ideas that we consider important today, without understanding the setting in which those ideas were originally formulated (Gould 1987, 5).

1 Human origins

An interest in origins may be a very early aspect of human consciousness. The possibility that the phenomenon of death led to reflections on afterlife or rebirth amongst early prehistoric peoples is suggested by burial rites. For example, around 23,000 years ago two young boys and a man were buried at Sunghir (200 km north-east of Moscow) with stone, bone and ivory objects including spears, pendants, beads and animal carvings (Gamble 1986, 188). Many societies have developed sophisticated mythologies to explain their origins, and, in association with religion, the whole environment may be fitted into an orderly system in which major natural features may be the work of gods (Trigger 1989, 29). Artificial mounds, abandoned occupation sites and ancient objects were often associated with deities, fairies, ancestors or other denizens of the world of mythology, and explanations of this kind abound in surviving folklore; an awareness of the physical remains of the past, and attempts to explain them, lie behind the modern disciplines of archaeology and history. However, the development of strictly archaeological (as opposed to antiquarian) thinking similar to our own belongs to very recent centuries.

Collections of antique objects and works of art were not uncommon in the Ancient World, from Babylon in the sixth century BC to the civilizations of Greece and Rome, and more sporadically in the medieval period (Trigger 1989, 29–35). Roman philosophical poetry of the first century BC contained ideas about the successive importance of stone, bronze and iron as materials for the manufacture of implements. Although this 'Three-Age System' was widely accepted by AD 1800, it was not applied in a practical way to ancient objects until 1816 (below, p. 26). Greek and Roman philosophers and travellers wrote accounts of peoples (real and mythological) whose lifestyles were more primitive than their own, partly out of curiosity but primarily in an attempt to judge their own societies (Blundell 1986, 187–201). It is difficult now for us to appreciate the basic problem that confronted historians or philosophers in literate societies right up to the eighteenth century AD. They were able to pursue their origins through surviving historical records, but beyond the earliest documents lay a complete void, containing unverifiable traditions that merged into a mythological and religious world of ancestors and gods. Most conspicuously lacking was a concept of the depth of time (Rossi 1984). Until the mid-nineteenth century, most historians found no difficulty in compressing the period before written records into a biblical time scale involving only six to seven thousand years. Interpretations of geology or evolution that demanded an unimaginable length of time were fiercely contested. Even today, the depth of archaeological and geological time is still grossly underestimated in the contemporary mythology of cartoons, in which no prehistoric man is complete without a stone axe or wooden club, a simple one-piece animal-skin garment, and perhaps a vehicle with stone wheels.

The fundamental problem of chronology did not change significantly between the Greek and Roman period and the eighteenth century AD. The only possible basis for the study of sites and artefacts was to link them to peoples and events known from documents, or otherwise dismiss them into a vacuum. Samuel Johnson stated: 'All that is really known of the ancient state of Britain is contained in a few pages. ... We can know no more than what old writers have told us' (Daniel 1963, 35). Historians of the Middle Ages (such as Geoffrey of Monmouth, who died *c.* 1155) filled out early periods with fantastic tales of mythological and real figures like Brutus the Trojan, King Arthur and Julius Caesar. The only real difference between Geoffrey and the 'enlightened' historians of the eighteenth century was in the quantity of mythology that they accepted; later writers tended to associate earthworks with Romans or Danes rather than Trojans or Druids, but a concept of prehistoric time was still missing. One positive development was that a greater understanding of the way of life of ancient peoples (such as the Britons described by Julius Caesar) could be gained from reports of 'savages' encountered by European traders and colonists in Africa or the Americas; prehistoric artefacts found in Europe could also be compared with those still in use in primitive societies (Trigger 1989, 53; below, p. 25–6).

1.1 Prehistory and history
(Daniel & Renfrew 1988)

Archaeologists today still tend to be divided into two categories – prehistorians and historical archaeologists. This division is not particularly helpful, but it does distinguish between the latter, who study people or places within periods during which written records were made, from the former, who are concerned with any period before the use of documents. Historical archaeologists usually possess a basic framework of dates and a general idea of the society of a particular period into which to fit their findings, while prehistorians have to create some kind of framework for themselves from artefacts and sites alone. The methods used by both kinds of archaeologist are very much the same, and there is considerable overlap between their ideas and interests; the most effective of today's scholars happily cross the boundary between prehistory and history. There was a distinct difference in the past, however. Ancient historians or biblical scholars could set out to locate physical traces on the ground of events and civilizations described in literature, unlike local historians, natural scientists or collectors who tried to make sense of artefacts or graves surviving from times before the earliest surviving written records. Because of early progress in classical archaeology, many historical archaeologists assumed that the written word had an innate primacy over physical evidence, and '... continued to regard prehistoric archaeology as greatly inferior to the archaeological study of periods that can be illuminated by written texts' (Trigger 1989, 40).

If early 'prehistorians' (the term only became current after 1850: Chippindale 1988) believed in a biblical Creation in 4004 BC (or some other date calculated from the Old Testament), at least there was an upper limit to the age of any of the items that they studied. If they did not, the potential questions were almost infinite, and at first sight insoluble. Which sites and objects were in use at the same time, and how many years elapsed between those that looked primitive and those that seemed more advanced? Did technical improvements represent a gradual series of inventions made by a single people, or did innovations mark the arrival of successive waves of conquerors with superior skills? The first step essential to any progress was a recognition of the amount of time occupied by human development in prehistoric times, and this advance took place in the first half of the nineteenth century. In the view of Bruce Trigger (1989, 70–3), the liberation of archaeologists from this 'impasse of antiquarianism' had two distinct consequences. The first was the invention of new dating methods in Scandinavia, and the second was the study of human origins in France and England, which 'added a vast, and hitherto unimagined time depth to human history'. I will examine dating methods below, after exploring the more fundamental and dramatic issue of human origins.

1.2 Human antiquity
(Grayson 1983)

The Society of Antiquaries of London was founded in 1717, and in 1770 it began to publish an impressive periodical, *Archaeologia*, whose style and format have changed little up to the present day. Volume 13 (published in 1800) included a minor item, whose full significance did not become apparent for sixty years. Amongst an assortment of papers on subjects ranging from a Roman fort in Germany to historical documents associated with British royalty was a short letter from John Frere, drawing attention to some observations he had made in a clay pit at Hoxne in Suffolk. He reported flint weapons found at a depth of twelve feet in a layer of gravel, overlain by a bed of sand containing bones of extinct animals and, remarkably, shells and remains of marine creatures, '... which may be conjectured to have been once the bottom, or at least the shore, of the sea'. Frere was evidently conscious of the problematic implications: 'It may be conjectured that the different strata were formed by inundations happening at distant periods. ... The situation in which these weapons were found may tempt us to refer them to a very remote period indeed; even beyond that of the present world ...' (1800, 205). Frere made no reference to the biblical Creation and Flood, and he died before an accumulation of similar finds began to suggest an alternative view of human origins.

Finds of human bones and artefacts associated with remains of extinct animals were noted with growing frequency in Europe in the early nineteenth century – and were as often explained away by theologians as accidental. By the time of Frere's death in 1807 a key figure was already becoming interested in archaeology in France: Boucher de Perthes (fig. 1.1) spent many years studying the gravel quarries of northern France and was a strong advocate of two ideas. First, he was impressed by the great depth and variety of the deposits of sediments and he felt that they were far too complex to result from the biblical flood, although he did not reject the authority of the Old Testament. Second, he fought hard to convince contemporaries that the flint tools that he had collected from the gravels were made by humans, and that they could be recognized by their artificial shaping (fig. 1.2). It was an uphill struggle: he commented that 'at the very mention of the words "axe" and "diluvium", I observe a smile on the face of those to whom I speak. It is the workmen who help me, not the geologists'

1.1 Jacques Boucher de Perthes, portrayed by Grèvedon in 1831. He published many ideas about artefacts and their stratification derived from Casimir Picard without acknowledgement. His bombastic manner diminished the credibility of his own beliefs: 'Few people took his book seriously; of those who had met him, none' (Evans 1956, 282). Despite this, Boucher de Perthes' central idea – that human artefacts of great age were to be found in the gravels of northern France – was confirmed by Evans and Prestwich in 1859. *Society of Antiquaries, London*

(Daniel 1981, 52). Because he was able to prove that these tools came from within ancient gravel beds, he concluded that humans had existed before 'the cataclysm that gave our country its present configuration', and that these humans were therefore also contemporary with a wide range of extinct animals. Because Boucher de Perthes did not abandon the idea of floods, he suggested that Adam and Eve resulted from a later and separate Creation, long after the Flood whose results he observed had wiped out earlier humans. 'Let us not bargain over the duration of ages; let

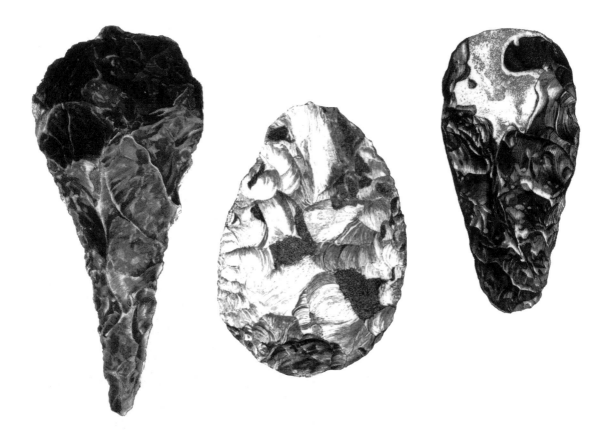

1.2 These flint implements from the Somme valley were published by John Evans soon after his visit to the sites where they were found. 'That they really are implements fashioned by the hand of man, a single glance at a collection of them placed side by side . . . would, I think, be sufficient to convince even the most sceptical. There is a uniformity of shape, a correctness of outline, and a sharpness about the cutting edges and points, which cannot be due to anything but design' (Evans 1860, 288). The 'hand axe' (centre) is approx. 17 cm long. *Evans 1860, pl. 15*

1.3 Geologist Joseph Prestwich (left) examining flint implements of the kind found in gravel pits in northern France, where Boucher de Perthes claimed to have found them in deep deposits together with bones of extinct animals. Prestwich and John Evans were convinced of the authenticity of these finds, and published reports that led rapidly to acceptance by most scientists and archaeologists. *Prestwich 1899, facing p. 126*

us believe that the days of the creation, those days that began before our sun, were the days of God, the interminable days of the world. Let us remember, finally, that for this eternal God a thousand centuries are no more than one second ...' (Daniel 1967, 62). Whether people accepted this modified view of the Creation or not, not only was the Earth becoming increasingly ancient, but humans were also being drawn back into a void of seemingly immeasurable depth.

Not all geologists treated Boucher de Perthes' work with disbelief and amusement. An English geologist, Joseph Prestwich (fig. 1.3), together with an authority on ancient implements, John Evans (fig. 1.4), organized a visit to France to meet him and to see the celebrated gravel pits. On the first of May, 1859, they were rewarded with the opportunity of seeing a flint axe still firmly embedded in an ancient gravel deposit, and any remaining doubts were removed (fig. 1.5). Prestwich read an account of their observations to the Royal Society in London before the end of May, and a summary of his paper

1.4 John Evans (1823–1908) combined a busy life in the paper industry with interests in geology and the collection and study of ancient coins and artefacts. This photograph demonstrates his continuing involvement in archaeology thirty years after his visit to the Somme valley in 1859; he is the figure in shirtsleeves, excavating a Roman burial at Youngsbury, Ware, in Hertfordshire. *Society of Antiquaries, London*

appeared in print in 1860. He referred to John Frere's letter published in 1800, and pointed out that Frere's observations conformed with the new findings from France.

In 1869 an important pioneer of many aspects of archaeology, Pitt Rivers, successfully sought and found flint implements in association with bones (elephant, hippopotamus, extinct deer, etc.) at Acton, near London. They occurred in a gravel terrace 25–30 metres above the River Thames; however, Neolithic and Bronze Age finds from the river itself demonstrated that its present course was over 2000 years old: '... this gives us some

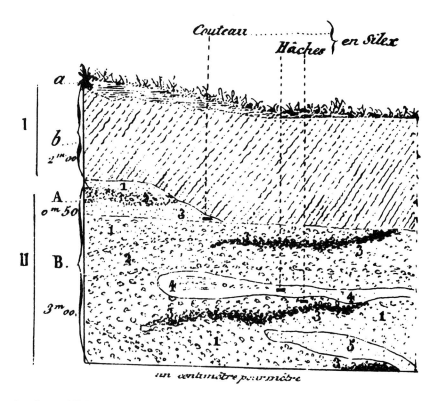

1.5 Section drawing published by Boucher de Perthes in his *Antiquités celtiques et antediluviennes* (1847) showing the geological strata in which he had found flint implements (labelled *couteau/haches en silex*) in the Somme valley gravels. The carefully numbered and delineated layers and artefacts, with a vertical scale in metres, illustrate how geologists used this method of recording, decades before it was adopted by archaeological excavators (compare figs 1.15 and 3.9 below).

idea of the great length of time it must have taken to erode the whole valley ...' (Bowden 1991, 74). He designed a particularly elegant method of proving the antiquity of early flint artefacts in Egypt, by looking for them in the walls of tombs constructed around 1500 BC near Thebes. The tombs had been dug into hard gravel that included (along with other artefacts) a flint flake cut by the builders; the geologist who accompanied Pitt Rivers commented: 'It belongs to the geological delta formation, and beyond question it is older beyond calculation than the tomb which was cut into the gravel, and cut through the end of this particular flint flake' (Bowden 1991, 91).

1.3 Catastrophists and fluvialists
(Gould 1987)

In some ways, the recognition of authentic associations between flint axes and the bones of extinct animals increased the problems of dating faced by geologists and historians: how long ago did these humans and animals live? The predicament was expressed particularly well by Joseph Prestwich:

The author does not, however, consider that the facts, as they at present stand, of necessity carry back Man in past time more than they bring forward the great extinct Mammals towards our own time, the evidence having reference only to relative and not to absolute time; and he is of the opinion that many of the later geological changes may have been sudden or of shorter duration than generally considered. In fact, from the evidence here exhibited ... the author sees no reason against the conclusion that this period of Man and the extinct Mammals ... was brought to a sudden end by a temporary inundation of the land. (Prestwich 1860, 58)

Prestwich reveals that the idea of sudden catastrophes survived as late as the 1850s, but Charles Lyell (1797–1875) had published a series of books in the 1830s (entitled *Principles of Geology*) that asserted that gravel, sand and clay deposits were formed by the same processes of erosion and deposition by weather and water observable today. Lyell, and subsequent historians of geology, have expressed the debate in terms of catastrophists and uniformitarians. In fact, after AD 1800 few geologists still believed that layers of gravel and sedimentary rocks were formed simply by the catastrophic floods described in the Book of Genesis, and few were constrained by the very short time span for the Earth derived from the Old Testament (Gould 1987, 112). 'Fluvialists' and 'catastrophists' both studied and interpreted sequences of rocks and fossils, and their methods offered a solution to the problem of early human tools and weapons. If the levels observed by Frere and Boucher de Perthes really *had* been laid down by slow erosion by wind and water, and gradual deposition by rivers and oceans, an immense length of time must be involved. It could not yet be measured, but if these processes were assumed to have operated uniformly in the present and the past, their duration could perhaps be sensed and visualized rather more easily than mysterious catastrophic floods.

During this period, human bones as well as stone tools were found in early geological deposits in many parts of Europe. In 1863, Lyell finally combined the 'new' geology with this archaeological evidence in a book entitled *The Geological Evidences of the Antiquity of Man*. This book also took full account of the evolutionary theory, perhaps the most significant scientific advance of the nineteenth century. Charles Darwin's theory, proposed in *The Origin of Species by means of Natural Selection* (1859), did not just provide an appreciation of the depth of time demanded by geology. It also provided a linear, almost historical, notion of progress that could be adopted easily by archaeology. Science in the nineteenth century was not divided into small specialized compartments in the way it is today, and Darwin was well aware of the implications of recent geological thinking. Darwin and the geologists both demanded the acceptance of the same concept: the present surface of the Earth, and the plants and animals (including humans) that inhabited it, resulted from an immense period of change.

The slow development and acceptance of a clear concept of human antiquity have been described here to illustrate how archaeology progressed by changing the explanations that prevailed at the time, and to remind us that new ideas normally meet resistance. Individuals were forced to look at fresh evidence in a scientific manner and work out its implications, rather than simply fitting new information into an existing framework of ideas in the least offensive way. This attitude is equally necessary today; we must never forget that we are trapped in the outlook of our own time. The study of changing attitudes to the past should act as a constant reminder of this, and we must avoid a smug satisfaction that we may distinguish the 'right' ideas of the past simply because they accord with the prevailing judgements of the present. Gould's thoughtful examination of the different concepts of time held by early geologists (including Lyell) contains many implications about our attitude to the work of such pioneers (1987).

2 Avenues of investigation
(Casson 1939)

Although human antiquity was the most important single idea that had to be established before archaeology could develop into its modern form, it was far from being the first field of study. Archaeology is still fundamentally concerned with sites and objects, and the growth of research into the material remains of past human activities throws further light on the basic principles that underlie the work of modern archaeologists. Considerable progress in setting these tangible remains into meaningful contexts had been made by the sixteenth century, with the help of travel, the collecting of artefacts, and anthropological information that began to reach Europe from the New World after AD 1500.

Speculation about the past was not uncommon amongst the Greeks and Romans. Something akin to modern anthropology (rather than archaeology) was prominent in ancient Greece, where intense interest in his own society and political system probably led Herodotus to travel amongst 'barbarian' (i.e. non-Greek) peoples such as the heavy-drinking, head-hunting Celts in the sixth century BC. His observations of institutions, customs and ways of life earned him the respect of one twentieth-century historian of anthropology, Stanley Casson (1939, 42–53). Greek and Roman travellers may have felt that an understanding of other peoples would give greater insight into their own society, but on a more practical level, their observations were useful to other travellers, for Greek and Roman culture and commerce embraced the whole Mediterranean as well as parts of its barbarian hinterland. These studies were paralleled by advances in anatomy, astronomy and biology, to the extent that ideas of biological and social evolution were emerging (Blundell 1986, 73–97). These ideas were taken up again during the Renaissance and advanced to a stage where true archaeological research could begin.

With few exceptions, Roman writers were content either to ignore barbarian cultures, or simply to rehash observations made by earlier Greek investigators. A notable exception was Tacitus, who wrote an interesting account of the Germans in the late first century AD. However, it was not simply scientific curiosity that motivated his description of the simple life and virtues of these barbarians; he wished to make a political point by contrasting them with the corruption of Roman society. His *Germania* is an early example of the creation of a 'Noble Savage' myth, a literary form that has remained popular ever since. Unlike his Greek predecessors, Tacitus made no attempt to gather first-hand information by travelling amongst the Germans. He embellished and updated Greek writings through conversations with senior army officers and civil servants from his own social circle who had held appointments in the Rhine provinces on the frontiers of the Roman Empire. His book could have formed the basis of a comparative study of the origins of Roman society, but in practice it provided an opportunity to make a political and philosophical point.

Some features of modern archaeology did exist in the Roman world. Collections of Greek sculpture and vases were popular, various stages of architectural development were appreciated and

tourist visits to ancient monuments had already become common, not only in Italy and Greece but also in Egypt. The Emperor Hadrian (AD 117–38) is a good example of a traveller and collector: during tours of the Empire, he visited ancient Greek shrines and restored or completed Greek buildings. He designed a country villa inland from Rome at Tivoli that housed a library and a collection of Greek sculpture, and incorporated gardens and lakes reminiscent of places he had visited in Egypt and Greece. He changed a century-old fashion by wearing curly hair and a beard in the Greek manner, in contrast to the severe clean-shaven and short-haired appearance of his predecessors.

This kind of self-conscious antiquarianism was unlikely to lead to any scientific inquiry into matters relating to archaeology. It was in any case swept away by the political and economic chaos of the third and fourth centuries AD, after which the western half of the Roman Empire gradually disintegrated and passed under the control of the descendants of Tacitus' Germans – tribes from northern and eastern Europe who invaded and settled in the old Imperial lands in the fifth and sixth centuries. Because the remaining Roman culture of these areas and the surviving eastern Roman Empire had become largely Christian, philosophical speculation was replaced by rigid biblical doctrine.

2.1 Medieval attitudes to antiquity

The attitudes of Christian theologians help to explain the lack of significant progress in archaeological thinking before the nineteenth century. It took revolutionary developments in geology and biology to force a new scientific view of human origins upon the Christian world. For most of its history, Christianity has been founded on total belief in the Bible; to doubt its word offended not only God, but also the political organization of Church and State that enforced its acceptance. Thus, independent thinking was discouraged by both intellectual and social circumstances, and new ideas were likely to be treated as heresy. In particular, archaeological speculation was hampered by the account of the Creation given in the Old Testament, together with a description of the subsequent settlement of known lands by descendants of Adam and Eve.

The credibility of the Bible was enhanced by the fact that its later books contained episodes set in contexts with independent historical records such as Egypt or the Roman Empire.

Some of the aspects of antiquarianism found in the medieval Church are superficially similar to those associated with Romans like Hadrian, but on closer inspection are usually found to be motivated by religion. 'Tourism' was common, in the form of pilgrimages to ancient shrines, as was the collecting of manuscripts and relics. Many travellers combined both purposes; collections of relics enhanced the status of churches as centres for pilgrimage, and good libraries improved the reputation of monastic centres of learning. Since these libraries might also contain the works of some of the more acceptable pagan Latin and Greek authors, educated ecclesiastics could gain some knowledge of the Classical world and its culture.

A medieval bishop of Winchester made a purely aesthetic collection of Roman antiquities in the twelfth century, including at least one ship-load of marble sculptures from Rome itself; his interest had presumably resulted from visits to Italy and the reading of Roman authors such as Pliny and Vitruvius on art and architecture. A growing number of ancient Greek authors became known in western Europe in the twelfth century AD, thanks to the translation into Latin of important Greek manuscripts.

2.2 Archaeology from the Renaissance to the 'Age of Reason'

(Piggott 1989)

In theory, when the west broke up into 'barbarian' kingdoms in the fifth century, classical culture should have survived in the Byzantine Empire, where 'Roman' rule lasted until the capture of Constantinople by the Turks in 1453. However, the civilization that emerged from the ruins of the former eastern Roman Empire was very much a Greek Christian culture. Although much of Greece was ruled by Italian states in the final years before the Turkish conquest, they took little interest in its ancient monuments. The heritage of ancient Rome was of more immediate interest to Italians involved in the Renaissance, an intellectual resurgence that began in Italy during the fourteenth century.

Scholars, artists and architects turned to pre-Christian Roman sources for largely forgotten information, ideas and new inspiration. The rapidly disappearing monuments of the city of Rome itself were studied by Poggio Bracciolini and Flavio Biondo in the fifteenth century, using every possible source of written evidence to elucidate the physical remains (Weiss 1969, 59–72). In some ways the Renaissance attitude to the examination of the past resembled that of the Romans, for it involved travel, the study of buildings and the collection of works of art and manuscripts. One scholar with this outlook who looked beyond Italy to Greece was Cyriac of Ancona, who was born in 1391, well before the fall of Constantinople (Weiss 1969, 131–44). He spent twenty-five years of the early fifteenth century in Greece, visiting sites and libraries for himself and publishing commentaries on his observations.

Cyriac embodied some of the principal components of a modern archaeologist, notably the active recording and study of physical remains of the past, whether sites or objects, through extensive fieldwork. In addition, as a historical archaeologist, Cyriac carried out his researches with the help of the literary background of the culture that he investigated. On the negative side, Cyriac displayed a typically selective attitude to what he recorded, and failed to record or comment upon changes that had affected the condition of Athenian monuments: 'A true child of the Renaissance, he was the first in a long line of travellers eager to overlook the barbarous rubbish of a barbarous people' (McNeal 1991, 52). By the sixteenth century, 'The testimony which could be extracted from ancient ruins, from statues and mosaics, but particularly from coins and inscriptions, was now fully appreciated, and any serious historian who dispensed with it, obviously did so at his personal risk' (Weiss 1969, 206). One important element – the idea of using systematic *excavation* of buried remains to supplement information gained from the surface inspection of sites – still lay far in the future.

The Renaissance atmosphere of discovery and speculation gradually spread to the rest of Europe, including areas in the north whose connection with the Classical world had been either brief (like Britain) or non-existent (like much of Germany and Scandinavia). In these countries the same spirit of enquiry was also directed towards the non-Classical past, and the first steps began to be taken towards the methods of prehistoric archaeology. Some of this research was undertaken by individuals whose means did not permit them to travel widely in southern Europe. Thus, most of the advances towards scientific archaeology occurred in northern Europe, and the methods and ideas fostered on the fringes of the Classical world were only applied to sites in Greece and the Near East much later.

The Renaissance also coincided with many voyages of discovery, which began shortly before AD 1500 and continued into the sixteenth century. Many societies at different levels of savagery or civilization were encountered in the Americas, and the world was finally proved to be a sphere; both discoveries conflicted with the authority of the Bible. The significance of these discoveries was potentially dramatic, but few dared to state the logical conclusions. Peoples unknown to the Bible in other parts of the globe could not have spread out from the Garden of Eden over a single flat continent, and they could not be related easily to the creation story surrounding Adam.

If this were indeed true, perhaps human races similarly unrelated to Adam could have existed in the Old World before the Creation described in the Bible. One writer, Isaac de la Peyrère, voiced these doubts; he was a French protestant who proposed in a theological book published in 1655 that Adam was simply the 'father of the Jews, not of all men' (Casson 1939, 115). His views were founded upon knowledge of the ancient civilizations of the Near East and the newly discovered inhabitants of various parts of the world. Peyrère was forced to recant by the Inquisition and his book was publicly burned in Paris. Many must have sympathized with his views, but they were quite beyond proof until developments in geology and biology in the nineteenth century (outlined above) enabled archaeologists like Boucher de Perthes to prove the existence of 'antediluvian' tool-using humans by observation and fieldwork.

The Renaissance interest in pagan classical literature, combined with New World discoveries, created an favourable atmosphere for archaeological work. Herodotus and Tacitus had written about primitive peoples who lived on the fringes of their (Greek and Roman) world, and this area included Germany and Britain, which were both now involved in the new scholarship. The precedent of these ancient authors made it respectable to investigate the primitive state of Europe; for example, John Shefferius (a Swedish professor of law) published a study of Lapland in the 1670s, inspired by Tacitus' *Germania*. Since primitive peoples like the Lapps were not readily available for study in the rest of Europe it is not surprising to find that the alternative in other countries was the examination and description of archaeological remains. Rising sentiments of nationalism enhanced the interest of searching for the origins of peoples such as the Celts, Germans or Slavs (Sklenář 1983, 24–8). As we have already seen, the exploration of this kind of material was more complicated in northern Europe than in Mediterranean countries, where research was dominated by classical sites recorded in documentary sources. Prehistoric earthworks, tombs and artefacts offered a greater challenge of classification and explanation precisely because they lacked direct historical evidence.

3 Archaeology and the Enlightenment

The age which set the 'light of reason' against the darkness of medieval and baroque superstition and prejudice based its philosophy primarily on the results achieved in the natural sciences (Sklenář 1983, 47)

The most important change in attitude to the past caused by the Enlightenment of the seventeenth to eighteenth centuries AD was the abandonment of a view that humans had degenerated since the time of the Creation. The economic and technological development of Europe encouraged an alternative idea involving progress in human material, intellectual and spiritual culture (Evans 1982, 17; Trigger 1989, 57–8). This shift in outlook was reflected in the work of many French and Scottish philosophers – rather than antiquaries – who used reports of 'primitive' cultures in an attempt to define stages of social evolution: 'The ancient state of mankind was the proper study of the philosophers untrammelled by the petty facts of the antiquary' (Piggott 1989, 151). Nevertheless the adoption of an evolutionary frame of mind clearly favoured the acceptance of the implications of scientific investigations into geology, biology and artefacts. As we have seen above, by the early nineteenth century European scholars finally possessed a range of essential concepts suitable for confronting the problem of human antiquity.

3.1 Antiquarian fieldwork in Britain
(Piggott 1989)

The aims and concepts of research into the past that followed the diffusion of Renaissance thinking into northern Europe may be illustrated by the work of a series of antiquarians who engaged in active field archaeology in Britain between the early sixteenth and mid-eighteenth centuries: Leland, Camden, Aubrey and Stukeley. Before the sixteenth century, historical writers occasionally referred to monuments, but with little purpose other than to display sheer wonder, or to add circumstantial detail to some actual or invented episode in their works. For example, a recognizable illustration showing Stonehenge being built by the magician Merlin appeared in a fourteenth-century British manuscript (Trigger 1989, 32, fig. 2). The Tudor dynasty coincided with an increase in national consciousness, which produced rational attempts to examine the continuity of Britain from Roman times. The founding of Britain was no longer attributed to unlikely or imaginary individuals and tribes (such as Brutus the Trojan or Phoenicians); instead, greater reliance was placed on references contained in Classical sources, and analogies from the New World. This was the atmosphere in which systematic attention was first paid to field monuments in Britain, by individuals who, from the sixteenth century, were described by their contemporaries as 'antiquaries'.

John Leland (1503–52)
Leland was educated in London, Cambridge, Oxford and Paris and held the post of Keeper of King's Libraries under Henry VIII. Like Cyriac of Ancona a century earlier, Leland travelled extensively, perusing the libraries of monasteries and colleges; unlike Cyriac, his fieldwork did not involve the rediscovery of sites belonging to a well-known and documented culture, but ill-understood remains of unknown age, or at

best fleetingly documented monuments like Hadrian's Wall or Offa's Dyke. His interests were primarily directed towards historical documents and genealogy. His records of items that attracted his attention (whether ancient or contemporary) in the landscape through which he travelled may have been intended to accompany a map or an annotated gazetteer. Leland's significance lies in his general idea of recording non-literary evidence as part of wider researches. Although never published, his work anticipated the many county histories of the eighteenth century, and illustrated a breadth of interest in the landscape that was characteristic of the new, wider horizons of Renaissance scholarship.

William Camden (1551–1623)
Like Leland, Camden (fig. 1.6) progressed through a sound education and eventually held a state appointment that gave him ample opportunity to further his antiquarian researches. After teaching and holding the headship at Westminster School, he became Clarenceux King of Arms in the College of Heralds. He was less devoted to the study of heraldry and genealogy than Leland, but it nevertheless formed an essential part of his historical writing. Antiquarianism was Camden's passion from childhood, and he consciously acquired the necessary skills for his purposes. Any educated person would possess Latin, but Camden learned Anglo-Saxon and Welsh to study place-names. He travelled extensively and was already an authority of European standing in his twenties; when only 35, his major work was published: *Britannia*, the 'first general guide to the antiquities of Britain' (Daniel 1967, 36).

Camden's intention was to set Britain into a respectable position in European culture, largely by emphasizing the importance of the Roman occupation, which linked Britain to the Continental centres of the Renaissance. The book proceeds through the Saxon and medieval periods, stressing the relationship of the Roman province to the recent historical past; no trace of the wild foundation myths of many Tudor writers is found in the reasoned prose of Camden. His descriptions of antiquities are thorough and detailed, and sections on coins and language were also included. As with Leland, descriptions of the present configuration of the places he visited

1.6 Engraving of William Camden used as a frontispiece to Gough's translation of Camden's *Britannia* in 1789

1.7 Engraving of John Aubrey by William Fairthorne, dated 1666. *Bodleian Library, Oxford*

form an inseparable part of his account of Britain; indeed, Camden made extensive use of Leland's unpublished manuscript. Camden is noted for a concise account of crop-marks, the visible effects of buried structures on growing plants that are so important in the detection of sites by aerial photography today. He also identified pre-Roman coins minted by the late Iron Age tribes of south-eastern England – a notion rejected by Leland (Piggott 1989, 133–4).

Part of Camden's achievement was to organize an enormous collection of information into published form, a feat Leland never managed. His interest in material culture, and the recognition of the part it could play in elucidating the past, was fundamentally important. His *Britannia* enjoyed great popularity, and its careful organization allowed additions not only in his lifetime, but for nearly two hundred years after Camden's death. The first edition of 1585 was in Latin, with only one illustration, but further illustrations were added to subsequent editions. The first English edition appeared in 1610, and a notable expanded version was produced by Edmund Gibson in 1695. 'An annotated copy of the 1695 or subsequent editions of Camden formed the almost inevitable nucleus around which comment and additions would grow as local investigations were carried by these amateurs who were beginning to build up the

tradition which crystallised into the great nineteenth-century county histories and the foundation of regional archaeological societies' (Piggott 1985, 18).

John Aubrey (1626–97)

John Aubrey (fig. 1.7) lacked the education of Leland or Camden, and was described by his biographer Anthony Powell as a 'Wiltshire Squire fallen on evil days' (Daniel 1967, 37). Nevertheless, Aubrey participated in a new kind of scholarship that came to prominence in the seventeenth century, centred upon the Royal Society. It was characterized by a scientific outlook, and a wish to approach any subject from a sound basis of classification and comparison, whether astronomy, medicine, botany, or antiquities. This new attitude was expressed clearly in 1686 by a contemporary of Aubrey, Dr Robert Plot, Keeper of the Ashmolean Museum in Oxford: 'I intend not to meddle with the pedigrees or descents either of families or lands, it being indeed my Designe ... to omit, as much as may be, both persons and actions and chiefly apply myself to things; and amongst those too, only of such as are very remote from the present Age' (Piggott 1989, 26). This is the approach of an archaeologist, rather than a historian who happened also to be interested in monuments, and it contrasts with that of Leland and Camden.

One attitude that did remain firmly established from the time of Leland and Camden was that antiquities formed only one part of a complete study of the landscape. Aubrey included all kinds of natural and artificial phenomena in accounts of his beloved Wiltshire. Sadly, his great work of a purely archaeological nature, *Monumenta Britannica*, was never published, except for some parts included in the 1695 edition of Camden's *Britannia*. The contents of *Monumenta Britannica* reveal Aubrey's interests and approach. The first part was focused on the great prehistoric monuments of Wessex, including Stonehenge, Silbury and Avebury; he was one of the earliest writers to assign these sites to the pre-Roman Celts and their priesthood, the Druids, known from the writings of Tacitus and other Roman authors. Part two concerned pre-Roman and Roman camps and forts, and Roman civil settlements, again predominantly those of Wessex. Part three was more diverse, including barrows, pottery, burials, linear earthworks, roads and trackways, mosaic floors and coins. The fourth part (never finished) contained assorted material of medieval date, including a study of architectural features from which he deduced (correctly) that windows were particularly diagnostic for dating purposes: 'the windows ye most remarqueable, hence one may give a guess about what Time ye Building was' (Piggott 1976, 17). Aubrey was right, but because his deductions were not published they had to be worked out again when interest in church architecture was renewed in the nineteenth century.

The most significant feature of Aubrey's work was the idea that information was worth collecting and classifying for its own sake, rather than simply to illustrate a particular theory. The same approach is found in the work of his contemporaries in other fields of learning such as botany and the study of fossils. Aubrey's observations and interpretations also reveal the effects of another important feature of his age – the dissemination in Europe of accounts of American Indians. He did not share the 'Noble Savage' view of native Americans that might have resulted from reading the *Germania* of Tacitus; this is clear from analogies he drew between ancient Britons and Indians: '. . . the inhabitants (of northern Wiltshire) almost as savage as the Beasts whose skins were their only rayment . . . They were 2 or 3 degrees I suppose less savage than the Americans . . . The Romans subdued and civilized them' (Piggott 1989, 62). Clearly, Aubrey shared Camden's view that the Roman period made Britain acceptable in the eyes of European post-Renaissance scholarship. Remnants of this concept survive today; the archaeology of Roman Britain is normally studied in the wider context of the Roman Empire, but rarely with sufficient reference to the periods that preceded or followed it.

Aubrey was not able to escape from the conundrum of dating ancient monuments. Although he was right to place Stonehenge and Avebury in a ritual context of pre-Roman date, he attributed Iron Age hillforts to Britons, Romans or Danes with wild inconsistency (Piggott 1989, 118–20). Sadly, death cut short the activity of Edward Lhwuyd (1660–1708), a younger scholar and friend of Aubrey. He had participated in preparing Gibson's edition of Camden's *Britannia*, but died before the publication of his own account of the monuments of Britain that should have followed his book of 'staggering brilliance' on Britain's Celtic languages (Piggott 1989, 30). Aubrey's style of scholarship had a final successor in the eighteenth century – William Stukeley.

William Stukeley (1687–1765) (Piggott 1986)

The early eighteenth century saw a decline in the spirit of objective scientific inquiry that had characterized the Royal Society, and a shift in taste away from Classical art and architecture towards fanciful 'Gothic' buildings incorporating medieval features; the same period also saw the development of 'Romantic' art and literature. Stukeley (fig. 1.8) reflected these changes in the spirit of the age; his early researches belonged to a passing tradition, but his later interpretations of them belonged to the new era. Stuart Piggott (Stukeley's principal biographer) pointed out the contradictions contained in his work by suggesting that '. . . perhaps we should see William Stukeley's greatness as a field archaeologist not in his being an innovator, but in his being provincial, old-fashioned and out-of-date, continuing the high tradition of Restoration antiquarianism unaware of the changed intellectual mood of the metropolis' (1982, 24).

1.8 A drawing by William Stukeley (1687–1765) showing him engaged in fieldwork with friends. Even in this light-hearted sketch a number of antiquities and features of the landscape are drawn and labelled; his observations and plans remain an important source of information.
Bodleian Library, Oxford (Ms Eng Misc b 65 fol 43r)

Stukeley was trained in medicine at Cambridge and became a Fellow of the College of Physicians in 1720, having practised as a doctor. He had also studied botany, and this experience probably led him to an appreciation of the ancient monuments in the countryside that captured his imagination, especially after reading the manuscript of Aubrey's *Monumenta Britannica* in 1718. Extensive fieldwork in Wessex followed in the 1720s, including accurate and thorough surveys of Avebury, Stonehenge and Silbury. He went on to travel extensively throughout Britain, from the south coast to Hadrian's Wall, making surveys and excellent sketches. So far, Stukeley was a typical scholar of the 'Age of Reason'; but signs of 'unreason' are evident in his taste for dramatic landscapes such as the Lake District, and for Gothic architecture (to the extent of designing mock-ruins or 'follies'). His life changed direction from medicine to religion in the 1720s, and he was ordained in 1729.

From this point, Stukeley attempted to use the results of his collected fieldwork from Wessex to establish a theological connection between the Druids and Christianity. Aubrey had made obser-
vations, sorted them into a sensible order and drawn limited conclusions from common sense and historical information; for him, Stonehenge and its related monuments did not fit into the Roman period, so he attributed them to the pre-Roman Britons. Since the sites were obviously ritual, not functional, Aubrey had assigned them to the only known cult and priesthood attested by Classical authors, the Druids. Stukeley accepted this attribution (while failing to acknowledge his debt to Aubrey), but went on to invent a vast theological system for the Druids, supported by quite unwarranted connections with features of the monuments: 'The form of that stupendous work [Avebury] is the picture of the Deity, more particularly of the Trinity'. He published two major books – *Stonehenge* (1740) and *Avebury* (1743) – that he claimed to be part of a larger enterprise entitled *Patriarchal Christianity or a Chronological History of the Origin and Progress of true Religion, and of Idolatry*.

Stukeley's reputation as a field worker rests not on these publications, but on the unpublished manuscript of 1723 from which he selected his information. One early historian of archaeology summarized the curious dualism of Stukeley particularly clearly: 'Just as Dr Stukeley may be said to be the patron saint of fieldwork in archaeology, so can the Rev. William be held to be the evil genius who presides over all crack-brained amateurs whose excess of enthusiasm is only balanced by their ignorance of method' (Casson 1939, 150). Nevertheless, Stukeley's basic evidence still forms an invaluable record of monuments that have suffered severely since his day. He recorded an avenue of stones leading from Stonehenge to the river Avon that was subsequently destroyed; it was only relocated by aerial photography in 1920 (Piggott 1985, 92). His observations were careful and logical, and included the ability to relate groups of separate earthworks in an area into a coherent pattern. Stukeley also made analytical observations, such as deducing that a Roman road on Oakley Down, Dorset, must have been constructed later than some 'Druid' burial mounds, because it cut across the ditch of one barrow (Piggott 1989, pl. 27). Skills like these are still essential today. It is noteworthy that Stukeley was already aware of the role of fieldwork as part of rescue archaeology: as it 'perpetuates the vestiges of this celebrated wonder & of the barrows avenues cursus &c for I forsee that it will in a few years be universally plowed over and consequently defaced' (Piggott 1989, 127).

3.2 Fieldwork elsewhere
(Malina & Vašíček 1990)

Advances in antiquarian research and fieldwork were not restricted to Britain, of course. Historians of ideas, science or archaeology can all point to similar phenomena taking place elsewhere in Europe at this time. In Scandinavia, Johan Bure and Ole Worm undertook antiquarian research – with royal patronage – in the early seventeenth century (Trigger 1989, 49), and similar efforts were devoted to Roman and earlier antiquities in central Europe (Sklenař 1983, 6–43). A German pioneer of the systematic investigation of Roman art and architecture in Italy, Johann Winckelmann, was a near contemporary of William Stukeley. An indigenous archaeological tradition had also emerged in America by the nineteenth century (Trigger 1989, 104–9). Inevitably it began with ethnographic accounts of the native Americans, but gradually extended to sites and artefacts. The literate civilizations of Central and South America attracted comment as early as the sixteenth century, for their architecture, sculpture and inscriptions offered the same kind of possibilities for study as those of Greece or Italy. By the end of the eighteenth century, it was generally accepted that the native population of North America had migrated from

Asia by way of the Bering Straits. Nevertheless, speculation about the origins of Indians was still influenced by a desire amongst European colonists to justify their conquests by proving that the natives were in some way inferior to themselves. This was frequently achieved by claiming a glorious past for areas that they now occupied. Some archaeological fieldworkers who recorded ritual earthworks, such as burial mounds reminiscent of those found in northern Europe, attempted to explain them in terms of 'lost races', identified with Israelites, Danes or even Welshmen. Willey and Sabloff aptly categorize the phase of archaeological study in America from 1492–1840 as 'the speculative period' (1980, 12–27).

From a methodological point of view, field archaeology in Britain could develop no further after Stukeley until some new element was introduced ('For prehistoric earthworks the utter confusion and ignorance of 1695 was to persist into the present century' – Piggott 1989, 120). Accurate recording was continued and extended, and many county histories maintaining the style of their work appeared into the nineteenth century; however, the interpretation of recorded monuments remained static, because historical evidence scarcely stretched back beyond the Roman period. Historical events could be shuffled into a different order, or fanciful theories could be constructed to expand them, but no new source of evidence was available until the idea of excavation was adopted on a large scale in the nineteenth century, and refined in the twentieth. This development will be followed in the appropriate chapter below, but a further stage in the unravelling of the past requires comment. The collection and study of objects, rather than sites, ran parallel to the development of archaeological fieldwork but triumphed in the nineteenth century when excavations began to provide growing quantities of pottery, metal and stone artefacts for study.

3.3 Touring and collecting
(Impey & MacGregor 1985)

The Renaissance revived the Roman penchant for visiting monuments and collecting works of art for aesthetic reasons, in contrast to the medieval Church's concentration upon shrines and relics.

The concept spread to northern Europe, and educated people of sufficient financial means began to visit the Mediterranean centres of classical civilization in Italy, Greece, Turkey and the Near East. Naturally, travellers purchased 'souvenirs' to adorn their northern residences (constructed and decorated, of course, in a classical manner), and the process was accelerated by agents sent to seek out further items and to arrange for their shipment to the new owners' homes. An early example of an English 'Grand Tour' aristocrat was Thomas Howard, Earl of Arundel (1585–1646), who first travelled with a large entourage to Italy in 1612; there, he bought, and even dug for, antiquities. His agent, William Petty, extended the search to Greece with the help of the local ambassador, who described him as 'all things to all men that he may obtain his ends' (Casson 1939, 128). Petty built up a collection (at a bargain price compared with buying in Italy) that became a centre of great learned interest, known throughout Europe after its publication in 1628. Although Arundel's collection suffered neglect and dispersal after the Civil War, it had already generated similar desires amongst other noblemen and even royalty. Indeed, King Charles I stated that 'The study of antiquities is by good experience said to be very serviceable and useful to the general good of the State and Commonwealth' (Daniel 1975, 19).

Tours had other effects too; learned societies, such as the Society of Dilettanti (an organization of British antiquaries) sponsored expeditions to record Classical sites, rather than simply to loot them. Individuals of lower social status and wealth also began to form collections that included a wider variety of items (fig. 1.9). For example, John 'Gardener' Tradescant's collection was created in the first half of the seventeenth century, and a catalogue of its contents appeared in 1656. Although largely made up of botanical specimens, it also comprised 'Mechanick artificial works in carvings, turnings, sowings and paintings' and 'warlike instruments', mainly from Polynesia, Africa and America (Casson 1939, 136). After his death, the material passed to the University of Oxford through Tradescant's friend, Elias Ashmole. A new museum was opened in Oxford in 1683 by the future King James II, and it moved in the nineteenth century to the building known throughout the world as the Ashmolean Museum; the original building, now a museum of the history of Science, still exists. Thus, the Renaissance fashion for collecting contributed to the establishment of public museums attached to centres of learning or to cities. Museums have become the first point of contact with archaeology for many members of the public. The essential features of the early Ashmolean (collecting, scholarship and public display) have become accepted as integral parts of the cultural life of almost every modern country. The interest of antiquaries like Aubrey and Stukeley in prehistoric sites and objects was connected to the same phenomenon; indeed, many travelled in Britain because they could not afford to go abroad. However, early field archaeologists naturally concentrated on sites, because the potential for using objects to distinguish between stages of development in prehistory remained extremely limited until a meaningful concept of time became accepted. We have already seen that this acceptance came only in the second half of the nineteenth century. The history of the study of objects, like that of fieldwork, provides a useful illustration of some basic principles that still underlie the subject to this day.

4 The recognition of human artefacts

There was not normally any doubt that Roman and later artefacts were the work of humans, but ordinary artefacts from historical periods attracted little interest unless they were considered to have aesthetic qualities. Unlike works of art, they were only recovered by accident until excavation became an essential part of archaeology during the nineteenth century. Sophisticated prehistoric objects made of cast bronze were commonly assigned to the Romans or Danes, because antiquarians lacked a clear idea of what to expect from prehistoric material culture. For these reasons the systematic study of objects began with simple stone tools from very early periods. Casual finds of finely worked flint arrowheads or polished axes must always have

1.9 Ole Worm's collection of natural and archaeological curiosities, illustrated in 1655, illustrates the breadth of such collections, which embraced natural, geological, ethnographic and archaeological specimens. *Bodleian Library, Oxford*

suggested human manufacture to anyone who actually thought about them, and it would not have been difficult to reach the idea that they might have been used before metals were known. Concepts of successive ages of stone, bronze and iron, suggested by actual finds, are known from Chinese literature as early as the first century BC, and Shen Kua made remarkable studies of artefacts in the eleventh century AD (Evans 1982, 13–14).

A number of Italian collectors made accurate identifications of human artefacts in the sixteenth century (Piggott 1989, 89–90), but the concept spread slowly, so that it still seemed a novelty when the seventeenth-century French theologian, Isaac de la Peyrère, proposed that

stone implements were not 'thunderbolts', but the tools and weapons of peoples who had preceded the creation of Adam (Piggott 1989, 45–7). The matter was soon placed beyond doubt when similar items became available for study in ethnological collections from the South Seas and the Americas, where they could still be observed in use (fig. 1.10). In 1800, John Frere's celebrated letter published in *Archaeologia* (above, p. 11) included drawings of typical flint hand-axes of the Old Stone Age, '... evidently weapons of war, fabricated and used by a people who had not the use of metals ...'. However, fifty years later, Boucher de Perthes was still fighting for the acceptance of similar artefacts as the work of early humans. Interestingly, bronze artefacts caused more problems than those made of stone or iron for, while early travellers could observe Stone Age communities in America and Australia, and Iron Age societies in many parts of Africa, no Bronze Age peoples had been encountered. Bronze artefacts were normally assigned to

25

1.10 Stone artefacts from the Old and New Worlds. Recognition of prehistoric implements in Europe was helped by observations of similar objects, still in use, in other parts of the world. In 1699, Edward Lhwuyd, keeper of the Ashmolean Museum and an authority on fossils and antiquities, wrote: 'I doubt not but you have often seen of these Arrowheads they ascribe to elfs or fairies: they are just the same chip'd flints the natives of New England head their arrows with at this day; and there are also several stone hatchets found in this kingdom, not unlike those of the Americans' (Piggott 1989, 86). The artefacts on the left come from North and South America; those on the right are from northern Britain, and date to the later Stone Age and the Bronze Age. *Hancock Museum and Museum of Antiquities, Newcastle upon Tyne*

the Romans, because they seemed too complex to have been made by 'savages', but suggestions of an earlier date by Camden were built upon by Edward Lhwuyd and others, and found some support by the eighteenth century (Piggott 1989, 95–100).

4.1 Scandinavia and the Three-Age System
(Graslund 1987)

Why has Scandinavian archaeology, generally speaking, an advantage over foreign archaeology, if not because Scandinavian archaeologists have had an opportunity to study in their museums not isolated specimens but whole series and their development? (Hans Hildebrand, 1873, quoted in Graslund 1987, 16)

The archaeology of Scandinavia is particularly rich in finely made artefacts dating from the pre-historic to Viking periods, and many of them are found in good condition in graves. Hildebrand was right to stress these factors, for increased building, agriculture and excavation in the nineteenth century had provided a plentiful supply of discoveries. Fortunately, Scandinavia also had museums where objects could be preserved, studied and displayed. An Antiquities Commission was set up by the Danish government in 1807 to protect sites, promote public awareness of antiquities, and to establish a museum. The first curator of the resulting National Museum in Copenhagen was Christian Thomsen (fig. 1.11), who held the post from 1816 to his death in 1865.

Thomsen would have been well aware of the concept of successive ages of stone, bronze and iron; it was particularly well expressed by Simonsen in 1816:

At first the tools and weapons . . . were made of stone or wood. Then the Scandinavians learnt to work copper and then to smelt it and harden it . . . and then latterly to work iron. From this point of view the development of their culture can be divided into a Stone Age, a Copper Age and an Iron Age. (Daniel 1967, 90–1)

Thomsen was the first to demonstrate the validity of these hypothetical ages by examining 'closed finds' (graves, hoards, etc.) in which artefacts had been discovered. He restricted his central definition of the Three Ages to cutting weapons and tools, and established their relative order. Some finds contained only stone tools, plus a few stone with bronze, but never iron. Bronze weapons were also found without iron, and bronze continued to be used for other kinds of objects during the Iron Age, which was observably the most recent age because of associations with Roman and medieval coins. Once this analysis had established the order of weapons and tools, Thomsen was able to observe

1.11 C J Thomsen in the Oldnordisk Museum in Copenhagen thirty years after its foundation in 1816. His enthusiasm for increasing public awareness of antiquities is well illustrated by this drawing by Magnus Pedersen. *National Museum, Copenhagen*

their association in closed finds with artefacts made from other metals and materials, as well as specific burial practices and grave forms. The basic objectivity of these observations meant that later finds elaborated and refined his system, rather than replaced it. Effective classification was indispensable to the advance of the study of prehistory, and the Three-Age System provided a framework that survives (with modifications) today.

Thomsen presented the evidence for his chronological deductions in his museum by displaying together groups of objects that had been found in association. He was keen to show them to visiting archaeologists, and also to peasants, who were likely to discover objects that could be added to the collections. The displays were described in a guide printed in 1836, and received wider attention after it was translated into English in 1848. The phenomenon of collecting antiquities was initially a hobby of a social elite, typified by the Earl of Arundel, but by the nineteenth century it had been transformed in a remarkably democratic fashion. Happily, the popularizing approach of Thomsen was reinforced by other archaeologists, such as Pitt Rivers, and it remains characteristic of most museum curators today. However, unlike Pitt Rivers, Thomsen did not attempt either to study the development of the forms of individual artefacts ('typology') or to explain the reasons for the changes that he had observed (Graslund 1987, 26–8).

Thomsen's successor as Director of the Danish National Museum was another remarkable man, Jens Worsaae (1821–85). His recommendations for the use of systematic excavation were inspired by the need to recover still more artefacts from specific contexts that would allow Thomsen's broad classifications to be refined. Glyn Daniel (1967, 99–100) noted a key phrase in Worsaae's writings, published in 1843: 'As soon as it was pointed out that the whole of these antiquities could by no means be referred to one and the same period, people began to see more clearly the difference between them.' In 1861 Worsaae subdivided the Stone Age into three periods according to the nature of stone artefacts. The earliest period was characterized by hand axes and large flakes, found in the gravels and caves of western Europe; these were followed by finer tools found in Denmark in 'kitchen middens' (mounds of shells and bones left by hunter-gatherers). Finally, polished stone tools were associated with elaborate tombs that occasionally also contained the earliest metal objects. These divisions of the Stone Age were soon named Palaeolithic, Mesolithic and Neolithic (old, middle and new) by Sir John Lubbock in his book *Prehistoric Times* (1865). Worsaae used a different method to divide the Bronze Age. He identified a series of different burial practices and grave forms, and was able to place them into chronological order either by reference to artefacts found in them, or by observation of excavated sites where examples of different forms had been found in a stratigraphic sequence. Like Thomsen, Worsaae relied primarily on the contexts of artefacts, rather than a typological study of the artefacts themselves.

4.2 Typology

Typology differs fundamentally from mere classification. It studies classes of artefacts from the point of view of developments and changes that may allow them to be placed into a hypothetical chronological order (below, p. 104). Until recently, the development of typology has been linked to the Three-Age system and the influence of Darwin's theory of evolution. However, Bo Graslund (1987) has demonstrated that this was not the case by means of a thorough study of the original writings of Thomsen, Worsaae, H. Hildebrand, Montelius and many other Scandinavian scholars (few were ever translated from Danish or Swedish). Studies of artefacts were based primarily on the contexts in which they had been discovered, and in Scandinavia these were sufficiently plentiful for virtually all classes of artefacts to be placed into chronological order *without* the use of typology. Once this had been done, typological studies could begin on a secure basis. Evolution provided a convenient, if rather misleading, metaphor, and it undoubtedly stimulated the development of typology from the 1870s onwards.

The influence of classical archaeology on typology has been underestimated because most histories of archaeology have been written by prehistorians. Systematic studies of Greek and Roman architectural and artistic styles began during the Renaissance, and were formalized by Johann Winckelmann in the eighteenth century. Ancient coins were even more significant: Petrarch studied inscriptions and portraits in the fourteenth century, and classifications of large coin collections were published from the sixteenth century (Berghaus 1983, 19–23). Joseph von Eckhel's *Doctrina numorum veterum* (1782–98) and similar works by other authors provided comprehensive geographical and chronological classifications that must have been useful reference tools for C. J. Thomsen and his successors. Graslund has rightly stressed the importance of the numismatic knowledge of Thomsen, Hans Hildebrand and Montelius, who all appreciated the importance of coins as dating evidence that could be used to subdivide the Scandinavian Iron Age (1987, 66). It is also important to recognize that coins are artefacts, and that their study by means of stylistic sequences of portraits or other ornamentation, combined with changes in size and weight, bears many similarities to typology. The styles of classical sculptures and Greek painted vases were also studied primarily from the objects themselves, largely because their contexts were rarely recorded.

Augustus Lane-Fox (1827–1900, also known as Pitt Rivers, after taking this name under the terms of an inheritance in 1880) collected artefacts from all over the world from the early 1850s while serving in the Grenadier Guards. He was involved in replacing muskets by rifles in the British army, and in testing various models and modifications for reliability and efficiency. This probably contributed to the way he sought to illustrate progressive improvements and developments of various classes of artefacts in his personal research. He liked to collect examples of the principal stages involved, and, in contrast to earlier collectors like John Tradescant, he assembled artefacts '... not for the purpose of surprising anyone, either by the value or beauty of the objects exhibited, but solely with a view to instruction. For this purpose ordinary and typical specimens rather than rare objects have been selected and arranged in sequence' (Daniel 1981, 140). Pitt Rivers' concept of typology was very different from that of Montelius, for he invoked analogies with Darwinian evolution as early as the 1860s (Bowden 1991, 54). His scheme for

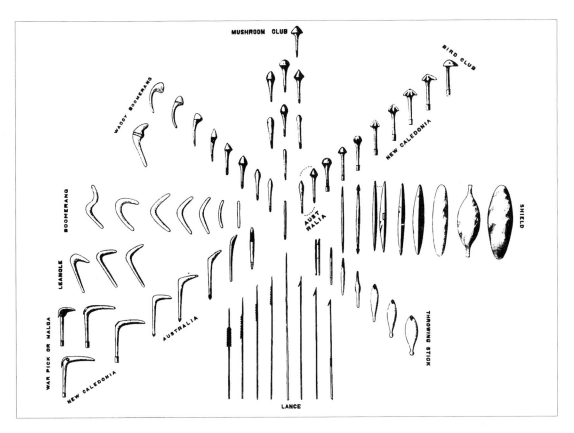

the derivation of Australian weapons placed a variety of clubs, boomerangs, throwing sticks, shields and spears into sequences from simplicity to complexity (fig. 1.12), but a little critical thought soon undermines this idea. A shield is only a shield when it is broad and flat, and a boomerang is not a boomerang if it does not fly; Pitt Rivers' model failed to take account of invention. Nevertheless, the analogy derived from Darwin's concept of linear evolution still underlies many modern studies of typology (Basalla 1989).

As soon as Scandinavian prehistory had been subdivided according to studies of groups of artefacts found together in graves and other contexts, attention was turned to the artefacts themselves. The work of Oscar Montelius encompassed the whole of Europe from the 1880s, and he used his broad knowledge to fix dates for the Bronze and Iron Ages by cross-referencing north European finds to datable objects exported from the civilizations of Egypt and the east Mediterranean (see p. 104). Fellow Swedes Salin and Aberg continued typological

1.12 Pitt Rivers justified his idea of typology by deriving a wide range of Australian aboriginal weapons from a plain cylindrical stick. '...I only ask you to glance at the sequence shown in this diagram ... in order to convince you of the truth of the statement ... that although, owing to the complexity of modern contrivances and the larger steps by which we mount the ladder of progress in the material arts, their continuity may be lost sight of, when we come to classify the arts of savages and prehistoric men, the term growth is fully as applicable to them as to the development of the forms of speech ...' *Lane-Fox 1875, pl. III and p. 514*

research in the twentieth century by studying objects and ornamental styles associated with Germanic tribes of the Roman and 'Dark Age' periods. Like Montelius, they used dated finds from southern Europe to provide fixed points in the archaeological sequences of Scandinavia. The introduction of radiocarbon dating in the 1960s revealed major errors in the dating of European prehistory, and cast typology in a bad light. Nevertheless, with appropriate caution, the

29

technique remains fundamental to the classification and study of artefacts of virtually any kind or date found anywhere in the world. Unfortunately, the classification of objects and cultural stages preceded the general development of improved excavation techniques by several decades.

Modern archaeologists should not allow the years that have elapsed since Thomsen, Worsaae or Pitt Rivers to provide an excuse for ignoring the intellectual context of their work, or forget that they underpinned the political attitudes of their day. Alice Kehoe expresses strong scepticism of their portrayal in 'Whiggish consensus histories' by Glyn Daniel and others:

> The three-age system was a variant of a myth in a standard, familiar format, the three offers or tests to which the culture hero must respond. Stone, Bronze, Iron – like the Three Little Pigs, he who persevered in working the least tractable material in the end won out. ... When the great historical change from landed estates to industrial capitalism and bourgeois democracies had been achieved, the format for a sanctioning myth was already given. Archaeology furnished the hero – mankind – and the substantive details – stone, bronze, iron – to lend verisimilitude to the myth. ... To ignore this context is to miss the forest for the trees. (Kehoe 1989, 106)

5 The Discovery of Civilizations
(Daniel 1981)

Interest in material remains, and in particular the concept of excavating sites for information rather than in search of treasures, developed long after the great period of descriptive study characterized by antiquarians like Camden or Aubrey. Archaeological exploration usually began for one of two reasons. Some structures, such as Hissarlik (Schliemann's Troy), were investigated because they were thought to relate to historical people, periods or events. Conversely, mysterious monuments such as the pre-Columbian North American mounds were dug into in the hope of revealing their nature and date (Daniel 1981, 90–2). A third factor existed almost universally:

treasure hunting, either for purely financial gain, or, on a more intellectual plane, in search of curiosities or *objets d'art* for collectors.

The Mediterranean civilizations of Greece and Rome formed an important background to European culture, and they received special attention during the Renaissance and Enlightenment periods. This degree of familiarity reduced classical archaeology's potential for introducing new techniques and concepts, in contrast to the stimulus given by difficult questions such as Human Antiquity, or the exploration of Egypt and Mesopotamia. In the years around 1800, Europeans first began to turn to more systematic forms of excavation. By a happy coincidence, the declining Turkish Empire was allowing easier access to these regions, resulting in the presence of diplomats and soldiers from France and Britain (and later Germany) around the Red Sea and Arabian Gulf – the strategic routes that connected the Mediterranean to the Indian Ocean. Many of these individuals came from the same educational and social background as antiquarians, who had studied the classics and travelled to historic sites on the Grand Tour, and who, increasingly, turned to the investigation of ancient sites on their estates. It is therefore not surprising to find that Claudius James Rich (agent of the East India Company at Baghdad from 1807) or Paul Emile Botta (French consul from 1842 at Mosul, the ancient Nineveh) investigated the remains of Babylon and Nineveh and other sites in Iraq near the towns where they were based (Lloyd 1980). National prestige became embroiled in the pursuit of antiquities, and as a result vast sculptures and even large portions of buildings were transported to the museums of London, Paris and Berlin. Napoleon's invasion of Egypt in 1798 was even more striking; although Nelson ensured that it was not a military success it certainly was an academic triumph. The 200 scholars who accompanied Napoleon's army established the foundations for decades of subsequent research into Egypt's civilization and prehistory (Trigger 1989, 39).

The failing grip of the Ottoman Empire in the nineteenth century also stimulated the exploration of Greek civilization. Greece gained its independence in 1831 and foreign excavators rapidly cleared the Acropolis of Athens, releasing the remains of such buildings as the Erechtheum and Parthenon from the encumbrances of a harem and mosque respectively (fig. 1.13). This action also illustrates that archaeological research is highly selective when combined with nationalism. Societies tend to select the past that they wish to emphasize; the removal of physical reminders of Turkish rule and its religion, Islam, allowed the new Greek nation to underline its connections with the European roots of classical culture.

5.1 Egypt and Mesopotamia
(Maisels 1993)

Interest in Egypt and Mesopotamia was not entirely separate from the investigation of classical Greece and Rome. Both areas had fallen within the power of Alexander the Great in the fourth century BC, and both were absorbed into the Roman empire in the first century BC. Thus some indications of the early history and antiquities of Egypt and Mesopotamia could be gleaned from classical writers, while even earlier references abounded in the Old Testament. A further important aspect was that a wide public could take a safe interest in news of discoveries made in the Near East, for they promised to enrich and confirm two major roots of European culture –

the Classics and the Bible. In contrast, unsettling claims were being made about unspectacular stone tools of dubious human manufacture found in France and elsewhere in the early nineteenth century (above, p. 11). Many geologists related these finds to the ideas of Charles Darwin, and had the effrontery to deny both the date and nature of the Creation recorded in the Book of Genesis: 'To the side of scholarship and literary interest there gravitated, imperceptibly, the bulk of those religious-minded traditionalists who were alarmed at the tendency of the times' (Casson 1939, 207).

The methods developed since the Renaissance

1.13 Stuart and Revett's engraving of the Parthenon, Athens, published in 1787, shows Turkish houses and a mosque that were removed when Greece became independent in 1831. They published five volumes of architectural studies and views of buildings between 1762 and 1830, and placed great emphasis upon accurate recording, for these books were intended for use by architects building in the neo-classical style. Fortunately for modern researchers with a wider interest in these sites, they began by sketching the actual condition of each monument. *Stuart & Revett 1787, pl. 1*

for the study of classical Greece and Rome, based upon a co-ordinated investigation of literature, art and architecture, provided a model for the study of Egypt and the Near East (Trigger 1989, 35–40). Literary interest was soon given a tremendous boost, for the written languages of both regions were deciphered by the middle of the nineteenth century. An inscription on the Rosetta Stone (discovered in Egypt by a French officer in Napoleon's army in 1799) turned out to have been written in two different Egyptian scripts and also in Greek. The stone was taken to Britain after Napoleon's defeat, but attempts to use the Greek text as a key for understanding the Egyptian scripts culminated in success by a French scholar, Jean François Champollion, who published a grammar and dictionary of Egyptian hieroglyphics in the 1830s (Andrew 1992). The cuneiform script of Mesopotamia was first translated around the same time, and the early Babylonian language of the region was deciphered with the help of a gigantic inscription carved on a high cliff at Behistun in Persia, recorded by Henry Rawlinson, a soldier and diplomat in the region who eventually became curator of the British Museum in 1876. It included identical texts written in Persian, Babylonian and Elamite to proclaim the authority of the Persian king Darius over his conquests, and the study was completed by 1857.

The implications of these translations were tremendous: 'The development of Egyptology and Assyriology in the course of the nineteenth century added 3000 years of history to two areas of the world that were of particular interest in terms of biblical studies, but for which no direct documentation had been available' (Trigger 1989, 40). Countless Egyptian hieroglyphic inscriptions were already known (their use had continued under Greek and Roman rule until at least the end of the fourth century AD), and buildings could now be dated according to the names of Pharaohs inscribed on them. The decipherment of 'cuneiform' writing allowed the translation of thousands of clay tablets found on excavations throughout the area; these tablets frequently provided details of palace stores and accounts, as well as historical information. Egypt and Mesopotamia thus joined Greece and Rome in having a detailed historical framework for the study of their culture and physical remains.

The increasing interest in Near Eastern civilizations was not entirely beneficial, for it led to intensive plundering of sites for carvings and inscriptions to satisfy greater demands from museums and collectors. In Mesopotamia, even palaces and temples were largely built out of sun-dried mud brick (see fig. 3.33) – unlike their stone counterparts in Egypt. Fragile structures and perishable or unimpressive artefacts were neglected for most of the rest of the nineteenth century, along with any earlier prehistoric levels underlying historical sites. Casson pinpointed the problem: 'Scientific method existed. But for the archaeologists of the various phases of civilized man there were no scientific collaborators.... This divorce of science from archaeology, in so far as the later phases of civilization were concerned, was largely due to the fact that historical sites fell automatically under the control of literary men' (1939, 215). Frere, Worsaae and Boucher de Perthes observed and recorded the stratigraphical contexts of prehistoric artefacts because it was the only possible source of chronological evidence; but with historical records written in hieroglyphs or cuneiform, who needed strata?

So far, then, planned fieldwork was almost absent from the process of discovery, and it was inhibited by the nature of the study of literate civilizations. As a result of the publicity surrounding Schliemann's major discoveries at Troy in the 1870s, a request was made in England to obtain financial support from the Treasury for work on burial mounds in the same area of Turkey, on the grounds that they were of as much potential interest as the Temple of Diana at Ephesus, which was already receiving financial support. The official reply was mortifying: the work at Ephesus was undertaken '... not for the purpose of ascertaining the site or the form of the Temple, objects quite beyond the scope of the Trustees [of the British Museum], but for the sake of such relics of ancient art as might be found buried among the ruins. The ascertainment of the site was a mere incident. ... The question then is: are excavations undertaken for the purpose of illustrating the *Iliad* a proper subject for the expenditure of public money? I am sorry to say that in my judgement they are not' (Rt. Hon. Robert Lowe, 1873). Mention of Schliemann does hint that clearer objectives were finally coming into the study of early civilizations. The late nineteenth century also witnessed a more systematic approach to the recording of surface remains of monuments, using improved surveying techniques, combined with the rapidly developing technique of photography.

5.2 Schliemann and Troy
(McDonald & Thomas 1990)

Heinrich Schliemann was born in Germany in 1822. His commercial skills and gift for languages allowed him to close down his business interests in 1863 to devote himself to travelling and studying the ancient Greek world until his death in 1890. Part of the enduring appeal of Schliemann's life-story lies in his rather dubious role as an outsider who took on the academic establishment and outwitted the Greek and Turkish authorities in the relentless and successful pursuit of his theories. How far this view is correct may be debated, but the persistence, discipline and intelligence that brought him commercial success and a rapid rise from shop assistant to Californian banker would have been helpful in approaching excavation: 'The grocer who unpacks crates is better equipped to unpack the middens of antiquity than the polite scholar who has never seen the inside of his own dustbin' (Casson 1939, 224). However, Schliemann was not the only archaeologist in Greece or Turkey to pay attention to the recognition and recording of stratigraphy and finds during an excavation. In the 1870s an Austrian, Alexander Conze, working at Samothrace and a German, Ernst Curtius, at Olympia both applied rigorous methods of excavation inspired by the recent work of Guiseppe Fiorelli at Pompeii in Italy (Trigger 1989, 196–7).

Nineteenth-century German literary scholars considered that the *Iliad* (Homer's epic poem recounting stories of the Trojan Wars) was not based on a historical reality, but involved miscellaneous accounts of mythical heroes. Schliemann held the opposite view and, having combined study of the Homeric text with fieldwork in Greece and Turkey, he published observations about Mycenae and the location of Troy in 1869 – two years before he began to excavate the latter site (fig. 1.14). He drew wide attention to his findings through the rapid publication of his work at Troy and related sites, as well as popular reports to newspapers such as *The Times*. His results have undergone considerable reinterpretation, initially by his co-worker Dörpfeld, who only three years after Schliemann's death, redefined the occupation level at Troy that was considered to have belonged to the Homeric period.

Although Schliemann's excavations and research around the Aegean were initially motivated by the desire to elucidate a specific literary text, they brought the Greek Bronze Age and its antecedents to light for the first time. He conducted his work as a conscious problem-oriented exercise, rather than simply to recover attractive finds from a known historical site; he also paid attention to the whole stratigraphic sequence at Troy, not just a single period. His approach was in stark contrast to Mariette's discovery of the Serapeum, at Memphis in Egypt, in 1851. Mariette knew about the site from an ancient Greek traveller's account and from references in Egyptian papyri, but only discovered it thanks to a good memory and the chance observation of the head of a sphinx sticking out of the sand; four years of excavation followed (Daniel, 1967, 229). Happy accidents of this kind were the rule rather than the exception. Many sites mentioned in historical sources or the Bible were only identified because their names appeared on building inscriptions or clay tablets found during plunder for museum exhibits. One example of this kind was the site of Sippar in southern Mesopotamia (the biblical *Sepharvaim*) where Rassam excavated for the British Museum in 1881. Ironically, one of the cuneiform inscriptions that he found recorded an excavation carried out by the Babylonian king Nabonidus in the sixth century BC. Nabonidus dug beneath the foundations of a temple dedicated to the Sun-God Shamash to find out who had built it, and discovered an inscription that answered his question (Lloyd 1980, 156). Nabonidus was evidently a rather more problem-oriented excavator than Rassam.

5.3 Evans and Knossos
(McDonald & Thomas 1990)

One of the final stages in revealing the early civilizations of Europe and the Near East took place when Sir Arthur Evans investigated the origins

1.14 Schliemann's excavations at Troy (Hissarlik, Turkey) were not a good model of archaeological technique. Only solid structures were noticed and recorded, and they were rapidly demolished to reveal earlier features. Schliemann's awareness that a succession of cities had occupied the site, and his determination to find the Homeric level, did at least force him to take note of the occurrence of artefacts in different levels. His motivation for digging is of particular interest; it was the culmination of a long programme of literary research, fieldwork and excavations on other sites, all aimed at identifying the geographical setting and physical remains of an early Greek culture known only from literature. *Schliemann 1880, facing p. 265*

of the Mycenaean civilization revealed by Schliemann in Greece. Soon after the independence of Crete in 1898 Evans excavated the Minoan palace at Knossos, where a 'literate' civilization had developed around from around 2000 BC. Evans, like Schliemann, was testing a hypothesis suggested by prior research. He was aware that engraved seal-stones bearing a pictographic script had been found in Crete, and that their script (now known as Linear A) was independent of those of Egypt or Turkey. It indicated that a system of writing had been developed well before the adoption of an early form of Greek by the Mycenaeans. Unlike Schliemann, Arthur Evans did not suffer opposition or ridicule; he had an impeccable academic background, and worked in the Ashmolean Museum, Oxford. He had even accompanied his father John on the famous visit to Boucher de Perthes at Abbeville in 1859 (above, p. 13); eight-year-old Arthur actually found a flint implement.

Unlike Egypt, Mesopotamia, or even Homeric Greece, the Minoan world was almost entirely unknown; the notion of a civilization preceding that of Classical Greece was a real revelation. As at Troy, earlier levels were found below the palace at Knossos; they extended back into the prehistoric period and emphasized the depth of time that preceded the literate stages of these early civilizations. Thus, archaeology alone had provided almost everything that was known about Minoan civilization, and this achievement paralleled the contribution made by prehistorians to the understanding of human antiquity. The excavations at Knossos were directed at the solution of a specific cultural problem, using a variety of evidence, including some small previous excavations on the site: the results were spectacularly successful (fig. 1.15). Evans was helped by the fact that the Minoan palace was not overlain by extensive remains of subsequent occupation. He was able to make really detailed interpretations because it had been destroyed by volcanic activity, and contained the remains of most of its artefacts and furnishings.

5.4 Beyond Europe and the Near East
(Fagan 1977)

After the discovery of Minoan Crete, the only early European or Near Eastern civilization to remain unknown until the twentieth century was that of the Hittites in Turkey. Like the Mesopotamian civilizations, it was known from

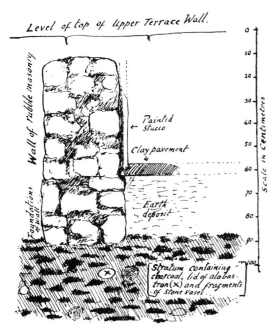

1.15 A section drawing from Arthur Evans' report on excavations at Knossos, Crete. In an unusually careful manner at such an early date, Evans illustrated the precise location of a vital piece of dating evidence (an imported Egyptian lid) beneath the wall and floor of part of the palace. Perhaps his father, John Evans, had made him familiar with geological sections such as fig. 1.5 above. *Evans 1899–1900, p. 64*

the Bible; it was illuminated in 1906–8 by the discovery of large numbers of inscribed tablets at the large fortified city of Hattusha (now Bogazköy). Further East, fieldwork and excavation in the twentieth century in India and China produced evidence of urban civilizations, dating back to before 2000 and 1000 BC respectively.

In the New World, Spanish colonists and churchmen had reported the existence of sophisticated urban civilizations since the fifteenth century, but the literate civilization of the Maya that flourished in Yucatan was first described by John Stephens and Frederick Catherwood in the 1840s. Fortunately, the objectivity and accuracy of their fieldwork set an example for work elsewhere in Central and South America. High-quality excavation of Maya sites, organized by the Peabody Museum of Harvard University, followed in the 1890s. Further south, fieldwork and excavation took place from the 1850s onwards, notably by Max Uhle in Peru and elsewhere. All of this exploratory work falls within Willey and Sabloff's 'classificatory-descriptive period (1840–1914)' of American archaeology, and it was of course influenced by European work both on human antiquity and early civilizations (1980, 34–76). In contrast to the languages of Egypt and Mesopotamia, the exciting breakthrough of deciphering Mayan script did not take place until the 1960s (Coe 1992).

6 Achievements of early antiquarians

The purpose of this chapter has been to demonstrate that the basic principles of contemporary archaeology are illuminated by studying how they developed in the first place. I hope to have done so without conflicting with Piggott's demand to avoid both hindsight and period charm: 'What we are left with, and surely should be our aim, is an attempt to see the early development of archaeology as far as possible in terms of its own past, with its individual exponents thinking and acting as children of their age (as we are of our own), and assessing what now seem for us their praiseworthy or unfortunate contributions to the subject in relation to their contemporary social and intellectual context, and their individual world-picture' (1982, 19).

The discovery of the 'lost' civilizations (other than Greece and Rome), the appearance of scientific excavation techniques, and the increasingly sophisticated interpretation of past societies, all belong to a phase of archaeology that had scarce-ly begun before the nineteenth century. However, the rapid developments of the nineteenth and twentieth centuries incorporated several of key factors established during the Renaissance and the Age of Reason. Pursuits that were considered respectable in intellectual circles happened to include the study, recording and collecting of ancient sites and artefacts, as part of a wider scientific interest in natural history. The efforts of individuals, usually amateurs and often eccentrics, established the methods of fieldwork, and led to the opening of museums that had to be staffed, displayed and catalogued. Others extended the existence of humans on Earth from a mere 6000 years back into an immeasurable period. As a result of all these achievements, greater efforts were made to collect human artefacts, and to organize them in more sophisticated ways to provide a new source for the documentation of human technical and social progress.

Unfortunately, the discovery of the great civilizations did little to advance archaeological techniques until conscious problem-solving investigations began in the late nineteenth century. Luck, accident and careless plunder were commonplace; historians and art-historians were interested in documents and works of art, and these could be gained without much attention to stratification or planned research. These awaited the growth of a sense of responsibility about antiquities, and the systematic approach of people like Pitt Rivers or Uhle. New methods had to be developed to investigate problems such as the prehistoric background of Egypt, or the Neolithic communities accidentally revealed beneath the Minoan palace at Knossos and at the bottom of many Near Eastern tells. Because radiocarbon dating only began to provide independent dates for prehistoric sites in the 1950s, these problems demanded the kind of study that had been developed in northern Europe, involving careful excavation (taking account of stratification), and typological study of pottery and other artefacts to provide relative dating.

Co-operation between specialists in separate disciplines was much easier in the restricted circles of learning that existed before the twentieth century. Fortunately, the multi-disciplinary approach that brought such beneficial results to the study of early humans in the mid-nineteenth century has grown ever since, with the result that archaeology remains one of the few subjects available in the educational world that forms a genuine bridge between science and the humanities. Two less welcome traditions were also established early. One was the inability of some scholars to complete their work for publication; another was the distortion of evidence to support fanciful theories. Although characteristic of early antiquaries such as Aubrey and Stukeley respectively, both phenomena are still very much a part of archaeology today, and they will be examined further in later chapters.

Note: a guide to **further reading** that includes topics covered in this chapter begins on p. 185.

2 Discovery, Fieldwork and Recording

This chapter aims to introduce a variety of traditional and modern techniques used in discovering and examining archaeological sites. I hope to emphasize that there are many non-destructive ways of looking at sites in their local and regional settings; excavation should be a last resort, since it involves irreversible physical intervention. It is remarkable how much can be revealed about a site using surface observations alone; however, these depend on a reasonably good state of preservation of visible structural remains or earthworks. In densely populated, intensively cultivated countries well-preserved sites are very much the exception. In much of western Europe many prehistoric sites must already have been ploughed flat by the end of the Roman period. In these circumstances, anything that can 'see beneath the soil' has an important role, from broad-scanning techniques such as aerial photography to geophysical devices used on individual sites. Twentieth-century technology cannot claim all the credit, however, for Camden and Stukeley made sensible observations and interpretations of buried features or structures revealed by variations in growing crops in the sixteenth and eighteenth centuries (Daniel 1967, 37; 45).

1 The discovery of new archaeological sites

Chapter 1 explained how antiquaries like Cyriac of Ancona and William Stukeley, or the tell-diggers of the Near East, relied on straightforward visual inspection to find ancient sites. Some travelled to investigate unknown areas, others made systematic attempts to increase knowledge about regions that had already proved productive. Limitations of transport continued to impose severe restrictions on fieldworkers until at least the mid-twentieth century. Although many technical devices are used today, the human eye remains an extremely important and sensitive instrument. Chance discoveries of artefacts or structures during farming or building work have been particularly important in adding to the basic corpus of archaeological knowledge in the nineteenth and twentieth centuries, and finds made in this way may be followed up by more informed examination. The pattern of discovery of artefacts and settlements in Denmark illustrates this well (fig. 2.1; Hedeager 1992, 14–21).

Discovery is pointless without recording, but observers (ancient or modern) only record what they see, and what they see is determined by what they consider to be significant. Early antiquaries did of course make invaluable observations about sites which in some cases have since disappeared, but they normally left frustratingly inadequate accounts. There was slow progress from terse descriptions to schematic illustrations, and then from picturesque drawings to accurate surveys (Piggott 1979). The scientific attitudes that accompanied the Enlightenment involved an increased interest in classification, which naturally required more careful observation. Recording was revolutionized in the 1840s and 1850s by the rapid development of photography (Feyler 1987). British and French expeditions carried out extensive photography in Syria and Egypt; when the Crimean War began in 1854, the Society of Antiquaries of London requested the English Army to instruct its photographer 'to take and transmit photographic views of any antiquities which he may observe' (Evans 1956, 291).

Perhaps the greatest contrast with the past is that fieldwork today is rarely directed at a single site. It usually forms part of a comprehensive study of an area selected either because it is threatened with destruction, or because it offers potential answers to questions generated by wider archaeological research. One of the first major fieldwork projects carried out in central Italy

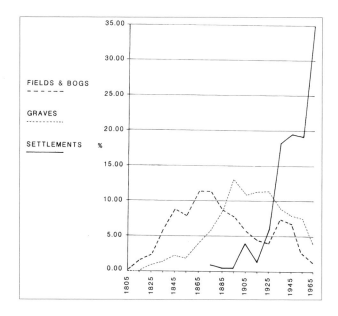

2.1 Sources of archaeological finds in Denmark changed markedly in the nineteenth and twentieth centuries. The expansion of agriculture led to many accidental discoveries in fields and bogs, but these were overtaken by finds from graves as archaeological work increased later in the nineteenth century. However, it was only after 1930 that the changing focus of archaeological excavation made settlements the predominant source of new finds. It can be seen that there was a plentiful supply of finds to nineteenth-century antiquarians who, like C J Thomsen, were primarily interested in typology. *Hedeager 1992, 14–20*

began in the 1950s because redistribution of agricultural estates to small-scale farmers led to a sudden increase in ploughing. Fortunately, archaeologists from the British School of Archaeology in Rome realized the implications of this change, and walked over large areas of farmland recording finds and traces of sites or structures. The result was a view of the distribution of rural sites over a long period, from later prehistory to the early Middle Ages. Interesting variations in the location and intensity of sites in different periods required careful interpretation to explain the changes in terms of settlement patterns, population and methods of farming. Partly as a result of this early success, studies in Greece or the Roman Mediterranean provinces shifted from the investigation of individual sites to the study of regions.

Formerly, significant sites (most commonly towns) were surveyed and excavated because their plans, buildings and inscriptions were expected to reflect the political and military history of their area. Now, studies are more likely to involve extensive analysis on a regional scale, designed to elucidate the broad agricultural, economic and social developments within which individual sites operated (Greene 1986, 98–143). Prehistoric archaeology has also undergone a similar shift in focus away from individual events to the consideration of longer-term processes (see chapter 6). An example of a recent multi-period Mediterranean field survey project in Dalmatia (Croatia) is described in a case-study below (p. 54).

Fieldwork underwater is not unlike that on land, for it relies on visual scanning of areas of the seabed by divers. Photography, recording and surveying practices on wreck sites and cargo scatters use the same general principles employed on dry land, but they are of course more time-consuming and cumbersome. Echo-sounders and sonar scanners replace aerial photography for detecting anomalies on the seabed, except in clear shallow water, and magnetic location devices are very effective in surveying wreck sites (Dean 1992, 128–46).

2 Fieldwalking and site recording
(Brown 1987)

Although fieldwork projects are often conducted on a very large scale today, they continue to employ techniques developed in the past for the study of individual sites or small areas. The simplest (and oldest) procedure is **fieldwalking**, which relies upon the observation of minor fluctuations in the character of the ground surface, and, where possible, the recognition of ancient artefacts lying upon it. If fieldwalking is conducted systematically the results can be analysed to reveal significant patterns of finds. The area selected for examination is marked out with a regular grid for the guidance of teams of walkers, to ensure that the ground is inspected evenly. Any finds, whether artefacts or surface features, must be recorded accurately in relation to this basic grid, and plotted on to a master-plan to give an overall distribution of the results (figs 2.2–3). If an area is too large to be explored in its entirety, it should be sampled in such a way that the results may be assessed statistically, and extrapolated to the whole area with some confidence; computer programs now allow this to be done with ease. Clusters of potsherds, flint flakes or building debris lying on the surface may suggest likely centres of occupation or other human activity in the past. A lack of obvious concentrations does not mean that no occupation existed, of course; agricultural exploitation or geological weathering of the land may affect the results in different ways, even in a small area.

Traces of structures, or earthworks such as

2.2 A team from the University of Bradford recording surface traces of a medieval monastic settlement and village on the Isle of May in the Firth of Forth, Scotland. It is important that all field recording, whether of sites or artefacts found on the surface, is conducted on a carefully planned basis. The surveying equipment used on this site included a site included a GRID-pad write-top, held by an operator in the foreground. This specialized portable computer has a screen that can display a general plan of the area, and is connected to an EDM (electronic distance meter). The exact location of features indicated by the archaeologist in the middle distance can be logged accurately and added to the site plan. *Steve Dockrill*

ditches or field-boundaries, should be surveyed straight away with simple equipment, but a more detailed follow-up may be desirable if greater accuracy is required for the interpretation of a complex site (fig. 2.2). A grid of measured spot-heights provides contour plans that may reveal subtle surface variations not immediately apparent to the eye. If the results are logged by a portable computer the readings may be processed to enhance variations before plotting the contours. Large sites are more easily understood when the features recorded in a survey are drawn out at a small scale; inconsistencies requiring further investigation will be more obvious. Relationships between the various components (enclosures, trackways, building plots, etc.) are more likely to be evident on a plan than on the ground. The analysis and interpretation of site-plans are an important aspect of archaeology, and a combination of field observations and the examination of plans may elucidate the sequence in which overlapping earthworks were created, altered or superseded. It must not be forgotten that Stukeley was perfectly capable of making deductions of this kind in the eighteenth century, however (above, p. 23).

2.1   Sites and Monuments Records
(Larsen 1992)

The more elaborate scientific techniques of archaeological prospecting outlined below are

Date: _____   LEPTI SURVEY 1990   Site #: _____
Time: _____   Team : _____   Field #: _____
Map Coord: _____

Recognized Chronological Periods : (Check all that apply)

☐ ? ☐ Prehistoric	**Rom-Lib:**	**Post Roman**
☐ ? ☐ Bronze Age	☐ ? ☐ Republican	☐ ? ☐ Vandal
☐ ? ☐ Protohist	☐ ? ☐ Early Imperial	☐ ? ☐ Byzantine
Phoenician:	☐ ? ☐ Mid Imperial	☐ ? ☐ Fatamid
	☐ ? ☐ Late Imperial	☐ ? ☐ Hafsid
☐ ? ☐ Archaic		☐ ? ☐ Ottoman
☐ ? ☐ Classical		☐ ? ☐ Modern
☐ ? ☐ Hellenistic		

Aspect:
NW N NE
W E
SW S SE

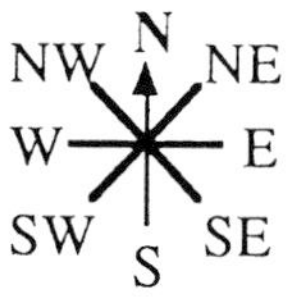

○ N
○ NE
○ E
○ SE
○ S
○ SW
○ W
○ NW
○ None

Geology:
○ No info
○ Visible
○ Concealed

Soil Color:
_____

Soil Composition:

Gravel	Sand	Silt	Clay
○ 0%	○ 0%	○ 0%	○ 0%
○ 25%	○ 25%	○ 25%	○ 25%
○ 50%	○ 50%	○ 50%	○ 50%
○ 75%	○ 75%	○ 75%	○ 75%
○ 100%	○ 100%	○ 100%	○ 100%

Topography:
○ No Info   ○ Upper
○ Artif Terrace ○ Middle
○ Foreshore   ○ Lower
○ Hilltop   ○ No Info
○ Gully   Other: _____
○ Plateau

Land Use:
☐ Vines
☐ Olives
☐ Fruit Trees
☐ Vegetables
☐ Pasture
☐ Cereals
☐ Fallow
Other: _____

Geological Description:
_____

Field Transect Plan   (with N. point and dimensions):

+   +   +   +   +

+   +   +   +   +

Locational Directions:
_____

Sketch:

Comments:
_____

2.3 A systematic approach to discoveries is illustrated by this standard form for recording sites during a survey project around Leptiminus, a Roman port in Tunisia. Fieldworkers can note most traces that they encounter simply by ticking boxes, and the information from the completed forms is ready for entry into a computer database. *Lazreg & Mattingly 1992, fig. 3*

normally applied to individual sites to maximize the understanding of their nature and extent before excavation. Broader methods, such as aerial photography or field survey, are more likely to be employed in a regional research project, with the aim of collecting information about all periods thoroughly. Ideally, a database should be created to serve a number of different purposes, including further research by individuals who may not have been involved in its collection. 'Rescue' archaeology has provided a stimulus to this kind of recording, and many countries now have a policy of maintaining **Sites and Monuments Records** on a regional basis. A good knowledge of the number and distribution of known sites makes it much easier to assess the implications of plans for building construction or other development threats. If planning authorities and contractors are able to consult these records at an early stage, they may be able to adjust developments to avoid sites, or, at least, to take account of them so that excavation can be arranged well in advance without costly disturbances to construction schedules.

Sites and Monuments Records are normally stored on computers for rapid access, and the details of each site include cross-references to maps, publications and aerial photographs. They are very useful for research, and provide an obvious starting point for anyone who wishes to study sites or finds of a particular type or period. Research of this kind increases our understanding of regions and their sites, and makes it easier to draw up priorities when difficult choices have to be made about their preservation or destruction. Thus, fieldworkers have many responsibilities besides the discovery and recording of sites; they have an obligation to interpret the results in the light of the latest research, and to present their conclusions in a convenient and comprehensible form for consultation by non-specialists.

3 Aerial photography
(Wilson 1982; Riley 1987)

The greatest single contribution to fieldwork and recording has undoubtedly been made by aerial photography. Besides giving a bird's-eye view of surviving sites, aerial photography can, in favourable circumstances, record details of buried sites revealed by discolorations in the overlying soil or vegetation (fig. 2.4). The visual effectiveness of aerial photographs had been appreciated since the 1850s; occasional archaeological shots were taken from balloons, but the First World War stimulated the practice of taking high-altitude reconnaissance photographs from aeroplanes both for mapping and strategic purposes. Many pioneers of archaeological aerial photography gained their experience in this way, including O G S Crawford, who published a manual on the subject in 1929. The use of the technique has expanded exponentially since then, and the understanding of the conditions for its optimum application has also increased. Cameras and film-types used in conventional photography are now very versatile, and remote-sensing from satellites is becoming a valuable additional source of high-altitude images (Shennan and Donoghue 1992).

3.1 Visible sites

Aerial photography provides a useful supplement to observations made during fieldwork on visible earthworks (figs 2.5–6). Isolated features may become more coherent when seen in an overall view, and new features not easily noticed on the ground may be revealed; a common example is the relation of outlying field boundaries and trackways to a farming settlement. The best conditions are provided by low light, because it emphasizes irregularities by highlighting bumps and filling hollows with deep shadow (fig. 2.5). Clear sunlight cannot be guaranteed at exactly the right time of morning or evening in temperate countries, of course, and the best shadow effects do not last long. This form of aerial photography is most suitable for adding details to known sites, rather than for prospecting for new sites. Frost or light snow may enhance both shadow sites and buried sites, either because of their reflective qualities or because of variations caused by

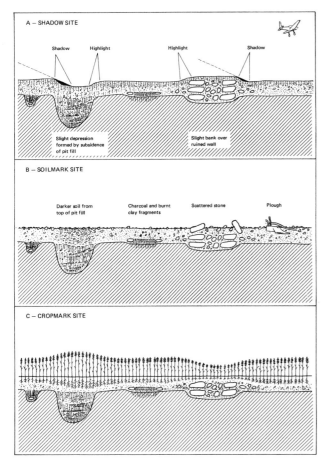

A — SHADOW SITE

Shadow Highlight Highlight Shadow

Slight depression formed by subsidence of pit fill

Slight bank over ruined wall

B — SOILMARK SITE

Darker soil from top of pit fill

Charcoal and burnt clay fragments

Scattered stone

Plough

C — CROPMARK SITE

2.4 Circumstances leading to the formation of characteristics visible on aerial photographs.
A: Slight surface variations, which might not be apparent to an observer on the ground, are enhanced by highlights and shadows produced by low sunlight in the early morning or evening.
B: Even if these surface features have been removed, subsequent disturbance of the soil by ploughing may still reveal variations in colour or texture. C: Irregularities in the depth and moisture content of the soil may lead to marked variations in the height and colour of a cereal crop during its growth or ripening. Severe drought conditions exaggerate these effects and may also reveal much smaller features, not only in cereal crops but also in permanent pasture like A. Note that the post-hole and hearth at the left and centre of these diagrams would not be likely to be revealed, even in extreme conditions. Fig. 2.10 illustrates the results of geophysical prospecting over the same buried features. *Audio Visual Centre, University of Newcastle*

2.5 The ditches of Roman military earthworks at Chew Green, Northumberland, are enhanced by shadows cast by low sunlight. This extensive site lies on sloping rough moorland in the Cheviot Hills, and is very difficult to understand on the ground because of its complexity and size: the most distinctive earthwork in the centre of the photograph is approximately 150 metres square. *Tim Gates, National Monuments Record*

differential thawing. Such conditions are of course rare, and are more likely to be recorded by luck rather than planning.

3.2 Invisible sites

(Whimster 1989)

Many of the most impressive photographs taken by pioneers like Crawford and Keiller were of known sites, but aerial photography has been much more important in providing information and discoveries about sites that have been levelled, and are therefore unlikely to be spotted during normal fieldwork. Even when sites are discovered by fieldwalking, after ploughing has scattered finds on the surface, their form and extent are rarely evident. Such sites are commonest in areas of heavy agricultural exploitation,

2.6 A new plan of Chew Green earthworks compiled by surveyors and investigators from the Royal Commission on Ancient and Historical Monuments. There are four overlapping square or rectangular military camps and forts, besides other features that probably result from more recent farming activities.

© Crown copyright: RCHME

where different settlement patterns and field systems may have come and gone several times during the evolution of the modern landscape. Their detection relies on a number of phenomena that influence vegetation or the soil. **Crop-marks** are created when buried features either enhance or reduce the growth of plants (figs 2.7–8). Since a key factor is the availability of moisture to their roots, abnormal conditions emphasize the height and colour of crops (particularly cereals) during growth and ripening. These effects are not consistent or easily predictable, and a complex site should be photographed over many years, under different conditions, to compile a cumulative record of its features. As with shadow sites, the optimum conditions do not last long; root crops and pasture are very insensitive, and only reveal marks during extreme drought conditions.

Soil-marks may be observed when land has been ploughed; human activity in the past may lead to variations in the character and colour of the topsoil, and like crop-marks, subtle variations are best seen from above to reveal a coherent plan. The most dramatic sites discovered in this way are Roman villas photographed by Roger Agache in north-eastern France; ploughing has brought fragments of their chalk foundations to the surface and revealed detailed plans of buildings, clearly visible as white lines against dark brown soil (Greene 1986, 116–18). Unfortunately a site that shows up as a soil-mark is probably being severely eroded, and may soon disappear altogether if regular ploughing contin-

ues. Some soil-marks are merely 'ghost sites', made up of soils of differing consistencies and colours derived from pits, ditches and other features that have been destroyed by deep ploughing (Clark 1990, 110–12).

Aerial photography is not to be undertaken lightly; like fieldwork conducted on the ground, it must be well planned and systematic. Photography should be carried out with a good knowledge of the sites, crops and geology of an area, so that it is timed to coincide with the best conditions. Expertise is required in selecting the optimum cameras and films, for some colour film emulsions are specially sensitive to particular colour ranges. The use of infra-red photography, or multispectral scanners that record the reflective properties of the ground, may clarify the results (Shennan and Donoghue 1992). Variations in colour or contrast can be enhanced by special developing or printing processes, or by computer scanning and filtering (fig. 2.9). Sites must of course be mapped to be used by archaeologists on the ground. Oblique views of sites require complicated adjustments to be plotted on to a horizontal plan, and even the best cameras suffer some distortion away from the centre of their lenses. Computer-based techniques have been designed to overcome these problems, but they are restricted to specialized mapping centres. It is important that aerial photographs include several fixed reference points that can be identified on large-scale maps, to enable archaeologists to create working plans by hand, using geometry – and a considerable amount of patience.

Experience is also required not only to photograph meaningful things from the air, but to recognize and interpret the results. It is not always easy to distinguish between archaeological features and natural geological phenomena, and a deep knowledge of archaeology is required for

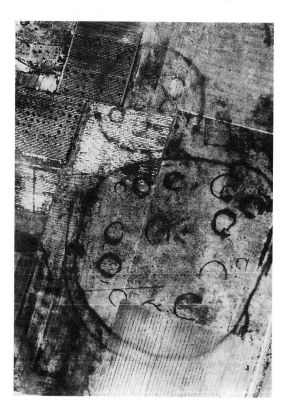

2.7 At La Panetteria, Foggia, Italy, a neolithic settlement is revealed by particularly clear crop-marks that mark enclosure ditches and circular foundation trenches for timber roundhouses. Many further dark lines and patches appear within and outside the enclosures; excavation would be necessary to determine whether these are natural geological effects, prehistoric features, or the result of modern farming. *Sherratt 1980, p. 147*

2.8 Dry conditions have revealed the remains of three concentric ramparts that once belonged to a fortified late prehistoric settlement at Chatton, Northumberland. The crop has ripened most where the subsoil is shallowest, producing a visual effect exactly opposite to that observable at La Panetteria. A further set of irregular enclosures may be seen in another part of the field. *Tim Gates, National Monuments Record*

the most promising regions. Proper research programmes are less exciting and more expensive than unplanned exploration, but their results allow much firmer conclusions to be reached about site distributions, settlement patterns and other features of ancient landscapes.

A different problem is that land that was once ploughed may subsequently have remained under pasture for a considerable period; in Britain, many fields used for grazing today show the tell-tale traces of medieval ridge-and-furrow ploughed strips. Medieval ploughing will not only have destroyed any earthworks that preceded it, but today's mature pasture will prevent the detection of earlier buried sites except under extreme drought conditions. The use of land for modern arable or pasture depends on factors such as the surface geology, drainage, climate and altitude. Thus, a map of archaeological sites in any area is incomplete unless it shows how the sites were discovered (shadow, crop- or soil-mark), and

2.9 Aerial photographs may be digitized for computer analysis, and then processed by programs that filter out irrelevant background variations and enhance significant details. Oblique photographs can also be adjusted to compensate for distortions of angle, and matched precisely to maps. This illustration shows an inexpensive PC-based imaging system in which a video camera is examining a negative. The graphs on the left represent scales of tones found in the photograph; they can be altered to produce modified images on the other screen. *Booth* et al., *1992, fig. 27.1*

any attempt to classify and date sites by their form. This problem is reduced by using an objective method of describing the traces recorded on photographs, and by using a computer database system to enforce standard methods of description (Edis, MacLeod and Bewley 1989). It is also important to recognize areas where sites are absent, and to decide whether they really did not exist there, or if modern conditions simply do not provide circumstances that will bring them to light. One of the first effects of aerial photography in Britain and elsewhere was to reveal crop-mark and soil-mark sites on heavy valley soils previously considered unsuitable for cultivation; it had been assumed that they were covered by dense forest until comparatively recent historical times. The discovery of these sites caused an upward revision of estimates of early populations and their agricultural technology. However, areas where earthwork sites had already been recorded have perhaps been neglected as a result; photographers understandably concentrate on records the conditions likely to reveal visible traces.

A final comment on the value of aerial reconnaissance was provided after an exceptional number of sites was photographed in the dry summer of 1989 in Britain. Flying funded by state organizations and private individuals covered much of England and Wales, at a total cost well below that of a season's excavation on an average urban site (Griffith 1990).

4 Geophysical surveying
(Clark 1990; Scollar 1990; Spoerry 1992)

Some sites never show up on aerial photographs at all, and some show different features at different times; others are revealed only in part because they extend into adjacent land where conditions are unsuitable for photographs. When excavation is planned on a site of this kind, further details may be required about areas that do not appear clearly on photographs. It may even be difficult to establish the precise location of a site known only from oblique photographs that lack clear reference points that can be found on a map. In these circumstances a selection of geophysical prospecting devices is available for detecting buried features. It must be stressed that these instruments are only suitable for use on sites whose location is already known or suspected, for their operation is much too time-consuming to be applied 'blind' to large areas. As with aerial photography, their main purpose is to distinguish anomalies, hopefully of human origin, from the natural subsoil (figs 2.10–11).

Geophysical prospecting devices are useful wherever details need to be checked, or where trial excavation would be an inefficient method of locating buried features. For example, at Usk, Gwent, the position of the southern defences of a Roman legionary fortress was thought likely to be in fields under pasture, insensitive to crop-marks. It was a comparatively simple exercise to take measurements along a line that began within the known eastern and western ramparts; two major anomalies were found, consistent with the presence of buried ditches lying outside the former rampart (Manning 1981, 86–8). Geophysical surveying is also used within known sites to suggest areas where excavation might be most profitable. Anomalies suggesting occupation debris or structures are a very helpful guide in 'rescue archaeology' situations where a large exploratory excavation would not be feasible; indeed, the first significant uses of geophysical instruments took place in exactly these circumstances. At Dorchester, near Oxford, prehistoric ditches (known from aerial photographs) were located in 1946 by using a resistivity meter, and they were excavated before their destruction by gravel extraction. Magnetometers were first used in Northamptonshire in 1958 to find pottery kilns of Roman date (known from the writings of a local early nineteenth-century antiquary) before road construction (Clark 1990, 12–17).

A great advance in geophysical surveying occurred in the late 1960s, when portable instruments became available that could supply *continuous* readings, rather than readings taken with the instrument positioned at a series of individual points. Geophysical instruments normally require a second operator to record readings in relation to the surveying grid, but an automatic logging system is faster (fig. 2.11). Early examples produced immediate visual output by means of graphs plotted on paper, but these were superseded in the 1980s by portable computers that could compile and display larger site plans on their screens (Clark 1990, 19–26). Results are normally presented in the form of linear graphs, whose peaks and troughs indicate points of high and low resistance that indicate the position of buried anomalies (fig. 2.12). Alternatively, if a series of linear surveys has been compiled over an area, it is possible to convert the readings into a contour plan. The data can be 'filtered' by computer programs to eliminate natural variations, so that archaeological features are emphasized when plotted on a plan. The availability of laser printers has enhanced the subtlety of filtered plans in a way described by Clark as 'nothing short of a revolution' (1990, 147).

It is dangerous to place too much reliance on the results of geophysical surveys, however. At South Cadbury Castle, Somerset (an Iron Age hillfort with additional 'Dark Age' occupation) an area of the interior was excavated because anomalies identified by a survey suggested the presence of a rectangular building – possibly, the excavator hoped, a timber hall of early medieval date. On

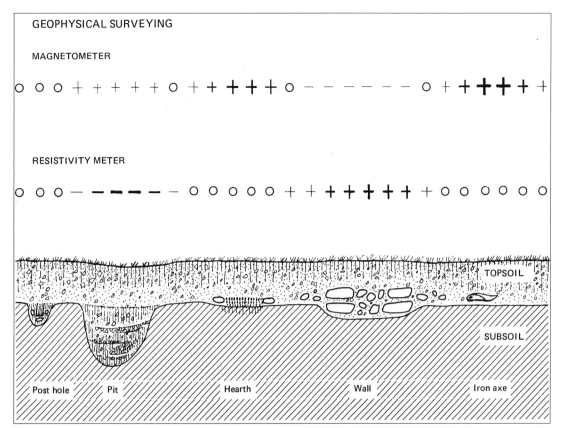

2.10 Diagram showing the ability of the two principal methods of geophysical prospecting to detect buried features. '+' indicates a positive reading from a strong magnetic field, or high resistance to the passage of an electrical current, and '–' shows a negative response (lower magnetism or resistance) in comparison with the site's average background reading ('O'). The size of the symbols gives a rough impression of the relative strengths of these results. The different kinds of instruments do not react to anomalies in the same way, and neither can be expected to detect minor features such as a post-hole. The nature of the site and the operator's experience will determine which method is employed. The same soil profile is also used in fig. 2.4 to illustrate how these features would show up on aerial photographs. *Audio Visual Centre, University of Newcastle*

excavation it was found to be a fortuitous combination of entirely unrelated features of different dates. However, a timber hall was indeed found in an adjacent area, but its construction was based on post-holes too small to have shown up in this kind of survey (Alcock 1972, 71, fig. 8).

Two main classes of instruments are used in geophysical prospecting. **Resistivity meters** detect the resistance of subsoil to the passage of an electrical current, and **magnetometers** measure variations in the subsoil's magnetic characteristics. Related instruments obtain useful information by measuring the magnetic susceptibility of the superficial soils, rather than that of features dug into the subsoil.

4.1 Resistivity surveying

When an electric current is passed through the ground between electrodes, the resistance to its flow may be measured. A current will pass relatively easily through damp soil, but drier compact material such as a buried wall or a cobbled road surface create higher resistance. Resistivity surveying is rather cumbersome, because it normally requires a number of electrode probes (usually four) to be pushed into the ground at precise intervals for each reading. A variety of configurations has been tried to speed up the surveying procedure; for instance, instead of forming a line, 47

2.11 Unlike aerial photography, geophysical surveying is never used on its own as a method of discovering sites. It is best used for checking details that are not clear from surface remains. Here, a resistivity meter is being used to record a traverse across a suspected medieval fortified farm at Easter Bradley in Northumberland. The operator is following a precise line (marked by tapes) which can be related to a precise site-plan by the EDM (electronic distance meter) visible in the foreground. *Jim Crow*

probes have been fixed in a square table-like arrangement with the instrument mounted on top for single-handed surveying (Clark 1990, 45–7, figs 35–8). An even, well-drained subsoil with features buried at a fairly constant depth is best for resistivity; otherwise, natural disturbances and variations may confuse the readings. In temperate climates, the best conditions for the moisture content of the soil occur in the months from July to September.

Because of the laborious procedure involved, resistivity is best suited to the detection of linear features such as roads, walls or ditches by taking measurements along a straight line at 90° to their suspected position. Some electromagnetic instruments measure soil conductivity without probes, and although less sensitive they have proved particularly successful on arid sites in desert areas.

4.2 Magnetic surveying

Magnetometers also detect deviations from the general background of the subsoil, in this case indicated by variations in its magnetic field. Several aspects of past human occupation cause suitable anomalies. Heating at approx. 700° C or above by hearths, kilns, furnaces, etc., causes the randomly aligned magnetic particles present in most soils and clays to realign along the prevailing magnetic field of the Earth, and to retain this new alignment on cooling. The alignment of magnetic particles is also affected by digging and refilling ditches and pits; solid features, such as walls or road surfaces, contain fewer magnetic minerals and therefore provide lower readings than their surroundings.

Magnetic surveying does not require probes in the ground; the instrument can be carried along a line or a grid by its operator, and it is generally preferred to resistivity for this reason when conditions are favourable. One form of instrument, the **proton magnetometer**, takes readings of the absolute magnetic field at given points on a grid. The **proton gradiometer** is less sensitive, but in many ways easier to operate; it measures the difference between two separate detector bottles at either end of a pole held vertically by the operator. Buried anomalies affect the lower bottle more than the higher, and the difference is recorded, rather than the absolute field. This permits rapid

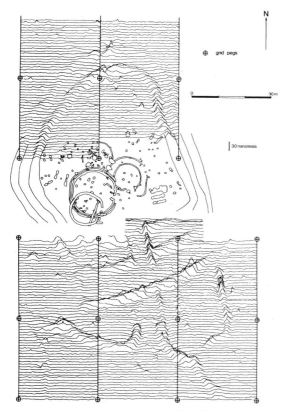

grid pegs

N

0   30 m

30 nanotesla

2.12 Magnetic survey of a site at Groundwell Farm, Wiltshire. As at La Panetteria (fig. 2.7) the site is a prehistoric settlement consisting of banks and ditches surrounding timber houses constructed in circular foundation trenches. The excavated central portion of the site confirms that the survey has been successful in detecting ditches. Each line represents a continuous reading along a measured traverse, and is in effect a graph of magnetism. Because the readings are higher over ditches, the visual effect makes them look more like raised banks; their positions are very clear, however. The survey technique would not have been sufficiently sensitive to detect the complexities of the overlapping foundation trenches of houses in the interior, however. *Clark 1990, fig. 99; Gingell 1982*

surveying of areas threatened by development, especially if a 'bleeper' mechanism produces an audible sound when an anomaly is detected. Even more rapid is the **fluxgate gradiometer**, which takes continuous, rather than spot, readings ('... the workhorse – and the race-horse – of British archaeological prospecting' (Clark 1990, 69)). Gradiometer results are easier to interpret than magnetometer readings, which are more easily disturbed by natural variations in the subsoil, or by the effects of wire fences, electrical storms or railways. Magnetometers are also an effective aid in surveying shipwreck sites on the seabed, where metal rivets or larger objects such as cannons may have been dispersed over a large area and covered by sediments (Green 1990, 81–5).

Some additional types of magnetometers and soil conductivity meters are employed in the surveying of archaeological sites. Unlike normal magnetometers, they inject a signal into shallow surface deposits and record the way the response is altered by magnetic susceptibility. Since susceptibility is influenced by human occupation and other activities, particularly when burning has been involved, it is particularly useful when it is necessary to deter-

mine the full extent of a site, for only a few very widely spaced measurements need be taken. On a smaller scale, susceptibility is a good indicator of intensively utilized domestic or industrial areas within sites; it provides a useful complement to the results of phosphate analysis, which reflect different kinds of activities such as waste-disposal or animal husbandry (Clark 1990, 107–9).

4.3 Metal detectors

Metal detectors are not only popular with members of the public who regard their use as an innocent hobby, but also with professional treasure-hunters who plunder sites for profit. The fine dividing line between these types of users accounts for the bad press metal detectors have received from archaeologists. Most types penetrate the soil only to a very limited extent, but they have been used by archaeologists to locate dispersed metal artefacts – for example, a hoard of Roman coins scattered by ploughing. A more sophisticated device (the **pulse induction meter**) gives a warning of metal objects in graves that are about to be excavated. This is not normally necessary if the site has already been surveyed by magnetometer, for when these instruments encounter iron objects they produce readings that are distinguishable from archaeological features. Some archaeologists and museum curators work in partnership with metal detector enthusiasts to make full records of any artefacts that they discover, and to provide expert

49

assistance when important antiquities are found. At Snettisham (Norfolk) several hoards of gold and silver coins and ornaments dating from the first century BC had been found by accident during ploughing, and by metal detector users. After the most recent find, archaeologists from the British Museum removed the topsoil mechanically, and located further undisturbed hoards buried at a depth that was beyond the range of metal detectors used on the original surface. The topsoil that had been removed was also thoroughly checked both by eye and by metal detector. The law of treasure trove ensured that the original finder received the market value of his discovery, and this provided an important incentive to report the finds immediately. Thus, the thrill of discovery and financial reward were combined with full archaeological details about the nature of the site and its buried metal objects (Stead 1991).

4.4 Radar and sonar location devices

A recent development with considerable potential for the examination of buried sites in future is the use of radar, but a disadvantage is that it performs best on very dry deposits. It works in the same way as sonar scanning, but electronic (rather than sonic) signals are transmitted into the soil, and bounce back into a receiver. The signals are altered by the density and position of whatever they encounter, and the patterns received from the ground are plotted as a diagram. When colour is used to enhance the variations, it is possible to see the shapes not only of solid features, such as buried walls, but also the profiles of pits or ditches. Radar images have been used in England at the Anglo-Saxon burial ground at Sutton Hoo to look for signs of possible ship-burials below mounds and at York to examine sites before excavation (Stove and Addyman 1989). Sonar scanning is a routine technique used in sea-bed surveys and it is able to detect archaeological anomalies such as shipwrecks as well as natural rocks and sand banks. The *Mary Rose*, a Tudor warship subsequently excavated and lifted for display in a museum at Portsmouth, was first located with the help of this method by a nautical archaeologist who knew, from documentary sources, the approximate position where it sank in 1545 (Green 1990, 50–1).

4.5 Soil analysis
(Courty 1989)

Scientific location instruments have not replaced all traditional pre-excavation techniques for examining sites. For example, if the ground is struck with a mallet it should produce a light resonance over a buried wall or thin topsoil, but a dull thud over a humus-filled ditch. Probing or augering are also useful for testing the depth of soil, or to remove samples to gain some idea of buried stratification. The latter is dangerous on a small complex site, for a regular series of boreholes could easily damage slight traces of structures or fragile artefacts. Augering is more commonly used to provide soil samples for pollen analysis, or to measure variations in their phosphate content to detect areas of a site used for habitation or related activities (Bethell & Maté 1989). An early medieval site at Vallhagar, on the island of Gotland in the Baltic, was thoroughly sampled for phosphate analysis. The site consisted of scattered buildings and enclosures representing a farming community; concentrations of phosphates derived from animal urine and dung were found next to some buildings, as well as in open areas that may have been used for milking and byres.

4.6 Dowsing

An unpredictable prospecting technique is dowsing, traditionally employed to locate underground water sources. Exponents use a Y-shaped twig (or whatever else they find suitable) and carry it above the ground, noting places where it twists downwards. Apparent successes in finding archaeological features, such as the plans of demolished Anglo-Saxon churches, are difficult to explain scientifically, for they rely heavily on the intuition of the dowser (Bailey 1988). I have witnessed the survey of a buried rock-cut ditch that enclosed a Romano-British farmstead in South Devon; the farmer had observed it as a crop-mark, and located its position by dowsing with a forked hazel twig, cut unceremoniously from the nearest hedge. A small trial excavation confirmed its position and recovered dating evidence (Greene and Greene 1970).

5 Archaeology and the landscape

(Wagstaff 1987)

Landscape archaeology places humans into a broad context where they are seen to have been in a state of continuous interaction with the environment; sometimes their actions helped to shape the physical form of the natural world, normally their lives were shaped by it to a large extent. The study of the environment had already come to form an important part of Stone Age studies by the 1870s, for Edouard Lartet had divided the upper Palaeolithic into phases, such as the 'cave bear period' or the 'woolly mammoth and rhinoceros period', according to the dominant species represented by animal bones found with human artefacts in France (Trigger 1989, 95). By the 1920s, studies of plant remains and microscopic pollen had revealed a very elaborate sequence of climatic phases since the last Ice Age, marked by changing patterns of vegetation (below, p. 145). Aerial photographs contributed to a stronger appreciation of the essential integration of finds, sites and their natural setting, and the potential significance of these relationships.

Environmental approaches also formed part of the 'new' archaeology of the 1960s, when attempts to understand ancient societies were based upon an analysis of their place in an ecological 'system'. The position of settlements in relation to each other, and to their agricultural and material resources, was an important research goal in processual archaeology (below, p. 170). It might involve **spatial archaeology**, which adopted mathematical methods and statistical techniques developed by geographers to elucidate modern settlement patterns. Mathematical approaches are useful for examining many kinds of information, from broad regional studies down to the positions of individual artefacts recovered from the surface of a single field. One basic element is to determine whether scatters of sites or artefacts contain significant clusters or a regularly spaced pattern, or whether their disposition is purely random. When the distributions of more than one kind of artefact or settlement have been recorded, comparisons may be made to establish connections (correlations) between them. The results are likely to be expressed in levels of statistical probability, rather than a simple 'yes' or 'no'; reliability will depend upon the quality of the information being used and the statistical techniques employed. Two early exponents of spatial analysis in archaeology presented these problems in a very positive light:

> It is important that most of the techniques ... demand good data. ... it is to be hoped that archaeologists will be stimulated by the possibilities offered by the techniques to collect in the future more data of high standard. (Hodder & Orton, 1976, 238).

5.1 Landscape archaeology

(Aston 1985; Rackham 1987)

The mathematical techniques associated with spatial archaeology are most commonly used in the context of prehistoric archaeology. Much more information survives from recent historical periods, not only in the form of evidence in the field, but also in documentary archives (Hoskins 1988). Traditions of field archaeology that stretch back to Aubrey and Stukeley were revived and strengthened in the twentieth century by a growing interest in **local history**, in particular its social and economic dimensions. It has incorporated research into all kinds of documents, including charters recording the extent and ownership of estates, tax registers, parish registers of births and deaths, and analyses of place-names. This kind of research leads not just to studies of the physical remains of sites and buildings mentioned in documents, but to the idea that archaeological observations about the landscape and settlements may be used to fill in gaps in the documentary record. Thus, landscape archaeology now requires a thoroughly integrated approach, involving both written and material evidence. One manual summarized its objectives with particular eloquence:

> The landscape is a palimpsest on to which each generation inscribes its own impressions and removes some of the marks of earlier generations. Constructions of one age are often overlain, modified or erased by the work of another. The present patchwork nature of set-

tlement and patterns of agriculture has evolved as a result of thousands of years of human endeavour, producing a landscape which possesses not only a beauty associated with long and slow development, but an inexhaustible store of information about many kinds of human activities in the past. The landscape archaeologist needs to develop an eye and a feeling for patterns in town and country and, even more important, to recognize anomalies in, for instance, the large isolated medieval church of the deserted medieval village; the straight stretch of stream channelled by monks in the thirteenth century; the regular eighteenth century Parliamentary enclosure hedge lying across medieval ridge and furrow; the lumpy ground next to the church, marking the site of an old settlement; and even a fine Jacobean building in an otherwise apparently poor area, indicating a former prosperity linked to a long forgotten trade or industry. Ideally it should be possible to look at any feature in the landscape, know why it is there in that form, and understand its relation to other features (Aston & Rowley 1974, 14–15).

This process may sound rather intuitive, but it is of course based on informed fieldwork and documentary research. It is also an essential accompaniment to the interpretation of aerial photographs; changes in land-use in the past may have determined whether surface features of ancient sites survived, or whether they will only appear as crop-marks. The term **retrogressive analysis** is sometimes employed to describe how landscape archaeologists work back from modern features to the fragmentary remains of earlier landscapes. In a fascinating study of a hill farm in Derbyshire, the medieval and modern field systems associated with Roystone Grange were subjected to aerial photography, detailed surveying and selective excavation. Features of known date were gradually eliminated, and by means of identifying changes in the design of enclosure walls, the outlines of Roman and prehistoric settlements were revealed:

The typology of walls permits us to strip off – layer by layer – the succession of changes made to Roystone over the past six millennia. By plotting the gates, tracks, stiles and sheep-creeps too we can begin to build up a picture of how the modern landscape has been shaped. Walls were employed in different ways at different stages in the history of Roystone. To understand these stages we have investigated the archaeology of the succession of farming communities themselves. Their farms, yards, pens and even their rubbish enable us to put flesh upon the skeletal picture formed by mapping the walls. With this mixture of information we can begin to reconstruct the history of the farm and its place in the making of the White Peak. (Hodges 1991, 43)

Landscape archaeology is also inseparably connected with environmental archaeology, notably in the context of the soils and surface deposits that have influenced agriculture and the exploitation of other resources for food-production or crafts and industries (Simmons 1989). If a 'systems theory' approach is adopted, it will be assumed that, given a free choice, a settlement is likely to be located wherever its inhabitants have optimum access to all the necessary parts of their economic system; this concept gave rise to **site catchment analysis**. A line is drawn around a site to determine the potential resources that lie within a day's walking distance; an arbitrary circle is less informative than a 'territory' constructed to take account of the actual terrain, however. Although rather mechanical, this technique does at least allow a clear perception of a site's potential, and it also allows finds from an excavation to be related to its resources. A standardized unit, such as an arbitrary 10 km circle, allows statistical comparisons to be made between the territories of different sites. In a 'classic' application of this technique at San José Mogoté, Mexico, Kent Flannery looked first at finds recovered from an excavated site dated to around 1000 BC, and then considered how large a catchment area would have been required to supply them. He determined that all essential agricultural needs could be obtained within 2.5 km, and all but the most exotic materials obtained within 5 km. When the distribution of other local sites was studied, it was found that a 2.5 km circle could be drawn around each one to define a 'territory', without overlapping (Flannery 1976).

Catchment analysis is open to the same criticisms that are levelled at systems theory and processual archaeology (below, p.170). It assumes a purely physical interaction between people and their environment, in which every detail of their life was ruled by the location of material resources. Settlements and the landscape are perceived in very different ways in many non-European cultures, where aspects may be related to social or spiritual factors rather than mere subsistence. A visit to Wessex today emphasizes this alternative view, for the landscape is still dominated by surviving Neolithic and Bronze Age ritual monuments such as Stonehenge, Avebury and Silbury Hill, while hundreds of burial mounds are dotted along the crests of nearby hills and ridges (Richards 1990). It is very unlikely that people who invested time and energy in the construction of conspicuous monuments to death and ritual would make a clear distinction between the world of deities and ancestors and that of their everyday lives. It would be dangerous to analyse the economy of a farming settlement of this period solely by examining the potential of soils within its hypothetical territory through catchment analysis. A settlement might have been constructed in a particular location according to spiritual factors, and its economy could have involved gifts and exchanges of food and raw materials between relatives scattered over a wider region.

Anthropological studies and local history both underline the view that human settlement is a very complex subject with an indisputable social component (Arensberg 1968). The growth of large-scale field survey projects in the 1970s and 1980s went some way towards integrating fieldwork, environmental science, and the social and economic development of regions over extended periods of time. These projects also focused attention on some very basic aspects of archaeology, notably the concept of a 'site'. Few archaeologists would find any difficulty in defining an artefact found on the ground, or a feature such as a stone wall or a burial mound. But what exactly is a site, what are its limits, and how should it be recognized from artefacts or features surviving on the surface? Ethnoarchaeological studies of hunter-gatherer societies suggest that individual 'sites' are meaningless if they are not viewed in

terms of the shifting patterns of activities that make up the overall manner of subsistence (Smith 1992, 11–26). The term 'site' is an artificial concept invented in the present, with no meaning in the past; it is only with the growth of twentieth-century fieldwork that functional words like 'monument', 'camp', 'village' or 'fort' began to be replaced by the objective term 'site' (Dunnell 1992, 22). Some purists would like to abandon it:

> In the last analysis, site, as an archaeological concept, has no role to play in the discipline. Its uses are not warranted by its properties, it obscures crucial theoretical and methodological deficiencies, and it imparts a serious and unredeemable systematic error in recovery and management programs. In spite of the technical problems its abandonment will cause, the concept of archaeological sites should be discarded. (ibid., 36–7)

A more practical solution for archaeologists involved in survey projects is to continue to use the term as a descriptive label for a place where a particular concentration of artefacts and/or features occurs, while remembering the many distorting factors of human and natural origin that determine whether a 'site' survives in a form that may be recognized today. 'Most of the time we have one or a very few sites that must guide our appreciation for the types of systems that once existed. If we are to use site information we must learn to see a past system from a site perspective.' (Binford 1992, 56)

6 A Mediterranean field survey project
(Barker & Lloyd 1991)

It was stressed at the beginning of this chapter that fieldwork today is rarely directed at individual sites. It is normally part of a regional study, devoted to answering questions generated by wider archaeological research. The most successful projects have been aimed at the analysis of long-term changes in settlement patterns, seen in the perspective of environmental factors that influenced, or were affected by, human exploitation.

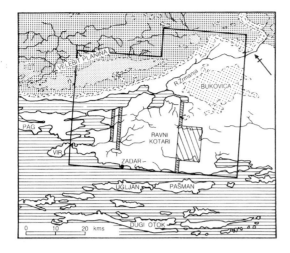

2.13 Location map of the Neothermal Dalmatia Project's survey area. It consisted of a survey block and linear transects across a peninsular on the Adriatic coast of Croatia, near the modern city of Zadar. *Chapman & Shiel 1993, fig. 4*

6.1 The Neothermal Dalmatia Project
(Chapman & Shiel 1991, 1993)

The Neothermal Dalmatia Project was designed to investigate the development of the landscape and human settlement over the 12,000 years since the end of the last Ice Age. It was centred upon an area near the modern city of Zadar in Dalmatia, a province of Croatia (fig. 2.13). Dalmatia is characterized by an indented coast and limestone mountains, with little in the way of level plains. The survey was conducted by John Chapman and Robert Shiel (an archaeologist and a soil scientist) from the University of Newcastle upon Tyne, and Šime Batović from the University of Zadar. John Chapman had written a doctoral thesis on neolithic agriculture and settlement in Yugoslavia, and Šime Batović had already made a detailed study of prehistoric sites in Dalmatia. The aim of the survey was to conduct an integrated programme to investigate the origins of food production, and the relationships between agriculture, society and environmental changes. Robert Shiel's role in studying the agricultural potential of soils was fundamental to the project. In addition, it was hoped that the emergence of social hierarchies in later prehistory could be investigated, along with the relationships between the native population and the Roman empire.

6.2 Research design and methods

Zadar lies on the coast of a short peninsula approximately 35 km long and 25 km wide. The survey selected three strips of land ('transects'), 1 km wide, running across the grain of the geological structure of the peninsula with the purpose of sampling different types of soil from the edge of the sea to the highest ground. Fieldwalkers were deployed in a uniform manner to cover the ground evenly, and when archaeological sites were encountered, samples of finds were collected from units of a standard size. Physical traces of sites, such as hillforts, buildings, ditches, or boundary walls, were surveyed, and trial excavations were carried out on some examples to recover dating evidence and other finds that would help to explain their function.

Besides fieldwalking for archaeological finds, soils were recorded in detail, particularly where deep sequences could be studied in sections cut by wells or streams. Soils reveal the history of erosion that normally follows the clearance of forest for farming. On hilly ground exposed to extreme periods of heat and rainfall (typical of the Mediterranean region), soil erosion is dramatic, burying low-lying sites and removing others from hillsides. This distorts the pattern of discovery, and has to be taken into account when the distribution of sites is analysed (Greene 1986, 85–6; 140). Other factors that might distort patterns of finds (known as 'transforms') were also noted. For example, there was a lack of uniformity in finds of flint, because of local variations in its availability, while well-made pottery of the Roman period survived much better than its less durable prehistoric and medieval counterparts.

6.3 Interpretation

The benefits of a carefully designed sampling strategy for sites, dating evidence and soil types are apparent when the results are interpreted in human terms. A fundamental factor is that sites were discovered and finds collected on a uniform basis, so that valid comparisons could be made not only between the three linear transects, but also within a larger rectangular area (5 km x 11 km) around a prehistoric hillfort that eventually developed into an important Roman town. Furthermore, sites of all periods could be related to the agricultural potential of the soil type on which they were located. Fig. 2.14 summarizes the results of the Dalmatian survey very succinctly. It shows at a glance that, for example, in the Roman period, settlement of the limestone uplands (*Kras*) with the lowest agricultural potential was as intense as neolithic settlement of fertile low-lying arable land.

No trace of occupation by late Stone Age (mesolithic) hunter-gatherers was encountered, possibly because coastal sites disappeared when sea levels rose after the Ice Age, while inland sites were buried by later soil erosion. The first settled farmers of the Neolithic period lived in small sites dispersed over the highest quality soils. In the Bronze Age, settlement was wider (but still dispersed) and included monuments such as stone cairns and boundaries situated on stonier ground. In the Iron Age all available types of soil were used for the first time, and large defended centres appeared amongst the scattered settlements. This pattern was intensified in the Roman period, with evidence for higher population and the use of some low-potential soils for specialized crops such as fruit and nuts. Medieval sites were fewer, but they still occupied a wide range of soils; many survive to the present, but their chronological evolution is difficult to study because very uniform pottery has been used from the early medieval period to the twentieth century.

6.4 Analysis

It is one thing to collect and quantify survey data, but quite another to interpret it in human terms, when the only information available is whatever happened to show up on the surface during a season of fieldwork. The finds will also have been affected by numerous 'transforms' over the years, of course. However, archaeologists only make progress by testing ideas against data, for without the demands made by the process of interpretation there would be no reason to improve methods of data collection.

One theme that emerged from Chapman's discussion was the increase in investment of capital (in terms of labour) required by the intensification of agriculture. This phenomenon was

observed from the Bronze Age onwards in the form of stone-walled enclosures, boundaries and cairn-fields, coinciding with defensive structures built to protect these investments. Intensification reached a peak in the Roman period, when the participation of Dalmatia in an empire resulted in a move from local subsistence to agriculture on an 'industrial' scale. Chapman proposed that '... there are strong theoretical grounds for supposing that intensification is strongly correlated with increases in social hierarchies' (1987, 142). In a different publication, he used the survey data to test rival theories about the native population's adaptation to life under Roman rule: 'The strategy which we shall follow is a deductive test of two hypotheses which make almost diametrically opposed assumptions about these processes' (Chapman & Shiel 1991, 64). He concluded that one view (substantial immigration of settlers from Italy) was true in large towns, but that there was a considerable degree of continuity in the countryside and smaller towns.

The final publication of the Dalmatian survey will contain many more hypotheses and tests,

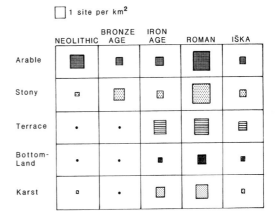

2.14 Settlement densities in the Dalmatian survey area are summarized by this chart. The larger the filled square, the greater the number of finds per square kilometre. Clearly arable land was popular throughout the history of the area, and exploitation of the less favourable land expanded through time to reach a peak in Roman times. Medieval finds are more difficult to recognize, but Iska pottery shows that all five categories of land were utilized to some extent. *Chapman* et al., *1987 fig. 10*

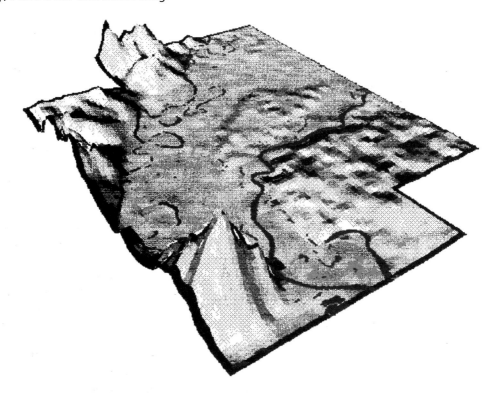

particularly where the interaction of agriculture and the environment is concerned. I hope that this short summary of an individual project makes it clear that data collected in a systematic manner may be used for many purposes by scholars interested in different themes or periods. Furthermore, it is very much more efficient (and less destructive) to collect survey data from a large area than to excavate a single site. Hard economics as well as changing research objectives led to the rapid growth of field survey programmes in the 1980s (Greene 1986, 98–101).

7 GIS

(Allen 1990)

The extraordinary pace of development in computer technology has transformed the potential of field survey and spatial archaeology by borrowing again from techniques employed in the study of geography. Computers that combine large data-storage capacity with fast mathematical processors and a high quality of graphic display, typified in the 1990s by Sun workstations, are very suitable for running programs known as **Geographical Information Systems**. In the

2.15 Greyscale image of part of the Upper Tisza Project's survey area in Hungary. The contours have been digitized from maps, and processed by a GIS program to give an oblique view with artificial shading; dark meandering lines show rivers. When integrated into maps like this, details of sites or the results of fieldwork give much deeper insights into the landscape than can be gained from two-dimensional maps. The results are normally displayed in contrasting colours that intensify the effects. *Mark Gillings & John Chapman*

Upper Tisza Project, data collected from a river valley in Hungary during a fieldwork project directed by John Chapman has been processed and analysed by Mark Gillings (fig. 2.15). It involved an immensely time-consuming preliminary stage in which large-scale maps of the survey area were **digitized**; the contours, natural features, geology and soil types were converted into mathematical form. All details recovered during archaeological fieldwork (notably site categories, locations and sizes, and the find-spot, type and date of artefacts) were also digitized.

One example of the potential of GIS was produced by calculating the effects on the river system of the thawing of mountain snows each spring. By fixing a specific depth of water, the map of the landscape could be transformed on the computer's screen by flooding the river and its tributaries up to a particular contour. Sites of a specific period could also be added to test ideas about their relationship to this phenomenon. Early farming communities in the Neolithic period were found to have been located near the water's edge or on temporary islands formed by the floods, with the implication that fishing may have provided an important supplement to the farmers' diet in spring, before crops were ready for harvesting. This idea is supported by studies of fish bones from sites where suitable samples have been recovered.

This exercise *could* have been performed manually by making tracings from contour maps, shading in the flooded areas, and adding neolithic sites recorded in files of survey data. The advantage of a GIS approach is that questions can be asked repeatedly in slightly different ways. What if the floods were deeper? Do burial sites of the same period have the same relation to water as the settlements? Do early Bronze Age sites share the same distribution? The answers can be displayed very rapidly, and results that look significant are measurable in statistical terms. Once maps and data have been entered into the system, they can be recalled in any combination or permutation. Some exercises could *only* be performed with the help of a computer; for example, if the investigator selects a specific site (such as a farmstead), it is possible to instruct the computer to display a view of the landscape from that location as it would have appeared to someone standing there, looking in any specified direction. By adding further information, perhaps by assuming that certain types of soil were still covered by mature trees while others had been cleared for fields, the view could be modified accordingly. Could a neolithic farmer see other farmsteads, and were 'ritual' monuments

and burials positioned so that they could be seen from settlements?

Thus, GIS provides an important new dimension to field archaeology that is very widely applicable to complex problems of location and distribution. As with other forms of computer-based data handling, an initial investment of time and energy in recording data in an appropriate form is repaid by the flexibility that it allows at the analytical stage. Similarly, publication is facilitated by printing out selected graphic displays rather than drawing them by hand. In the future, the actual data could be published on disks to make it accessible to other researchers, along with moving graphics to present a dynamic view of the director's own interpretation of developments over time, rather than traditional static printed maps of separate periods or phases.

8 Conclusions

Archaeological fieldworkers now require many skills, some of them traditional and subjective, others based on new scientific techniques. They also need to be experts in the use of documentary evidence and aerial photographs, besides understanding geology and geography. These skills have important implications for the process of excavation, which is examined in the next chapter. Our ability to investigate ancient landscapes and environments, without resorting to the destructive process of digging into sites, means that no excavation work should ever be carried out until a programme of fieldwork and documentary research has been completed. It is impossible to ask valid questions about an individual site *without* understanding its place in the historical and natural environment.

Note: a guide to **further reading** that includes topics covered in this chapter begins on p. 185.

3 Excavation

Archaeological evidence for past human activity is an irreplaceable part of our common heritage. Activities aimed at recovering this information can destroy all traces of the evidence unless it is preserved by adequate recording. Those of us who are involved in archaeology, whether as amateurs or professionals, have a duty to the rest of society to treat this heritage responsibly. Investigations should be conducted in such a way that reliable information is acquired, and the results then made available for others to study. These objectives should apply to all archaeological work, whether on land or underwater. (Dean 1992, 300)

Of all the archaeological activities described in this book, excavation has the highest profile in public perception, to the extent that anyone could be forgiven for gaining the incorrect impression that excavation is the primary activity of most archaeologists. This chapter aims not only to explain how excavation is conducted, but also to emphasize the background work that precedes it, and the time-consuming processing of site records and finds for publication that should follow. I hope that it will also explain the thinking that lies behind the ethical standpoint outlined above in the Nautical Archaeological Society's principles of conduct.

Along with fieldwork, excavation is the most important source of new information in archaeology. If reliable data are to be recovered, excavation techniques must be sound. Although major modern excavations involve complex technical equipment under the control of virtuoso directors, the basic principles are comparatively simple and have changed little since their importance was first recognized. The process of excavation incorporates two approaches that are frequently in conflict: the exposure of vertical sequences of layers, and the definition of horizontal plans of occupation levels or individual structures. In both cases full records must be kept of the contexts in which all artefacts and other finds were discovered. The most important development of the twentieth century has been an improved understanding of the vertical aspect, and the design of excavation techniques to reveal it with the utmost care. Recent large excavations have gone further, and have attempted to maximize the horizontal aspect while still recording the vertical sequence in necessary detail (Barker 1993; 1986).

1 The development of excavation techniques

Whatever their motives, very few excavations before the late nineteenth century were much better than treasure hunts. A few caves with prehistoric occupation, such as Brixham in Devon, were explored by removing the filling in layers to confirm that tools really were associated with bones of extinct animals (Grayson 1983). Most excavators sought to recover objects of commercial or aesthetic value by random digging on known sites, or by systematically plundering monuments such as burial mounds. Luck, accident and careless plunder were commonplace; historians and art-historians were interested in documents and works of art, and these could be gained without much attention to stratification or planned research. Other sites were uncovered in a more academic manner to reveal structures as well as finds. Frequently, the two objectives were combined; many ancient sites in Egypt and the Near East were extensively cleared, and the best sculptures and objects removed and transported to museums in Europe. Impressive foundations or ruins were left behind, but much important evidence about the sites had been shovelled away for ever; this phase has been described aptly as 'digging before excavation'

(Maisels 1993, 30). Finely engraved architectural plans and elevations are no substitute for the information that might have been gleaned from unspectacular layers of accumulated soil and debris, and the modest artefacts they once contained. The careful work carried out at Pompeii from 1860 by Fiorelli was very much an exception (Daniel 1981, 85–7). Most familiar views of ancient Greek or Egyptian sites frequented by tourists today are the product not of abandonment and natural decay, but of eager clearance by archaeologists in the nineteenth century.

The discovery of civilizations did little to advance archaeological techniques until the late nineteenth century, when excavators such as Schliemann and other German archaeologists began to ask more sophisticated historical questions about classical sites around the eastern Mediterranean (Trigger 1989, 196–7). At about the same time advances in excavation and the study of finds also began to emerge from work on prehistory and ethnography, but only after a depressingly long period of careless barrow-digging that severely damaged the majority of prehistoric burial mounds in Europe (Piggott 1989, 153–9). Individuals such as Pitt Rivers and Flinders Petrie developed a sense of responsibility about antiquities, and began to formulate more sophisticated questions about sites. Many problems could *only* be studied by archaeological methods (including excavation), for example the prehistoric background of Egyptian and Mesopotamian civilizations or the origins of the prehistoric farming communities accidentally revealed beneath many Near Eastern tells. Without historical texts or radiocarbon dating, these problems required the use of techniques developed in northern Europe, notably excavation conducted with reference to stratification, combined with classification and typological study of pottery and other artefacts to provide relative dates.

Two positive products of the depth of tell deposits were that awareness of stratigraphy increased, and sequences of various kinds of artefacts from successive levels were recognized. One of the first and most famous tell excavations was by Schliemann at Troy (Hissarlik, in Turkey). Many of his assistants went on to apply high standards on classical sites in Greece, while

Koldewey and Andrae, who investigated Babylon and Ashur in Mesopotamia, came from the same background (Daniel 1981, 122–3). These excavators were well aware of the horizontal and vertical aspects of their work. They were interested both in exploring large areas of buildings on individual levels of tells, and in excavating complete stratigraphical sequences from the top to the bottom. Glyn Daniel summarized the context of their work:

> In Egypt every monument was built of the stone or cut in the solid rock, and the arid climate permitted the preservation in a remarkable manner of objects . . . which would have been destroyed elsewhere. It was, therefore, in Mesopotamia that the classical techniques were reshaped and that new techniques of stratigraphical excavation, and of the excavation of perished and semi-perished materials, were developed. The architecture of Mesopotamia is executed in sun-dried bricks; the techniques of tracing these were quite unknown to earlier excavators. Koldewey and Andrae first successfully traced the walls of sun-dried brick, and this work reached its highest technical achievements in the work of Delougaz, at Khafajah, where every single brick was articulated, the chips being blown away by compressed air. The excavations at Ur were a noteworthy model of the whole modern technique of archaeology, from extraction and preservation to interpretation and publication. (Daniel 1975, 290–1)

One of the most prominent excavators of Ur in the 1920s was Sir Leonard Woolley, who made his first fumbling beginnings in archaeology at Corbridge in Northumberland in 1906, while Koldewey and Andrae were already at work in Mesopotamia (below, p. 70).

Arthur Evans' excavations at Knossos (above, p. 33) were directed at the solution of a specific cultural problem, using a variety of evidence, including some small previous excavations on the site; his results were spectacularly successful. He was helped by the fact that, unlike many sites, the Minoan palace was not overlain by extensive remains of subsequent periods of occupation. He was able to make really detailed interpretations because it had been destroyed by fire (possibly

3.1 This Anglo-Saxon ship burial (Mound 2) at Sutton Hoo, Suffolk, had been disturbed by nineteenth-century barrow-diggers, who had cut steps down the far side of the burial chamber. The process had been repeated in 1938 by an archaeologist, but full examination had to wait for the campaign of excavations mounted in the 1980s. Many significant details were deduced by fragments of artefacts left behind by the earlier excavators, but most information about the burial itself had been irretrievably destroyed. However, most of the structural details of the mound, which had covered an upturned ship placed over a wooden chamber, could still be discerned. © *Sutton Hoo Research Trust; photograph by Nigel Macbeth*

caused by an earthquake or volcanic activity), and still contained the remains of most of its artefacts and furnishings. In contrast to most Near-Eastern excavators, Evans made a conscious effort to preserve the crumbling gypsum masonry of the palace at Knossos while the excavation proceeded. His earliest photographs show a meticulously cleaned site, and the text demonstrates close attention to the stratigraphic positions of finds (see fig. 1.15), both as dating evidence and as a means of interpreting the

destruction of the palace (Evans, 1899–1900). In Britain, Pitt Rivers was paying similar attention to detail in the closing years of the nineteenth century (below, p. 61–2), and his work must have been familiar to Evans. However, these high standards were far from universal, and were certainly not reached in the excavations at Corbridge between 1906 and 1914. Unlike Pitt Rivers, Evans did not publish *full* excavation reports; fortunately, his detailed commentaries and the notebooks kept by his assistant, Donald Mackenzie, have allowed more recent archaeologists to review the evidence in detail. For example, it was possible in the 1960s for Popham to carry out a review of pottery from deposits associated with the destruction of the Minoan palace, thanks to careful labelling during the original excavations (Popham 1970).

1.1 The destruction of evidence
(Mytum & Waugh 1987)

It is instructive to consider the circumstances of one of England's richest discoveries to realize just how much information has been lost on other sites (fig. 3.1). The Anglo-Saxon barrow cemetery at Sutton Hoo in Suffolk was excavated in an exploratory manner in 1938 and 1939, and an undisturbed burial was found in one mound in 1939 (Evans 1986, 19). A deposit of extraordinary richness was excavated, including armour, weapons, silver tableware and other items from an Anglo-Saxon royal household. Years of laboratory work in the British Museum have been devoted to the conservation and reconstruction of corroded iron and bronze items such as a magnificently decorated iron helmet. Historical documents, together with dates derived from gold coins found in a purse in the burial, suggest that it was the grave of King Redwald, who died in *c*. AD 625.

The burial deposit had been placed in a chamber in a 24-metre ship that had been hauled from a nearby river, placed in a deep trench and covered by a large mound. Robbers dug a hole into the centre of the barrow in the sixteenth or early seventeenth century, but, fortunately, earlier erosion of the mound meant that the burial chamber no longer lay directly below its centre. Since the hole was not taken below the surrounding ground level, the excavators missed all signs of the ship as well. If this early 'excavation' had been successful, very little would now be known about the find. Some objects would have been melted down or sold off immediately; others might have survived as fragments, but the majority would have been discarded immediately as worthless corroded metal. We would know nothing about the ship itself, which would have survived only as discoloured sand and iron nails, or the layout of the grave goods in the burial chamber. The date, identity and cultural connections of the dead king would remain unknown, together with the light that the boat burial has shed on *Beowulf*, an important early Anglo-Saxon poem.

Although these hypothetical effects of early excavations at Sutton Hoo represent an extreme case, the analogy is applicable to most of the 'great' excavations or discoveries made before the twentieth century. Even in comparatively well protected countries like Britain, the proliferation of metal detectors has revived the plundering of sites. The problem is much greater in areas of the world where sites regularly produce items desired by museums and collectors. What suffers from uncontrolled treasure hunting is the quality of information: coins, precious objects, or carvings have little meaning when divorced from their stratigraphic level or structural context.

1.2 The concept of stratification

(Harris 1989)

John Frere's observations published in 1800 (above, p. 11) clearly embodied the common sense notion that in a series of layers, those at the bottom will be older than those at the top. Geologists had already used the same principle to arrange fossils from different strata into developmental sequences, and it was well established among students of human origins, such as Boucher de Perthes and McEnery, by the early

nineteenth century. Unfortunately, other archaeologists whose studies were focused on later periods paid little or no attention to stratification. A modern excavation peels away these layers in reverse order, and records the finds and structural evidence that they contain.

Good examples of stratigraphic observations on excavations took place at least as early as the seventeenth century in Scandinavia (Trigger 1989, 49), and J J Worsaae wrote with lucidity and intelligence on the requirements of controlled excavation in the 1840s (Daniel 1967, 103–6). The recovery of closed groups of artefacts from stratified contexts had been an important element in Thomsen's development of the Three-Age System some years earlier, but these tended to be self-defining contexts such as graves, rather than individual layers found in a sequence (Graslund 1987; above, p. 26–7). However, the majority of nineteenth-century excavators observed stratification passively, rather than using it actively to guide their excavation strategy.

1.3 Pitt Rivers

(Bowden 1991)

Modern excavation practice does not have a single founder, but the kind of progress made in the late nineteenth century is exemplified by Pitt Rivers (1827–1900; fig. 3.2). His wide range of activities provides fascinating insights into the cultural atmosphere of late Victorian England.

3.2 General Pitt Rivers (1827–1900), portrayed by Frank Holl R.A. in 1882, shortly after inheriting a large estate in Hampshire and Dorset containing many archaeological sites. The prehistoric shield and a pickaxe relate to his interest in ancient weapons, which led him to conduct excavations, while the observant stance and notebook draw attention to his role in recording and protecting ancient monuments. *Pitt Rivers Museum, University of Oxford*

61

He would be remembered today even if he had not turned to excavation late in his life, for he had already played an important part in the development of the typological study of artefacts, besides conducting fieldwork and surveys in England and Ireland. Through an unlikely course of inheritance, Pitt Rivers came into possession of a large tract of Cranborne Chase in Wessex, one of the richest archaeological areas in England. He devoted the rest of his life (1880–1900) to the study of this area, while indulging in many other interests of an educational and 'improving' nature for the benefit of his estate workers and their families.

The wealth derived from his estates allowed Pitt Rivers to employ full-time archaeological assistants, and to use his own labourers to carry out excavations on a variety of monuments from a neolithic barrow to a standing medieval building (fig. 3.3). Pitt Rivers had conducted his first excavations in Ireland in the 1860s, and from the very beginning he devoted detailed attention to artefacts as well as to sites and their structures. The importance he attached to all finds, however trivial, led him to record not just the artefacts themselves but also the contexts in which they were found. Pitt Rivers' excavation technique was far from revolutionary, although it was neat, methodical and accurately surveyed, in accordance with his military training. The most remarkable novelty was that his excavations and finds were published in great detail in a series of

3.3 Pitt Rivers' excavation of Wor Barrow, a neolithic burial mound in Dorset, in 1893. Despite the quality of the recording, the actual excavation technique was crude (Bowden 1991, 131–4). The labourers simply moved forward against a vertical face on horizontal levels; sloping layers of barrow material are clearly visible on the sections, but no attempt was made to remove them individually. Worse still, the excavation was taken down into natural chalk well below the old ground surface, whose buried soil shows as a dark layer at wheelbarrow height in the left section. Fortunately, Pitt Rivers eventually realised his mistake when the large foundation trench of a timber mortuary structure was found underneath the barrow, but many minor features must have been dug away unnoticed. A scale model of the barrow before excavation can be seen propped up at the front of excavation. *Salisbury and South Wiltshire Museum*

massive volumes, containing copious illustrations and 'relic tables' that are still informative today.

1.4 Developments in the twentieth century
(Barker 1993)

The requirements of 'scientific' excavation were finally met when Pitt Rivers' approach to recording and publication was combined with a clear perception of the significance of stratification, and the ability to recognize and excavate it layer by layer. Contemporaries of Pitt Rivers, such as

Schliemann or Petrie, who were working in Turkey, Egypt and Palestine, possessed a more advanced understanding of stratigraphy and the use of artefacts for dating the observed layers.

> It is difficult to overestimate the contribution made to archaeological method in the last quarter of the nineteenth century by Schliemann, Pitt Rivers and Petrie. It would be no exaggeration to say that, with the experience of the Danes and the Swiss behind them, they forged the essential technique of archaeology. (Daniel 1975, 177)

Thus, three indispensable elements of excavation had emerged by the beginning of the twentieth century. *Horizontal* observations had improved considerably, and were combined with accurate recording, notably on German excavations of classical cities in Turkey (Trigger 1989, 196–7). *Vertical* sequences were increasingly important, particularly on deeply stratified tell sites in the Near East such as Ashur, excavated by Andrae (Daniel 1981, 123). Systematic attention to all classes of *finds* was the newest and most important element, and it led to a growing number of authoritative publications of sites and catalogues of artefacts that allowed archaeologists to make criti-

cal evaluations of the work of other excavators.

1.5 Mortimer Wheeler
(Hawkes 1982)

All three elements were combined in work conducted during the 1920s and 1930s by Mortimer Wheeler, a man who (like Pitt Rivers) developed an outlook and methods that reflected his military background; unlike Pitt Rivers, he trained many younger archaeologists who went on to have distinguished careers in archaeology. During a long career interrupted by two world wars Wheeler conducted excavations in Britain, France and India on sites selected for the investigation of specific research questions. For example, he explored the relationship between the pre-Roman hill-forts of southern England

3.4 Sir Mortimer Wheeler (1890–1976) and Tessa Wheeler during their excavations at Verulamium (St Albans) in the 1930s. Mortimer Wheeler first entered professional archaeology in 1913, and his perception of sites and the landscape was soon increased by artillery experience during the First World War. He remained a vigorous and colourful figure active in archaeology until his death.
Verulamium Museum

and northern France by excavating the defensive structures of several sites and comparing the styles of pottery found on them. In India, he used imported Roman coins and pottery (that could be dated by reference to sites in Europe) as a fixed point in a sequence of phases in Indian sites and finds. Wheeler also organized and published museum collections, wrote books and articles for the general public, and, in his later life, became a remarkably successful radio and television personality. His first wife, Tessa, played an underrated part in the development of Wheeler's methods, and also instigated the creation of the Institute of Archaeology at the University of London. She met a tragically early death in 1936 (fig. 3.4; Hawkes 1982, 122–43).

Wheeler is chiefly remembered for perfecting the 'box system' of excavation, whereby a site was uncovered by means of a grid of square trenches, with baulks left standing between them as a permanent record of the stratification of all four sides of each trench (fig. 3.5). Wheeler did not always excavate in this fashion, however, and his work at the Roman city at Verulamium (St Albans) or the Iron Age hill-fort at Maiden Castle (Dorset) involved uncovering large open areas in a manner similar to modern practice (Sharples 1991). His techniques emphasize the conflicting requirements of lateral and vertical excavation. Stratification is essential for understanding the sequence of a site, but an arbitrary grid of vertical baulks imposed on a site may mask important horizontal features (figs 3.6–8). Wheeler was of course aware of this basic conflict, and summarized the optimum compromise after discussing it at length (1954, 126–9):

> With the proviso, then, that all horizontal digging must proceed from clear and comprehensible vertical sections, the question of priority is fundamentally not in doubt. Careful horizontal digging can alone, in the long run, give us the full information that we ideally want (ibid., 129).

This compromise cannot always be reached even today, especially in urban rescue excavations constrained by limitations on time and access (see fig. 3.20). Wheeler was undoubtedly well aware of the comparable problems posed by tells in the Near East, where it had become standard practice to sink deep shafts ('sondages') to sample their successive occupations and artefacts, but where horizontal excavation of the lower levels was physically impossible. Wheeler's approach to stratigraphy (developed further by his student Kathleen Kenyon) included close attention to layers and features such as pits or walls, and the interfaces between these stratigraphic units. He continually stressed the need to excavate these units, rather than to follow the common practice of removing arbitrary horizontal levels ('spits'). Because Wheeler's whole approach was combined with systematic numbering of layers and the finds that they contained, Harris has compared its significance with that of the ideas about strata and fossils introduced into geology by Hutton and Smith in the late eighteenth century (1989, 11).

1.6 From keyholes to areas
(Barker 1993)

An opposite extreme to the open-area approach was the procedure of digging many very small widely spaced trenches on large shallow sites. A more specialized form of this approach (sometimes described as 'keyhole' excavation) was used extensively in Roman military archaeology (for example, at Corbridge: below, p. 72). Ian Richmond produced overall plans of many Roman forts and fortresses in northern Britain by the judicious excavation of small narrow trenches, carefully placed to check critical details of the fairly predictable layout of their internal structures. Richmond was also an astute observer of stratification; his pioneering drawings of occupation layers and their associated dated coins were included in a report on Wheeler's excavations in the Roman fort at Caernarvon in Wales published in 1923 (fig. 3.9).

The interwar decades saw the development of open-area excavations on sites lying on flat alluvial land in southern Scandinavia, northern Germany and the Netherlands, a region that contains many rural sites, ranging from neolithic farming settlements through to villages of the early medieval period (fig. 3.10). Because their buildings were constructed entirely from wood, there was little build-up of construction and demolition layers of the kind found on sites where stone or mud bricks have been used. Many sites were located on subsoils that facilitated the

3.5–6 Box trenches and open area excavation in The Tofts, part of an Iron Age fortification at Stanwick, Yorkshire, excavated by Wheeler in 1951–2. Fig. 3.5 shows a typical grid of unexcavated baulks that provided four permanent sections in each square trench; wooden pegs at their intersections are reference points for surveying and plotting important finds. In fig. 3.6, the removal of the baulks has revealed the foundation of a circular timber building. The shallow ploughsoil did not justify the numerous sections visible in fig. 3.5, and the baulks concealed important features. *Wheeler 1954a, pl. VIII, facing p. 8*

3.7–8 As part of a re-examination of the Stanwick fortifications since 1983, the area known as The Tofts has been investigated further by Colin Haselgrove. Wheeler's area excavation is marked A on fig. 3.8, which shows that he sampled only a very small part of the interior. A geophysical survey of most of the rest of the site demonstrated that it had been densely occupied, and placed Wheeler's excavation, and larger open-area investigation by Haselgrove (see B), into context. *Haselgrove 1990, fig. 11*

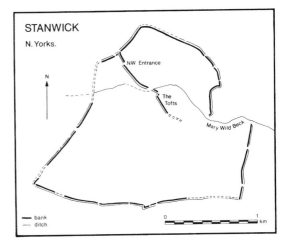

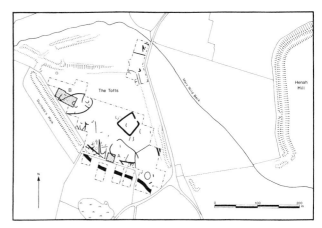

recognition of pits, post-holes and other structural remains of buildings. Unlike Roman forts, the plans of these settlements could not be predicted, and complete uncovering was essential to the understanding of their form and development (fig. 3.11). A German archaeologist, Gerhard Bersu, was invited to England in 1938 to carry out an area excavation of this kind on an Iron Age farmstead at Little Woodbury, Wiltshire (Evans 1989). He demonstrated that pre-Roman Britons lived in substantial round timber houses, not, as previously thought, in minute pit dwellings. The plans of their houses could only be recovered by stripping large areas, and by analysing the plans of post-holes and other features that had been carefully excavated and recorded (Bersu 1940). The site was excavated in strips rather than as a continuous open area, but the contrast with 'keyhole' trenches is nevertheless dramatic.

65

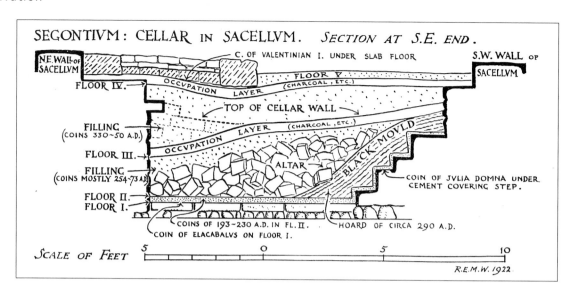

SEGONTIVM: CELLAR IN SACELLVM. *SECTION AT S.E. END.*

FLOOR IV.

C. OF VALENTINIAN I. UNDER SLAB FLOOR

N.E.WALL OF SACELLVM

S.W. WALL OF SACELLVM

FLOOR V.
OCCVPATION LAYER (CHARCOAL, ETC.)

TOP OF CELLAR WALL

FILLING (COINS 330~50 A.D.)

OCCVPATION LAYER (CHARCOAL, ETC.)

BLACK MOVLD

FLOOR III.

ALTAR

FILLING (COINS MOSTLY 254-73 AD)

COIN OF JVLIA DOMNA UNDER CEMENT COVERING STEP.

FLOOR II.
FLOOR I.

COINS OF 193~230 A.D. IN FL. II.   HOARD OF CIRCA 290 A.D.
COIN OF ELACABALVS ON FLOOR I.

SCALE OF FEET   5   0   5   10

R.E.M.W. 1922.

3.9 Drawing of a section through the filling of the strongroom (*sacellum*) beneath the headquarters building of Segontium Roman fort, Caernarvon, Wales. Because the phases of occupation of this military site were assumed to reflect the history of Roman Wales, particular emphasis was placed upon dating evidence in this drawing. Thus, for example, the layer of rubble cannot have fallen there before c. AD 290, for a hoard of that date was found in the soil ('black mould') beneath it. *Wheeler 1923, 55, fig. 17*

3.10 The Iron Age settlement at Nørre Fjand in Denmark, explored by Hatt from 1938–40, is an early example of open area excavation. The faint traces of timber buildings, fragmentary stonework and superimposed floor levels could only have been understood by uncovering large areas, and examining each feature and layer. *Hatt 1957, 75, fig. 50; National Museum, Copenhagen*

3.11 The neolithic settlement at Elsloo in the Netherlands illustrates a common problem on open-area sites where no occupation levels survive to provide stratigraphical relationships between separate structures. The only clues to the sequence are given by chance intersections between features in the few places where building plans overlap. It is also difficult to tell whether the site was crowded with buildings for a comparatively short time, or whether a few buildings existed at any one time, which were gradually replaced in slightly different positions over a long period. It may be helpful to examine the distribution of datable artefacts, such as pottery, to see whether they cluster in separate areas; this approach has proved fruitful at Mucking, in Essex (Hamerow 1993). *Modderman 1975, fig. 86*

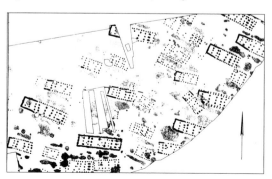

The history of the development of modern excavation techniques is completed by examining the extension of the concept of open-area examination to sites that possess a significant depth of accumulated layers. It should be repeated that good excavation should aim to satisfy the demands of both the vertical and horizontal aspects of a site. Even on sites excavated in the past by a grid system, or in the case of mounds excavated in quadrants, the final stages usually consisted of removing the baulks. Open-area excavations rarely use baulks at any stage. On sites of limited depth, this causes no problems, for the disturbed plough-soil can be stripped off to reveal various features for individual study. This process can be extended to sites with deep stratigraphy if the extent, contours, depth and consistency of each layer are carefully recorded before it is removed. If this is done properly, a section of the sequence of deposits could be drawn on any given line from the site records alone. Alternatively, lines are fixed before excavation at selected positions where a cross-section of each layer will be drawn, so that a cumulative drawing of the sequence is built up in stages as the layers are removed (Barker 1993, 113–17). These techniques both suffer from an unavoidable drawback, for unlike sections preserved in a baulk at the sides of a trench, they are never actually seen by the excavator all at once, and they can only ever be checked on paper. However, this is a legitimate sacrifice when it is very important to obtain the maximum exposure of each horizontal level on a site.

1.7 The interpretation of stratification
(Harris 1993)

Stratification can be defined, therefore, as any number of relatable deposits of archaeological strata (from a stake-hole to the floor of a cathedral) which are the result of 'successive operations of either nature or mankind'. Stratigraphy, on the other hand 'is the study of archaeological strata ... with a view to arranging them in a chronological sequence'. (Barker 1993, 21, quoting Harris)

All excavation is based on the fundamental principle of the succession of levels, which assumes that layers of soil (or any other material) were deposited in chronological order, with the oldest at the

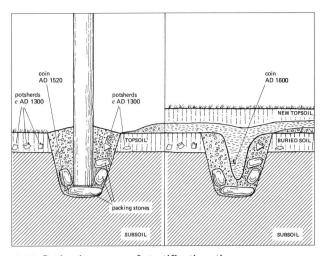

3.12 Dating by means of stratification: the excavation of a post-hole. Left: a post stands in a hole with packing stones added for stability. By chance, the rim of a pot datable to c. AD 1300 was included when the hole was back-filled with a mixture of topsoil and subsoil. A coin of AD 1520 found amongst the packing stones could not have got there *after* the post was erected and the hole refilled. Thus, the date of the potsherd is irrelevant, for it is 'residual' from earlier occupation of the site, but the coin provides a *terminus post quem* showing that the post was erected *after* 1520. Right: a layer has accumulated after the demolition or decay of the structure, filling the cavity left by the post, and a new topsoil has formed. The coin of AD 1600 could only have reached its position *after* the decay or removal of the post, but 1600 is only a *terminus post quem* for the formation of this layer. Thus, the life of the timber structure began after 1520, and ended before the new layer was formed, sometime after 1600. However, one or both of the coins might have been residual or old when lost. Greater precision could only be achieved by considering other evidence from the site. Without the coin of AD 1520, the residual potsherd would have given a *t.p.q.* at least two centuries too early. If the precise findspot of the second coin in the later layer of the post-hole had not been recorded, a false *t.p.q.* of AD 1600 would have been given to the structure. *Audio Visual Centre, University of Newcastle*

bottom. Today, even the simplest archaeological situation is still approached from the same point of view, whether it is a long sequence of layers

67

recorded in section, or a direct relationship between two intersecting features in an area excavation. The analysis of dating by means of stratification involves the clumsy but apposite phrases *terminus post quem* and *terminus ante quem* (fig. 3.12). The interpretation of sections is not strictly objective, and it is an important reminder that excavation is not a science. Excavators should prepare detailed reports and make them available to other archaeologists as soon as possible, so that they can decide whether the conclusions are based on reasonable interpretations of the evidence.

The first stage in writing an excavation report involves the integration of layers and structures with dating evidence recovered from them, whether it is pottery, coins, radiocarbon samples

3.13 The recording of a stratigraphic sequence using the Harris Matrix. The simple section (top left) and the exploded three-dimensional diagram (right) show the same stratigraphic units and the order in which they were formed. It should be noted that (2) and (6) are interfaces, rather than actual layers. Bottom left is a Harris Matrix showing all stratigraphical relationships; in the centre, these superfluous or duplicated lines have been removed to give a clear summary of the original section. This method of summarizing stratigraphy can be carried out during an excavation, and is useful in published excavation reports. *Audio Visual Centre, University of Newcastle, after Harris 1989, fig. 12*

or anything else of chronological significance. It is of course essential that all excavated material was carefully recorded in relation to the deposits where it was found. The **Harris Matrix** is a useful development that has brought considerable benefits to the study of stratigraphy; it was devised in the 1970s as a response to the overwhelming complexity of deeply stratified urban excavations (Harris 1989, 34–9; see fig. 3.13). Harris emphasizes the fundamental validity of Wheeler's approach to stratigraphy, but demands a more systematic approach. His term 'unit of stratification', rather than 'stratum' or 'layer', conveys the importance of interfaces between layers. Analysis of the stratification of complex excavations is simplified by the reduction of sections to diagrams, and the recognition of these interfaces.

Thus, although the sides of a silted-up ditch have no existence other than as the boundary, or interface, between its filling and the material through which the ditch was dug, they nevertheless represent a human action that should be assigned to its correct place in the sequence of layers. In the case of working surfaces, such as floors, it is not always fully appreciated that the interfaces represent an important period of human activity that may have lasted for a very long time, whereas a visible layer that overlies it may have been deposited very quickly. Harris stressed that the only way to make sense of a site is to study the whole extent of each interface to understand the activity that took place:

No amount of sectional drawing is of the slightest help in such a composition of these period plans, as it becomes clear that the horizontal record of stratification is far more important than the vertical.... What is needed is not a grain-by-grain plan, but a record of scaled drawings with each stratigraphic unit on a separate sheet, and which shows, at the very least, the area of the stratum and spot heights of its surface – as recorded prior to excavation. With such an archive any desired configuration of stratigraphic units can be made at any time. ... (Harris 1977, 94)

Harris Matrices have not replaced traditional section drawings in archaeological reports; site directors will still wish to illustrate relationships

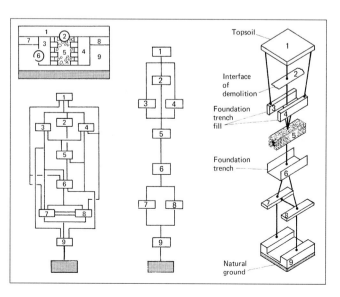

that are crucial to dating or interpretation. **Section drawings** remain a convenient method of summarizing individual features, for example the composition of silted-up ditches or rubbish pits; colour photographs rarely bring out sufficient detail, and they are expensive to publish. A drawing of a section is by definition an interpretation, and it can be expressed in a variety of different styles, from baldly diagrammatic to naturalistic (Harris 1989, 69–81). Section drawings can supply an impression of the actual appearance of a stratigraphic sequence that cannot be included in a matrix. Some excavators go much further, and attempt reconstruction drawings to explain how structures have decayed to result in a particular section. This valuable intellectual discipline can generate useful ideas that improve the quality of interpretation.

2 An example of the development of excavation techniques: Corbridge, Northumberland

The large Roman site commonly referred to as Corstopitum lies just west of Corbridge, a small medieval town in the Tyne Valley, 24 miles (38 km) from the mouth of the river. It lay at the junction of two important Roman roads: Dere Street led from York into Scotland, while Stanegate continued west to the Solway, and marked the northern frontier of the Roman Empire for around thirty years before Hadrian's Wall was built 4 km to the north. The history of exploration at Corstopitum illustrates the changing aims and techniques of archaeology, from treasure hunting to investigation, from research to rescue, and from excavation to publication and display. As early as the seventh century AD, Corstopitum was used as a convenient source of stone for local Anglo-Saxon churches, which were the first major stone buildings to be constructed in the area since the end of the Roman period. This kind of quarrying continued for more than 1000 years before any serious archaeological excavation began. The site was probably still impressive when it attracted the attention of King John in 1201; the terse contemporary record was elaborated in an eighteenth-century edition of Camden's *Britannia*:

> No inconsiderable remains of antiquity, however, are to be found here, among which King John dug for treasure supposed to be buried by the antients; but fortune mocked his vain pursuit, as he had formerly done Nero when searching for Dido's treasure at Carthage. He found nothing but stone with marks of brass, iron, and lead. Whoever views the adjoining heap of ruins called *Colecester* will pronounce it a station of Roman soldiers. (Gough 1789, III, 235)

The name Corstopitum came from an inaccurate medieval copy of a Roman document, and is certainly incorrect; modern interpretations vary, but a plausible view is that the place was called Coria by the local native Celtic population, and that it was adapted to Corioritum ('hosting-place by a ford') to describe the Roman military base at this important river crossing (Hind 1980).

2.1 Antiquarian observations

Many travellers commented on the visible ruins well into the eighteenth century, but besides stone robbing, the expansion of agriculture was already having severe effects. A notable local antiquarian, John Horsley (1684–1732), gathered information in the first quarter of the eighteenth century, and observed in his *Britannia Romana* that 'It is now almost intirely levelled . . . Pieces of Roman bricks and pots were lying everywhere on the surface of the ground in tillage, when I was on the spot' (1732, 397). Stukeley commented on both stone robbing and agriculture in *Iter Boreale*, an account of a tour made in 1729: 'They tell us with some sort of wonder, that it is the richest and best thereabouts for ploughing: they discern not that it is owing to the animal salts left in a place that had been long inhabited. Corbridge is built out of its ruins, which are scattered about there in every house' (1776, 63). A large area of the site was cleared for agricultural improvement in the first decade of the nineteenth century.

2.2 Excavation

Archaeological excavations were mounted in 1861: '. . . a labourer had been placed by Mr.

Cuthbert of Beaufront at the service of Mr. Coulson, ... for the purpose of making investigations at Corbridge.' Dere Street and the Roman bridge across the Tyne were examined along with some internal structures (Bruce, 1865, 18–19). Woolley did not benefit from this earlier work when he began a major investigation in 1906: 'the results obtained were apparently of great interest. Unfortunately the plans, reports, and drawings made by Mr. Coulson have entirely disappeared, and the only record of his work is an inadequate résumé given at second hand ...' (1907, 162). The excavations of 1906–14 were stimulated not only by past accounts of buildings and rich finds, but also by ignorance about the real significance of the site. The best insight is provided not in the excavation reports, but in an autobiography published in 1953 by the first director, Leonard Woolley (1880–1960):

My first experience of digging was at Corbridge in Northumberland, and I know only too well that the work there would have scandalized, and rightly scandalized, any British archaeologist of today. It was however typical of what was done forty-five years ago, when field archaeology was, comparatively speaking, in its infancy and few diggers in this country thought it necessary to follow the example of the great pioneer, Pitt Rivers. *The Northumberland County History* was being written and the writers wanted to know more about the Roman station at Corbridge, so proposed a small scale dig to settle the character of the site. The committee naturally appealed to Professor Haverfield as the leading authority on Roman Britain, and he, as he had intended to take a holiday on the Roman Wall, agreed to supervise the excavations. Somebody, of course, had to be put in charge of the work and because I was an Assistant Keeper in the Ashmolean Museum my qualifications were, in the eyes of an Oxford professor, *ipso facto* satisfactory. Haverfield arranged with Sir Arthur Evans, the Keeper, that I should go to Corbridge. In point of fact I had never so much as seen an excavation, I had never studied archaeological methods even from books (there were none at the time dealing with the subject), and I had not any idea of how to make a survey or a ground plan; apart from being used to hand-

ling antiquities in a museum, and that only for a few months, I had no qualifications at all. I was very anxious to learn, and it was a disappointment to me that Haverfield only looked in at the excavation one day in the week and then was concerned only to know what had been found – I don't think that he ever criticized or corrected anything. (Woolley 1953, 14–15)

The excavations of 1906–14 explored enormous areas of the site (fig. 3.14), and resulted in a series of prompt annual excavation reports that totalled 676 pages and were as detailed as the general standards of their day expected. In addition, Volume X of *The Northumberland County History* (1914) contained a 48-page synthesis of the results, written by Prof. Haverfield:

It seems plain that we have here something that was neither an ordinary fortress nor an ordinary town. The castramentation of the one and the street-planning of the other are alike, wanting. We may rather guess that Corstopitum was now a store-base for armies operating further north and possibly even for the eastern garrisons of Hadrian's Wall, with a half-military, half-civil population which would gather round such a base (op. cit. 479). As the [fourth] century advanced, Corstopitum declined. It survived . . . only as an ill-built town of hucksters and mechanics, whose mean shops intruded on the nobler ruins of the Antonine Age; a town of vanishing wealth, on the extreme border of a sinking empire (op. cit. 11).

Thus coins, pottery and dated inscriptions indicated occupation throughout the Roman period, from the late first century AD until the late fourth or early fifth century. Most structural information related to stone buildings of second-century date; what preceded or succeeded them was largely unknown, because excavation had consisted of stripping soil until stone structures were found, and either uncovering them completely or simply following the walls (fig. 3.15). Some digging was carried out beneath foundations, but earlier structures were rarely revealed, even though 'disturbed ground' containing recognizably earlier Roman finds was frequently encountered. The excavation was certainly superior to treasure hunting, for the horizontal

3.14 A large area was excavated at Corbridge before the First World War. Good plans were obtained of major stone structures in the centre of the site (the granaries and 'forum', labelled X, VII, and XI, and walled compounds south of Stanegate). To the north and west, many buildings had been at least partially constructed in timber, or had been disturbed by modern agriculture. The positions of shops opening onto Stanegate were indicated by stone gutters and by floors with gravel surfaces or stone paving. Earlier timber forts that lay beneath the stone structures were not discovered until excavations began again in the 1930s. *Craster 1914, facing p. 481*

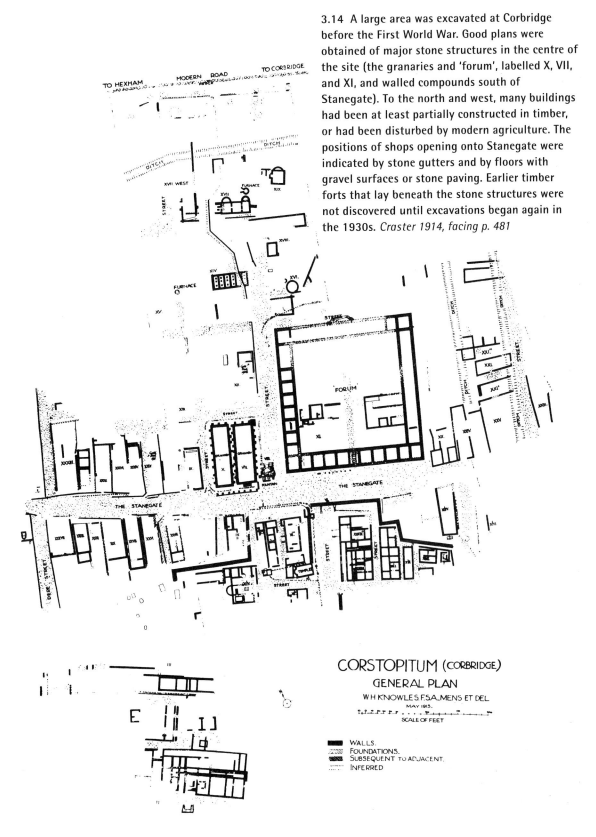

CORSTOPITUM (CORBRIDGE)

GENERAL PLAN

W.H. KNOWLES. F.S.A., MENS ET DEL

MAY 1913.

SCALE OF FEET

WALLS.
FOUNDATIONS.
SUBSEQUENT TO ADJACENT.
INFERRED

3.15 This illustration shows excavation techniques at Corbridge in 1909. The columns of porticoes belonging to two stone granaries (X and VII on fig. 3.14) had been partly buried by rises in the level of the Roman main street (Stanegate); its stone gutter can be seen resting against them. The excavators have removed the vital deposits between the road to the granaries. These stratified layers might have revealed important details about the date and nature of changes to the buildings and their entrances. However, everything except solid masonry was simply dug out, destroying evidence that later excavators would have liked to re-examine. *Knowles & Forster 1910*

aspect of the site – plans of buildings in particular – was being explored with the clear purpose of finding out more about the site. Attention had still not been devoted to the examination of vertical sections or sequences by the time that the Great War ended excavation in 1914.

2.3 Excavations between the wars

Durham University Excavation Committee began work at Corbridge in 1934, under the joint direction of Ian Richmond and Eric Birley, because His Majesty's Office of Works was in the process of preparing the central portion of the remains found in 1906–14 for public display. Birley had been asked to write an official guide to the site, and, as a result of his own recent excavations on Hadrian's Wall, he had hypothesized four firmly dated periods of construction, occupation and destruction for the frontier. Stratigraphic excavation had become familiar by the later 1930s (Richmond had worked with Wheeler in the 1920s), and artefact studies,

notably the dating of pottery, had improved considerably. The new excavations were therefore carried out with strict reference to individual layers and deposits, which could be dated by associated artefacts, and by the examination of stratigraphic relationships between structures (fig. 3.16). Furthermore, the directors had a distinct working hypothesis: 'It seemed axiomatic that the four main Wall periods should be reflected in the structural history of Corstopitum too' (Birley 1959, 3). Part of their work consisted of resurveying and analysing the stone structures that were to be conserved and displayed to the public, but this was combined with the excavation of new trenches to examine the relationships between the structures and to assign them to their appropriate historical period.

Richmond and Birley also wanted to explore below the stone buildings to investigate the layers that had been recognized, but not understood, since 1909. They knew how to recognize remains of timber structures, and were well informed about the nature and planning of Roman forts. Thus, a late-first-century fort gateway, together with its ditch system and parts of internal buildings, was identified by means of small trenches. Further layers were recognized as belonging to later forts constructed between this first phase and the overlying stone structures. The 1936–8 excavation report speaks with an air of confidence entirely lacking from the 1906–14 series:

> . . . it is impossible . . . to correlate with history all the periods of occupation so far discovered . . . The deep sections, however, by relating to the subsoil and to one another buildings of which the planning has long been known, mark a new departure in our understanding of the site. It is not possible both to describe and to date the work of later periods; while the fact that the problems concerned with early periods can be defined, may be regarded as the first step towards their solution. (Birley & Richmond 1938, 260)

After a second break caused by world war, excavations took place every year from 1947 to 1973 on a comparatively small scale, heavily constrained by the consolidated remains of the major stone structures in the central area. The site was used for training students as well as for research; new details were added, and old ideas were confirmed, modified or rejected. Four successive superimposed forts (two with additional phases of internal modification) were gradually disentangled by means of the detailed stratigraphic observation of intercutting features. In addition, a round timber house was discovered, belonging to a native farmstead that had existed before the first Roman fort was built. The phases of military occupation were correlated with dating evidence drawn from historical events, dated building inscriptions, coins and stratified pottery, while comparisons with other forts suggested the size and nature of the army units that occupied each phase.

The stone structures on the site, and in particular their histories after the second century AD, were more difficult to assess than the earlier forts because crucial overlying strata had been removed either by earlier excavators or during clearance in advance of public display. Debate has raged, complicated by the fact that it has had to rely on observations recorded in the early reports from the 1906–14 excavations that cannot be checked, for the evidence has gone for ever. The area surrounding the central military and official core lies outside the limits of the

remains open to public display under farmland, and it has not been touched by archaeologists since 1914. However, regular ploughing has clearly done further damage to the uppermost levels, for the cultivated areas are now up to a metre lower than those under pasture (Bishop & Dore 1989, 12). It is known that open-fronted shop buildings flanked a main street leading west, but we know nothing about their construction or subsequent history. Many were only recorded

3.16 Sections drawn by Ian Richmond in trenches dug at Corbridge in the 1930s to explore relationships between structures discovered before the First World War. The excavators related these buildings to road levels that they had assigned to specific historical periods (Antonine, Severan, etc.). Several layers belonging to timber forts of the late first and second centuries AD can be seen beneath the lowest road level, together with traces of timber structures cut into the subsoil. With hindsight, the interpretation of the site in terms of a rigid historical sequence seems oversimplified and arbitrary, but it was a considerable advance over the treatment of the same road a few metres away illustrated in fig. 3.15. *Birley & Richmond 1938, facing p. 254*

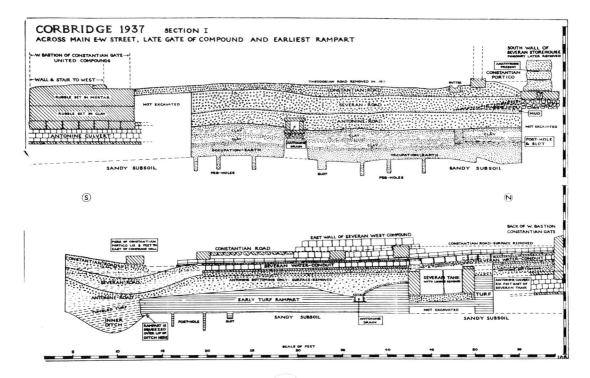

when traces of stone gutters, hearths or gravel levelling and floors were found; the actual buildings were probably constructed mainly of timber. Other structures may well have been missed completely, for the detection of timber buildings without stone drains or floors lay outside the technical competence of the early excavators. To the north, the plan is even less satisfactory. Fragments of buildings, minor roads, ditches and furnaces indicate intense activity in what was probably an industrial area, overlying the northern parts of the early timber forts. A few stratigraphic sequences were recorded on the plans in places where major features overlapped each other, and, occasionally, structures were dated by associated finds. Little else can be said about the overall development and decline of the whole Roman town of Corstopitum without further fieldwork and excavation.

2.4 Area excavations

The application of new excavation techniques at Corbridge did not end in the 1960s; it was brought up to date by two large open-area excavations in the 1970s and 1980s. The first of these, caused by road building, was a classic example of planned research, chance discovery, and systematic fieldwork that revealed a whole new phase in Corstopitum's early military history. During the final season of training excavations at Corbridge in 1973, several fragments of pottery were found in the foundations of the headquarters building belonging to the very first fort on the site, providing a textbook example of a *terminus post quem*. The pottery was a well-known form of samian ware with moulded decoration, imported from southern France. It could be dated by historical evidence from other sites, including Pompeii; experts agreed that it was unlikely to be earlier than *c.* AD 90, and certainly later than *c.* 85 (Bishop & Dore 1989, 219). This created an immense problem, for it had been assumed since the 1930s that the first fort was built by Agricola, the governor of Britain who garrisoned the region in the *early* eighties AD during his campaigns in northern England and Scotland.

A solution to this problem was offered by a Roman bath-house that had been discovered by accident in 1955, one kilometre west of the main

3.17 Location map showing the relative positions of Corstopitum ('main site') and the Red House site excavated in 1974 before the construction of a by-pass. The structures shown in black on the main site are those found in 1906–14 (see fig. 3.14), and the rectangular outline indicates the position of the underlying timber forts revealed between the 1930s and 1970s. *Hanson* et al., *1973, fig. 1*

site (fig. 3.17). Pottery dating to the time of Agricola had been found there, and it seemed almost certain that a military site must lie nearby, for civilian baths would be unthinkable in this area at such an early date. Since the early fort was definitely *not* situated on the main site, a level river terrace immediately to the east of the bath-house now seemed to be a possible location. By a remarkable chance, a new dual carriageway by-pass was about to be constructed, which had been designed to avoid the northern limits of Corstopitum but would cut right across the site of the newly suspected Agricolan fort. Rescue excavations were organized, and, thanks to co-operation from the road contractors, the fort's existence was confirmed; a continuous open strip over 150 metres long was excavated, and the remains of fifteen timber buildings were found (fig. 3.18). Pottery and coins found on the site could be dated to the time of Agricola, and were contemporary with the nearby bath-house. They proved that the first military occupation was on the Red House site, and that it shifted to the main site soon after AD 85/90, the date provided by those critical pottery sherds found there in 1973.

Publication standards had risen dramatically by the 1970s. The excavation of a small percentage of this single-period site, without occupation levels or rubbish deposits, generated a report of 98 pages in the 1979 issue of *Archaeologia Aeliana*. The same periodical had carried reports on the 1906–14 excavations, but although these earlier seasons involved incomparably larger and more complex areas, with abundant structures and other finds, the results were presented in an average of only 85 pages per season.

One very small research excavation was carried out on the Corbridge main site in 1976 to check an outstanding detail of the interpretation of the second-century forts. Then plans were drawn up to construct a new purpose-built site museum. This

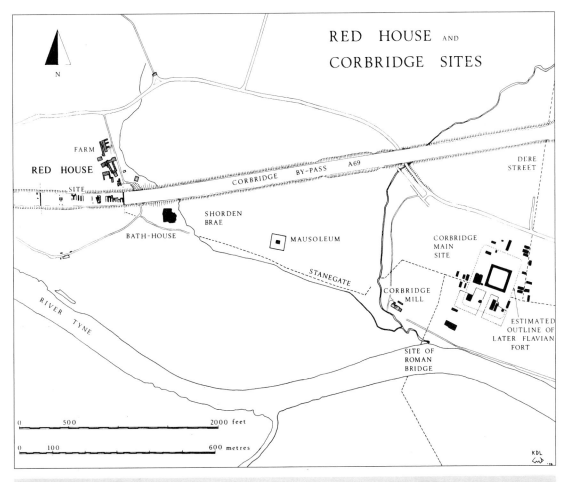

3.18 Open-area rescue excavations at the Red House site, Corbridge. A strip was cleared along the line of the new road, although space had to be left for contractors' vehicles working further along the route. The outlines of foundation trenches for timber buildings can be seen in the foreground. *Charles Daniels*

required a rescue excavation because the museum's basement would intrude into archaeological levels. As a result, the whole area was excavated to record any information that had survived disturbance by earlier trenches. A deep trench cut below stone buildings on this part of the site in 1908 had only found four to five feet of 'disturbed soil'. This trench was emptied again in 1980, and revealed the remains of successive west ramparts of the early forts; a useful cross-section of their structure was recorded by the excavators, John Dore and John Gillam.

2.5 Publication and cataloguing

Besides revealing a sequence of forts and civilian buildings, excavation conducted over 75 years had generated an enormous collection of artefacts. Many individual papers, notably on classes of Roman pottery, had appeared in the periodical *Archaeologia Aeliana* from the 1930s through to the 1970s. Ian Richmond published a particularly interesting paper in 1943, 'Roman legionaries at Corbridge, their supply-base, temples and religious cults', that related the rich collection of sculptures, inscriptions and excavated structures to the Roman army's calendar of religious ceremonies. Another landmark was John Gillam's 'Types of Roman coarse pottery vessels in northern Britain' (1957, subsequently reprinted in book form), a fundamental reference work that used finds and dating evidence from Corbridge and other sites in the northern frontier zone to provide dated typological classifications of the principal forms of pottery found in the region.

In common with other spheres of British archaeology in the 1980s, further work at Corbridge veered away from excavation towards publication. The Department of the Environment (in the form of English Heritage from 1984) put more of its resources into publishing a backlog of reports and finds generated by the boom in rescue excavation in the 1960s. This policy was extended to important sites in State care, such as Corbridge, and resulted in two major publications. The first, *Excavations at Roman Corbridge: The hoard* (Allason-Jones & Bishop 1988) was a detailed account of the discovery, in 1964, of the remains of a large wooden box that contained the most extensive remains of Roman legionary armour ever found, along with assorted weapons, tools and miscellaneous other

items. The authors concluded that the contents had been gathered together when a workshop was cleared out at the end of a phase of occupation of one of the site's series of forts. The items had been packed up ready for transport before a decision was made to bury them instead. Hundreds of detailed scale drawings of the armour and other artefacts were accompanied by a careful analysis of their form and function. Re-examination of the excavation records and the stratigraphic context dated the whole find to c. AD 122–38 – around 30–40 years later than had been thought in 1964.

The second book published by English Heritage, *Corbridge: Excavations of the Roman fort and town* (Bishop & Dore 1989), drew together all surviving information from the long series of excavations conducted between 1947 and 1980. Of its 323 pages, 140 were devoted to a detailed analysis of the myriad of small trenches (rather than open areas) excavated all over the site. Since it was very difficult to correlate finds and layers from so many different deposits, the results were published in elaborate tables and supplemented by four microfiches of further text and drawings. The remainder of the volume comprised reports by specialists on coins, pottery, glass and 'small finds' (miscellaneous objects made of metal and other materials). The sequence of dates for the forts built on the site was not significantly altered by this research, but the identification of exactly *which* contexts (and finds) were associated with each phase provided important supporting evidence for dating them. Thanks to this work, the report is not only a scholarly discussion of the structural history of a complex military site, but also a valuable reference work for dating finds from the late first to second centuries AD.

2.6 A new museum

The 1980s also witnessed a change in the management of ancient monuments in State care, particularly in the quality of their presentation to the public (below, p. 175). The construction of a new site museum at Corbridge allowed finds to be displayed in an aesthetically pleasing, as well as informative, manner, and it also provided an opportunity to improve the storage of the thousands of other items that are not on public display. The painstaking process of sorting out old records for publishing a report on the excavations was inseparable from improving the catalogues of the museum store. The resulting report and museum archives now offer a collection of accessible, well-documented material ready for future research. At the same time, an attractive modern museum enhances the appeal of the site to ordinary visitors (fig. 3.19).

3 Excavation procedure
(Barker 1993)

Every archaeological site is itself a document. It can be read by a skilled excavator, but it is destroyed by the very process which enables us to read it. ... when the site has been destroyed all that is left are the site records, the finds and some unreliable memories. (Barker 1993, 13; 1986, 108)

The account of excavation techniques at Corbridge gives an insight into the development of modern methods; most of the remainder of this chapter will attempt to explain how excavations are carried out today. Excavation can destroy a site just as thoroughly as ploughing, building construction or natural erosion; the only difference is that destruction by excavation is initiated by people who should (in theory) understand the value of ancient sites. This awareness brings responsibilities; no site should be touched without consideration of the need to carry out the excavation with the utmost skill, after making careful plans for the preservation and publication of the results. All excavators face the same ethical question: on what grounds can their action be justified? Some may claim that examination of a site will advance knowledge, others that they are rescuing a site from destruction. We should not forget that different motives may be involved, such as economics, through the enhancement of tourism, or politics, by promoting nationalism.

It must be remembered that fieldwork techniques have advanced to a high level of sophistication, making use of remote sensing from the air or geophysical surveying devices on the ground (Chapter 2). Field survey programmes are conducted by non-invasive observation of the ground and limited collection of artefacts from its surface. In view of these

3.19 Corstopitum, or Corbridge 'main site', today. The purpose-built museum is unobtrusive, and the façade echoes the colonnaded porticoes of the Roman granaries that lie immediately in front of it; their columns, seen in fig. 3.15, may be distinguished just left of centre. *Neal Askew, English Heritage*

alternatives, excavation should be a last resort. If excavation *does* take place, fieldwork techniques should have been exploited fully in advance to maximize the amount of information available about the site, and to assist in the preparation of the excavation strategy.

3.1 Selection of a site (fig. 3.20)

New sites are discovered with growing frequency, but resources remain limited; it is therefore important that sites for excavation should be chosen with care. Since the number of sites is finite, every excavation should form part of a wider programme of research, whether the site is threatened with destruction or not. One site might attract attention because it is particularly well preserved, another because it is going to be destroyed; are these good reasons for excavation? The answer depends on fundamental attitudes to archaeology. Should a picture of the past be built up from a gradual accumulation of independent observations (like clues in a detective story), or should there be overall strategies? The detective-story approach characterized most work conducted up to the early twentieth century, but

3.20 Richard Rogers' remarkable Lloyds building in the City of London overlooks an excavation of the Roman basilica; this was a large hall attached to the forum of Londinium, capital of Roman Britain. Apart from a period of near-abandonment in early Anglo-Saxon times, London has been an administrative and commercial centre linking the British Isles with Europe and the rest of the world for nearly two thousand years. This site also illustrates the pressures of rescue excavation in an urban setting. Procedures for excavation and recording must be adjusted to take account of the time scale and nature of building work. Large modern buildings require such deep foundations and basements that, unlike most constructions in previous centuries, they remove all trace of earlier occupation. *Museum of London*

our knowledge is now so detailed in most parts of the world that we have sufficient information for posing meaningful questions; it is now indefensible, both ethically and intellectually, to excavate a site simply to find out what is there.

The kinds of decisions facing archaeologists involved in excavation today may be illustrated by a hypothetical problem. Suppose that an area has been extensively examined by fieldwork of various kinds, and that twenty Roman sites of a similar form have been recorded. Ten are situated on marginal land, well protected from past or present destruction; of the other ten, nine lie on arable farmland, and are suffering from the effects of ploughing, while the remaining one is about to be destroyed by building work. Sufficient funds are available for the complete excavation of *one* site. What should be done? Some possible choices may be suggested:

a) the site threatened with complete destruction should be totally excavated to save a record of its information for posterity;

b) one of the well-preserved sites should be fully excavated, because it is in better condition. It can be approached at a more leisurely pace, since it is not threatened; the quality of information should therefore be higher than (a);

c) several sites, including the one threatened with destruction, should be examined partially in order to provide some basis for making comparisons between them;

d) none of this class of site should be excavated at all. Resources should be redirected to non-destructive fieldwork aimed at the investigation of a different period, or an area about which less is known. The destruction of one out of twenty similar sites is tolerable.

There are good points about all of these choices. It would require much confidence to take choice (b), for no two sites are ever identical and surface indications may be misleading. There is no guarantee that a well-preserved site will produce information of better quality than that found on a damaged site.

If (a) or (b) are selected, how safely can the results from one site be generalized to the other nineteen? Few scientists would accept results gained from only 5% cent of a sample. Choice (c) may seem to be a good compromise, but partial excavations always leave unanswered questions, and complete knowledge of one site might be more informative than one quarter of each of four;

opinions would vary over this solution. Whether (d) is better than any of the others depends on the interests of the decision-makers; a specialist on the Bronze Age would obviously prefer to increase aerial survey and fieldwork on prehistoric sites rather than excavate a Roman site.

English Heritage has added a variation on this theme of conflicting priorities (*Exploring . . .* 1991, 34):

> The management of the archaeological resource is based on a series of stages which form the framework for decision-making and the formulation of strategies. Three such stages can be proposed in the context of archaeological resource management and together these stages may be called the management cycle:
>
> Stage 1   Identification, recording and the understanding of the monument or historic landscape.
> Stage 2   Option 1 – curatorial management where the main aim is to arrest the natural and man-induced processes of decay through protection and management.
> Stage 2   Option 2 – exploitative management where the archaeological resource can be used for public enjoyment through interpretation and display, or for academic interest through investigation and excavation.
> Stage 3   Recording – in exceptional circumstances, when preservation is no longer possible, because the value of the archaeological resource is outweighed by some other factor, a site may be excavated to record as much as possible of its structure and form and thus in effect preserve it as a record.

Central to this cycle is the understanding of the resource which requires research and evaluation. For that reason the stages of the management cycle are preceded by the proposed framework of the academic objectives which English Heritage considers necessary in order to provide a framework for the future.

Although a cynic might be suspicious of the reference to 'public enjoyment', and question how 'the value of the archaeological resource' is to be measured, the emphasis on placing excavation within a 'framework of the academic objectives' is important. If resources are scarce, it is better that they should be distributed according to a strategic plan – even if no two archaeologists agree on the details of such a plan! The most dangerous phrase in this extract lies in Stage 3, however, where elegant phrasing makes it sound acceptable to 'preserve' a site 'as a record'; few archaeologists are sufficiently confident about the process of excavation to regard the results as nearly equivalent to the site itself.

A further question may be added at this point: what should be done about 'unique' sites? Stonehenge, Avebury and Silbury Hill are all 'unique' prehistoric sites in Wessex, if only because they are so much bigger than other contemporary stone circles, henge monuments or mounds. Should efforts be concentrated on more 'typical' sites, or can these monuments be expected to give clearer insights into their times because of their individual character? It is instructive to frame the same question in a historical period: which will tell us more about medieval Kent – an architectural and archaeological analysis of Canterbury Cathedral, or the study of a selection of churches from surrounding urban and rural parishes? Again, there is no clear answer without a statement of research objectives. In practice, the intellectual climate of the 1990s would not look favourably upon any further excavation of a major monument such as Stonehenge unless it was faced by a dire threat that could not be met by protection and management, rather than intervention. Perhaps the only conclusion to emerge from this discussion is the need for conscious decisions and policies about *all* ancient sites, based on a good knowledge of their significance in a particular region or country, and their relevance to current research questions.

3.2 Planning an excavation

The role of site director varies in scale and complexity. An individual engaged in a small research project might dig a minor site with a few volunteers, whereas the director of a permanent excavation unit involved in a major research or rescue project would employ a full-time team of special assistants and a paid labour force. An average excavation will probably be planned by a single director who takes responsibility for preliminary research, setting up and conducting the actual excavation, and writing up the results for publication. Even when a site has been selected as a result of a sensible programme of fieldwork and there is a clear reason for the excavation, an enormous amount of research and organization still remains to be done, irrespective of the period or geographical location of the site.

3.3 Background research

No excavation should take place without a careful study of previous work on the site, or without an appreciation of how it fits into a wider landscape. The amount of data that has been collected in advance will determine how well the director is able to draw up detailed plans for the excavation, and to respond to new information that is revealed as excavation proceeds. Much of this preparation must be conducted in libraries and archives where earlier accounts and illustrations of the site may be found. Records of previous excavations, or stray finds recovered from the site, may lead to material preserved in museum collections, which must be examined before a new excavation takes place, and, if unpublished, included in the final report. In countries where documentation extends far enough back into the past, archive offices may hold informative maps and plans, such as those drawn up to record the ownership of land. These might show features of the site itself or physical surroundings, along with forgotten but informative place-names and field-names. In England, a site or its area may even have been mentioned in an Anglo-Saxon charter, a form of land document that survives from as early as the seventh century AD. Ideally, this documentary research will form part of a programme of fieldwork to investigate the local landscape (above, p. 51).

The most important modern source of information that must be explored is aerial photography. Ideally, a number of photographs will have been taken over a long period under varied conditions, and may reveal slight surface earthworks or the effects of buried features on growing crops (see fig. 2.4). Maps of soils and local geology should also give insights into the natural subsoil conditions that will be encountered. The site should be visited to check knowledge gleaned from the above sources against its present state on the ground. If it is not visible, detailed surveys must be made to relate it to modern reference points, or, if necessary, to fix its exact position with the help of geophysical devices (above, p. 46). All visible traces must be recorded, especially on a research excavation where the original form of the monument must be restored from an accurate contour survey. If sufficient resources are available, new aerial photographs may be commissioned, along with more extensive exploration with resistivity equipment or magnetometers, and professional surveyors may be employed. With all this information, the director will be ready to decide what the priorities of the excavation should be, and to devise the optimum layout of trenches to explore them.

3.4 Staff and equipment

The number and nature of staff employed on an excavation are directly related to its size, resources and complexity; on small sites, many tasks will be performed by the director. Although it is impossible to generalize, certain basic requirements always exist. Because excavation destroys a site, **recording** is the most important part of the process. Site records come in three forms – written, drawn and photographic – and every excavation must have staff with appropriate expertise, both archaeological and technical, to compile and maintain them. A large excavation that produces large numbers of finds will also require a full-time finds assistant, with sufficient helpers to sort and wash pottery and other materials. Lists of finds from each excavated context must be compiled, and every artefact must be labelled, bagged or boxed for storage, in such a way that it is accessible for further study when required. An on-site conservation laboratory should be provided on sites where delicate finds are likely to be abundant; remains of wood, leather or textiles recovered from waterlogged deposits require immediate treatment, for example. The site should also employ someone with a good knowledge of environmental evidence, which involves the careful selection of soil samples, and the use of sieving or flotation equipment to increase the recovery of small bones, seeds, etc. Since all of these categories of information about the site and its finds are suitable for recording in computer databases, an excavation should also have a competent computer operator as well as appropriate computing equipment. The ultimate quality of the interpretation and publication of a site depends not only on the skill of the excavator, but also on the comprehensive nature of the recording and preservation of finds; these factors should guide the director's selection of staff.

3.5 Excavation strategy

The director's experience, combined with all the background research that has been carried out in advance, will determine how best to approach a site. Aerial photographs and the results of geophysical prospecting may suggest the most informative parts; this is particularly important if the site is being sampled, rather than totally excavated. Exploratory 'sondages', larger trenches or extensive open areas are employed in various configurations, according to the availability of resources and the nature of the site. Since even the best-prepared director rarely finds that a site conforms exactly to expectations, the strategy should allow for modifications. Flexibility is important, and it depends to a large extent on the quality of the excavation's specialist staff. Interpretation of excavated structures, combined with provisional dating and other observations about the finds, should provide continuous feedback that can help to reinforce, modify or reject the director's working hypotheses. It is now possible to compile up-to-date computer files of site information for this purpose during an excavation, and to carry out sophisticated analyses while the work progresses.

Stratigraphic excavation is sometimes compared to the dissection of a biological specimen, because layers or other features are removed in strict order, and detailed records are kept of each stage. The analogy is misleading in two major ways. First, if dissection goes wrong another specimen can be obtained, but no two sites are ever identical. Second, the structure of tissues, bones and organs is more predictable and easier to recognize than a sequence of archaeological features; layers of soil may merge into each other without clear interfaces, leaving the excavator to decide what divisions should be made for the purposes of recording.

However scientific a site's recording system may seem, it is inevitable that major subjective elements remain. Individuals working with trowels make continuous observations and judgements about the texture, colour and significance of soils, deposits or features (some samples should be taken for examination by soil micromorphology: Courty 1989). In addition, they must be able to recognize all kinds of finds, from solid stone or pottery and fragile corroded metal to the faint discolorations left by organic materials that have decayed away completely. The alarming early history of excavation shows how easily this information was lost.

3.6 Recording

The large size of many modern excavations means that the role of director resembles that of a general manager who balances objectives against resources, while site supervisors control the details of the excavation. In the past, directors kept an overall check on the entire process by writing descriptions of layers and features in site notebooks, and jotting down subjective insights that might eventually help in the interpretation of the basic plans and drawings. An increasing demand for objectivity and accuracy, combined with the complexity of, for example, a large open-area multi-period urban excavation, led to the design of pre-printed recording forms (fig. 3.21). These allow the director to impose standardized recording methods that considerably reduced the scope for errors or omissions. Individual record forms are used to describe the position, size and characteristics of each separate excavated context. Forms should be designed with future analysis of the site for publication in mind, so that the description of a feature is cross-referenced to all relevant photographs, plans and significant finds.

Further files are required for recording categories of excavated material such as pottery, bones or scientific samples, as well as for supplementary information like section drawings and photographs; all of these must also be cross-referenced back to their relevant excavated contexts. Ideally, site record forms and details of finds should be coded in such a way that the information can be transferred rapidly into data files on a computer during the excavation. It may even be possible to type information straight into

SOUTH SHIELDS 1993   AREA PSG   CONTEXT 5885

TYPE:	LAYER			
PERIOD:	ROMAN	7 CONSTRUCTION		
CUTS:				
CUT BY:	5815	5822		
OVER:	6132			
UNDER:	5877			
EQUIVALENT TO:				
OTHER RELATIONS:	See sketches on reverse			
DIMENSIONS	Maximum		Minimum	
WIDTH:	1M			
LENGTH:	3.57M SURVIVING			
DEPTH:	0.35M		0.20 M	
HEIGHT:	—			
DIAMETER:	—			
CO-ORDINATES:	(52.00) / (44.50)		(55.50) / (44.50)	
	( ) / ( )		( ) / ( )	
PLAN NUMBERS:				
UNDERLAY NOS:	PSG 269			
SECTION NOS:				
BLACK/WHITE:	FILM 80, FRAMES 7-9 COLOUR:			

DESCRIPTION: Demolition material between courtyard house and barrack, filling alley or passage. Cut on NW and SE sides by robber trenches 5815 and 5822. Mortar, fragments of sandstone and shattered tile, trampled into a compact surface. This surface reached from main street to SW by a ramp of the same material, overlain by late road surface 5877. Tile fragments occur in distinct tip-layers, and were uniformly frost-shuttered, suggesting that they were derived from a roof of considerable age when demolished.

EVENT: Period 7 Construction dump to raise level in alley between buildings

FINDS: /T118\ /T119\   ·TILE FROST SHATTERED· Bone

DATE : 21 /07/93   COMPILER: NH

3.21 A standard form for recording excavated features at South Shields Roman fort, Tyne and Wear. This layer has been given a unique context code (5885), and the excavator has assigned it to a phase ('construction 7') in the Roman sequence. Relationships with earlier or later contexts are identified by 'over' or 'under', 'cuts' or 'cut by'; these could be added to a Harris Matrix (see fig. 3.13). A series of recorded dimensions follows, together with references to plans, sections or photographic records; more general observations and interpretations are entered into 'description' and 'event'. 'Finds' provides space for mentioning important discoveries (in numbered triangles) and indicating other finds, which will be fully catalogued elsewhere. Finally, the date of the record and the initials of the recorder are added so that any discrepancies may be checked. When the form has been entered into a computer database, the context code will link it directly to other files that list photographs, plans and finds, or to other features excavated nearby. *Paul Bidwell* a portable computer, while the planning of excavated features is carried out with surveying equipment that logs its readings in electronic form for processing by computer. High-quality video cameras offer an additional photographic record of all aspects of excavation (Hanson & Rahtz 1988).

3.7 Computerized processing of site records

Information needs to be recorded with a clear idea of the questions that are likely to be asked about it at a later stage, and the archaeologist must be aware of these factors while recording features or artefacts. The presence or absence of a long list of attributes must be recorded for every layer of soil, post-hole, wall or whatever else is encountered, including dimensions, location, soil colour and texture, any finds, stratigraphic relationship to adjacent features, etc. This stage is tedious and time-consuming, but with forethought it is simplified and speeded up by abbreviated codes and well-designed computer programs that check the data as it is being entered.

Time devoted to computerized recording is repaid when the director comes to write the excavation report, for a comprehensive site database can be indexed in many different ways to produce specific information sorted into any desired order. For example, it may be suspected that post-holes filled with brown, stony soil have some particular significance. The computer can be instructed to search for all such features, and to select those examples that contained pottery or similar material suitable for dating, to see if they all belong to the same period. If it is suspected that these post-holes represent buildings whose plans are difficult to distinguish from other features on a plan by eye, a computer with suitable graphic software can plot them along with all other features that contained material of the same date, such as rubbish pits, fences, hearths, etc. If the dimensions of excavated features have been digitized, GIS systems allow data and plans to be combined in all sorts of combinations.

The advantages of computerized recording become particularly obvious if the alternative is considered: multiple card-indexes, masses of site plans, photographs, notebooks and perhaps only the memory of the excavator for some details. An enormous amount of time would be involved in sifting through all of these records manually to provide the information demanded by the straightforward enquiry outlined above, and the boredom it could generate might seriously affect the accuracy and completeness of the process. The cost and availability of computers are now well within the reach of small sites; no director of a large, complex site can possibly afford to ignore the value of comprehensive computer-based recording of all aspects of the excavation.

3.8 Publication
(Cunliffe 1982)

Publication was assisted by the invention of photogravure in 1879, for photographs could be reproduced without having to be printed individually or redrawn as engravings (Feyler 1987, 1045). For the next century it was generally assumed that a site should be published in book form, and this concept was boosted by the massive printed volumes produced by Pitt Rivers at the very end of the nineteenth century. By the 1960s it was taken for granted that an excavation report would consist of an 'objective' account of the excavated features and structures, followed by descriptive catalogues of each category of finds, along with scientific reports on bones, environmental samples, etc. (fig. 3.22). However, the unparalleled size and number of rescue excavations in the 1960s and 1970s, followed by spending cuts in the 1970s and 1980s, made it impossible to produce reports of this kind. A number of committees proposed new standards of publication, with varying emphases, but with a consistent recommendation that much material should be stored in archives, rather than published. Thus, the phrase 'preservation by record' was coined to minimize the reality of the destruction of a site at the same time that 'preparation of an archive' was substituted for compiling and publishing a traditional excavation report.

English Heritage recently set out a definition of minimum requirements for the contents of a published report (*MAP* 1991, 39):

i. the research objectives as expressed in the project design

ii. circumstances and organisation of the work

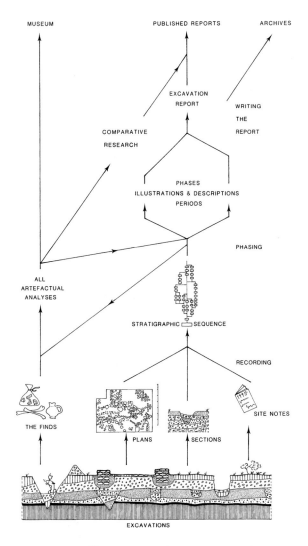

MUSEUM   PUBLISHED REPORTS   ARCHIVES

EXCAVATION
REPORT

WRITING
THE
REPORT

COMPARATIVE
RESEARCH

PHASES
ILLUSTRATIONS & DESCRIPTIONS
PERIODS

PHASING

ALL
ARTEFACTUAL
ANALYSES

STRATIGRAPHIC SEQUENCE

RECORDING

SITE NOTES

THE FINDS

PLANS   SECTIONS

EXCAVATIONS

3.22 There are many important stages between excavation and publication. Perhaps the most important is the amalgamation of plans, section drawings and recording sheets into a stratigraphic sequence, and its interpretation in terms of periods of occupation and abandonment, and phases characterised by particular activities. The finds should be processed at an early stage, for artefacts such as pottery and coins assist in dating and understanding the nature of occupation, while bones or samples of soil, plants, etc., help to elucidate environmental conditions and the economic functions of each phase. All finds, together with any information that will not appear in a published report, must be documented in full, ready for storage in a museum or archive. *Sandra Hooper, after Harris 1989, fig. 57*

and the date at which it was undertaken
iii. identity of the individual/organisation by whom the work was undertaken
iv. summary account of the results of the project
v. summary of the content of the project archive, where it is housed and how it may be consulted.

The same document also defined the specification of a research archive (37):

> The research archive will be derived from the work done during the analysis phase and will comprise: stratigraphical/structural, artefact, environmental, and other catalogues and all other records as well as details of the methods and selection strategies used in each case. Each separate data group should be cross-referenced to related data groups, to the final publication, and if necessary to a general context concordance. These should be supplemented by indices to allow the user maximum accessibility to the contents.

The move towards unpublished archives coincided with a growing use of standardized excavation records held on computers, and this has interesting implications for how publication might take place in the future. Why issue site records in an indigestible and expensively printed book, when they can be left in a computer archive to which specialists are allowed free access? Why not publish a short summary of the principal structures and finds, in a form that will be more interesting to general readers and simply inform specialists about the existence of archives? This attractive solution conceals the danger that excavations published only in summary form do not allow readers to check the details upon which the excavator's general interpretations are based. A solution may lie in the growing availability of videodisks and CD-ROMs, together with indexing and searching programs similar to the Hypertext systems that began to reach an advanced state of development in the late 1980s. In the twenty-first century, excavation reports may become multimedia experiences, with site records, photographs, drawings and video sequences stored on a single disk.

4 Excavation: special cases
(Schiffer 1987)

It has already been stressed at the beginning of this chapter that archaeology cannot be classed as a science because one of its primary sources of information, excavation, involves the destruction of unique specimens. The remainder of this chapter will look at various forms of excavation, without making any attempt to provide a comprehensive 'manual' of methods. My personal experience is limited to sites in Britain and north-western Europe, ranging in date from neolithic to medieval, involving everything from almost invisible traces of timber structures to elaborate Roman masonry. I have worked on urban and rural sites situated on a range of subsoils, from the relatively easy chalks and sandstones of southern England to the more difficult valley silts of south Wales, and the intractable glacial clays and dolerite of Northumberland. Before tackling the interesting problems involved in excavating and understanding various forms of buildings, it is important to look briefly at other categories of sites that are important in the archaeology of earlier periods or other parts of the world.

4.1 Camps and caves
(Smith 1992)

A sedentary lifestyle is a very recent innovation in human history. It began at different times in different parts of the world, normally when settled farming came to replace hunting and gathering as the predominant means of subsistence. Before this, human occupation revolved around numerous temporary and/or seasonal sites whose locations were determined by hunting or gathering activities. Archaeological traces of such sites should reflect their function, and the nature and length of occupation. Thus, the *home base* of a hunter/gatherer group might contain semi-permanent houses and other structures, while a *field camp* associated with hunting expeditions would be very different (Smith 1992, 29, fig. 3.1). From the point of view of excavators, the principal problem of open sites is that seasonal occupation and insubstantial buildings did not lead to the formation of an appreciable depth of stratified deposits. They are particularly susceptible to erosion and other forms of natural disturbance; exceptionally, sites occupied at the edge of water were covered by silt, and coastal sites were sometimes buried by blown sand. The priority of an excavator is to make exact records of the position of every fragment of bone, flint or other artefacts, for an analysis of their distributions may suggest the functions of different parts of a site and imply relationships between structures and activities (Smith 1992, 30, fig. 3.2):

Many repetitive tasks such as fine flint knapping or bone carving are often most comfortably carried out in a seated position and, requiring little space, may take place inside. Butchery requires space so that the operative can move around the carcass and, because it is associated with unpleasant smells, it is usually considered to be an outside activity. Stationary tasks may require warmth and need to be carried out by the fire while detailed tasks may require light and, if they are undertaken inside, will need to be located near an opening. It is inconvenient, and even dangerous, to walk on flint waste or fractured animal bone, and at a site occupied for a prolonged period such rubbish is likely to be cleared away. (ibid. 31–2)

The interpretation of sites as field camps or home bases, and the identification of the activities that took place on them, is based largely upon ethnoarchaeological observations of modern hunter-gatherers (below, p. 171).

Caves occupied from time to time offer much better possibilities for finding stratified deposits, but little in the way of structures; furthermore, their stratigraphy is likely to result from natural weathering and sedimentation as much as from human activities. Cave excavations were very important in the nineteenth century because assemblages of tools and other artefacts could be found in association with bones of animals and, occasionally, human burials or even cave-paintings. The bones and tools that Boucher de Perthes retrieved from gravel beds in the Somme valley were only associated in the sense that they had ended up in the same geological deposit. However, animal bones found in caves are very misleading if those that were brought there by human hunters are not distinguished from those introduced by carnivorous animals when humans were absent. This problem applies to most sites with signs of early human occupation, including those associated with fossil hominid remains in East Africa, with the result that opinions are divided over whether early humans were hunters at all, or mere scavengers. Donald Johanson's informative and entertaining account of interpretations of Site FLK in Olduvai Gorge provides an excellent historical outline of changing perceptions of sites and their finds since the 1940s (1991, 213–44).

4.2 Waterlogged sites

(Coles 1984)

Information about the indigenous peoples of the Americas and Australia gave early prehistorians in Europe valuable perspectives on the lifestyles of people known only through discoveries of stone tools. An important additional source of knowledge resulted from a drought in Switzerland in 1853–5, when low water levels revealed several hundred 'lake-dwellings' (probably settlements on the shore, rather than dwellings constructed on piles in the water itself, as originally thought). Ferdinand Keller published an influential book about these sites in the 1860s that included illustrations of a wide range of organic structures and artefacts, as well as bones and plant remains, that complemented the

stone and metal artefacts being studied by Scandinavian archaeologists (above, p. 26). In Trigger's judgement, '. . . the continuing study of these prehistoric remains attracted wide interest. It played a major role in convincing Western Europeans of the reality of cultural evolution and that ancient times could be studied using archaeological evidence alone' (1989, 84).

The growth of ecological perspectives on archaeology in the twentieth century enhanced interest in the range of information that could be retrieved from waterlogged sites. It led to the 'classic' investigation of a mesolithic site at Star

3.23 An early medieval timber round-house preserved in wet conditions at Deer Park Farms, Antrim, Northern Ireland. The walls were constructed from interwoven branches, whose inherent strength and light weight demanded little in the way of foundations or supporting posts; a length of wall that collapsed inwards can be seen in the foreground. The exterior would presumably have been made weatherproof with clay. Remains like these remind excavators of sites where wood does not survive that they must not underestimate buildings that lack impressive foundations. One of the excavation workers kneels beside a stone hearth, providing a useful indication of scale; a large number of people could be accommodated in a structure of this kind. C J Lynn

Carr in Yorkshire by Grahame Clark (Smith 1992, 110–21). This tradition continues in Britain, and includes major work prompted by 'rescue' archaeology, such as the Somerset Levels project (Coles & Coles 1986) or Flag Fen, near Peterborough (Pryor 1993); wetland archaeology also thrives in many other parts of the world (Coles & Lawson 1987; Coles 1992). Wet sites also enhance periods of historical archaeology (fig. 3.23). In Ireland, for example, the early medieval period is marked by the poverty of artefacts and absence of pottery from settlement sites. Fortunately, some were constructed on artificial islands (*crannogs*) in lakes, and finds from these illustrate what is missing on land – notably a range of barrel-shaped containers and lathe-turned wooden vessels that made pottery unnecessary for most storage and table purposes (Edwards 1990, 77, fig. 30). Crannogs also produce many finds of metal artefacts, for it was difficult to recover objects that were dropped into water or fell between gaps in timber floors.

John Coles gave the name **sensitivity analysis** to his outline of the most important components of the assessment that should take place before any wetland site is examined (1984, 36–8):

1. site *identification* (e.g. settlement, burial, etc.) and *chronological position*: the date and nature of any kind of site are fundamental to any research that is carried out.
2. site *content*: awareness of the types of evidence likely to be encountered will deter mine the excavation strategy.
3. *condition* of the site: the extent of waterlogging and the nature of the deposits may vary from soft peat to hard mud.
4. *recovery* techniques to be used: an excavator must make a hard-headed estimate of a project's resources and effectiveness in planning the tactics to be used.
5. requirements for *post-excavation* work: 'This is probably the most crucial element in any programme, and unless it is fully debated and agreed beforehand, and arrangements made, the excavation should not proceed. Sampling and extraction of materials for analyses, specialists and their specific requirements, and relevance of such work to the project's aims, must be laid down and fully understood by all' (ibid. 37).
6. *conservation* needs: a very careful excavation strategy is required to limit the exposure of these finds to the air during excavation, and to ensure that adequate facilities are available for immediate treatment and long-term preservation of organic finds.

Ideally, these six aspects should be applied to the excavation of *any* kind of site; the implications of insufficient planning are more immediately apparent on wet sites, however. The principal difference between 'dry' and 'wet' sites lies in the range of organic finds that will be encountered. Excavation trenches will be more difficult to manage, for it may be necessary to erect platforms suspended above the working surfaces to avoid walking on fragile remains. The greater complexity of structures complicates recording by planning and photography, while additional categories of finds make increased demands on the cataloguing system. Publication costs will also be affected by the scale and quality of the discoveries.

Perhaps the single most important development in wetland archaeology has been the extension of dating by dendrochronology into prehistory; it is now possible to provide accurate dates for timber structures back to about 9000 BC in Europe. Tree-rings can also be used to analyse periods of construction on complex sites (below, p. 110). This degree of precision allows a 'historical' perception of the construction and development of suitable prehistoric sites that is discussed in relation to dating methods.

4.2 Underwater archaeology
(Dean 1992)

As with wetland archaeology, the guiding principles and methodology of underwater archaeology are identical to those that should be employed on dry sites (fig. 3.24). However, the additional complexity of the tasks of discovery, excavation, recording and conservation forces directors of underwater projects to take a much more stringent approach to their objectives and ethics. The **Nautical Archaeological Society**, based in Britain but with one third of its members abroad, has clear principles of conduct (Dean 1992, 300):

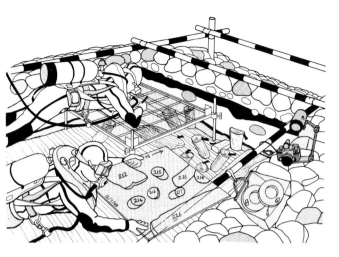

3.24 The principles of excavation and recording on an underwater site differ little from those employed on dry land, but many special techniques have been devised to maximize the effectiveness of divers who, for reasons of safety, can only spend limited amounts of time working. Here, a planning-frame with a measuring grid is being used to support rigid plastic sheets onto which features may be drawn accurately by eye.
Dean 1992, 168

   i. NAS members shall adhere to the highest standards of ethical and responsible behaviour in the conduct of archaeological affairs.

  ii. NAS members have a responsibility for the conservation of the archaeological heritage.

 iii. NAS members will conduct their archaeological work in such a way that reliable information about the past may be acquired, and shall ensure that the results are properly recorded.

 iv. NAS members have a responsibility for making available the results of archaeological work with reasonable dispatch.

Maritime archaeology is particularly troubled by the indiscriminate damage to shipwreck sites by looters and souvenir hunters. Much of this activity is not malicious in intention, for diving is a popular leisure activity whose attraction is enhanced by visiting wrecks. However, commercial salvage on modern wrecks shades imperceptibly into the destruction of historical evidence from older ships by unscrupulous treasure hunters. Shipwrecks

offer rare insights into the technology, warfare and commerce of the past, and individual ships provide a chance to study a range of artefacts that were all in use at a specific date. For this reason they are frequently described as 'time capsules'. On most dry-land sites, structures are found in the state that they reached after their useful life had ended, and artefacts often accumulated in rubbish dumps over an extended period. In contrast, finds from the *Mary Rose*, a Tudor warship that sank in 1545, illustrate weapons, clothing and personal items that belonged to members of the crew at the moment of the ship's loss. When sufficiently large numbers of ancient ships and their cargoes have been recorded and published carefully, each find contributes to a wider picture of ancient trade. We now have a good idea of the changing patterns of shipping and trade in the Mediterranean, thanks to a database compiled by Parker (1992) of 1259 wrecks dating from prehistoric times to AD 1500.

4.3 Graves
(Roberts 1989; Pader 1981)

Occasionally the concept of 'time capsules' is extended to burials, for the majority were placed in the ground at a single moment in the past. For an archaeologist, the most informative kind would consist of the skeleton of a dead individual who had been placed into a grave fully clothed, accompanied by **grave-goods** – a selection of personal items, or gifts to take into an afterlife – that might indicate the deceased's sex, social status and religion, and help to date the burial (fig. 3.25). Unfortunately, burials are normally more complicated; bodies were cremated in many periods, grave goods were not always included, and large numbers of individuals were sometimes buried together in collective tombs. Worse still, acidic soil conditions can remove virtually all traces of human bone, and cause severe damage to artefacts. Ethnoarchaeological studies provide many warnings about the interpretation of burials, which may just be the end-result of a complicated series of ritual practices (Humphreys and King 1981).

Burial practices also vary in terms of cemeteries and structures. Some graves were isolated, rather than placed in neat cemeteries with clear markers to indicate their position. Structures

3.25 Photograph of a recently discovered Anglo-Saxon burial at Sutton Hoo, Suffolk (see also fig. 3.1). Mound 17 covered an undisturbed grave containing a man in a coffin, placed in a large oval pit, along with assorted grave goods, including weapons and horse-gear. Close by was a separate burial pit containing the skeleton of a horse. The excavation of such complex and delicate remains requires considerable expertise, and a comprehensive understanding of the problems of lifting and conserving finds for future study and display.
© *Sutton Hoo Research Trust; photograph by Nigel Macbeth*

may range from simple wooden memorials to massive stone mausolea, such as those of the emperors Hadrian and Augustus that can still be seen beside the Tiber in Rome, or the pyramids of Egypt. In many parts of the world prehistoric burials were incorporated into earthen barrows or stone megalithic tombs whose monumental character attracted the attention of antiquarians, who 'excavated' them with little attention to anything other than the hope of finding grave-goods.

Because the process of burial was frequently accompanied by ceremonies, modern excavations should not just examine a burial, but also its surroundings, where remains of ritual feasts or religious structures might be found. In Christian contexts, there may be signs of cemetery churches or facilities for pilgrims visiting notable graves (Rodwell 1989).

The excavation of burials and cemeteries requires scrupulous recording for many reasons. If soil conditions do not favour the survival of bones it may nevertheless be possible to detect the former position of a skeleton from subtle changes in the texture of the earth, or by chemical analysis of soil samples from the grave. The exact positions of the remains of dead individuals must be recorded, for they may be related to factors revealed by pathology, such as signs of injuries on bones. If grave goods are present, their position may also be significant, particularly where items of jewellery or other clothing accessories are concerned, for these may suggest the form of costume worn by the deceased individual. Recent excavations at the royal Anglo-Saxon cemetery at Sutton Hoo in Suffolk illustrated the complexities that may occur on a single site. The burials include both cremations and unburned bodies, humans and animals, some plain graves and others under large barrows, graves without goods, and others amongst the richest ever found in Britain. The most famous barrow originally covered a wooden chamber, filled with grave-goods, in a complete ship that had been dragged up a slope from the nearby River Deben and lowered into a deep trench beneath the mound (Carver 1992).

5 The excavation of structures
(Barker 1993)

Early excavators cleared stone-built sites without any regard to traces of timber structures, and, in the Near East, only solid stone or fired clay structures were detected on sites whose buildings were constructed mainly from sun-dried mud bricks (see fig. 3.33). There is no substitute for experience, based on an understanding of the many processes involved in the formation of an archaeological site – how ruined buildings decay, how occupation layers accumulate, how ditches silt up, etc. Excavators should also have some technical understanding of the variety of constructional techniques that may be encountered on a site (fig. 3.26).

The study of buildings – whether fortifications, temples, palaces, houses or workshops – is fundamental to archaeology. Antiquarians and travellers from the Renaissance to the nineteenth century did produce many excellent publications of buildings, but the possibilities for recording them have been expanded by photography and film. At the same time, archaeological techniques have increased the quantity and range of information provided by structures from any area or period. Information gained from the excavation or analysis of buildings is of enormous value, whether it comes from early palaeolithic structures such as the oval wooden huts that date back to 380,000 BC at Terra Amata, Nice, in France, or from recent mills and factories associated with the Industrial Revolution.

5.1 The excavation of stone structures

Second only to burial mounds and other major earthworks, stone structures were the easiest form of site for early archaeologists to recognize and excavate. In many cases quite reasonable conclusions were drawn from them, for many more nineteenth-century excavators had an architectural training than those of today, paticularly where Greek and Roman archaeology were concerned. J T Wood, who excavated at Ephesus in Turkey in the 1860s, was able to explore Roman theatres and the Temple of Diana knowing roughly what to expect, and with an understanding of how fallen columns or fragments of architectural sculpture might have fitted into the original structures (Wood 1877). If less was known about a site it was common for narrow trenches to be dug to locate buried walls, and for digging to continue along the sides of walls looking for off-shoots or junctions in an attempt to recover complete plans. 'Islands' of unexcavated soil left in rooms by this procedure might then be cleared in the hope of recovering objects to indicate the date and function of various parts of the building. Vital stratigraphic relationships between walls, floors, and occupation or destruction levels were entirely removed, making it virtually impossible for modern archaeologists to make sense of the remains by re-excavation.

The use of stone for construction does not necessarily have any significance for technical ability, wealth or social status, except in obvious cases of monumental architecture such as Stonehenge or the Parthenon. Stone was used in areas where it was conveniently available; when it was not, timber, mud brick, or other useful local resources provided alternative building materials. The remains of stone or brick buildings are much easier to recognize than mud brick or timber; as a result, problems of differential survival distort evidence for human settlement in many parts of the world.

A great variety of construction techniques is employed when building stone is readily available. Dry stone walling is the simplest; uncut natural boulders or roughly quarried blocks are stacked up with care or laid in regular courses, relying on gravity and friction for their stability. Outcrops or boulders that might otherwise obstruct farmland would have provided very convenient sources of stone. Dry stone construction is not unskilled, but tools or other materials are not essential. The stones are bonded together with tough clay or mortar to increase strength and to improve the comfort of buildings by reducing draughts and water penetration. Many Roman buildings relied on the strength of the concrete cores of their walls rather than on the visible stone surface, which formed a mould for the concrete while it set. Some major buildings of

3.26 An understanding of construction techniques is very helpful in the interpretation of excavated remains of structures. This diagram presents eight imaginary examples of wood, stone and clay used in a variety of combinations (many other possibilities exist). Since only four of these structures have holes or trenches dug into the ground, the remainder might leave no trace on a site that had suffered from ploughing or surface erosion. The location of structures built directly on the surface may be detected on undisturbed sites by means of scrupulously careful open area excavations, such as those carried out at Wroxeter by Philip Barker (1990, 1993). *Audio Visual Centre, University of Newcastle*

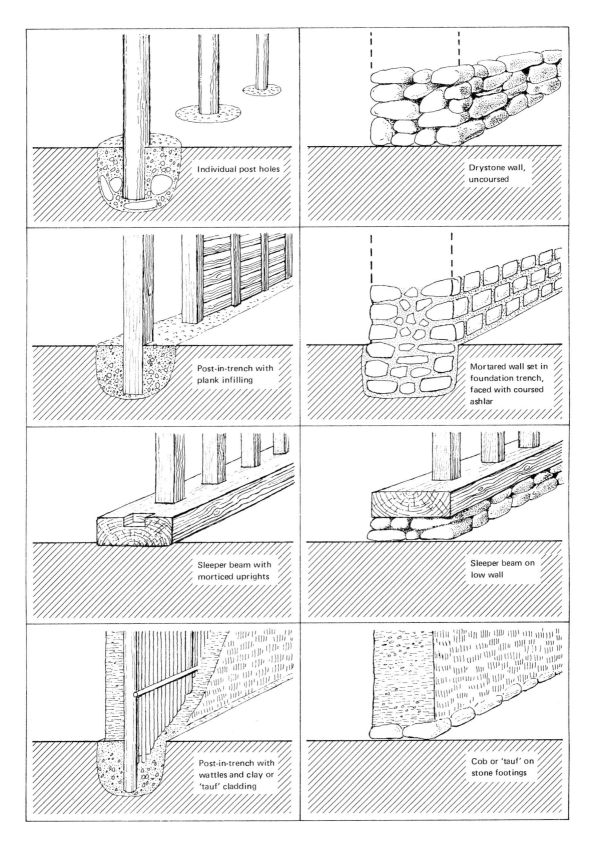

Individual post holes

Drystone wall, uncoursed

Post-in-trench with plank infilling

Mortared wall set in foundation trench, faced with coursed ashlar

Sleeper beam with morticed uprights

Sleeper beam on low wall

Post-in-trench with wattles and clay or 'tauf' cladding

Cob or 'tauf' on stone footings

the second century AD and later were made of thick concrete with occasional courses of stone or tile, and thin ornamental wall claddings made of marble or mosaics. They can appear unsightly today if the concrete cores have been stripped of their facing by later stone robbers, especially where good building stone is not easily available locally.

Much of the final work on Greek, Roman and medieval buildings made of finer stone was carried out on site. Blocks were roughly shaped at quarries to minimize their weight during transport, and trimmed to the exact requirements during building; decorative carving was usually completed at this stage, too. Small chippings of stone and discarded tools can often be detected during excavations, and they are useful in relating the stratigraphic record to the building. Debris left by masons cutting blocks of fine imported stone into geometrical shapes for decorative wall cladding was recognized at the Roman palace at Fishbourne, Sussex; the excavators also found spreads of builders' mortar, and splashes of paint from the walls (Cunliffe 1971, pl. 11).

Structure (Adam 1994)

Remains of stone walls uncovered on an excavation do not necessarily result from a stone building, for low stone walls were frequently used to provide firm dry footings for clay or timber buildings. Their effectiveness is shown by the large numbers of picturesque cob and half-timbered cottages that have survived for many centuries in the south of England; dry footings combined with an overhanging roof that throws rainwater well clear of the wall face are most effective. Mud or clay walls are ideal in drier climates, and quite complex structures were already being constructed on early agricultural sites of the eighth to seventh millennium BC in the Near East, such as Çayönü, in Turkey or Jarmo, in Iraq. Stone footings were used as a base for packed mud walls, while stone foundations in curious 'grill plan' formations supported floors made from bundles of reeds covered in clay (Oates 1976, 83–4).

Another variable is the presence or absence of foundations set in a trench dug into the subsoil. Substantial foundations would be superfluous for a structure of modest height, or if sound bedrock lay immediately below the surface. On farmsteads in Northumberland occupied during the Roman period, traditional round timber houses of pre-Roman origin were often rebuilt in stone. Their thick stone walls were erected on the surface of the ground without creating distinctive subsoil features such as the post-holes of their wooden predecessors. This can create a real problem for excavators, for agricultural clearance easily remove all trace of stone houses from a site. The only traces of stone buildings on a farmstead at Apperley Dene were large boulders in a surrounding ditch, mixed with late Roman pottery that also occurred in miscellaneous features elsewhere on the site (Greene 1978). At the other end of the architectural spectrum, the original specification for Hadrian's Wall was so broad that it did not require foundations for stability. When the plan was modified during construction, probably to save stone and mortar, it was reduced from c. 3 to c. 2.5 metres thick, and proper foundations were then considered necessary.

When a timber roof resting on stone walls decays through age it is possible to remove and replace it without disturbing the walls; it is therefore difficult to trace the full history of a simple stone building, even when the walls remain substantially intact. A long chronological span for artefacts from such a structure may be the only indication of its length of occupation. In contrast, the walls and roof supports of timber houses require frequent repairs that leave observable traces in the subsoil. A glance at any standing medieval building usually reveals inserted and blocked windows, changes in roof line, extensions and rebuildings stretching over several centuries. If nothing but the foundations and a few of the lower courses survive, this information will have disappeared, leaving only features such as blocked doorways or extended foundations to hint at modifications. If the excavator is fortunate, further details may be revealed by fragments of distinctive masonry showing architectural characteristics or decorative styles that are datable; stonework demolished at the end of one period is often reused in the next. Documents containing building accounts, or illustrations made before the building was completely ruined, may be found in archives. Indeed, these records should have been revealed during preparatory research before excavation began and used in the design of an excavation strategy. This was the case at Norton Priory, in Cheshire, where a medieval monastic complex and the secular houses that replaced it were analysed through an integrated programme of excavation and documentary research (Greene 1989).

Internal features of stone buildings, such as partitions, screens or flooring, were frequently constructed from wood, and they are difficult to detect unless parts of their structure extended below ground level. Floors of stone or beaten clay are more helpful because they were frequently laid on a foundation of rubble or other material containing architectural fragments from earlier phases, masons' chippings, and even domestic rubbish. Datable sherds of pottery or coins discovered in these layers provide a useful *terminus post quem* for the construction of the floor that covers them.

Survival of stone structures (fig. 3.27)

Much of what has been said so far assumes that stone structures have survived reasonably well. In reality, buildings that went out of use were normally treated as quarries, especially if they contained squared facing blocks. In areas where stone is particularly scarce even the foundations may have been carefully removed, leaving only unusable fragments and scattered mortar. The holes left behind are known as 'robber trenches', and they destroy the stratigraphic relationships between walls, floors and other surrounding levels in a similar manner to trenches dug by 'wall chasing' archaeologists. However, since stone robbers did not shift more than the very minimum amount of soil in their quest for stone, they normally followed the foundations very closely. An excavator can recover a 'negative' plan of the building by removing the filling of robber trenches. Mortimer Wheeler recognized 'ghost walls' at Verulamium (St Albans, Herts.) and excavated them in this way to reveal one of the city's monumental Roman gateways, of which not a single stone survived (Wheeler & Wheeler 1936, pl. 88a).

Standing structures (Rodwell 1989)

In the seventeenth century, John Aubrey was aware

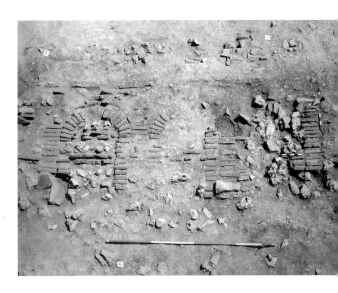

3.27 Part of a building façade excavated at Meonstoke, Hampshire, where the end wall of part of a Roman villa complex had collapsed outwards. This photograph shows a set of three windows (or decorative arcades) constructed from earthenware tiles that would have made a visual contrast with the surrounding stonework. Since the walls of most Romano-British villas rarely survive above their foundations, this was the first opportunity to gain any impression of the appearance of their upper levels. It also demonstrates the importance of careful cleaning and observation of stonework in open area excavations. If parts of the fallen wall had been encountered in small trenches, they would probably have been interpreted as flooring or a paved surface. *British Museum; King & Potter 1990, 198*

of the value of different forms of window styles for dating medieval buildings, while classical archaeologists deduced Greek and Roman architectural styles from ancient authors and surviving buildings in Greece and Italy. From the Renaissance to the eighteenth century architects examined and recorded classical buildings to incorporate details or designs into their own work. The Gothic Revival of the nineteenth century brought medieval buildings back into favour, and many architects reshaped existing buildings (especially churches) in a meticulously academic fashion – but destroyed genuine medieval features in the process. The notion that representative examples of old buildings should be preserved intact has only really gained hold in the twentieth century; ironically, it coincided with a phase of urban renewal that destroyed large areas of historic cities on an unprecedented scale. At the same time many rural churches have become redundant, while major European cathedrals such as York and Trier have undergone massive repairs. All of these factors have encouraged traditional architectural methods to be supplemented by archaeological activities.

The procedure of analysing a standing building relies on principles similar to stratigraphy (Harris 1989, 56–61). The objectives are to establish its original form, to work out the sequence of later alterations, and to relate them to any available dating evidence. There may be visible indications of changes such as the blocking of redundant doorways or the insertion of new windows. It is surprising how often existing walls were adapted to bring a building up to date with changes in function or new fashions, rather than being demolished and replaced. Pitt Rivers pioneered modern archaeological methods of examining buildings in his study of a medieval hunting lodge at Tollard Royal on his estate in 1889, doing such things as stripping wall plaster to reveal earlier decoration and original wall faces, and excavating both within and outside the building

3.28 Churches present some of the most complex problems of archaeological and architectural analysis, but offer rewarding results (Rodwell 1989). This photograph shows the excavation of structures and burials stretching back over 1000 years in the church of St Peter at Barton-on-Humber, Lincolnshire. Unfortunately, the earliest remains are likely to have suffered from considerable later disturbance, and they may also be masked by later masonry that cannot be removed. *Dr W Rodwell*

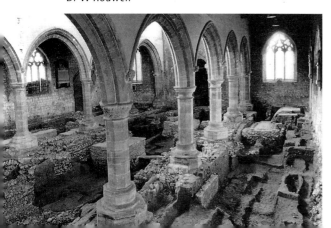

(Bowden 1991, 122–6). Additional techniques are available today. Samples of mortar compared in the laboratory may reveal different phases of construction; earthenware tiles or bricks are datable by thermoluminescence (below, p. 123), and the exact age of structural timbers may be determined by counting tree-rings (below, p. 109).

Medieval parish churches in many parts of Europe have provided some of the best examples of this kind of analysis, because they are small enough for comprehensive study (figs 3.28–29). They remind excavators who normally deal only with buried structures that many complex changes can take place in the history of a building without affecting the foundations. The combination of excavation with the study of standing remains can also tell architectural historians that significant phases may have come and gone without leaving visible traces on the surviving structure (Rodwell 1989). Meanwhile, new techniques of **spatial and functional analysis** have brought a deeper understanding of the significance of changes made to the plans of buildings that were used for many centuries. A study of a medieval castle at Edlingham in Northumberland identified changes in society, economics and the need for defence that were reflected very clearly by the way that people of different status gained access to various parts of the building (Fairclough 1992). Since this approach has been developed and validated in the context of documented historical buildings, it can be extended to the explanation of prehistoric buildings, although the results will always remain hypothetical.

5.2 Timber structures

Timber only survives where extremely wet or dry conditions have remained constant over a long period. Otherwise, it decays completely, leaving differences in the colour and texture of soil that are only detected by careful excavation. Three examples of archaeological discoveries of boats illustrate these conditions. One side of the hull of the *Mary Rose* survived in excellent condition near Portsmouth because the ship sank on its side into deep silt that protected the timber from erosion by currents and from marine worms that eat exposed hulls (Rule 1982). The world's oldest surviving ship was excavated in Egypt in 1954, beside the Great Pyramid of Cheops (c. 2590 BC);

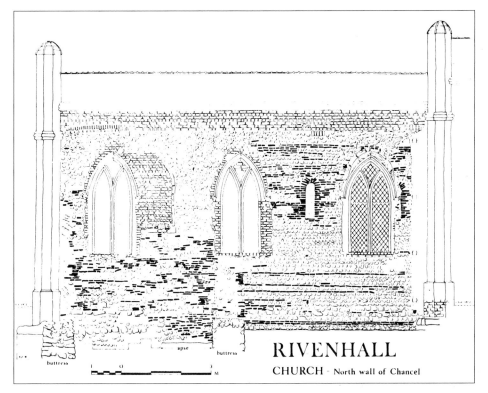

RIVENHALL
CHURCH - North wall of Chancel

apse   buttress

buttress

3.29 A detailed record of one external wall of a church at Rivenhall, Essex, drawn to emphasize differences in the masonry. The remains of distinctive small round-headed windows (marked in black) provide evidence that this wall was initially constructed in the Anglo-Saxon period. It was then retained throughout the life of the church, and larger windows were inserted later by knocking holes through the original Saxon structure. Because these significant details had been concealed behind wall plaster, the church at Rivenhall was thought to have been constructed much later in the medieval period, on the evidence of visible windows (Rodwell 1985). *Drawing: Dr W Rodwell*

it had been dismantled and placed in a specially constructed stone chamber where arid conditions preserved it from decay (Jenkins 1980). In contrast, the Anglo-Saxon ship containing a royal grave at Sutton Hoo in Suffolk was buried in a long trench and covered by a large mound. Alternating wet and dry conditions in the sandy subsoil caused complete decay of all but one fragmentary plank from the bottom of the hull. Fortunately, layers of stained soil marked the positions of decayed timber, and the outline of

the ship was revealed by meticulous excavation and confirmed by the positions of corroded iron rivets that had originally held the planks together (Evans 1986, frontispiece).

Construction of timber buildings
(Brunskill 1985)
A knowledge of construction methods is important if the remains of timber buildings are to be excavated and interpreted correctly (see fig. 3.26). Although most forms require foundations, it is possible for substantial structures to be built on the surface without leaving any traces in the subsoil. Timber-framed buildings and 'log cabins' made from interlocking timbers rely for their stability on joinery rather than earth-fast upright posts. Fortunately, problems with uneven ground and dampness usually made it wise to erect these structures on a spread of gravel or rubble make-up, or on low stone walls; even then, only indirect evidence for the actual timber building may remain. One of the most impressive achievements of modern open-area excavation has been the discovery of a phase of late Roman timber structures built at Wroxeter in Shropshire after the Roman baths were demolished (Barker 1993, 207–20).

Earlier excavators had used narrow trenches to trace the plans of Roman masonry buildings, digging through a layer of rubble lying near the surface that they dismissed as debris left by the demolition and decay of the Roman town, disturbed by later agriculture. However, open-area (and open-minded) excavation employed by Philip Barker revealed a hitherto unsuspected final phase in the occupation of the town. The implications of his work are universal: wherever timber buildings might have been erected on rubble levelling, leaving no detectable floor levels, an excavator cannot claim with complete certainty that buildings were *absent* during a phase when a site was apparently deserted. Unfortunately, this kind of excavation is virtually impossible on other Roman town sites, because, unlike Wroxeter, most have been disturbed by medieval and modern occupation, and assorted foundations, cellars, wells and pits reduce the area available for excavation. Deep ploughing also destroys traces of this kind on many open sites (e.g. Corbridge – Bishop & Dore 1989, 12); sadly, few places survive where the full benefits of the techniques learned at Wroxeter are applicable.

Barker's excavations also emphasize the importance of recording. The location of a building may be indicated by nothing more than slight differences in the size and character of one area of rubble compared to its surroundings. Artefacts also require the same kind of scrutiny; fragments of flint, pottery or small coins may be found outside the limits of such structures, where they were broken or dropped and trampled into the ground surface. It is possible to study their exact distribution only if each find has been accurately surveyed, and detailed plans may provide valuable guidance for interpreting the site. The significance of some of this information may only emerge after the excavation has finished, thus underlining the principle (first proclaimed by Pitt Rivers) that *everything* found should be recorded, even if its meaning is not apparent at the time of discovery.

Timber structures that *did* possess below-ground foundations are not without problems for excavators. One of the most recurrent archaeological features encountered on sites is the **post-hole**. The simplest method of erecting a firm upright is to dig a hole, stand a post in the bottom, and to pack the upcast from the hole

firmly back around it, perhaps with the addition of some packing stones. The subsoil is rarely suitable for large posts to be rammed directly into the ground without some pile-driving equipment, but this technique was certainly in use as early as the Roman period.

Although separate post-holes are commonly dug for each upright in a large complex structure, a continuous **foundation trench** may be more efficient if a building contains lines of regular posts. It is also a useful technique if large posts need to be set close together; individual holes would tend to intercut, and would be inconvenient during the manoeuvring of heavy timbers. Roman military granaries are amongst the best examples of structures making use of linear foundation trenches (Manning 1981), but the technique occurs widely. Gaps between individual posts of houses or fences were frequently filled in with planks, which sometimes extended below ground level, but perhaps only just penetrated into the foundation trench. Particular care is required to detect these traces during excavation of the top layers of the fill. Some walls or fences, and even large ramparts, consisted of a continuous **palisade** of posts or planks set into a trench. An alternative to setting vertical posts into the ground is to use **sleeper beams**. Large timbers are laid horizontally, and upright posts are mortised into them to provide the structure of a building; time and effort saved in digging post-holes is offset by additional carpentry, of course. The horizontal beams might sometimes be set into trenches or raised on low stone sleeper walls, but they frequently stood on a simple rubble platform; some of the buildings recognized at Wroxeter were probably of this form. Discussion of the sleeper beam technique merges into stone construction, for stone footings were commonly used together with timber or half-timbered superstructures.

These various methods of timber construction may coexist on different parts of a site, or even in a single building. Neolithic longhouses of the Linear Pottery culture in Europe (see fig. 3.11), Iron Age round houses in Britain, and early medieval aisled halls in the Netherlands and north Germany frequently combine two or more of these features. Many closely comparable (but unconnected) buildings have been erected over wide chronological and geographical spans. A large timber hall excavated at Balbridie in Scotland was initially assumed to be of early medieval date because it closely resembled one found on an Anglo-Saxon site in Northumberland; however, radiocarbon dates revealed that it had been occupied in the Neolithic period and was more than 5000 years old (Fairweather & Ralston 1993).

Interpreting timber structures (Dixon 1988) (figs 3.30–32)

As with stone buildings, interpretation is helped by

3.30 Foundation trench of an Anglo-Saxon timber hall (Structure C12) excavated at Cowdery's Down, Hampshire, before the construction of a new housing estate (Millett & James 1983). The magnificence of this building can be judged partly from its size, and partly from the lavish use of large timbers. *Royal Archaeological Institute*

3.31 Careful excavation within the foundations of Structure C12 at Cowdery's Down revealed alternating vertical planks set either side of the walling material, which was probably woven hurdles. Larger posts stood at the corners, and the side walls were flanked by large rectangular buttresses set at an angle to receive the thrust of the weight of the roof. *Royal Archaeological Institute*

3.32 Reconstruction drawing of the Anglo-Saxon timber hall (Structure C12) excavated at Cowdery's Down, Hampshire, based on observations of structural features illustrated in figs 3.30–1. The details of the roof are of course conjectural, but its overall form has been worked out from observations of post-holes and other indications of elements that reached the ground. It is likely that a high-status building would have been decorated with elaborate paintings and carvings similar to those found on surviving Anglo-Saxon metalwork. *Royal Archaeological Institute*

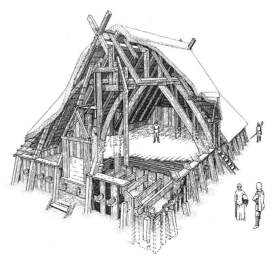

studying recent structures that are still standing, or well-preserved remains of ancient structures preserved by waterlogging or desiccation. Excavated remains of burnt buildings are also informative, for once timber has been converted into charcoal it resists further decay.

The dimensions of post-holes or foundation trenches are the best guide to the sizes of structural timbers and the loads that they were intended to bear; it is very important for excavators to record the exact location and measurements of every post by careful observation of the filling (see fig. 3.31). Features that did not support much weight, such as internal partitions, did not have to penetrate into the ground, and their traces are unlikely to survive on a site that has been damaged by activities such as modern ploughing. This problem can even affect the walls of a building if the main weight of its roof was supported on internal pillars. A further complication is caused by the perishable nature of wood, particularly in temperate climates. Decay affected timbers at different rates, and wooden buildings required running repairs. Posts were rarely replaced in exactly the same holes as their predecessors, and precise excavation and recording are necessary if the correct sequence of intercutting holes is to be sorted out and related to any significant dating evidence. When an entire building had to be replaced, a very similar structure was often constructed on almost exactly the same spot; this could possibly happen several times in succession. Careful open-area excavation is needed to recover the separate plans of successive structures, and to detect crucial points where post-holes or other features overlap, allowing the excavator to establish a stratigraphic sequence (see fig. 3.11).

If large numbers of apparently unrelated post-holes are found on sites that were occupied for long periods by structures that have left no complete or obvious plans, it may be possible to hypothesize numerous rectangular or circular structures. Sets of features that belonged together may be revealed if precise records have been kept of differences in the shape, depth, soil filling, etc., of post-holes and other structural evidence. A computer database of these records would be particularly suitable for analysis in this way, and possible structures could be plotted directly onto a digitized site plan (Bradley & Small 1985).

5.3 Other building materials

Along with stone and timber, one of the most important ancient building materials was clay, whether applied directly to wooden walls (**wattle and daub**), shaped into blocks and dried in the sun (**mud bricks**; fig. 3.33), or made into bricks or tiles fired in kilns. Building techniques are of course dependent not only on the availability of suitable raw materials, but also on climatic conditions. The use of hand made bricks of sun-dried clay began around 8000 BC in western Asia, where a move away from hunting and gathering towards food production and farming had led to a sedentary lifestyle, and the construction of permanent buildings. Hand-made bricks were used in circular houses at Jericho (Israel) in the 'pre-pottery Neolithic A' phase; rectangular mud bricks, shaped in a wooden mould, were particularly suitable for rectilinear buildings, and went on to become the standard building material of the first urban civilizations of Mesopotamia, Egypt and India. Mud bricks remain the dominant construction medium of the region today. Mud walls were sometimes provided with stone footings, and, where a more temperate climate made the unfired mud building technique less suitable, bundles of reeds or timber might be combined with clay walls to increase their strength; Nea Nikomedia in Greece and Karonovo (Bulgaria) in the Balkans provide good examples of mud and timber construction dated to between 7000 and 6000 BC (Piggott 1965, pl. 2a).

Mud-brick buildings have a limited life but are easily demolished and replaced, so that the build-up of levels over many centuries leads to deeply stratified deposits, such as the characteristic tells of the Near East. They are very difficult to excavate, because demolished structures compacted by overlying levels have a similar consistency to that of any surviving structural remains. Mud bricks decay rapidly once they have been exposed; many pioneering excavators in the Near East found that monumental structures simply crumbled to dust. More durable **fired bricks** form part of the archaeology of many parts of the world. They were in regular use in Mesopotamia by 3000 BC, but were mainly restricted to the ornate or exposed parts of ceremonial buildings. Roman brick buildings make a strong impression around the west Mediterranean and in Europe.

3.33 Unfired mudbricks bonded together with wet clay are notoriously difficult to locate and excavate. This scrupulously cleaned section at Tepe Ali Kosh, Iran, makes it perfectly clear why early excavators of tells in the Near East failed to find any structures other than those finished in fired brick or stone. *Hole et al., 1969, pl. 9b*

Although the emperor Augustus (27 BC–AD 14) claimed to have found Rome a city of brick, and left it a city of marble, surface appearance is deceptive: we have already seen that most marble-clad Roman buildings depended for their grandeur on brick arches and vaulting, backed by the strength of concrete.

The use of sun-dried clay is not restricted to the Old World; under the name 'adobe', it is in common use in Mexico, and is often found in combination with other materials. The vast pre-Columbian city of Teotihuacan (Mexico) is famous for a number of pyramids, made from adobe with a protective facing of stone or plaster – a combination reminiscent of Mesopotamia. The importance of local resources has been stressed throughout this discussion of stone, timber and other materials; at Teotihuacan, the same phenomenon is found in the private houses:

The basic building materials of Teotihuacan were of local origin. Outcrops of porous volcanic rock in the valley were quarried and the stone was crushed and mixed with lime and earth to provide a kind of moisture-resistant concrete that was used as the foundation for floors and walls. The same material was used for roofing; wooden posts spaced at intervals bore much of the weight of the roof. Walls were made of stone and mortar or of sunbaked adobe brick. Floors and wall surfaces were then usually finished with highly polished plaster. (Millon 1967, 43)

5.4 Reconstruction
(Drury 1982)

An excellent way of increasing understanding of an excavated building is to attempt to reconstruct the possible structure in a drawing or a scale model (fig. 3.34; see 3.32). Some information may be particularly helpful, notably the size and strength of foundations, pillars and walls. Fragments of architectural stonework such as window or door frames, voussoirs from arches or vaulting, or roofing slates and tiles, may help to date the building as well as to reconstruct it. Comparisons should be made with contemporary structures and relevant documentary evidence, but specialist help from an architect or engineer may be needed to estimate load factors on walls, roof structures or vaulting. Although the results are merely informed guesswork, the display of an ancient site for the public is enhanced considerably by a high-quality scale model that includes

3.34 Excavators rarely have an opportunity to test their interpretation of an excavated structure in a full-size reconstruction, rather than a drawing. The gate of Arbeia Roman fort (South Shields, Tyne and Wear) is based on extensive research into military architecture throughout the Roman Empire, but it is not clear whether the towers would have had tiled roofs or battlements. Although many significant aspects may never be resolved, the value of the structure for tourism and education is very important, for the rooms provide exhibition space, and the rest of the site can be understood much more easily when seen from the parapet. Because the building had to conform to modern planning and building regulations to allow public access, it was not possible to create an authentic interior. The cost of materials was too great to allow solid stone and mortar walls in the Roman manner; cheaper concrete breeze-blocks lie behind the sandstone facing.
Paul Bidwell

human figures and activities relevant to its function. Excavators also benefit, for the scrutiny of alternative reconstructions will require very detailed analysis of the excavated remains; new interpretations may be suggested, and attention is drawn to parts of the site that need further investigation. If several plausible reconstructions are deduced from a single plan it is best to offer more than one possible interpretation in the excavation report. Shakespeare's Globe Theatre in London provides an excellent example of the difficulties involved in relating excavated foundations to an above-ground timber structure, even when its form is known from contemporary illustrations (Blatherwick & Gurr 1992).

The elaborate nature of excavated remains of buildings is easily underestimated, especially if nothing more than post-holes remains. However, the complexity of joinery and the elaboration of purely decorative detail that survive on many medieval and later timber buildings must have existed in earlier times. Anthropological analogies point in the same direction. The timber buildings, boats, textiles and everyday objects of the native Americans of the Pacific coast of Canada still bear elaborate painted and carved designs derived from animals, birds and fish. Norwegian stave churches provide a good European parallel; if none had survived, who would have believed an archaeologist's reconstruction of the ornate superstructure and intricate carved ornamentation of Urnes church from its simple ground plan?

Note: a guide to **further reading** that includes topics covered in this chapter begins on p. 185.

4 Dating the past

Dating is the key to organizing all archaeological evidence. Furthermore, the development of dating methods, whether 'traditional' or scientific, illustrates the ingenuity and lateral thinking that make archaeological problem-solving such a fascinating exercise. This chapter will examine the use of historical evidence and some methods of relative dating based upon artefacts before looking at scientific techniques. As in earlier chapters, the historical development of the subject will be stressed at various points. It is interesting to see how tree-rings, varves and pollen analysis were used to construct relative and absolute dating for prehistory in the first half of the twentieth century. The intellectual appeal of this pioneering work is just as attractive as that of more recent methods.

1 Background

Chapter 1 described how the biblical accounts of the Creation, the Flood and the peopling of the world were gradually eroded, and how, by the 1860s, scientists had undermined Bishop Usher's date of 4004 BC for the Creation. An awareness of geological time scales, combined with Darwin's concept of evolution, emphasized the slow and gradual nature of developments in human societies and artefacts. Prehistoric time could be subdivided with growing confidence and artefacts could be subjected to more detailed classification. While observations of geological and archaeological stratification and contexts provided evidence for sequences of fossils and artefacts, they only placed them into a correct relative order. Absolute dating remained firmly in the hands of archaeologists working on the literate civilizations such as Greece or Rome. The scope of historical dating was extended to Egypt and the Near East when their scripts were deciphered in the early nineteenth century. By then, Thomsen had already used archaeological finds in Scandinavia to validate the concept of three

successive ages of stone, bronze and iron, but these remained essentially undatable before Roman imports appeared in Iron Age phases.

At the beginning of the twentieth century it must still have been inconceivable that reliable dates could ever be established for European prehistory, other than those that depended on tenuous connections between Egypt and the Aegean in the second millennium BC. Dating began later in most other parts of the world; apart from South America, India, China and other parts of the Far East where literate civilizations existed, dating began with the first contacts between native peoples and European explorers and colonizers. Not until 1950 did absolute dates become a reality for prehistoric archaeology in areas outside Scandinavia and the south-west of the United States, where varves and tree-rings had begun to provided a locally applicable dating method some decades earlier.

The dating of sites by stratigraphy was examined in Chapter 3 and the concepts of the *terminus post quem* and *terminus ante quem* were explored (p. 67). Many of the dating techniques surveyed in chapter 4 are independent of stratification, but it is important to stress that they are most valuable when objects or samples to be dated come from properly recorded, stratified contexts on excavations.

2 Historical dating
(South 1977)

Scientific dating techniques have received considerable attention since 1950, but their most spectacular successes have tended to affect prehistory. It is impossible for archaeologists working in historical periods to cause such dramatic changes as the destruction of the accepted framework for dating Neolithic and Bronze Age Europe, or the addition of several million years to the estimated age of tool-making hominids from the Olduvai Gorge in East Africa. Prehistorians had already constructed a framework from archaeological sources by the end of the nineteenth century, long before scientific dates became available; the introduction of independent dates caused adjustments to the framework, rather than complete rebuilding. Archaeologists working in a historical setting are in a very different position, for documentary sources have already been used to establish a framework of dates and cultures into which they are expected to incorporate archaeological evidence.

However, prehistorians sometimes overestimate the accuracy and detail of frameworks based on historical evidence; in practice, early written sources may provide little more information than a scatter of radiocarbon dates. The extent of documentation varied considerably in 'historical' cultures and the information that survives today is determined by a variety of factors. People wrote about a restricted range of subjects in the past; their successors only preserved what was still of interest to them, and they frequently rewrote it from their own point of view, introducing errors and misunderstandings. Historical writing has only recently attempted to aim at objectivity. It was normally written with a clear purpose, either to represent an individual or regime in a good or bad light (depending on the writer's point of view), or to convey a particular philosophical or religious point. A number of considerations have to be weighed up before a piece of information contained in a historical or biographical account is accepted: the date and quality of the surviving manuscripts; the distance (in time and place) of the author from the events described; the author's record of accuracy on items that may be checked independently; the quality of the writer's sources; and any personal biases or motives for distorting the truth.

Some documents were written with a clear historical purpose, but the value of others is a result of attention from modern historians and archaeologists. The first category includes narrative historical works or biographies such as those written by Tacitus or Bede, as well as the chronicles maintained in many monasteries in medieval times. Documents without a historical purpose include laws, land-charters, wills, accounts, miscellaneous letters and anything else written for use rather than posterity. This kind of material is often preserved today in archive offices, and it becomes more abundant as it decreases in age. Post-medieval and industrial archaeologists may find precise dates for sites and structures in company accounts, building designs and detailed maps.

Historical documents may be discovered in archaeological excavations; thousands of clay tablets with cuneiform inscriptions were found in Mesopotamia before Rawlinson deciphered their script, while everything from the lost works of Greek poets to gossipy letters, written on fragments of papyrus, have been recovered from the desiccated rubbish tips of Graeco-Roman cities in Egypt. Inscriptions carved on stone were particularly important in Egypt and the Greek and Roman world, and their content ranges from terse building dedications giving the date and builder's name, to lengthy historical, religious or legal material (fig. 4.1). Coins are historical documents of a kind, and besides dates they sometimes bear short inscriptions about rulers and events that may not appear in surviving documents. A datable coin provides an excellent *terminus post quem* when it is found in a significant stratigraphic position on an excavation (see figs 3.9; 3.12). The unique importance of these kinds of historical evidence is that they are *primary* documents that have not been copied out many times over the centuries by scribes who might introduce fresh errors at every stage.

Dates derived from historical information should be related to sites with care. Sometimes a direct association is established, perhaps by a coin in a stratified sequence, or an inscription from a specific building. Otherwise, there tends to be at least one remove between the evidence and the archaeology, whether it is the use of cross-dating by dated finds, or the identification of places named in texts with remains of sites found by fieldwork. Cross-dating is used extensively in the study of artefacts in historical periods. Roman Germany provides a good sequence of military sites established between the late first century BC and the later second century AD, resulting from advances, retreats and modifications along the Rhine–Danube frontier. Sites of the first century AD are particularly useful, for many new forts were founded and they may be dated very closely, thanks to the *Histories* and *Annals* written by

Tacitus towards the end of the century. By the early twentieth century German archaeologists had worked out detailed typologies for pottery and other artefacts by comparing finds from sites of different dates, and these dates could then be applied to undated sites in other areas where the same artefacts were discovered. In India, Mortimer Wheeler's cross-dating of sites near Pondicherry in 1945 involved Italian tableware (Arretine ware) that had been classified and dated thanks to its occurrence on early military sites in Germany (Wheeler, 1954, 119–25).

A danger of historical archaeology is that dates may have a rather mesmerizing effect. If a layer containing burnt debris and broken artefacts is excavated, there is an inevitable tendency to search the local historical framework for a reference to an invasion or warfare in the region, and to date the excavated context accordingly. Unfortunately, historical information is patchy even in the Roman period, and there may have been many unrecorded episodes that could equally well account for the remains found. In any case, buildings and even whole forts or towns could burn down accidentally; it happened to London in 1666. If an excavated context and the artefacts that it contains are dated incorrectly in this way, there is a real danger that cross-dating will apply inaccurate dates to similar artefacts found on other sites.

One of the most precise examples of historical dating is provided by Pliny the Younger's eye-witness account of the burial of Pompeii and Herculaneum by the eruption of Vesuvius in AD 79. The volcanic deposits that sealed these cities are a rare example of a *terminus ante quem*, for everything found beneath them must be earlier than AD 79. Objects found in circumstances that show that they were in use at the time of the eruption (such as pottery vessels left on a table) are particularly well dated, but finds from uncertain contexts could be several hundred years old. Thera, a Bronze Age city on the Greek island of Santorini in the Aegean, has been compared to Pompeii because it was buried by an even more cataclysmic volcanic eruption. The excavator dated the destruction to around 1500 BC, ultimately on the basis of cross-dating to historical records in Egypt, and the same eruption was thought to have destroyed Minoan palaces on

4.1 This stone slab, which is just over one metre long, is a primary source for dating the construction of Hadrian's Wall. It was found in the 1750s at the site of a milecastle that formed part of the original plan for the Wall, and probably once adorned its gateway. It was common for this kind of dedication slab to be carved to mark the completion of a Roman building. The inscription reads IMP CAES TRAIAN HADRIANI AUG LEG II AUG A PLATORIO NEPOTE LEG PR PR, which can be translated as 'This work of the Emperor Caesar Trajan Hadrian Augustus [was built by] the Second Legion Augusta under Aulus Platorius Nepos, propraetorian legate' (RIB 1638; Collingwood & Wright 1965, 520). It associates the Wall not just with Hadrian himself, but with Nepos, who was governor of Britain from AD 122–6, and shows that the first phase of the frontier structure had already been completed early in Hadrian's reign (AD 117–38). *Museum of Antiquities, University of Newcastle upon Tyne*

Crete, providing a valuable dating horizon for the Aegean Bronze Age.

The analogy between Thera and Pompeii proved to be misleading, for scientific techniques have produced a series of conflicting dates that still cause argument. On the whole, scientific evidence now favours an earlier date for the eruption and fails to support any connection with events in Crete (Hardy & Renfrew 1990). Many archaeologists now relate the destruction of Thera to a major volcanic episode that had been noted in Greenland ice-cores and has subsequently been dated by tree-rings to 1628 BC (below, p. 114). Considering the warning (issued above) about the danger of using historical dates, it is interesting to note that scientific dating may have now the same effect: 'Any sloppily dated archaeological event, within a century or so, tends to be "sucked in" to the precisely dated tree-ring events. We all have to be on our guard against circular arguments' (Baillie 1989, 313). Ultimately archaeologists and historians share the same general objectives; the principal contrasts lie in the kinds of evidence that they explore, and the different aspects of the human past that they are able to address most successfully with the material or documentary information available to them.

3 Typology
(Graslund 1987)

Although Pitt Rivers was an early exponent of typology, his ideas of its universal validity were too abstract to have any chronological promise (see fig. 1.12). In Sweden, Oscar Montelius advanced typology into the realms of firmer dating by producing comprehensive publications of European artefacts from the 1880s. He sought **associations** between artefacts of different forms buried together, such as grave-goods in individual burials, or collections of objects buried in ritual deposits. Each form of artefact was classified in a **type-series**, and the sequence of find contexts normally confirmed progress from simplicity towards greater elaboration or efficiency (figs 4.2–3). These procedures are perfectly acceptable today.

A third technique used by Montelius, **cross-dating** (or *synchronism*), was entirely logical in theory, but, in retrospect, has been very misleading. In its strongest form, cross-dating takes account of artefacts made in historically dated areas, such as Egypt or Mesopotamia, found in association with other artefacts made in undated areas. For example, in 1891 Flinders Petrie found pottery from Crete on Egyptian sites, in contexts dating to around 1900 BC (fig. 4.4). He subsequently identified Egyptian exports at Mycenae in mainland Greece that could be dated to *c.* 1500 BC (Drower 1985, 182–5). Thus, dates derived from Egyptian historical records were extended to sites and cultures in Crete and Greece that lacked internal dating evidence. An

4.2 In an explanation of his methods for studying typology, Montelius illustrated the transition of the axe head from stone to metal. The first copper axes (top row) were very similar to their stone counterparts (extreme left), but it was soon realized that metal could be saved by making them thinner, while increasing their effectiveness by hammering out a wider cutting edge (bottom row). *Montelius 1903, 22*

obvious limitation was that no historical dates extended beyond 3000 BC, so that the age of earlier artefacts could only be guessed. Whereas Petrie's links were based on direct associations with Egyptian material, Montelius extended cross-dating right across Europe into Britain and Scandinavia by noting associations between artefacts found far from their area of manufacture and local types. These fixed points allowed type-series of different areas to be interlocked, but unfortunately every step away from Egypt increased the possibility of a weak link in the chain (see fig. 6.1).

Two further criticisms are apparent: objects imported from distant sources may have been treasured for long periods before being lost or

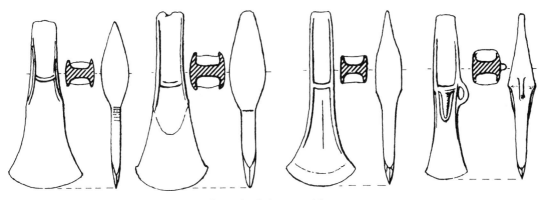

Growth of the stop-ridge

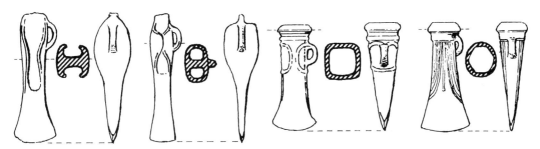

Growth of the wings

4.3 Some technical reasons for further modifications of Bronze Age 'celts' (axes) were explained by Pitt Rivers in 1875: '... the celt of the neolithic period, chipped only at first and subsequently polished ... gave rise to the copper celt of the same form having convex sides, which grew into the bronze celt with flat sides. Then the bronze celt was furnished with a stop to prevent its being pressed too far into the handle by the blow. Others were furnished with projecting flanges to prevent them from swerving by the blow when hafted on a bent stick. Others had both stops and flanges. By degrees the flanges were bent over the stops and over the handle, and then the central portion above the stops, being no longer required, became

thinner, and ultimately disappeared, the flanges closed on each other, and by this means the weapon grew into the socket celt. On this socket celt you will see that there is sometimes a semicircular ornamentation on each side. This ... is a vestige of the overlapping flange of the earlier forms out of which it grew, which, like the rings on our brass cannon, are survivals of parts formerly serving for special uses.' (Lane-Fox 1875, 507)

The development of copper alloy axes ended at this point, for the introduction of iron from c. 1000 BC provided a superior metal for edge tools, with radically different manufacturing techniques. *Audio Visual Centre, University of Newcastle, after Smith 1920*

buried in association with local items; and superficially similar artefacts found in different areas may be unconnected and not contemporary at all. However, confidence in Montelius' cross-dating was increased by the assumption that all cultural advances in Europe were inspired by the civilizations of the Aegean and Near East. The

effects of this 'diffusionist' view survived into the 1960s, when radiocarbon dates suddenly snapped the chain of connections into many unrelated links.

Typology has not been superseded, but radiocarbon dates have reduced the burden of prehistoric chronology that it was once made to

4.4 Cross-dating by pottery: Arthur Evans used imported Egyptian artefacts to date his excavation of the Palace of Knossos in Crete (fig. 1.15). Local Cretan pottery found on this site could also be dated because similar sherds had been found in Egypt. A, B and D are from Crete and bear decoration of Evans' Latest Middle Minoan II Phase, while C was found at Kahun in Egypt. *Evans 1921, fig. 198*

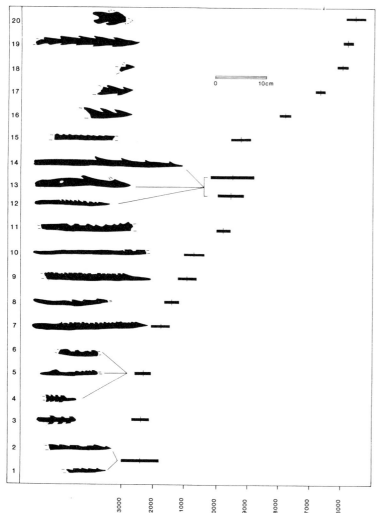

4.5 Unlike Bronze Age axes, the shapes of harpoon points used by hunters in Britain after the end of the last Ice Age show no clear typological development. However, small samples of the bone from which they were made can now be dated by the AMS radiocarbon technique, and these dates may be used to place them into chronological order. *Smith 1992, fig. 1.2*

carry (fig. 4.5). Type-series remain an extremely useful means of describing and classifying artefacts of any period, and for understanding their technology and function. Radiocarbon dating (below, p. 115) now allows the typology of prehistoric bronze objects to be checked independently, for remarkably precise results can be derived using the AMS technique from small fragments of wooden handles or shafts that occasionally survive in the sockets of spears or axes (Needham 1986). Association and cross-dating are still important in the historical period; Roman metal-work, pottery, glass and coins were traded to Scandinavia, Central Europe and even India, where they provide valuable dates when found with local artefacts. In the early medieval Migration period (fourth to sixth centuries AD), typological analyses of brooches and buckles linked to Germanic peoples (such as the Goths, Huns or Franks) are still important in the study of 'barbarian' settlements within the former Roman Empire (Greene 1987). It is important to realize that cross-datings and associations obey the same principle as a *terminus post quem* in an excavation (p. 67); dated finds only establish fixed points *after* which the contexts that they were discovered in must be dated.

4 Sequence dating and seriation

These dating techniques rely on careful excavation and recording, for they both place **assemblages** of artefacts into relative order. Petrie used sequence dating to work back from the earliest historical phases of Egypt into Pre-Dynastic Neolithic times, using grave-groups that could be assumed to consist of contemporary artefacts deposited together at a single time (Petrie 1899; Drower 1985, 251–4). Decisions were made about 'early' and 'late' artefacts in graves by typological judgements about their form. Grave groups were then arranged in a sequence according to their combinations of artefacts of early or late character, in a kind of 'simultaneous typology' that weighed up the development of every item found in each grave. Petrie drew graphs of pottery types that occurred in his sequence of fifty pre-dynastic phases, and showed that types did not appear and disappear abruptly, but became popular gradually before declining equally gradually (1920, pl. L). This phenomenon is confirmed by the ways that modern clothing and jewellery go in and out of fashion at different rates.

Seriation is based on the same principle, and it has been applied to finds from grave groups, strata or other kinds of assemblages, whether found on individual sites or over a wider area. It works best on assemblages that contain a range of definable characteristics, such as types of pottery or flints, especially those that are subject to change rather than continuity. The numbers of selected artefact types found in each assemblage are converted into percentages to make them comparable. The figures are then arranged into the best possible sequence on the assumption that the percentages of artefacts will have increased and declined in an orderly manner. This process may be carried out by eye if the percentages are marked on individual strips of graph paper to represent each assemblage and shuffled to find the best fit. Random statistical variations and possible differences in the character of the assemblages that are being compared make it very unlikely that the results will form perfect 'battleship curves'. Seriation is only a relative dating method, but it remains useful in the study of finds that do not occur on stratified sites where the sequence is revealed by excavation; like artefact typologies, it is now used within an absolutely dated framework. Petrie's desperate, but inconclusive, attempts to establish an absolute date for the *beginning* of his prehistoric Egyptian sequence underline the enviable position of modern archaeologists (Petrie 1899, 4–6).

5 The advent of scientific dating techniques
(Zeuner 1946)

For Prehistory, no calendars are available. Up to not many years ago, the time-scales suggested for the evolution of early man and his cultures were pure guesses, not to say imagination. From a scientific point of view they were worthless. (Zeuner 1946, 1)

This quotation underlines the complete transformation of archaeological dating that began around 1950 and continues to this day (figs 4.6–7). However, archaeologists tend to forget that geology had already undergone a revolution in scientific dating during the first half of the twentieth century. Seen in the context of the development of dating methods over the previous century, radiocarbon does not seem quite as dramatic as it is sometimes portrayed.

Frederick Zeuner's book *Dating the Past: An introduction to geochronology* (first published in 1946) integrated geological dating with archaeology in an exemplary manner. The text was updated and expanded several times up to 1958, by when Zeuner was able to document the introduction of new techniques such as radiocarbon and potassium-argon dating. Because it gives

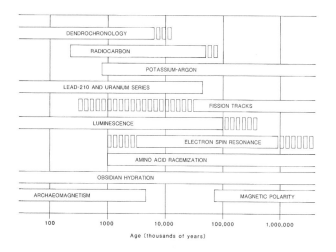

4.6 The leading scientific dating methods are applicable to widely differing periods of the past. Each horizontal bar indicates the range of an individual method; interrupted bars show periods where the potential is less good. Techniques with the greatest time-span are not necessarily the most useful: see fig. 4.7. *Sandra Hooper, after Aitken 1990, fig. 1.2*

such a vivid impression of the difficulties and triumphs of archaeological dating as it emerged from the nineteenth century, Zeuner's book provides an excellent companion – and contrast – to Aitken's 'state of the art' survey, *Science-based Dating in Archaeology* (1990). While Aitken organized his book according to the scientific basis of each dating technique, Zeuner had adopted a very different approach that began with techniques applicable to the recent past and worked back towards measurement of the age of the Earth. My account will group methods together according to their scientific basis, but it will begin with some of the earliest methods to emerge into general use in the hope of retaining some of the atmosphere of discovery that characterizes Zeuner's writing.

5.1 Geological time scales

Nineteenth-century geologists were preoccupied with the age of the Earth, and Darwin's demand for gradual evolution underlined the length of the time scales involved. Glimpses of 'deep time' could be gained by estimating the rate of erosion

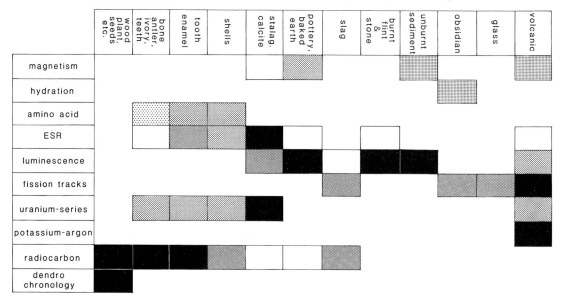

4.7 Summary chart of materials that can be examined by different scientific dating techniques; the best results will be obtained from the techniques and samples with the darkest shading. Thus, wood and other plants respond well to dendrochronology and radiocarbon, but no other techniques are applicable; conversely, volcanic materials are un-

suitable for either of these methods, but offer many other possibilities. Archaeologists need an understanding of figs 4.7–8 to take the right kinds of samples for dating methods, appropriate to the period with which they are concerned. *Sandra Hooper, after Aitken 1990, fig. 1.1* of geological formations; Darwin suggested 300 million years to produce the modern form of the South Downs. Lyell used the rate of evolution of certain shells to calculate the age of the Earth and arrived at around 240 million years for the time that had elapsed since the appearance of life (Zeuner 1946, 307–8). However, Lord Kelvin's estimate of as little as 20 million years, based on the rate of cooling of the planet, was widely accepted (ibid. 315–16). The problem was solved by a growing understanding of radioactive decay and measurement of the rate that uranium decayed to produce lead. From around AD 1900 Arthur Holmes and other scientists used the radioactivity method to extend the date of pre-Cambrian rocks back to an age of nearly 2000 million years (Zeuner 1946, 333).

Thus, estimates of geological time underwent a transition from informed guesswork to scientific precision in the fifty years that followed the publication of Darwin's *Origin of Species* in 1859. Accurate knowledge of the age of the Earth was of little direct help to archaeologists, but it emphasized the potential of scientific dating techniques. The first half of the twentieth century witnessed a similar transition that began with the dating of recent geological periods when early humans first lived, and ended with the introduction of radiocarbon dating. As a result, by 1950 absolute dates were available for important stages of recent prehistory, such as the inception of farming and the first use of metals.

While some geologists concentrated on the age of the Earth, others studied distinctive surface traces left behind by changes in the extent of the polar ice cap. They established the existence of a succession of Ice Ages and worked out a sequence of climatic phases based on evidence for alternations between glaciations and more temperate conditions. If these could be dated, much could be learned about the emergence of modern humans and their interaction with different environments. Some calculations were attempted by measuring the depths of deposits and comparing them with the formation rate of similar deposits in modern times, but there was no way that these estimates could be checked (Zeuner 1946, 134–5). However, an attractive idea that had been developed with increasing precision since the 1780s was that glaciations

coincided with changes in solar radiation and that these changes were caused by regular and measurable variations in the Earth's orbit. However, the correlation between periods of glaciation and periods of low solar radiation remained hypothetical until independent dating was achieved with the help of ocean-bed deposits and potassium-argon dating between the 1950s and 1970s (Aitken 1990, 17–19).

6 Environmental methods
(Aitken 1990)

6.1 Tree-ring dating (dendrochronology)
(Schweingruber 1988)

It had been recognized since at least the fifteenth century that trees produce annual growth rings, and their physiology was well understood by the eighteenth century (Schweingruber 1988, 256–7). Well-documented examples of their use for dating begin in North America in the late eighteenth century; for example, the Reverend Cutler counted 463 rings in a tree that had grown on a native American burial mound at Marietta in Ohio and deduced (correctly) that the mound must antedate Columbus (Daniel 1981, 40–2). Because annual growth rings are subject to seasonal factors that affect their thickness, distinctive patterns recognized in different samples of timber may be compared and used to establish their contemporaneity (figs 4.8–9). In 1901 A E Douglass had begun to study fluctuations in solar radiation and their effects on climate by looking at patterns of varying ring thickness in trees in Arizona and his work became inseparably linked to archaeological dating in the 1920s. Many timbers preserved in *pueblos* (prehistoric native American sites in arid areas of Arizona and New Mexico) could be dated by cross-referencing them to his series (fig. 4.10). An overlapping series of rings was gradually built up from many timbers found on sites in the south-west of the United States, and the sequence was extended back to the fourth century BC. In 1954, bristlecone pines still growing in California were found to be as much as 4000 years old, and a combination of specimens from living trees and old trunks preserved in the White Mountains now provides a continuous record

4.8 Apparatus for measuring tree-ring thicknesses. The screen in the centre of the photograph shows a series of rings from a sample mounted beneath a microscope and video camera on the left. Individual rings can be measured precisely and recorded by a microcomputer, while the more sophisticated computer on the right runs programs to match the series of measurements with sequences of known date. *Laboratoire de Chrono-Ecologie de Besançon; photograph by Olivier Girardclos*

back to 6700 BC that is of vital importance for checking radiocarbon dates (below, p. 116). An even more impressive achievement is the establishment of a tree-ring sequence that extends beyond 5000 BC, based on a large number of trees from north-western Europe. Many of the early samples have been taken from ancient tree-trunks preserved in peat bogs. Some earlier 'floating' sequences that could not yet be linked to absolutely dated timbers were dated approximately by 'wiggle matching' with the radiocarbon curve (p. 117) and extended the range of dendrochronology back to around 9000 BC. By 1993, the sequence in Germany had reached 9494 BC by following pine trees back beyond a period that was too cold for oaks to grow (Becker 1993).

Tree-rings may also be used for relative dating on waterlogged sites where successive timber structures have been excavated. At Charavines (Isère, France), a large scatter of wooden stakes was found preserved on a neolithic village site submerged in a lake, but no coherent plan was apparent. However, when posts made from trees felled in the same year were plotted, they revealed the plans of two rectangular structures built in successive years (Bocquet 1981). This technique became even more valuable when the tree-rings were dated absolutely. Many studies have been conducted in medieval buildings – such as the cathedrals at Trier in Germany or Chartres in France – to identify or date periods of construction that were not fully documented in surviving historical records. Roman forts and bridges in Germany and the Netherlands have also been investigated in the same way; the precision of tree-ring dating is impossible to achieve by any other means. Once dated, the sites can be integrated into historical accounts of the area.

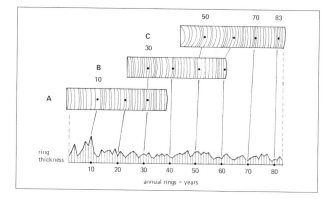

4.9 Dating by dendrochronology: A, B and C are sections from three different trees showing annual growth rings that cover a period of 83 years, from the innermost ring at the left of timber A to the outermost of C. The overlapping (contemporary) portions of the timbers can be matched by observing similarities in the pattern of their rings, especially when unusually wide or narrow rings reflect particularly good or bad growing seasons for the trees. The graph records the average annual ring thickness for each year, allowing for the fact that the outer rings are always narrower than the inner because their volume of wood is spread thinly around a large trunk. Long overlapping sequences from dated timbers provide a reference graph against which individual undated samples can be compared. Thus, if this graph began in AD 1000, timber B was felled in AD 1060, and this is a *terminus post quem* for any structure into which it was incorporated. *Audio Visual Centre, University of Newcastle*

4.10 Pueblo Bonito, in Chaco Canyon, New Mexico, is an extensive native American site built mainly from stone but with timber beams, lintels, roofs, etc. Since the arid desert environment had ensured the preservation of wood for hundreds of years, it was the first site to be studied system-atically with the help of tree-ring dating. A com-bination of dendrochronology and architectural analysis revealed a detailed picture of the devel-opment of Pueblo Bonito from c. AD 900–1100 (Judd 1964). The end of a large beam and a hori-zontal lintel visible in this photograph provide useful sources for dating this part of the struc-ture. Although the latest (outer) tree-ring will provide a *terminus post quem* (the date after which the structure must have been built), there is always a possibility that old timbers were re-used from an earlier phase of the building. The obvious blocking of the doorway suggests that the func-tion of these rooms changed during the life of the building. *Neil Judd, 1926; copyright: National Geographic Society*

Unfortunately there are many problems in the direct application of dendrochronological dating. Not all tree species are sufficiently sensitive to display distinctive variations in their ring charac-teristics, particularly when growing in temperate climates. Wood only survives under exceptionally wet or dry conditions, and large timbers must be recovered to provide sufficient rings for valid comparisons, because they rely on patterns that accumulated over several decades. Timbers used in buildings were normally trimmed into regular shapes, removing the evidence for the exact date of their felling, and they may have been stored for many years before use. Worse still, timbers were frequently reused several times in repairs or reconstructions of wooden buildings, whose foundations rot long before their roof. Re-use is a particular problem on arid sites, where timbers do not decay easily. Despite these problems, tree-rings are perhaps the only source of truly absolute dates, in terms of a single year. Unfortunately, they will never be universally applicable, partly because of regional and envir-onmental variations in the growth of trees, but principally through the rarity of suitably wet or arid conditions that ensure their preservation.

The provision of samples of known age for test-ing the accuracy of radiocarbon dates is not the only indirect use of tree-rings. Variations in ring widths reflect climatic conditions, and there are several instances of extreme disturbances to nor-mal growth. A series of exceptionally narrow rings indicates an episode of cold, wet weather from 1159 BC that was almost certainly the result of a volcanic eruption marked in ice-cores at 1100 ± 50 BC. Ash in the upper atmosphere reduced solar radiation to such an extent that human settlement patterns and farming practices were disrupted for sufficiently long to cause an abandonment of upland areas of northern Britain. Thus, tree-rings provide not only dates for sites, but also for environmental catastrophes that influenced changes in human behaviour (Baillie 1989).

At a more intimate level, the precision of tree-ring dates adds an exciting dimension to other finds associated with dated timbers. In the late 1980s timbers from the Somerset Levels track-ways were tied in to the dated European series; suddenly, their construction ceased to be 111 'somewhere in the early fourth millennium', and became an event that took place in 3807/6 BC. This precise date extended to other finds, such as tools and pottery, found in the same context (Hillam 1990). The impact is similar in historical periods; it is now known that a wooden grave chamber erected within the famous Viking ship burial at Oseberg in Norway was constructed from trees felled in AD 834 (Bonde and Christiansen 1993).

6.2 Varves

Every summer, the melting of glaciers causes erosion by streams and rivers, and the resulting sediments are eventually deposited on lake beds (fig. 4.11). The sediments become sparser and finer as the year progresses, for the flow of water is reduced when temperatures begin to fall; winter freezing then stops erosion until the next summer. Sections cut through lake beds in glacial regions reveal a regular annual pattern of coarse and fine layers, known as varves. Variations in climate produced observable differences in the thickness of sediments, and, like the patterns of variation in tree-rings, this allows comparisons to be made between deposits in separate lake beds. Varves had been recognized and understood as early as the 1870s in Sweden. From 1905 onwards, Baron de Geer carried out extensive fieldwork with the aim of establishing a continuous sequence from overlapping deposits preserved in beds of the hundreds of lakes that formed during the retreat of glaciers after the last Ice Age. Whereas tree-rings can be counted back from a tree felled today, de Geer lacked a secure fixed point at the end of his sequence. However, a lake known to have been drained in AD 1796 gave an approximate pointer, and he published a sequence covering around 12,000 years in 1910.

Varves allowed the end of the last Ice Age to be dated with confidence to around 6800 BC and provided the first extension of 'calendar' dates into European prehistory. They also made it possible to date individual sites if their positions could be related to former lakes or seashores. Work on varves continues, particularly in North America, and it may one day be possible to tie the sequence of Scandinavian varves to some areas of the New World. Varves also contribute information to archaeomagnetic dating, for they contain a record of the Earth's magnetic field in their iron-rich clay particles (below, p. 121). Even more important, until radiocarbon dating was introduced after 1950, varves provided the only method that could be used to date the climatic sequence revealed by changes in vegetation known from pollen analysis.

6.3 Pollen analysis
(Dimbleby 1985)

Microscopic wind-blown pollen grains survive well in many soil conditions, and the ease of distinguishing different plant species is of considerable value in the study of past environments (p. 143). Pollen that has accumulated in deep deposits such as peat-bogs supplies a sequential record of changes in vegetation since the last Ice Age, for variations in temperature and rainfall resulted in periods of markedly different plant and tree populations in the past. Work on pollen began in Scandinavia in the 1920s and it confirmed the general pattern of climatic change that had been proposed from visible plant remains. Fortunately, since these changes were also reflected by varves, each distinctive climatic phase could be dated.

The value of this technique for archaeology lay in the fact that climatic phases were likely to have been fairly uniform throughout northern Europe. Thus, plant species found in a sample of pollen from an archaeological site could be fitted into the climatic sequence. Correlations could be established between sites belonging to similar climatic phases in different countries, and this form of cross-dating did not have to rely on dubious links between artefacts. However, even individual artefacts could be dated if they were found in peat-bogs, or if they had sufficient soil attached to them for the identification of pollen. For example, a mesolithic bone harpoon dredged from the bottom of the North Sea was placed into the period when pine was declining in favour of trees that preferred warmer conditions around 7000 BC (Zeuner 1946, 91–2).

A further benefit of dating sites and artefacts to climatic phases was that new insights could be gained into their environmental context. The significance of the location of settlements was increased by understanding the state of contemporary vegetation and the landscape, and the functions of tools also took on more significance. Since climatic zones established from pollen have been dated absolutely by radiocarbon, they are no longer required as chronological indicators; nevertheless, pollen analysis continues to supply important evidence for the interpretation of the ancient environment (below, p. 143).

6.4 Sea-bed deposits

An approach to geological dating analogous to varves was developed during the 1950s. Deep sediments exist on the sea-bed, representing a slow accumulation of shells and skeletal material from dead marine creatures. Cores (typically 10 metres in depth) extracted from these deposits reveal variations in oxygen isotopes in the shelly material, caused by fluctuations in the volume of the ocean that reflect global temperatures and ice ages. A pattern of climatic variation is derived from temperature-sensitive species of marine fauna and from measurements of oxygen isotopes. It correlates with geological evidence for cold and warm periods that are dated according to deviations in the Earth's orbit around the sun (above, p. 109). Sea-bed sediments also contain material derived from the erosion of land containing iron particles; their magnetic alignment has been measured to produce a dated sequence of changes in the Earth's magnetic field, which undergoes complete North–South reversals from time to time. As a result of studies of deep-sea cores, geologists and archaeologists interested in the earliest stages of human development now possess an integrated dated record of global temperature and magnetism. Thus, if bones or tools associated with early hominids, such as the famous series from East Africa, are found in geological deposits related to periods of extreme temperature or magnetic reversals, they are now datable (below, p. 128).

6.5 Ice-sheet cores

Yet another form of dating based on a cumulative natural phenomenon has been developed by climatologists who have extracted cores from the ice sheets of Greenland. Each winter's snowfall creates a distinct layer, and the annual layers have been counted back almost 6000 years in a core more than 2 kilometres in depth, with an excellent level of reliability within around 50 years

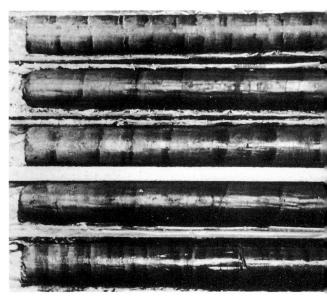

4.11 These cores bored from sedimentary lake deposits in Sweden show distinctive varves; each band of light to dark silt marks a single year's deposition of water-borne sediment. Varves vary in thickness from a few millimetres to several metres; these average approx. 2.5 cm. *Prof. D Tarling, University of Plymouth*

(standard deviation ±10). The thickness of each layer varies, as do the proportions of different oxygen isotopes whose formation is known to reflect temperature; thus, long-term patterns of variation reflect changes in climatic conditions. A further factor of value for dating is the recognition that even when the individual layers are no longer distinguishable by eye, they contain annual fluctuations in dust and acidity that have extended the annual record back almost 10,000 years, at which point the layers become too thin for counting (Aitken 1990, 23).

Some layers of ice contain high levels of dust and acidity caused by volcanic eruptions (fig. 4.12). Volcanoes known from historical records, such as Krakatoa (1883) or Vesuvius (AD 79), can be correlated with ice-cores; further undocumented eruptions in prehistoric times may also be detected. Ideally, prehistoric eruptions dated by ice-cores would provide precise dates for sites, especially when calibrated with tree-rings, which may show abnormal growth patterns caused by volcanic disturbance of the climate. The massive eruption that destroyed much of the island of

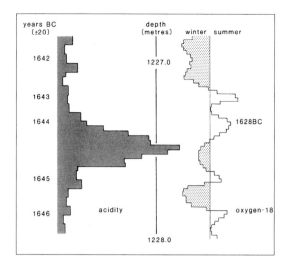

4.12 Major volcanic eruptions affect the atmosphere by emitting large quantities of acidic ash; it may be revealed by abnormal acidity in layers within cores taken from deep ice-sheets in Greenland. Even when the annual layers are not clearly visible, the pattern of yearly temperature variations is indicated by changes in oxygen isotope levels. Here, an eruption that left its mark around 1644±20 BC was almost certainly the same event that caused damage to trees in rings dated to 1628 BC; it is usually assumed to have been the explosion of Thera in the Aegean. *Sandra Hooper, after Aitken 1990, fig. 2.10*

Santorini in the Aegean should probably be linked to signs visible in ice-core and tree-ring data from 1628 BC, but many interesting conflicts between archaeological and scientific dating remain unresolved (Hardy & Renfrew 1990). Akrotiri, a Bronze Age town on the island, was buried under deep volcanic ash, and the same ash also fell on Crete and Turkey, offering the potential for dating sites over a wide area. Volcanic eruptions may also give indirect dates for wider changes in settlement patterns, for ash in the upper atmosphere may cause severe disturbances to the weather, and if these circumstances were prolonged for many years they could lead to the abandonment of adversely affected sites (below, p. 183).

Finally, ice-cores and varves provide an additional way of checking the reliability of radiocarbon dating in periods beyond the range of samples from precisely dated tree-rings. Abrupt signs of climatic change dated by ice-cores and varves to around 8750 BC, are underestimated by approximately 700 years by uncalibrated radiocarbon dating.

7 Absolute techniques
(Aitken 1990)

The proper meaning of absolute dating is that it is independent of any other chronology or dating technique, that it is based only on currently measurable quantities. (Aitken 1990, 2)

We have seen that, by 1950, a number of dating techniques had emerged that could offer chronological frameworks for the study of prehistory at least as reliable as those used by historical archaeologists. Unfortunately, all required special circumstances, such as the survival of timber for tree-rings, the proximity of glacial lakes for varves, or the existence of soil conditions that favoured the preservation of pollen. However, the successful development of dating methods for geological periods, whether they relied upon radioactive decay or variations in the Earth's orbit, offered the possibility that a similar, generally applicable, technique might one day be found that would give absolute dates for prehistoric archaeology.

7.1 Radioactive decay

Several scientific dating techniques exploit the phenomenon of **radioactive decay**, including those first used to date the age of the Earth in the early years of the twentieth century (above, p. 109). Many elements occur in different forms, and some are unstable; these **isotopes** have extra neutrons besides their standard number of protons and they are designated by a number representing their atomic weight (carbon-14 or ^{14}C). Unstable isotopes are radioactive and emit rays of particles at a known rate. Some isotopes become stable after emitting these particles, while others (such as uranium) go through a protracted series of 'daughter' elements before reaching a stable form (e.g. uranium to lead: p. 123 below). The speed of decay is expressed as the **half-life**, the time taken for half of the total radioactivity to decay; this may vary from seconds to millions of years.

7.2 Radiocarbon dating
(Bowman 1990)

Amongst the numerous peaceful by-products of accelerated wartime research into atomic physics and radioactivity in the 1940s was **radiocarbon dating**. The rate of decay of carbon-14, which has a half-life of 5730 years, is long enough to allow samples of carbon as old as 70,000 years to contain detectable levels of radioactive emissions, but short enough for samples from periods since the late Stone Age to be measured with reasonable precision. However, the feature of carbon-14 that makes it exceptionally important is that it is absorbed naturally by all living organisms, but ceases to enter them when they die (fig. 4.13). In theory, all that needs to be done is to measure the radioactivity of a sample from a dead animal or plant and to calculate from the level that remains the time that has elapsed since its death. The practicalities of age estimation are rather more complicated, and the discussion that follows will attempt to highlight the principal advantages and disadvantages of carbon-14 rather than to provide a comprehensive account.

This simplified description does not do justice to the inspired formation and testing of hypotheses carried out by Willard F. Libby in Chicago in the 1940s for which he received a Nobel Prize in 1961. However, the publication of his preliminary results in 1949 was only a beginning. By a happy chance, the period of the past where it promised to be most effective from the outset was one of particular significance to prehistoric archaeologists, for it encompassed the transition from hunting and gathering to farming, and the emergence of the first civilizations. There are now more than 80 radiocarbon laboratories all over the world and upwards of 30,000 archaeological dates have been calculated. Accuracy and precision are improving, and the introduction of **Accelerator Mass Spectrometry** laboratories in the 1980s allowed very small samples, one hundredth of the size required in the 1950s, to be dated. AMS allows direct dating of actual artefacts and bones, rather than just the contexts where they have been found. It therefore offers particularly exciting prospects in early prehistory, for example in dating fragments of fossil bones associated with the disappearance of Neanderthals and the appearance of modern humans in Europe and Asia between 50,000 and 30,000 years ago (Stringer 1986).

Radiocarbon dating has grown exponentially, and many problems and inaccuracies have been isolated and examined, some leading to major adjustments of the results. Despite many problems, radiocarbon dates now provide a framework for the prehistory of the world; for the first time, its study has become more like that of historical periods, and emphasis has shifted away from pure chronology towards more fundamental social and economic factors.

Positive factors
- **radiocarbon dating is universal**, because the radioactive isotope carbon-14 is formed continuously throughout the Earth's atmosphere by the effects of cosmic radiation.

4.13 This drawing by Robert Hedges illustrates the basis of radiocarbon dating with unusual clarity. The arrows follow the formation of the carbon-14 isotope in the atmosphere by cosmic radiation, and its incorporation into a tree through photosynthesis of carbon dioxide. It then passes to a deer that has eaten the foliage, but this animal ceases to take in fresh carbon-14 when it dies. Thus, a bone is placed at the top of a graph that shows the steady decline of the radioactive isotope over time. *Research Laboratory for Archaeology, Oxford University*

- carbon-14 has a known **half-life**, and decays at a constant rate.
- the rates of **formation and decay are in balance**; cosmic radiation in the past should have maintained carbon-14 and the other isotopes of carbon in the atmosphere at constant levels.
- **all life-forms contain carbon**, and living organisms absorb carbon from the atmosphere, mainly in the form of carbon dioxide photosynthesis by plants is one common mechanism. Animals and plants therefore maintain the same proportion of newly formed carbon-14 as the atmosphere until their death, when it begins to decay.
- **dendrochronology** provides an independent 'benchmark' of dated samples of wood from annual tree-rings stretching back nearly 10,000 years. The initial source was bristle-cone pine trees found in the south-west of the USA; some are still growing after more than 4000 years. Older samples come from dead trunks that had resisted decay in this semi-arid habitat, and from trunks of oak trees preserved in bogs or river sediments in Europe.

Thus, if a sample of ancient wood, charcoal or other organic matter is processed in a laboratory so that carbon is isolated, the amount of radioactivity that remains can be measured; the older it is, the fewer radioactive emissions of beta-particles will occur in a period of observation. Ten grams of modern carbon-14 produce 150 disintegrations per minute; the age of an ancient sample of the same weight that produced only 75 counts should therefore be equal to the half-life of the isotope, around 5730 years.

The measurement of radiocarbon requires highly accurate laboratory equipment to keep the margins of error within reasonable limits. By the 1950s the technique had moved rapidly from using solid carbon to gases such as carbon dioxide, and in the 1960s **liquid scintillation counting** joined **gas counting**. All of these radiometric methods require some means of detecting natural cosmic radiation that may penetrate the apparatus, to ensure that only radioactive emissions derived from the sample itself are recorded. A new technique, **accelerator**

mass spectrometry, was developed in the late 1970s; AMS is fundamentally different because it measures the concentration of carbon-14 in a sample (relative to carbon-12) rather than its radioactivity.

Negative factors

Several aspects of radiocarbon dating require careful examination to achieve a correct understanding of the interpretation of its results. Some of Libby's original assumptions were incorrect, and the method of calculating dates has been revised several times since the technique began to be employed.

- the **half-life** has been shown by more accurate measurement to be too low by around 3%; it is now judged to be around 5730 years, rather than 5568.
- different isotopes of carbon are taken into organisms at different rates (**fractionation**); the proportions of carbon-13 and carbon 14 must be checked and an adjustment made to the estimated date.
- the level of **cosmic radiation** has fluctuated over time, perhaps in relation to sunspot activity and the Earth's magnetic intensity. This means that the formation of carbon 14 in the atmosphere has varied; thus, samples from organisms that absorbed abnormally larger or smaller amounts of carbon 14 will give misleadingly younger or older dates.
- a **calibration curve** must be used to convert 'radiocarbon years' into calendar years (fig. 4.14). Tree-rings have not only revealed short-term fluctuations in carbon-14 levels,but also a divergence between carbon 14 dates and 'real' calendar years that becomes increasingly serious before c. 1000 BC. Samples with a radiocarbon age of 5000–7000 years require upward adjustment of as much as 500–1000 years, and this trend increases as dates extend further back in time; at a point when Uranium-Thorium dating measures coral as being around 30,000 years old, its age in radiocarbon years is only around 26,000.
- calibration reveals that dates from the **southern hemisphere** are around 30 years too old compared with those from the North;

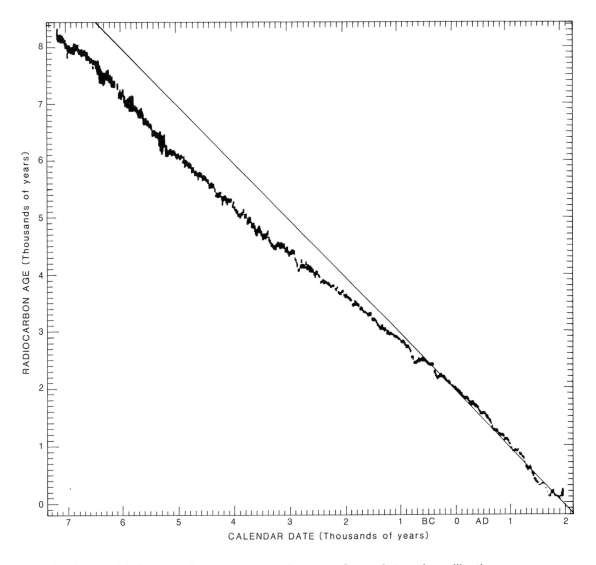

4.14 Pearson's tree-ring calibration curve for radiocarbon dates. The straight line shows what the relationship would have been had the amount of carbon-14 in the atmosphere had remained constant over the last 10,000 years: i.e. 4000 radiocarbon years would be equivalent to c. 2000 BC. However, beyond 500 BC there is an increasing divergence, so that a radiocarbon age of 8000 years has to be increased by almost 1000 years, from c. 6000 to c. 7000 BC. The process of calibration looks deceptively simple at this scale, but the 'wiggles', combined with other statistical uncertainties, make calculations much more complicated. *After Pearson 1987*

this is probably because the greater area of oceans has affected the distribution of carbon 14 in the atmosphere.

• a statistical estimation of error, expressed as a **standard deviation**, is attached to laboratory counts of radioactivity. Since isotope decays occur at random, a reasonably long counting period is needed to reduce this inherent error. Several counting sessions of the same fixed length are normally carried out and the range of differences between the separate results is conveyed by a figure that follows the date, preceded by '±'. Fig. 4.15 shows how the reliability of a date should be envisaged.

117

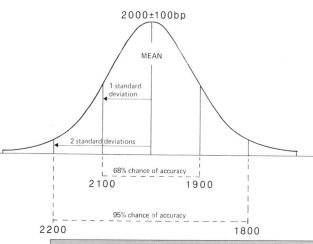

2000±100bp

MEAN

1 standard deviation

2 standard deviations

68% chance of accuracy

2100   1900

95% chance of accuracy

2200   1800

4.15 Every radiocarbon measurement has a statistical margin of error, which is quoted in terms of the mean and one standard deviation (e.g. 2000±100 bp). A normal distribution curve shows how it should be interpreted: one standard deviation either side of the mean will give a 68% probability of the true date lying within a 200-year bracket (and consequently a 32% chance of it not doing so), whilst two standard deviations increase the probability of accuracy to around 95%. *Audio Visual Centre, University of Newcastle*

Summary table

POSITIVE	NEGATIVE
Radiocarbon dating is universal because carbon-14 is distributed throughout the atmosphere	There is a 30-year difference between dates from the N and S hemispheres
Carbon-14 has a fixed half-life and decay rate	The half-life is now known to be 5730 years, rather than 5568
The formation and decay of atmospheric carbon-14 are in balance	Variations in cosmic radiation have caused carbon-14 levels to fluctuate
All life-forms contain carbon	Isotopes of carbon are taken into organisms at different rates (fractionation)
Plants and animals take in newly formed carbon-14 until their death	Marine creatures absorb old carbon from deep-sea water
Dendrochronology provides an independent measure of accuracy	Radiocarbon underestimates the true age of tree-rings to an increasingly serious extent beyond 2000 BP
Pearson's calibration curve converts radiocarbon estimations into calendar dates	The curve contains many sections where calibration is imprecise or ambiguous
Conventional and AMS dating now provide very accurate dates	The results are still subject to a statistical margin of error, indicated by the standard deviation
Excellent results may now be obtained from small samples	Good results depend on the careful selection of appropriate samples, and the quality of the archaeological context remains crucial

7.3 Presenting and interpreting a radiocarbon date

(Stuiver 1993)

Health warning! Proper calibration is not easy for the non-mathematician, but doing it incorrectly, wrongly interpreting the result, or even not understanding the potential of calibration may seriously damage your archaeology. Take advice from the experts – know what calendrical band-width is necessary for correct interpretation and discuss this with the dating laboratory, preferably before taking and certainly before submitting samples. Think first, not after you get the radiocarbon date. (Pearson 1987, 103)

Because interpretation is so complex, all radiocarbon dates included in an archaeological publication must be presented in a standard manner. For example, a series of charcoal samples obtained from a late neolithic site at Galgenberg (Bavaria) is shown in Table A below (Aitchison 1991, 113).

The first column contains the code for the Groningen radiocarbon laboratory (GrN) together with a unique serial number for this particular sample, so that it could be checked with laboratory records if any problem arose. The archaeological number refers to an excavated context at the Galgenberg site, and its nature is explained in the final column. The determined age of this sample is expressed in 'raw' uncalibrated form in years BP (before the 'present', standardized to AD 1950), complete with an unavoidable counting error estimated by the laboratory (±35). The 'raw date' has already been adjusted to compensate for fractionation, but it is calculated according to Libby's half-life of 5568 years rather than the more recently determined estimate of 5730 years; this practice is maintained to avoid confusion in comparisons with older results. The standard counting error of 35 years means that the (uncalibrated) date has a 68% chance of lying between 4350 and 4420 BP, and a 95% chance that it lies between 4315 and 4455 BP. This emphasizes the importance of regarding radiocarbon ages as ranges of possibilities, rather than 'dates'.

This 'date' has not yet been calibrated. Reference is normally made to the calibration curve, derived from dated tree-ring samples, published by Pearson in volume 28 of the periodical *Radiocarbon* in 1986 (supplemented in 1993 by volume 35.1). A rapid inspection of the curve suggests that the radiocarbon estimation will be transformed into a calendar date with a range falling roughly between 2900 and 3100 BC. However, closer inspection of this particular age determination reveals a common problem: a 'wiggle' in the calibration curve at around 4400 BP means that it could represent three different 'historical' dates (fig. 4.16; Aitchison 1991, 113); see Table B below. The tree-ring calibration curve is itself subject to statistical variations; for this reason the standard deviation should be considered as only a *minimum* estimate of unreliability. Furthermore, precision varies according to which part of the curve is being consulted; if

(A)

lab no.	arch. no.	uncalibrated determination B.P.	archaeological context
GrN-12702	T14 1P	4385±35	collapsed palisade fence in W ditch

(B)

uncalibrated determination B.P.	corresponding historical dates BC	estimated standard errors
4385±35	2947	59
	2973	80
	3025	30

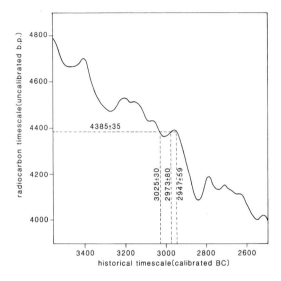

4.16 This diagram shows how a single radiocarbon age estimation (from the Galgenberg, Germany) may produce three different calendar dates of varying reliability if it happens to coincide with a difficult 'wiggle' in the calibration curve. For the purposes of dating a neolithic sample, it would normally be sufficient to know that the calibrated date lay somewhere between 2800 and 3100 BC, but a margin of error of this size would be too great for historical periods. *Sandra Hooper, after Aitchison* et al., *1991. fig, 4*

the line is steep, the prospects are good, but if it is flatter, the date range will be very wide. Thus the 'date' of 3025 has the lowest of the three estimated levels of error. When all thirteen samples from Galgenberg were examined together, the main period of the whole site's occupation was estimated to lie between 2810 and 3100 BC.

Thus, Galgenberg illustrates some of the problems that lie between the receipt of an age estimation from a laboratory and its interpretation in meaningful chronological terms for a site or an artefact. This is why Pearson advised archaeologists to consider the 'calendrical bandwidth necessary for correct interpretation' before submitting samples. In the context of later prehistoric Britain, a sample from the British late Bronze Age and early Iron Age that was expected to give calibrated results between 1100 and 800 BC would be very worthwhile, for it would coincide with a steep slope on the calibration curve. In contrast, samples from the period

between 800 and 400 BC are almost useless, for this part of the curve is much flatter, and does not permit refinement within a range of around four centuries; traditional forms of dating would be more accurate; see fig. 4.14; Bowman 1990, 55–7.

It should be noted that in many British publications, uncalibrated dates are indicated with a lower-case 'ad' or 'bc', while calibrated dates are cited as '1000 BC' or '1000 AD'. This practice has not been followed elsewhere; an International Radiocarbon Convention in 1985 recommended that uncalibrated age determinations should always be quoted in the form '1000 BP' (*Before Present*; for this purpose, the 'present' is standardized as AD 1950). If dates are calibrated according to 'an agreed curve', they should be cited in the form '1000 cal BP'. In areas of the world where the AD/BC division is useful, calibrated dates can be converted to '1000 cal BC' or '1000 cal AD' (Gillespie and Gowlett 1986, 160). 'Perhaps with the benefit of hindsight it might have been preferable if radiocarbon measurements had never been expressed as "ages" or "dates"; then there could be no misunderstanding' (Bowman 1990, 49).

Radiocarbon samples
Most materials containing carbon are suitable for dating; the lower the carbon content, the larger the sample needs to be. Charcoal derived from the burning of wood is a common find on archaeological sites and samples of around 10–20 grams dry weight are adequate for conventional counting, compared with around 50–100 grams of peat, or 100–500 grams of bone (Aitken 1990, 91). 'Mini-counting' methods cope with samples less than a tenth of this size (e.g. 0.1–0.5 grams of charcoal), while AMS requires only around one hundredth (e.g. 0.01–0.1 grams). Many other materials may be tested, including cloth, flesh, pollen, shell, soil and even iron, which usually contains some carbon impurities. The collection of samples needs to be scrupulous and their storage and handling must avoid contamination, even though they are subjected to a chemical 'laundry' process before being tested.

Archaeologists must know exactly *what* is being dated and, in the case of samples from excavations, their precise stratigraphic relationship to the site. The nature of charcoal and wood samples is very important – twigs or nuts are ideal, because they only contain carbon-14 taken in during a short growing season, whereas the central portion of a large tree will obviously give a date decades (or even centuries) earlier than its use for fuel or construction. Thought must also be given to the extent that samples are related to the objects or contexts that they are intended to date. Thus, the same significance must not be attached to fragments of charcoal from a general occupation level and to a sample taken from part of a wooden artefact or a human body. One of the most widely publicized examples of direct dating was the examination of the Turin shroud; since only very small samples of linen could be provided from this unique artefact, AMS was an ideal method. By good luck the result (691 ± 31 BP) matched a favourable part of the calibration curve and gave a date of 1275–90 cal AD at the 68% confidence level (fig. 4.17); whatever the nature and date of the strange image painted(?) on the shroud, the linen from which it was woven

grew no earlier than the thirteenth century AD, making it impossible that it was ever associated with Jesus.

Even in prehistory radiocarbon raises questions of a 'historical' nature. For example, evidence of very early human settlement linked with a hunter-gatherer economy was recently found on the island of Cyprus, whereas it had previously been thought that farming communities had settled there in the Neolithic period. However, since the relevant radiocarbon dates were too early for the conventional calibration curve, it was difficult to provide a calendar date for the earliest occupation. Evidence from varves, floating tree-rings, Uranium-Thorium dates from coral, and various other forms of dating suggest a date around 10,000–11,500 BC in 'calendar' years – but this may be changed or refined in future (Manning 1991). Technical limitations upon radiocarbon dates are just as significant in the case of relatively recent (in European terms, historical) periods. The question of the date of colonization of New Zealand is a good example: estimates ranged up to 2000 years ago, with a majority favouring around 1000 years ago. A large number of radiocarbon estimations now demonstrates that it took place as recently as the fourteenth century AD, but many samples derived from shell, bone and old wood had given misleading earlier dates (Anderson 1991).

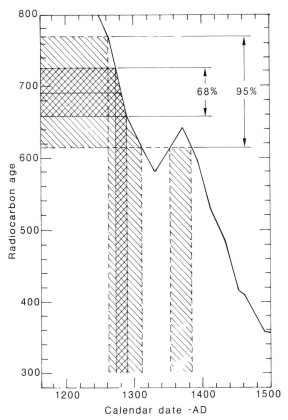

4.17 The precision of AMS radiocarbon dating gave an unambiguous answer to questions about the age of the Turin shroud, a mysterious piece of cloth that bears such a striking image of Christ that it was believed possible that it really had been preserved from the Crucifixion in the first century AD. Accelerator dating was able to test very small samples of the cloth, and the age estimation matched a particularly favourable part of the calibration curve. Results from three different laboratories combined to give a remarkably precise indication that there was a 68% chance that the cloth dated from AD 1275–90; the safer 95% significance level increased this to 1275–90 and 1355–85. Thus, whatever explanation for the image on the shroud is proposed, it must start from the knowledge that the cloth is of medieval date. *Sandra Hooper, after Aitken 1990, fig. 4.10*

First-order radiocarbon dating

Emphasis on accuracy and precision in radiocarbon dating is not always appropriate. Occasionally, results from a much quicker and simpler method may be quite sufficient for some needs – at only one four-hundredth of the cost. First-order radiocarbon dating is applicable to carbon dioxide gas derived from shells using the liquid scintillation counting technique. It has proved very effective on shell middens up to at least 20,000 years old, and it can be checked against samples of charcoal from the same deposits. It revealed exploitation of marine resources in Victoria (Australia) three to five thousand years earlier than had been thought, because it could be employed on older, less well preserved shell middens that had not been considered good enough to be tested by more expensive conventional methods (Frankel 1991). The advantage was summarized well in a recent article: 'We believe that in many archaeological situations it is better to have 10 dates with standard deviations around the mean of 200 years, than one date with a 40-year standard error' (Glover 1990, 566).

The impact of radiocarbon dating
(Taylor 1987; 1992)
Without doubt, radiocarbon dating has made the greatest single contribution to the development of archaeology since geologists and prehistorians liberated themselves, a century earlier, from the constraints of historical chronology by rejecting the biblical Creation. The major stages of human development from hunting through to urbanization are now well dated over most of the world. However, so few radioactive carbon-14 isotopes remain in a sample more than 40,000 years old that it is difficult to measure the small number of particle emissions. The technique is therefore unsuitable for studying most of the Palaeolithic period; fortunately, a related method based on an isotope of potassium allows the examination of early hominid developments beyond the range of radiocarbon.

7.4 Potassium-argon dating

Potassium is abundant throughout the Earth's crust. Among its isotopes is a small percentage of K-40 that decays into calcium-40 and a gas, argon-40. This gas escapes while new volcanic rocks are being formed, but as minerals crystallize they begin

to trap Ar-40, which can be released from samples in the laboratory and measured. At 1250 million years, the half-life of K-40 is staggeringly long in comparison with that of carbon-14. Its potential for geological dating had been realized by 1940, but archaeological applications began in the 1950s. Dates are arrived at by measuring the amount of Ar-40 trapped in potassium-rich minerals in comparison to K-40; the less there is, the more recent was the formation of the material involved. The inaccuracies inherent in measuring minute quantities of Ar-40 make it difficult to use in periods less than 100,000 years old. However, improvements in the measurement of comparatively recent samples will allow checks to be made on thermoluminescence dating in the period beyond the effective range of radiocarbon dating (at best 50,000 years).

Potassium-argon is ideal for dating early hominid fossils in East Africa, for they occur in an area that was volcanically active when the fossils were deposited between one and four million years ago. Layers containing bones and artefacts may be found 'sandwiched' between volcanic deposits of ash or lava that provide excellent samples of newly formed minerals for measurement. Very occasionally the association between human remains and volcanic deposits may be much more intimate, as in the case of human footprints around 3.6 million years old found on a layer of freshly deposited ash at Laetoli, Kenya (Leakey and Lewin 1992, 103).

Independent radioactive techniques, including uranium series and fission-track dating, give similar results that support dates derived from potassium-argon. Margins of error measured in thousands of years are unimportant in periods of such long duration, but they are useless in later prehistory, when, for example, the entire European Bronze Age lasted for only around 1000 years. A more serious problem involves the nature of the material required for sampling; few areas in the world provide archaeological remains that are stratigraphically related to sequences of freshly formed but undisturbed volcanic material, containing crystallized minerals of the kinds best suited to measurement. Potassium-argon has also been very important to geologists for checking the dates of some major reversals of the Earth's magnetic field (below, p. 128) and climatic patterns revealed by sea-bed cores (above, p. 113); both sources of information are valuable for dating purposes in places where volcanic minerals suitable for the potassium-argon method are not available.

7.5 Uranium series dating

The dating of geological periods followed the discovery of radioactivity, and the age of rocks back to the Pre-Cambrian was assessed by measuring the proportions of uranium and lead or uranium and helium. Uranium could be used in this way because it remains radioactive for very long periods; elements with shorter decay periods are of course more helpful for recent geological and archaeological dating. Thorium-230 is a useful isotope because it has a half-life of 75,400 years. Although coral is the ideal sample material, calcite crystals contained in stalagmite may also be sampled, and this makes it suitable for dating early human activity in caves, anywhere between 5000 and 350,000 years ago; calcium carbonate deposits from springs also provide suitable material. Large samples of around 50 grams are required unless mass spectrometry is available. In any case, the precise relationship between the sample and an archaeological event or activity must always be established. Uranium series dating is frequently used in conjunction with ESR (electron spin resonance – below, p. 124), for the latter may also be carried out on the kinds of samples typical of cave finds, such as teeth, shells and stalagmite calcite. Uranium-Thorium dating of coral has also allowed radiocarbon dates to be calibrated back to around 20,000 BC, because coral, a living organism, also contains carbon.

8 Radioactive effects on crystal stucture
(Aitken 1990)

The following absolute techniques do not simply measure radioactive emissions or the products of radioactive decay; instead, they examine the effects of radioactive impurities on the crystal structure of minerals.

8.1 Thermoluminescence dating
(Aitken 1985)

TL dating is most effectively applied to fired clay, which normally contains crystalline impurities, or burnt flint. In addition to being subjected to continuous cosmic radiation, these materials are also affected by radioactivity from uranium, thorium and potassium, contained in the artefacts themselves or in the soil where they have been buried until excavation. Crystals have defects in their structure that 'trap' electrons produced by this radiation; 'deep traps' do not begin to release these electrons unless they are heated above 300°C. When electrons *are* released, some recombine immediately with a **luminescence centre** (another type of defect) and emit light in proportion to their number. As soon as heating is over, electrons begin to accumulate again, until reheating to the same temperature occurs.

The first stage in calculating a date is to measure the amount of light released by a suitably prepared sample from an appropriate material and to plot its 'glow-curve' on a graph as the sample is heated up to 500° – the 'natural' glow-curve. This is then compared with another, 'artificial', glow-curve derived from an identical sample subjected to a known amount of radiation in the laboratory (fig. 4.18). The relationship between the two curves gives information about the reliability of the sample, as well as revealing the amount of energy that had accumulated since it was last heated (the **palaeodose**). The palaeodose does not reveal the age straightaway. It is necessary to measure the **annual dose** derived not only from radioactive impurities in the sample itself, but also from the radioactivity of the soil where it had been buried. When this has been done, and a number of additional factors have been allowed for, the age is equivalent to the palaeodose divided by the annual dose. Thus, a palaeodose of 8.5 Gy divided by an annual dose of 5.18 Gy (Grays, a standard measurement of absorbed radiation) would give an age of 1640 years – around AD 350 (Aitken 1990, 151).

The most important material for TL is fired clay; hearths, kilns and especially pottery form an important part of the archaeological record in most parts of the world. Since pots are fired at a temperature well above that required to release all the electrons that have been trapped in their crystal lattices, the energy released in the laboratory today will have built up from the date of their firing. The older the pots, the more energy that should have accumulated. Unfortunately, there

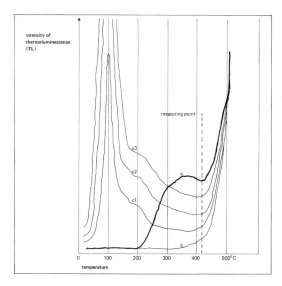

4.18 Thermoluminescence apparatus provides a graph of light released by a sample prepared from an ancient artefact as it is heated (a). A second measurement of the same sample provides a different graph for the same material without its ancient energy (b); the bulge in curve (a) between 300° and 400°C resulted from the electrons trapped in the sample. Curves c1–3 are further measurements taken to study the luminescence produced after the sample has been exposed to known levels of modern radioactivity in order study its sensitivity. When further factors about the context in which the artefact was found have been taken into account, a date may be calculated. *Audio Visual Centre, University of Newcastle*

are many problems connected with measurement. Clays contain a variety of mixed minerals of differing particle size that vary in their ability to trap electrons. Samples require elaborate preparation to separate particles of the optimum size, and extremely sensitive equipment must be used to record the very slight amounts of thermoluminescence emitted. Furthermore, measurement of the radiation absorbed from the soil that surrounded a buried clay artefact is difficult, but crucial for an accurate calculation of the age; this is even more critical in the case of flint. Obviously, it is not possible to measure this form of radiation in objects from museum collections whose precise find spot is unknown; TL will still detect modern forgeries that lack trapped electrons, however.

The TL dating technique is particularly valuable for dating in situations where no suitable materials for radiocarbon dating have been found, or if the age exceeds 40,000 years, when radiocarbon is of rapidly diminishing usefulness. Fortunately, site finds from early periods of prehistory usually include stones and flint implements burnt in fires in caves or camp sites at a sufficiently high temperature to release their trapped electrons. Flints found in deposits with relatively low radioactivity may have a potential datable range of up to 500,000 or even a million years. In areas where volcanic materials suitable for potassium-argon dating are absent, this is of great significance. Stalagmite may also be dated, and so too can volcanic materials or the soil over which molten lava has flowed (Aitken 1990, 172). It is even possible to date deposits of soil or sediment that were subjected to intense sunlight and subsequently buried. It has been established that this kind of exposure to heat and light is sufficient to remove trapped electrons ('bleaching'), but they begin to accumulate again as soon as it is covered (ibid. 173–5).

8.2 Electron spin resonance (ESR)

The basis of ESR has much in common with thermoluminescence, for both measure electrons that have become trapped in the crystal lattice of minerals. It differs from TL in the nature of suitable samples, which include teeth, shells and stalagmite calcite. The method of measurement is also unlike TL, for ESR does not release the electrons, but subjects them to electromagnetic radiation in a magnetic field. At certain points of interaction between the magnetic frequencies and the magnetic field, the electrons resonate and absorb electromagnetic power. The strength of resonance reflects the number of trapped electrons, and their quantity is related to the time that has elapsed since the crystals were formed. The radioactive content of samples, combined with the external radiation that they have received, must always be measured so that their age can be calculated by dividing the palaeodose by the annual dose – in exactly the same manner as TL (see above).

ESR sample materials favour the study of the Palaeolithic period, for stalagmites may be related to cave occupation, and fossil teeth from large mammals such as mammoths may provide effective dating. Tooth enamel is required, for the dentine of the core – like bone – is porous, and new minerals continue to form long after the death of the animal, giving an underestimate of the true age. Aitken cites some convincing examples of ESR dates derived from samples of mammoth and rhinoceros teeth from Canada and Germany; the resulting dates of around 100,000 and 350,000 years old correlated well with the climatic stages to which the finds could be assigned, and with uranium-series dating (Aitken 1990, 198–9).

8.3 Fission-track dating

This method involves counting microscopic damage trails in minerals such as zircon, and glass, whether volcanic (e.g. obsidian) or of human manufacture. The trails are caused by fission fragments when the nucleus of uranium-238 splits during radioactive decay. In practice the most useful samples come from zircon, and from obsidian, a material used extensively for making tools. However, the sample must have been subjected to heating at the time of the archaeological context or event that is to be dated. Obsidian tools or waste flakes from tool production that have been dropped into a hearth would be ideal, for heat removes the fission-tracks that have accumulated since the obsidian first solidified after its volcanic formation. Glass, or a vitreous glaze on pottery, should *not* have been re-heated in this way if the date of its manufacture (rather than its last heating) is to be discovered. Fission-track dating, along with potassium-argon, has also assisted in checking the age of volcanic deposits associated with early hominid remains in East Africa (Aitken 1990, 135).

9 Derivative techniques
(Aitken 1990)

Aitken draws a clear distinction between absolute and derivative dating methods (1990, 2); the latter may only be used for dating by comparing their results with a time scale or reference curve that has been established by other dating methods. Thus, the level of thorium-230 found in a sample of stalagmite is a product of its urani-

um content, and the sample's age is calculated from the known radioactive half-life of thorium-230, which is not affected in any way by its environment; this method can therefore be described as **absolute**. In contrast, measurement of one form of amino acid changing to another (outlined below) is a **derivative** method, for the rate of alteration is entirely dependent on the temperature of the context where the sample has been buried.

Fluorine, uranium and nitrogen testing was one of the first scientific dating methods used in the examination of bone. It did not attempt to provide an estimate of age, but addressed a more fundamental problem that affects bones or artefacts of any kind: are the finds excavated from a single level – for example, a layer containing artefacts and bones in a cave – really contemporary? Does the stratum contain older items that have eroded out of earlier contexts, or items dug up accidentally during a later phase of occupation? Amino acid racemization and obsidian hydration dating may also be used to detect stray items, for bones and artefacts buried in uniform conditions over the same length of time would produce identical results; if they do not, some disturbance must have taken place and the excavated material is of limited value for *any* dating method.

9.1 Fluorine, uranium and nitrogen tests
(Price 1989)

Buried bone absorbs water containing elements that react chemically with the bone, adding fluorine and uranium, while nitrogen decreases through the decay of bone protein (collagen). Bones found in a single context should have been subjected to the conditions that cause these changes in a uniform manner, and their levels of these three elements should therefore be very similar. Older survivals and recent intrusions should therefore be distinguishable because of unusually high or low levels. The technique remains useful for checking bone samples that are to be submitted for radiocarbon dating, but other methods (such as ESR) are now more informative for dating purposes. Fluorine/uranium/nitrogen testing holds a special place in archaeological history because of its role in proving that the skull and jaw of 'Piltdown Man', excavated in Sussex in 1912 and claimed as evidence of an early hominid, was a forgery (Spencer 1990). Analysis showed that the find had been assembled from bones of several different ages and origins.

9.2 Amino acid racemization

Samples taken from bone, teeth or shells contain detectable amino acids that undergo gradual change (racemization) from L-form to D-form over time; the ratio of the two is measured to indicate age. Since the rate of change is highly dependent on temperature it is necessary to use an independent method, such as radiocarbon, to date a sample from the same burial context. Once this has been done, the speed of racemization may be determined and other samples may be dated by this means alone. The upper limit for successful dating may range from 100,000 to several million years, according to the kind of sample material available and the amino acids selected for study.

9.3 Obsidian hydration dating

Like amino acid racemization, this dating technique relies on a transformation that takes place over time and, likewise, it is highly dependent on the temperature of the context where the sample of obsidian has been buried. Obsidian is a natural volcanic glass that was a popular alternative to flint for making flaked tools in many parts of the world (see fig. 5.2). As soon as a fresh surface of obsidian is exposed, for example during the process of making it into a tool, a microscopically thin 'hydration rim' begins to form as a result of the absorption of water (fig. 4.19). Furthermore, obsidian from different geological sources may weather at different rates. However, in regions where supporting dates are supplied by radiocarbon (notably Japan and South America), large numbers of measurements can be compiled to provide a calibration curve that may be used for checking the rim thicknesses of individual artefacts or assemblages found on similar sites.

4.19 This photomicrograph shows a section through the hydration rim of an obsidian artefact. The interior of the specimen is on the left; the diagonal band is a layer of weathering on the surface, and its depth is demarcated by a diffusion front that shows up as a paler line. This can be measured quite accurately, even though it is only three microns thick in this sample. *Prof. J Michels*

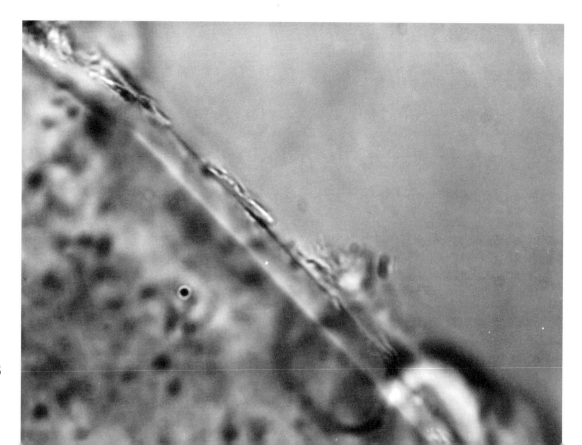

This technique may also be used to check the contemporaneity of material from a single deposit and to detect modern forgeries. The thickness of the hydration rims of large numbers of artefacts from individual sites are plotted on a graph; if the site was occupied continuously they should display a reasonably smooth progression with age, while discontinuities may represent periods of abandonment. In warm climates where hydration is rapid, obsidian dating is useful for quite recent centuries, but, generally a margin of error of at least ±1% must be expected – in other words, a bracket 100 years either side of an age of 1000 years.

9.4 Archaeomagnetic dating
(Tarling 1983)

Fine grains of iron oxide are present in most clay and soil, and they take on a new magnetic alignment in two main ways. **Thermoremanent** magnetism is acquired when they realign according to the Earth's magnetic field after having been disoriented by heating above 650°C; some grains may retain the new field for hundreds of thousands of years. Magnetism is also acquired by means of the **deposition** of sediments, for instance in lake beds, where particles may settle into alignment with the prevailing magnetic field. Magnetic North wanders at random around the North Pole (and indeed reverses completely to the South Pole for long periods). From any reference point its position is measurable in terms of two components: movement up or down (**inclination** or 'dip') and from side to side (**declination**).

Magnetic dating measures the alignment in an ancient sample and attempts to relate it to a record of past changes in the magnetic field (fig. 4.20). However, although records of magnetic alignment have been made by scientists in Britain since before AD 1600, they began much more recently elsewhere in the world. Thus, information about the pattern of past variations has to be derived from suitable samples from archaeological sites that have been dated *independently* by some other means, such as historical evidence or radiocarbon dating. The reference curve of inclination and declination has been extended back to 1000 BC in Britain in this way. Unfortunately, the Earth's magnetic field varies from region to

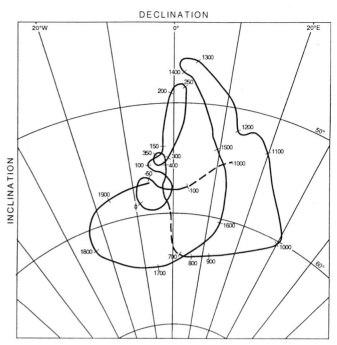

4.20 The movement of Magnetic North, measured from Britain. The graph shows *declination*, in degrees east or west of true North, and *inclination*, in degrees below the horizontal. These wandering lines are compiled from contemporary observations as far back as records allow, but samples from *dated* deposits or structures on archaeological sites must be found to project them further back into the past. Samples from *undated* sites can be measured in the laboratory, and dated according to where their magnetic alignments coincide with the curve established for the relevant geographical area. Difficulties do exist, however: identical readings occur wherever the curve crosses itself, for example between AD 1600, when the curve also matches late-Saxon measurements.
Prof. D Tarling, University of Plymouth

region, so that results from Britain are not even applicable in France. Thus, magnetic dating clearly illustrates Aitken's definition of a derivative method, for it is necessary to establish a separate independently dated series of measurements for every region where the technique is required. When multiple dates result from overlaps in the record of the magnetic field, one particular date may be selected on archaeological or historical grounds. Fortifications that were possibly erected by Charles the Bald at Pont-del'Arche on the Seine in France produced dates around 360 BC, AD 580, AD 860 and AD 1580; obviously only AD 860±20 was appropriate for a historical reference to a Viking attack in AD 865 (Dearden and Clark 1990).

This technique may only be used on archaeological sites where solid clay structures that have not moved since becoming magnetized are found; kilns, hearths and burnt clay walls or floors are ideal. Small samples are selected, and their positions are carefully recorded in relation to the present magnetic field. This allows their alignment to be duplicated in a laboratory, so that differences between the ancient and present alignment can be measured. It is also possible to examine the 'dip' angle of portable fired objects such as bricks or pots, as long it is possible to assume that they were fired in a horizontal position.

One further dimension of archaeomagnetism is **magnetic intensity**, a measure of the strength rather than the direction of the magnetic field. Like magnetic alignment, it may be retained after heating or acquired through deposition, and it also varies from area to area. A dated reference series of measurements is therefore needed for any region before it may be used as an independent dating method. Insufficient variation has been discovered for it to become a useful chronological tool (Aitken 1990, 252–3).

The direction and intensity of the Earth's magnetic field are of an interest that extends beyond dating, for they probably have an influence upon global climate and cosmic radiation. The general pattern of major variations (such as North–South reversals) has been established by geologists, and it has considerable implications for archaeologists involved in the study of early human remains found in geological deposits in East Africa and elsewhere. Furthermore, absolute dates for the major reversals have been determined by the potassium-argon method. Thanks to the occurrence of iron oxide particles in sea-bed deposits, magnetic reversals have also been correlated with the climatic changes indicated by oxygen-isotope variations recorded in cores taken from ocean-floor sediments (above, p. 113). Thus, fossil bones or tools found in a stratum with magnetic characteristics that can be linked to a datable magnetic reversal may be dated *and* placed into their correct environmental context.

9.5 Cation-ratio dating (CR)

Prehistoric rock carvings ('petroglyphs') are not uncommon in arid areas where suitable surfaces have escaped erosion by the action of rain and frost. However, their age is notoriously difficult to determine unless they are found in contact with a datable stratified deposit. Petroglyphs are commonly covered by a so-called 'rock varnish', a chemically changed layer that builds up after around 100 years through weathering, enhanced by the action of micro-organisms. Using a method first put forward by Ronald Dorn in 1983, samples are taken by scraping the 'varnish' from petroglyph surfaces back to original rock surface. A separate cation (positively charged ion) leaching curve must then be established for different geographical areas, because local soil and moisture conditions affect the speed of its formation (Dorn 1988, 683). The date of the surface layer that has formed over the carvings may sometimes be checked by AMS radiocarbon dating, if sufficient carbon from micro-organisms was included in the initial 'glaze'.

Forty-six petroglyph samples from Piñon Canyon, an arid site in south-eastern Colorado, were dated to between 300 and 2000+ years before the present (Loendorf 1991). The results were consistent with a relative sequence established on typological grounds according to the style of the designs, and they also matched radiocarbon dates from associated sites. The first use of cation-ratio dating on carvings outside the USA was in the arid zone of south Australia, where it suggested exploitation of the area for over 30,000 years (Dorn 1988). However, Lanteigne has sounded a note of caution, because many underlying assumptions have not yet been fully tested (1991). As with radiocarbon and the derivative techniques (notably obsidian hydration), many modifications will no doubt be required before the potential and limitations are properly understood. It may also be possible to use this technique to date stone artefacts found on the surface of deserts; it would at least provide a minimum age for the time that has elapsed since they were exposed by erosion.

10 The authenticity of artefacts

(Jones 1990)

It is inevitable that major museums that buy items for their collections become involved in expensive commercial dealings in the fine art market. The profits to be made not only stimulate illicit plundering of ancient sites, but encourage skilful forgeries. Scientific dating techniques bring obvious benefits, for precise dates are rarely required, simply an assurance that an artefact is not a modern fake. Thermoluminescence and archaeomagnetism provide adequate checks on pottery and a variety of highly priced elaborate ceramic 'terracotta' sculptures from Africa and South America. Where they survive, the remains of clay cores left inside bronze statues or objects after they were cast in moulds also provide suitable samples. It is very unlikely that a forger could create artificially the precise levels of radioactive energy or magnetic conditions that should be found in genuine items. Radiocarbon dating by the AMS technique now allows very small samples to be taken from small wooden, bone or other organic artefacts without affecting their appearance. Dendrochronology is helpful in the study of wooden panels used in furniture and early paintings, while paints and pigments may be examined by means of various forms of radioactive isotope dating.

11 Conclusions

> Thus scientific dating is not just a boring necessity that tidies things up by providing numbers, it is vital for valid interpretation. (Aitken 1990, 1)

Traditional forms of archaeological dating have been strengthened immeasurably by the growth of an extraordinarily diverse range of scientific techniques that helps to demonstrate the truly multi-disciplinary nature of modern archaeology. Traditional methods have *not* been replaced, however. The definition of sequences by means of stratigraphic excavation remains the basis for observations about sites and for typological studies of artefacts. Scientific dating techniques add precision and allow specific hypotheses about the relationships of sites, regional cultures or forms of artefacts to be tested. The transition from hunting and gathering to agriculture and the emergence of early civilizations may be interpreted in meaningful human terms now that we know – thanks to radiocarbon dating – when they occurred and how long the processes of transformation took. Similarly, potassium-argon dating (in association with several other methods) has provided a framework for the study of human evolution at the important point when there are the first clear signs that stone tools began to be used.

Scientific dating techniques play more of a supporting role in historical periods, and they are particularly valuable where there is doubt over historical dates, or where gaps exist in the historical framework. It must not be forgotten that even absolute methods such as radiocarbon had to be validated first by testing samples of known historical date. Libby used finds from Egyptian pyramids up to 5000 years old, dated by historical records of the reigns of pharaohs, to test the consistency of carbon-14 measurements beyond the range of tree-rings (Aitken 1990, 58, fig. 3.2). The refinement of radiocarbon dating, combined with dendrochronology, now feeds information back into this process; recent detailed scientific dating of the late Bronze Age around the Aegean confirms the sequences built up from artefact typologies and historical records over the last century (Manning & Weninger 1992). As with other scientific approaches to archaeology, the whole procedure is founded on cooperation, and the increasing complexity of methods used to refine the accuracy of scientific dating techniques demands ever closer collaboration between scientists, historians, prehistorians and excavators to produce results that benefit all in different ways. The best of the old should accompany the best of the new.

Note: a guide to **further reading** that includes topics covered in this chapter begins on p. 185.

5 Science and Archaeology

1 Is archaeology a science?

So much of the evidence left behind by past cultures has been destroyed that archaeologists have a duty to employ whatever methods are available to extract the maximum possible information from what still survives. Since archaeology has always borrowed concepts and techniques from other disciplines, it is not surprising to find that science has had just as dramatic an effect on archaeology as it has had on all other aspects of modern life. To demonstrate the fundamental role of science in archaeology it would almost be sufficient to refer readers to the many forms of scientific dating described in chapter 4. The 'radiocarbon revolution' exemplifies the nature of most relationships between science and archaeology. Its development was entirely dependent upon advances in nuclear physics, and the archaeological applications are a very minor diversion from the central issues of physics. Likewise, the location devices described in chapter 2 were not originally devised for archaeological research, but they were applied and adapted to archaeological situations either by scientists who happened to be interested in archaeology, or by archaeologists who understood the scientific principles sufficiently well to be able to recognize their potential.

The use of scientific methods does not make archaeology into a science. The many scientific techniques that may be applied more or less directly to the investigation of sites or objects fall into a sub-discipline generally known as **archaeological science**. On a deeper level, a 'scientific' attitude of mind rejects individual observations or subjective conclusions, and demands that questions about the past should be posed in the form of hypotheses that can be *tested*. In this manner, archaeological research should ideally proceed as a series of laboratory experiments designed to verify or refute these hypotheses. However, this analogy contains a flaw: archae-ological experiments are rarely (if ever) repeatable under laboratory conditions, because no two sites or artefacts are ever exactly the same.

In practice, there are few questions about the past that would *not* benefit from investigation with the help of the natural or biological sciences; indeed, many questions may only be answered with the assistance of scientific methods. One of the principal educational virtues of archaeology is that it is truly multi-disciplinary, and that it defies all attempts to pigeon-hole it either as a science or as one of the humanities. This chapter will attempt to illustrate parts of the wide range of information that science contributes to archaeology.

2 The examination of objects and raw materials
(Henderson 1989; Bowman 1991)

Any archaeological object, whether found casually or during a controlled excavation, poses questions about its date, origin, function and method of manufacture. A museum curator who deals with visitors' enquiries will know that some of these questions may be answered superficially by a combination of common sense and experience. Scientific analysis offers many insights into ancient objects, but, as with dating methods, there must be full cooperation and communication between archaeologists and laboratory scientists to ensure that the most appropriate methods are applied to suitable samples. There is little point in conducting analyses without clear questions in mind, and those questions should be the result of archaeological research. Occasionally an archaeologist will only require a straightforward 'yes' or 'no'; the course of further scientific investigation might depend entirely on the answer. In the case of the 'Ice Man' found in the Alps (Spindler 1994; Barfield 1994), it was important to know the composition of a metal axe found with the body. Whereas the typological form of the axe suggested a date in the early Bronze Age, radiocarbon dates indicated that the man died in the late Neolithic period. Fortunately, metallurgical analysis was able to reveal very quickly that the axe was made of pure copper, which was acceptable at this early date, rather than bronze, an alloy of copper and other metals that was not introduced until the early Bronze Age.

Thus, the initial question about the Ice Man's axe was very simple; once it had been answered, further information from the analysis might help in the investigation of subsidiary questions, such as the likely source of the copper, or the precise method of its manufacture. If the axe *had* turned out to have been made from bronze, a very different range of questions would have been posed. The most important problem would not have been related to the axe itself, but to the possibility of errors in the radiocarbon dating of the body. If a Neolithic date for a bronze axe had been confirmed, a further programme of analyses would have to be conducted to check whether other early 'copper' objects were also made from bronze. This example demonstrates how interactions between archaeologists, analytical scientists and radiocarbon dating laboratories are essential if the right questions are to be posed, and the implications of the answers are to be understood.

It is not only finished artefacts that provide interesting sources of information about raw materials. Mines and quarries illustrate extraction methods, and industrial sites offer insights into manufacturing processes through the excavation of furnaces, kilns or workshops. Waste products, such as the slags that flowed out of metal smelting furnaces and solidified, can be subjected to the microscopic and analytical procedures similar to those explained below in relation to objects found on occupation sites (Craddock 1991). A wide range of techniques may be applied to sites as different as the scatter of stone fragments discarded by a prehistoric hunter-gatherer making tools in a temporary camp in East Africa, or the ruins of a nineteenth-century lead mining complex in the Pennines in northern England. Many details of the very recent industrial past either went unrecorded, or the relevant documents have not survived.

Scientific excavation and the recovery of carefully chosen samples for analysis will help to clarify both types of site.

2.1 Microscopic examination
(Olsen 1988)

Not all questions of scientific analysis require complex analytical methods; traditional study by microscope allows many aspects of stone or metal artefacts to be examined. Geologists have used microscopes to enhance visual observations for several centuries, and metallurgists may still learn a lot about a metal object by examining a magnified cross-section. Archaeologists now use microscopes in **use-wear analysis** of artefacts, in particular tools, for patterns of wear or damage on working surfaces may suggest how a tool was used. Evidence for manufacturing techniques may also be revealed by microscopic examination; decorated metal objects were frequently ornamented by means of a range of engraving tools whose shapes may be identified when magnified. Visual examination in use-wear studies is enhanced dramatically by a **scanning electron microscope** (SEM), which projects a magnified image onto a screen (Olsen 1988). An SEM sweeps a band of electrons over a surface to provide images that possess a depth of focus unobtainable from conventional microscopes (see fig. 5.13). This, combined with a dramatic increase in the power of magnification, reveals not only traces of use-wear on tools, but also traces of tissues from animal or starches from plants that were cut by them. SEM photomicrographs of cross-sections of pottery are also very informative, for they reveal the texture and structure of clays and glazes with remarkable clarity, revealing techniques of manufacture and decoration (Tite 1992).

Petrology (Kempe & Harvey 1983)
Besides the more sophisticated analytical techniques described below, traditional geological methods have much to offer the archaeologist, whether in the context of early prehistoric cultures that relied heavily on the use of stone for tools, or in more sophisticated societies where fine building stone was transported over long distances. Petrology involves the examination under a microscope of thin sections cut from samples of stone. Many minerals may be identified by eye,

and distinctive rocks are recognizable without the help of spectrographic analysis to measure their elements. Axes made in stone from volcanic outcrops in western Britain were distributed all over England in the Neolithic period, and more than 7500 examples were studied by petrological microscope from the 1940s onwards (Clough 1988). However, the majority of neolithic (and earlier) stone axes, along with other stone tools, were made from flint, which has such a uniform appearance that its source can only be traced with difficulty by spectrometry; inspection under a microscope is of no help.

Geologists occasionally pour cold water on attractive theories held by archaeologists. It was thought for several decades that the volcanic stones from outcrops in south-western Wales used in the construction of Stonehenge had been transported by water and overland in an impressive display of prehistoric organization and technology. Although a recent petrological survey has confirmed the Welsh origin of these 'bluestones', some geologists claim that they were carried to Wessex by glaciers during the last Ice Age. The builders of Stonehenge would have been able to find them locally where they had been dropped (along with many other 'erratic' boulders) when the glaciers melted (Williams-Thorpe & Thorpe 1992). The identification of the sources of building stone is also very important in historical archaeology, right up to recent times: Roman villas, medieval cathedrals and nineteenth-century town halls provide insights into the technical skills, communications, and prosperity of the societies and individuals who created them. The sources of stone used in the Roman palace at Fishbourne (Sussex) demonstrate that a wide range of appropriate building stones had been identified all over southern England within a few years of the Roman conquest, and that Roman engineers were capable of selecting, quarrying and transporting specific types of stone for different parts of the building (Greene 1986, 154–6).

Petrological techniques are applicable to bricks and pottery if their clay includes distinctive minerals related to the geology of the areas where they were manufactured. The forms and fabrics of the millions of Roman amphorae that were traded all over the Empire have responded particularly well to petrology, with the result that we now know where most types were manufactured. As a result it is possible to study the sources and distributions of important agricultural products such as Italian wine, Spanish fish sauce or North African olive oil; Roman documentary sources tell us very little about trade, but amphorae are very common finds on excavations and in shipwrecks. Petrological study is helped by the fact that amphorae are occasionally found still bearing hand-written inscriptions, written in black ink before their shipment, giving details of their contents and origin (Peacock & Williams 1986).

Metallography (Tylecote & Gilmour 1986)
The Ice Man's axe required full analysis to determine whether it was made of pure copper or an alloy with other metals, but many other aspects of metalworking are suitable for study under a microscope. Indeed, according to Northover, '... it should become a rule that analysis and metallography (and hardness testing) should always be combined, since a full interpretation of one is impossible without the other' (1989, 214).

It was realized long ago that, before bronze was made, unalloyed copper was used, because (like gold) it occurs naturally, and can be worked to a certain extent without smelting. However, all but the simplest artefacts required the metal to be poured molten into a mould. Their form, and surface traces left by flaws in the casting, usually makes it clear if this happened, but a metallurgist is able to determine the kind of mould used (metal, stone or clay) and to distinguish cold-worked from cast objects by examining a cross-section under a microscope (fig. 5.1). The crystalline structure of cold-worked objects is severely distorted and flattened by hammering. Because these traces are more difficult to detect than minerals in a petrological sample, the section has to be polished and etched to enhance the edges of crystals, and it may be necessary to use SEM magnification to reveal subtle distinctions (Bowman 1991, 86, fig. 5.11).

Iron objects also reveal their production techniques when studied in section. Since cast iron did not appear until the medieval period in Europe, all the traces visible in earlier iron objects are the result of laborious hammering by smiths. Treatment of the surface to harden it by

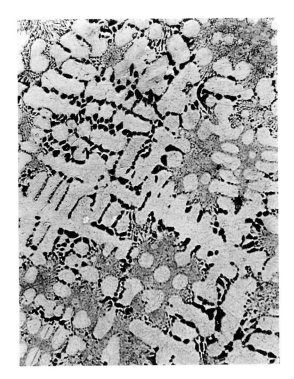
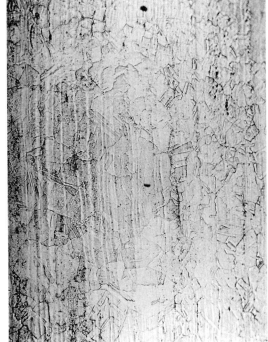

5.1 The structure of metals, seen under a microscope, can reveal the processes involved in their manufacture. The cross-section on the left (c. 0.5 mm across) shows the crystalline structure of an Egyptian figurine cast from an alloy of silver and copper; in comparison, the section on the right (c. 0.5 mm across) shows considerable flattening and distortion by extensive hammering and reheating during the making of a Roman silver bowl. *Vera Bird/Janet Lang, British Museum*

quenching in water or roasting in charcoal was important in the production of iron weapons, and it also leaves visible traces that can be confirmed by analysis of their carbon content. Large or complex objects were constructed from several pieces, and their joins are more easily studied in X-ray photographs than by the destructive process of cutting sections for microscopic inspection; this is also necessary for badly corroded objects (see fig. 5.6).

2.2 Analysis and characterization
(Jones & Catling 1986; Hughes 1991)

Many of the dating methods discussed in chapter 4 are based upon scientific procedures, but few involve analysis of exactly what artefacts are *made*

from, or how they were made. For example, although thermoluminescence dating of pottery requires analysis to measure the radioactivity of its minerals, it is not necessary to know their geological origin. The basic aim of the analysis of an artefact is to identify the materials from which it was made, and to measure accurately the relative quantities of its constituent minerals or chemicals. When this information is interpreted it may be possible to define the sources of the raw materials, to suggest a place of manufacture, and to deduce techniques involved in the manufacture of an object. Analysis is not restricted to objects, however; structures such as buildings offer many possibilities for the analysis of stone, bricks and mortar.

Many forms of analysis are conducted by means of **spectrometry**. A sample is subjected to radiation, and each element then emits radiation with a distinctive wavelength that may be identified and measured. The presence or absence of significant elements may thus be detected, and the actual quantity of each is measured from the amount of radiation recorded. Besides their principal elements, most types of stone, metal or ceramic material also contain small quantities of impurities; it is possible to detect and measure these

133

'trace elements' down to a few parts per million by spectrographic means. Trace elements are extremely helpful in tracing the origins of raw materials, and this approach has been very useful in **characterization studies**. Characterization aims to provide individual 'fingerprints' for *sources* of raw materials (whether stone, metal ores or clay deposits) by detecting significant trace elements. The results normally require complicated statistical processing to determine whether a distinctive combination of elements found at one source genuinely differs from that found at all other sources; if so, the figures can be plotted onto reference graphs (see fig. 5.3). Obviously, a large number of specimens from *known* sources must be analysed before any artefacts of unknown origin are tested.

An important consideration in the choice of analytical methods is the size and nature of the sample that is required. Traditional geological and metallurgical examination under a microscope involves the removal of a portion of an object sufficiently large to be ground flat and mounted on a microscope slide; many stone axes on display in museums show visible traces of this kind of sampling. Most spectrographic techniques based on radioactivity (such as **neutron activation analysis**) are conducted on very small samples drilled from an unobtrusive part of an artefact. **X-ray fluorescence** is completely non-destructive, but it only detects the composition of the surface. Thus, the choice of technique must depend on full consultation between a museum curator or archaeologist and the laboratory where an analysis will be performed. Many major museums have their own laboratories; the British Museum in London is a leading centre for programmes of research involving active cooperation between the museum's staff and scientists that benefit both sides (Bowman 1991).

Obsidian (Taylor 1976)

This volcanic glass occurs widely in both the New and Old Worlds, and it has attracted considerable attention from archaeological scientists. Like flint, it has excellent working properties for chipping, flaking and grinding into tools with sharp cutting edges (fig. 5.2). In some parts of the world, such as New Zealand, straightforward visual inspection or microscopic examination has

5.2 Obsidian, a natural volcanic glass, formed an important raw material for tool production in many parts of the world and was often traded over long distances. Since sources are rarely identifiable by eye, petrological analysis is required to study the distribution of obsidian from different sources. This flake of semi-translucent obsidian is from Greece, and the flake, core and arrowheads are from Patagonia. *Hancock Museum, University of Newcastle upon Tyne*

proved sufficient to isolate different sources. Around the Mediterranean and the American Cordillera, however, there are numerous varieties of obsidian that require more subtle differentiation. Most analyses have attempted to study patterns of prehistoric trade by identifying sources that supplied sites; this has been particularly successful in the Near East and around the Mediterranean (fig. 5.3). Their distribution patterns provide insights into extensive connections between early neolithic sites in the Near East as early as the seventh and sixth millennia BC.

This valuable information about undocumented cultures could not have been gained without the use of scientific analysis. However, the interpretation of the results in human terms remains an archaeological problem. Geology may reveal the sources of obsidian, but archaeologists must attempt to explain why any particular site should have received its raw material from one source rather than another. Analysis will not indicate whether artefacts arrived on a site as finished objects, or if blocks of raw obsidian were broken up and fashioned into tools on each site. Experienced archaeological observers may answer this question by looking for waste flakes chipped off cores during the manufacturing process. The nature of 'trade' is also a matter for archaeological interpretation, with the help of economic anthropologists: was the raw material bartered for other goods in a commercial manner, or was there an elaborate system of gift-exchange conducted on a ceremonial basis?

Bronze Age metallurgy (Oddy 1991)
Bronze usually consists of copper alloyed with tin, and varying percentages of other metals. The composition of an artefact made of copper or bronze is usually examined by a technique known as **atomic absorption spectrophotometry.** It requires a small sample drilled from the artefact, which is tested by repeatedly burning parts of the sample, and shining a beam characteristic of each element's wavelength through the flame. The quantity of an element is indicated by the amount of light absorbed by atoms of that element in the sample, to an accuracy as precise as five parts per million if necessary; this allows trace elements to be measured along with the principal metals. It is theoretically possible to use trace elements to identify areas from which ores came, by analysing ores and products in a manner similar to the study of obsidian. Unfortunately it was normal practice for scrap objects to be used as a source of metal, in addition to freshly quarried or mined ores. The resulting mixtures obviously confuse any attempt to pinpoint the sources of metal alloys.

Programmes of analysis of finished objects have been carried out since the 1930s in Europe and elsewhere, and a clear general pattern has emerged, although the changes took place at different dates in different areas, according to the availability of metal ores. Pure copper (i.e. with only naturally occurring impurities) and copper alloyed with arsenic were soon superseded by 'true' bronze made by adding tin to the copper.

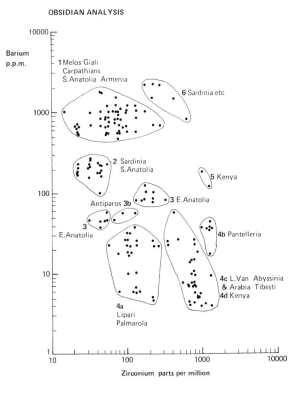

5.3 Sources of obsidian in the Near East and Mediterranean: samples from known sources have been analysed, and the results processed to find trace elements that differ significantly. In this diagram, barium and zirconium are plotted against each other on a logarithmic scale, and form clusters of results. Artefacts from sites can be tested against these clusters to determine the origin of the raw material from which they were manufactured. Some clusters are more convincing than others; relationships between several different trace elements may be needed to improve the characterization of each source. The same technique is also useful in the study of pottery, and other kinds of stone. *Audio Visual Centre, University of Newcastle, after Cann* et al., *1969*

This change was normally accompanied by the use of more sophisticated moulds that required less further work to be carried out to finish the artefact after casting. In some areas (at various dates) lead was also included as a major constituent along with tin. This required a balance to be achieved between two conflicting factors: lead made the metal easier to cast into long elaborate

135

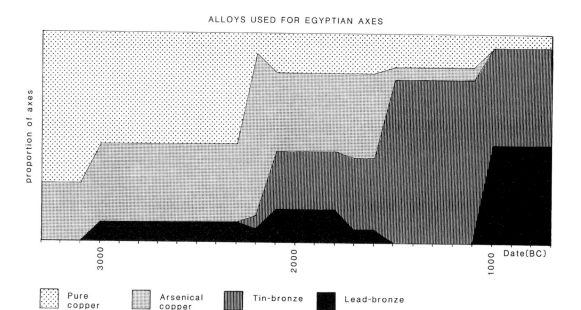

ALLOYS USED FOR EGYPTIAN AXES

proportion of axes

Date(BC)

3000   2000   1000

Pure copper   Arsenical copper   Tin-bronze   Lead-bronze

5.4 Analysis of the composition of metal alloys reveals interesting changes over time. This graph illustrates the changing proportions of Egyptian axes made from pure copper and three different alloys of copper. Axes used as weapons were primarily tin-bronze, and those used as tools might be copper or arsenical copper; decorative axes were cast in weaker lead-bronze. *Sandra Hooper, after Cowell & La Niece 1991, fig. 5.4*

swords or axes with hollow sockets, but it could make it weaker in actual use. In Egypt, the alloys of copper used for making axes were carefully matched to their function (fig. 5.4). Those used as weapons were primarily tin bronze, while tools might be copper or arsenical copper; lead bronze was only utilized for axes that were decorative rather than functional.

Roman coins (Oddy 1980)
The use of information derived from the analysis of metals is not restricted to the prehistoric period. Roman metallurgy has been extensively studied through examinations of ores, ingots, coins and manufactured objects. Evidently alloys could be prepared very accurately to match the properties of the metal to the function of the end product (Greene 1986, 143–9). Of particular

interest is how the principal Roman silver coin, the *denarius*, gradually lost its content of silver as successive emperors debased the metal in a desperate attempt to outstrip inflation. Under Augustus (27 BC–AD 14) *denarii* were as pure as possible, and contained 98% silver, but by the middle of the third century AD, when inflation and political chaos reigned, the silver content had fallen to 2–3%. Coins left the mint with a thin silver coating that soon wore off in use, leaving a coin that could only be differentiated from contemporary bronze issues by its size. The difference between early and late examples is obvious to the eye, but analysis has charted the decline in detail; it provides an interesting commentary on the contemporary economy and the political problems of rulers who authorized debasements (Greene 1986, 60–2).

Isotopic analysis (Sealy 1986)
Individual elements can be examined in more detail to establish which isotopes (elements with an abnormal number of electrons) are present, and in what proportions. The same procedure is used in AMS radiocarbon dating, where the proportion of carbon-14 in a sample relative to carbon-12 is measured. Studies of stable isotopes now assist in the study of Greek and Roman

architecture and sculpture. Although some forms of marble may be distinguished visually or under a microscope, the fine white marbles of Italy, Greece and Asia Minor have always presented difficulties. Analysis of the oxygen and carbon isotopes contained in their chemical structure now provides a method of separating them, and it allows styles of carving to be related to the areas where stone was quarried and prepared for use (Walker 1984; Hertz 1987). As in the case of obsidian, isotopic analysis had to begin with samples taken from quarries known to have been in use in the past, to characterize each of the main sources, before their products could be identified. In cases where quarries are not distinguishable by means of stable isotopes, trace elements provide a successful alternative approach.

Isotopic studies of metals show some promise for the examination of ancient trade (Gale 1991; Gale & Stos-Gale 1992). Four different isotopes occur naturally in lead, and their ratios have been used to characterize the sources of lead ores, and those of copper that contained natural lead impurities. The technique works well on ingots of metal that were lost before use, or objects that were made from fresh lead or bronze. It may even be possible to extend the technique to other artefacts that contained lead, but its usefulness will always be limited by the same problem of mixing scrap metal from several sources that also complicates the characterization of trace elements in bronze.

2.3 Provenance by date

Scientific dating and analysis occasionally converge. For example, geologists are able to determine the age of deposits of obsidian formed by volcanic activity by means of fission track dating (above, p. 125). If fragments of obsidian found on an archaeological site are examined by the same method, the dates obtained do not apply to the artefacts themselves, but to the formation of the raw material at its volcanic source. This date can then be matched to a deposit of obsidian formed at a corresponding date. As in obsidian characterization studies, accuracy depends on how many potential sources have been sampled and tested. Potassium-argon dating has been used in a similar way to identify the *origins* (rather than the date) of hones and whet-

stones found on Viking period sites in Britain; again, the raw material has been matched with volcanic rocks of the same type and geological age in Norway (Mitchell 1984).

3 Conservation
(Cronyn 1989; Oddy 1992)

Although conservation is one of the most important aspects of archaeological science experienced by visitors to sites and museums, it is easily overlooked.

3.1 Ancient objects
(Black 1987)

Whenever an ancient object is removed from the ground during an excavation it is immediately placed at risk, for the stable environment that has protected it from total decay since its burial has been lost. Objects in museum collections also require constant attention, whether during storage or in public displays. It is essential that an exact identification of the composition and structure of an object is made before conservation begins. The structure may sometimes be revealed by visual inspection, using a microscope if necessary, but a particularly complex artefact (or one that has become encased in a thick layer of corrosion) may require X-ray radiography to understand it (figs 5.5–7). Further analysis may be necessary to find out exactly which metals or other substances are involved, for these will dictate the form of treatment to be employed.

The most important task of conservation is to neutralize decay, whether caused by the corrosion of metals or the rotting of organic matter, and this requires a detailed knowledge of chemistry. The next stage is to stabilize the object so that decay will not start up again; even when treated successfully, objects that are intended for display in a museum will have to be monitored carefully to ensure that changes in temperature and humidity do not trigger further deterioration. Ethical issues are involved in conservation; a responsible archaeologist must plan the finance and facilities necessary for the preservation of finds, and no excavation is complete without at least 'first aid' facilities to minimize the onset of decay until full treatment is carried

137

5.5–7 Conservation of archaeological finds and their presentation for archaeological display involves many scientific and practical skills. This corroded metal object is an Anglo-Saxon buckle (seventh century AD) from the St Peter's Tip cemetery, Broadstairs, Kent. Iron corrosion had encrusted the entire object, and its decorative inlay of silver and brass was only visible in an X-ray (fig. 5.6). Conservation stabilized the decay of the artefact, and removed corrosion from the decorated surface (fig. 5.7) while preserving it on the back, where traces of the leather belt and textiles could be seen. *English Heritage/Cathy Haith, British Museum*

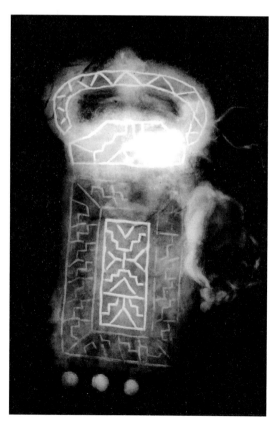

out. This is particularly important in the case of waterlogged or desiccated sites where artefacts made of wood, leather or textiles are likely to be found, for these organic materials decompose extremely quickly once they have been removed from a stable environment. The restoration of artefacts is also sensitive from an ethical point of view. A severely corroded or damaged object has little commercial value, but cleaning, stabilization and repair not only improve its display quality for a museum, but also increase its monetary value in the antiquities trade. Since the borderline between a heavily restored genuine artefact and a fake is sometimes difficult to draw, conservators must keep detailed records and photographs of all work that they have carried out. This is also important in cases where further treatment may be required later, or where researchers need to know the original form of the object. Video recordings now provide a convenient additional medium for recording conservation work.

3.2 Historic buildings and archaeological sites

(Hodges 1987)

Newly excavated structures soon suffer from exposure, and require permanent supervision if they are to be left on display. Wind, rain, frosts, plant growth and human erosion (by visitors or vandals) soon destroy apparently sound masonry structures. Buildings that have been visible for hundreds of years are increasingly vulnerable, for ancient stonework is easily damaged by air pollution in modern urban environments. Famous monuments, such as the Parthenon in Athens or Trajan's Column in Rome, have been disfigured by deposits of dirt, while fine details of their carvings have disappeared since accurate drawings and photographs were made in the nineteenth century. These problems will only be solved by a combination of science and good environmental management.

4 The Environment

(Shackley 1982; Bell & Walker 1992)

It is late November, outdoor work has come to a standstill. The winter rye has been sown and the young plants cover the fields already with a thin green carpet. Most of the cattle are still kept outside as long as the weather permits. The longer they can graze on the stubble of the summer crops, the better. It saves time in cleaning out the stalls and having to transport the farmyard manure to the fields. Moreover, one has to be economical with winter fodder nowadays. The pregnant cows have already been brought in to protect them from the early night frosts . . . The sheep, by day herded on the heath, are penned in during the nights in the outfield. The pigs fattened on acorns and beech-nuts in the forest are now again grubbing around the house, rooting up the soil of the garden plot and feeding on the remains of last summer's yield. (Groenman-van Waateringe & Wijngaarden-Bakker 1987, 4)

These 'reflections of a farmer in the early 10th century' are included in the report on an early medieval site excavated at Kootwijk, in the Netherlands. They provide an illuminating example of the value of environmental studies, for every detail is based upon evidence found on the site; they also emphasize the very human purpose of archaeological science.

The tendency to treat environmental archaeology as a separate discipline obscures the diversity of specialist skills that it draws upon. For example, an archaeologist engaged in studies of the early Stone Age requires a detailed knowledge of the plant and animal resources available to hunter-gatherers, an understanding of the prevailing climatic conditions, and information about human diet, diseases and life expectancy (Smith 1992). For this reason, from the early nineteenth century onwards excavators of prehistoric cave sites paid close attention to animal and plant remains, as well as to human bones and artefacts. A drought that lowered lake levels in Switzerland in 1853 led to the examination of many neolithic and Bronze Age settlements where not only wooden and bone artefacts were preserved, but also many remains of plants. The plentiful occurrence of waterlogged conditions in Scandinavia stimulated research into the environmental setting of humans in the past, notably through the definition of a series of 'climatic zones' characterized by changes in plant species since the last Ice Age (above p.112). Awareness of this work led Grahame Clark to excavate a waterlogged mesolithic hunter-gatherer site at Star Carr (Yorkshire, England) in 1949, with the express purpose of recovering a wide spectrum of botanical and zoological evidence to understand the economy and society of its inhabitants (Trigger 1989, 264–8).

Environmental factors have not always been taken sufficiently seriously in Roman and medieval studies, whether in the interpretation of sites or in the consideration of climatic influences upon history. The archaeology of Roman villas was for many years dominated by comparisons of architectural plans, wall paintings and mosaic floors, with little reference to the agriculture that formed the basis of the site's prosperity. Only rarely did excavation extend beyond the principal dwelling house to its barns and animal sheds, let alone to a full examination of excavated animal bones and plant remains (Greene 1986, 89–94).

4.1 The concept of 'sites'

The dubious significance and serious limitations of what archaeologists call 'sites' has been discussed in relation to landscape archaeology (above, p. 53). Few techniques used in environmental archaeology are restricted to individual 'sites' or excavations; humans are just as much part of a wider ecological system as other animals or plants. Broader aspects, such as climate and vegetation, provide a background setting for human activity, and the primary sources of evidence for these aspects do not come from excavations of habitation sites. More specific aspects, such as food gathering and production or the exploitation of natural resources, *can* be studied by means of evidence recovered from occupation sites, in the form of bones, shells and any organic materials that happen to survive.

4.2 The survival of environmental evidence

Archaeology in the New World has always taken a close interest in environmental aspects of sites because of the many different ways that native American cultures developed in diverse settings, from tropical rain-forests to temperate woodlands, and from plains to deserts. The superb preservation of organic remains on settlement sites in arid desert conditions in the south-west of the United States made the observation and examination of environmental evidence an obvious part of archaeology, in contrast to most European sites, where organic remains had disappeared through decay. The American sites also provided samples of ancient timber that could be used in early studies of climatic changes reflected by variations in tree-rings.

Although bones are normally found in tremendous numbers on most archaeological sites, with the addition of shells near coasts, damp acidic soils are likely to destroy everything except burnt bone. The most favourable conditions are alkaline subsoils and well-drained sands or gravels. Arid, waterlogged or permanently frozen conditions also assist the preservation of other organic materials besides bones, and whole bodies of humans and animals have been preserved in many parts of the world. Egyptian mummies are widely known, but equally striking are some Iron Age bodies found in bogs in Scandinavia and Britain, including 'Tollund Man' and 'Lindow Man', two individuals who both met a particularly grisly end as sacrificial victims. Frozen bodies, such as the Greenland mummies (medieval Inuits) or the late neolithic 'Ice Man' from the Alps, have been found complete with clothing and personal possessions that would have decayed completely under normal conditions. Amongst the Ice Man's property were a bag of dried mushrooms and some sloes, which indicate the good potential for the survival of very delicate substances (Spindler 1994).

Plant remains are also preserved in arid or wet conditions: wood survives well, as do pips, seeds, and the fibrous matter from leaves, stalks, etc. A surprising amount of information may still be gained from sites with ordinary soils, too. It has become common to be employ 'flotation' techniques on excavations to improve the recovery of very small bones from rodents, birds, reptiles and fish, as well as small shells and the remains of insects and plants. Burning may convert plants into charcoal under the right conditions, and many species of wood, grain, and other plant material may be identified. All of these have considerable significance for the final interpretation of the economy and environment of a site or other discovery.

Leather and textiles (some made from animal hair, others from plant fibres) were important raw materials in the past, but finds are absent from most sites. The study of those that have survived is therefore particularly significant if a fuller understanding of the exploitation of natural resources is to be achieved. The Basket-maker stages of the Anasazi tradition in the American south-west take their name from an organic raw material that normally perishes under European climatic conditions. Every archaeologist should make regular visits to a museum of ethnography or folk-life, and take note of the large number of significant items that would not survive on a normal archaeological site. Hairstyles, body paint, head-dresses and costume all play an important role in the identity of cultures and personal status (even in contemporary urban civilization), and it is impossible to have too many reminders about this major loss of knowledge about the past.

5 Climate

(Roberts 1989; Wigley 1981)

Long-term climatic change has been a fundamental factor in human development, seen at its most dramatic during the periods of extensive glaciation that have been known to geologists for more than 200 years. Recent research has not only confirmed the dates of major Ice Age episodes, but has also given accurate indications of global temperatures. Evidence over a geological time scale comes from variations in oxygen isotopes in **sea-bed deposits** (above, p. 113), while more recent indications are derived from annual layers in **ice-sheet cores** (above, p. 113). Ice layers overlap with records from tree-rings, and the results can be correlated with precise documentary evidence in recent centuries.

While long-term change is obviously important from an archaeological point of view, short-term fluctuations may have had an important impact on human life in the past – especially in farming communities. Ice-sheet cores are very interesting in this respect, for they contain clear records of volcanic eruptions, represented by layers containing high levels of dust and acidity. Volcanic ash in the upper atmosphere may cause severe disturbances to the weather by blocking solar radiation, and if these circumstances were prolonged for many years they could lead to changes in settlement patterns. The abandonment of upland settlements in northern Britain around the twelfth century BC has been attributed to this phenomenon, and supporting evidence comes from tree-rings that indicate a period of around twenty years' appalling cold and wet weather from 1159 BC.

Vegetation is an important measure of regional climatic change that has direct archaeological implications. Plants are very sensitive to temperature and moisture, and most species produce pollen. Fortunately, pollen grains resist decay well, so that cores taken from bogs or lake beds contain excellent records of wind-blown pollen (below, p. 143). The general pattern of change since the last Ice Age has been well known since the 1920s (see fig. 5.10), but samples are now dated by radiocarbon to produce a detailed history of vegetation on a regional level. The interpretation of pollen analysis as an indicator of human, as opposed to climatic, influences will also be examined below.

6 Rocks and soils

(Davidson & Shackley 1976; Holliday 1992)

The earlier the period of archaeology that is being studied, the more important geology is likely to be – particularly in phases related to Ice Ages. Geology and geomorphology are essential for understanding the present landscape and its past configurations, along with changes in sea level, erosion and the deposition of new land by sedimentation or volcanic activity. This information not only influences our concepts about the environmental context of human activities in the past, but also provides vital insights into the likelihood of finding sites and artefacts. The significance of early finds of bones and flint tools in deep gravel beds was only fully appreciated when geologists had studied their formation and understood the principles of stratification. In cases such as the hand-axes discovered at Hoxne or in the Somme valley (above, p. 11), the artefacts and the bones 'associated' with them had been eroded from their original resting places and redeposited in river gravels. Geology is also a key component in the study of early hominid fossils in East Africa, where many finds have been made in layers of sediment separated by volcanic material. It is very important to understand the stratification of these deposits, and to date them by the potassium-argon method and magnetic reversals (above, p. 128); expeditions around Lake Turkana in Kenya are actually planned according to the location of deposits already dated in this way (Leakey 1992).

6.1 Soil science

(Courty 1989)

A knowledge of geomorphology is also vital for reconstructing the wider environment of ancient sites in terms of natural resources. Surface deposits and outcrops of rock, combined with evidence for rivers and lakes, dictate the forms of vegetation and animal life available to hunter-gatherers or early farmers. An understanding of soils adds further detail, for soils with differing colours, textures and other characteristics are formed and changed both by natural and human activities (fig. 5.8). Maps of modern soils and 141

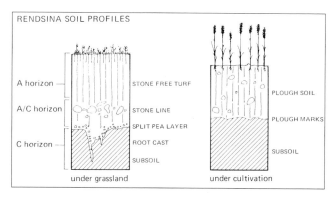

RENDSINA SOIL PROFILES

A horizon —
A/C horizon —
C horizon —

STONE FREE TURF
STONE LINE
SPLIT PEA LAYER
ROOT CAST
SUBSOIL

under grassland

PLOUGH SOIL
PLOUGH MARKS
SUBSOIL

under cultivation

5.8 The profile of a rendsina soil, commonly found on chalk, limestone, or gravel, has a clear structure if it has been under pasture for a long time (left). Earthworm activity will have made stones sink to a distinct layer, along with any large artefacts, such as coins or pottery, that have been deposited in the soil. Since it takes a considerable time for this structure to re-form after it has been disturbed by ploughing (right), a soil buried by an ancient earthwork can be examined to ascertain which kind of agriculture was responsible for its formation. *Audio Visual Centre, University of Newcastle, after Evans 1978, fig. 29*

their present agricultural potential are published in many countries, but they are not a reliable indicator of their state in the past. Modern fieldwork projects, such as the Neothermal Dalmatia survey outlined in chapter 2 (p. 54), take samples of soils to determine the history of land-use. Soil scientists need to take deep samples and are particularly keen to examine deposits that have been cut through by erosion or modern construction. When forests on hills are cleared for cultivation or grazing, an increase in erosion normally leads to the deposition of sediments in valleys, covering up earlier phases of valley-floor cultivation and settlement. Archaeological earthworks such as ramparts or burial mounds usually preserve an earlier ground surface (see fig. 3.3) that may also provide samples of pollen and/or molluscs (below, p. 151). Buried soils in these situations give important information about the vegetation or form of cultivation that took place immediately before they were built. Dated structures (such as the Antonine Wall in Scotland, constructed in the 130s and 140s AD) act as a *ter-*

minus ante quem for a buried soil.

Other characteristics of soils give clear indications of concentrations of settlement and agriculture, notably a high phosphate content (above, p. 50). Samples taken systematically over a wide area may help to define the limits of a settlement without extensive excavation; measurement of the levels of trace metals offers an addition or alternative to phosphate testing (Bintliff 1990). The acidity of a soil is a useful guide to the prospects for the survival of pollen and molluscs; if it is unfavourable, time need not be spent on fruitless collection and processing of inadequate samples.

Soils also provide evidence of past climate through **soil micromorphology** (Courty 1989), which is based on microscopic analyses of soil structures. The sizes and shapes of soil particles deposited by water during damp periods may be distinguished from wind-blown material that accumulated during periods of low rainfall. Soils are classified into types that provide interesting insights into human disturbance of the environment. A good example is provided by 'podsols' characteristic of heath and moorland. They only support a thin surface layer of vegetation, and overlie a layer of leached soil from which rain water has washed iron and humus down to the surface of the subsoil. However, the soils found under prehistoric earthworks erected on what is now moorland are frequently 'brownearths' typical of woodland, not podsols. Brownearths are stable when covered by trees, but when woodland is cleared, rainfall causes a deterioration to poorer podsols. Thus the harsh inhospitable soil conditions characteristic of open moorlands in much of upland Britain result from human interference. Clearance for occupation and agriculture eventually exhausted them and rendered them uninhabitable for later farmers, and the process was possibly accelerated by the spell of rapid climatic deterioration caused by volcanic activity (indicated by tree-rings: see p. 111). The destruction of the world's rain forests in the twentieth century is leading to a similar result, as the stable recycling of nutrients by trees is brought to an end, and alternations of extreme wet and dry conditions break down the structure of the soil.

7 Plant remains

(Jones 1988; Pearsall 1989)

The conditions that favour the survival of plant remains have been indicated above (p. 86). The larger the sample, the more reliable the results of their study are likely to be. Botanical identifications are time-consuming and expensive, but they are extremely important to the interpretation of an individual site or vegetation in general. Nineteenth-century botanists concentrated on large fragments of plants, but the focus in the twentieth century moved to microscopic pollen grains. Large items such as seeds and pips remain important, however, for they not only reveal the existence of plant species but also give insights into the collection and processing of wild fruits or crops from domesticated plants. Finds of particular species of cereal grains have implications for farming and harvesting methods, and further enlightenment about soil conditions is gained from studying seeds of weeds that grew amongst cereal crops (Veen 1992). One spectacular example of the study of plant remains is the investigation of the gardens of Pompeii, where the volcanic eruption of AD 79 sealed vineyards, orchards, vegetable plots and ornamental gardens under a thick layer of ash (Jashemski 1979). Grape-pips, nuts and fruit stones were recovered, but a bonus discovery was the existence of cavities in the earth where the roots of trees and other large plants had decayed. It was possible to pour plaster into these holes and then excavate the root system, which could be identified from its size and pattern. One open area once thought to have been a cattle market was found to have been filled with vines and olive trees, and to have had open-air dining couches amongst the foliage (Greene 1986, 94–7).

In contrast, indirect evidence of plants is also recovered in surprising ways. Impressions of grain are occasionally preserved on pottery; damp clay vessels were dried before firing, and their bases frequently picked up fragments of straw or grain from dry material that was probably spread out to prevent them from sticking. The organic matter burnt out completely during firing, leaving hollow voids from which casts can be taken with latex or plaster. These are examined under a microscope to identify the species present. Pottery can also be examined to detect food residues absorbed into the clay during cooking. Evidence for cabbage (or turnip) was identified from epicuticular leaf wax components at the Anglo-Saxon settlement at Raunds (Northants); no other evidence for soft plant tissues had survived (Evershed 1991; 1992). Work on a site on the Solomon Islands has recently demonstrated that starch residues from plants are occasionally visible on stone tools, if they are examined under high magnification by a Scanning Electron Microscope (Loy 1992). This kind of evidence extends the range of information about plants to food preparation and cooking.

The domestication of wild plants in the early stages of settled farming is a process of profound significance that may be investigated through the remains of plants. Research in Central America and south-east Asia indicates that a much wider range of species was involved than in Europe and the Near East. Maize was a key food source in Mesoamerica, and finds of cobs in stratified deposits show that their size gradually increased. American food plants are of particular interest because they spread to the rest of the world after European contacts began in 1492; the European diet would be very much less varied today without potatoes, tomatoes, peanuts, peppers and pineapples (Gowlett 1984, 170–1). The prospects for future research are expanding now that methods for extracting ancient DNA from ancient seeds or cereal grains are beginning to succeed (Allaby 1994). In a reflection on recent progress, Jones concluded that:

> . . . advances in molecular, chemical and radiometric analyses have set a new agenda for bio-archaeology. The direct examination of surviving fragments of past human food webs is gradually being liberated from those questions they were least suited to answer, and instead, through analyses with these newer techniques, can provide the qualitative framework for a much more structured examination of the particular place of humans in past food webs. (1992, 216)

7.1 Pollen analysis

(Dimbleby 1985; Moore 1991)

The most productive technique that has been applied to archaeological plant remains is undoubtedly **palynology** – the study of pollen.

All hay-fever sufferers know that the air is full of wind-borne pollen during the summer months. Fortunately for archaeologists each minute grain of pollen has a tough outer shell of a different shape for each species (fig. 5.9). These shells survive well in soils whose acidity is sufficiently high to reduce the bacterial activity that would normally cause them to decay. The loss of pollen from alkaline soils, such as those of the densely occupied and farmed chalklands of England and northern France, is unfortunate, but these soils are favourable to the survival of molluscs that also provide environmental information (below, p. 151). The toughness of pollen grains allows them to be separated from samples of soil collected on sites by straightforward laboratory methods, but they must then be identified and counted under a microscope by an experienced palynologist – a very time-consuming task. Most grains are less than 100th of a millimetre in diameter (fig. 5.9); their abundance makes counting a tedious procedure, but it has the advantage that statistically significant quantities are easily obtained from small samples of soil.

Since palynology is able to monitor general changes in climate and vegetation over long periods, it is of considerable interest to climatologists, ecologists, botanists and geographers as well as to archaeologists. Samples of pollen taken from cores bored from deep peat bogs or lake sediments are stratified, with the earliest part lying deepest. A deposit that has formed over thousands of years should reflect overall changes from tundra to forest or from forest to farmland, and indicate fluctuations in the prominence of individual plant species (fig. 5.10). Sufficient analyses have been made to give a fairly clear picture of the major changes of vegetation since the last Ice Age, and to define a series of climatic 'zones' that formed a valuable form of dating before the arrival of the radiocarbon technique (above, p. 112). These zones of climate and vegetation provide a general context for human activities, such as early Stone Age hunting on the open tundra, or mesolithic hunting and gathering in forests. When a picture of background vegetation is added to other plant remains, artefacts and animal bones from an excavated settlement, there is an increased possibility of accurate interpretation of past economies and the functions of tools and weapons. The application of palynology is world-wide, and its value is not restricted to prehistoric times. It can be used to examine the environment of individual sites or regions in periods before documents provided such information in sufficient detail.

One key issue that may be studied through pollen analysis is the appearance of the first settled neolithic farming communities. It represents a momentous stage in human development, both in terms of exploitation of the environment and social organization. The neolithic economy required permanent buildings to be erected and for land to be cleared of trees for pasture and arable land. The destruction of woodland is

5.9 Different plant species have distinctive pollen grains whose tough outer shells can be identified by specialists in the laboratory. This drawing shows important trees found in postglacial deposits: alder, birch, hazel, hornbeam, oak, elm, lime, beech and pine. *Zeuner 1946, fig. 21 (after Godwin)*

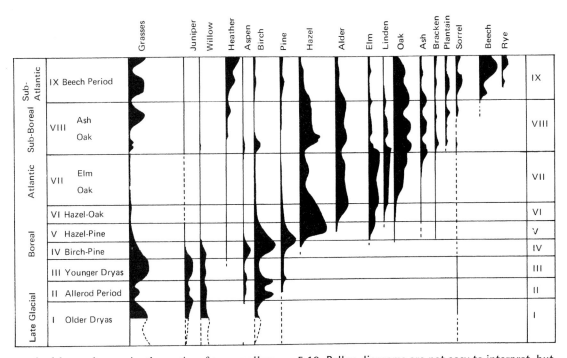

5.10 Pollen diagrams are not easy to interpret, but the method of presentation is similar to that of seriation in that the thickness of the line for each individual species reflects its relative importance. This diagram of vegetation in Jutland incorporates Dr J Iversen's results from numerous samples that revealed the recolonization of Denmark by significant plants since the last Ice Age. The earliest period is at the bottom of the diagram, where in stages I–III, grasses and small hardy trees (birch, willow, juniper) dominated the cold landscape. From V onwards, temperate tree species appeared as warmer conditions developed, replacing open grassland. Human actions began to have marked effects in VIII, when forest was cleared to supply fuel, timber and open land for cultivation and grazing. Grasses became common again, and signs of farming are evident from cereals and the 'weeds of cultivation', such as plantain, associated with them. *Audio Visual Centre, University of Newcastle*

marked by a change in the ratio of tree-pollen (TP) to non-tree-pollen (NTP) in stratified deposits; thus, even if no neolithic sites have been discovered in a particular region, the pollen record may indicate their existence. TP declines, NTP rises, and tell-tale species of grasses and cereals appear, together with 'weeds of cultivation' that thrived in the new conditions. Fine particles of charcoal may also be detected, showing that forest clearance involved burning. The appearance of signs of a Neolithic economy in a pollen sample can be dated by radiocarbon, and their presence may provide a spur to fieldwork to locate the settlement sites that belonged to the first farming communities. In comparison with their use in prehistoric archaeology, environmental approaches to historical periods are still in their infancy, but have great potential (Greene 1986, 72–6; 126–8).

Because most pollen is deposited within a few miles of its source, it can provide a picture of the plant population in the immediate surroundings of an individual site. A site that occupied a small clearing in a forest would have a high proportion of tree-pollen (TP) to non-tree-pollen (NTP), whereas a settlement in open country would show the reverse. TP and NTP may also be examined in terms of individual species or groups of related plants. NTP may highlight different proportions of grasses and cereals that indicate the relative importance of grazing and grain production in the economy of a site, while pollen from plants such as legumes, flax and hemp may indicate other forms of food production and raw materials

145

for textiles. Samples of pollen taken from soil buried beneath mounds or ramparts may tell the archaeologist whether the land was forested or covered with scrub before its occupation. The soil that formed after the abandonment of a site may show whether the land returned to scrub and then forest, or remained open, perhaps as part of the farmland of another settlement nearby. Further questions of direct relevance to an excavator may be answered by palynology. Mounds and ramparts can be examined to see if their material was dug from the subsoil, in which case it will contain a mixture of contemporary and older fossil pollen, or whether they were formed by scraping up turf or topsoil from the surface. This kind of information may help in the interpretation of ditches, pits, etc., on a complex site, and clarify their relationships to the construction of earthwork features (Shackley 1982, 31).

7.2 Tree-rings

(Schweingruber 1988)

Besides their value for dating (above, p. 109), tree-rings provide a continuous annual record of climate. The correlation between modern meteorological records of temperature and precipitation and the width of individual rings seems sufficiently close to allow them to be used to make estimates of conditions in the past before such records began (Schweingruber 1988, 170–5), but caution is still advised (Baillie 1992). At the opposite end of the scale, the pattern of tree-rings in an individual trunk is influenced by the location of the tree. Minor fluctuations in the immediate locality, such as fire damage, insect attack, clearance of surrounding trees, drought or flooding, may all leave tell-tale indications in the rings (ibid. 176–83). A useful result of this degree of sensitivity is that timbers used in a building or a ship reflect the nature of the woodland where they grew. Trees from dense forests display different ring patterns from those that grew in open spaces or hedgerows, for example. Ring patterns characteristic of a particular area allow the origins of wood to be determined, revealing, for example, that a Viking ship excavated in Denmark was constructed in Ireland.

An unexpected by-product of tree-ring dating is the detection of phases of exploitation of the landscape, reflected by the age of tree trunks preserved in river silts. During the Roman occupation of southern Germany, very large numbers of trunks from mature trees up to 400 years old ended up in the Danube. It is likely that agriculture was intensified in response to the presence of Roman forts and towns, and that there was an increased demand for timber, both for building purposes and fuel. These factors led to woodland clearance and soil erosion, resulting in an increase in the amount of sediment that was washed into rivers. This caused flooding that swept away mature trees growing some distance from the normal course of the river (Schweingruber 1988, 186).

Many other precisely dated climatic episodes are suggested by tree-rings. That they are so closely dated provides an invitation for archaeologists to scrutinize all sorts of evidence to seek wider evidence for changes caused by climatic phenomena. Even major changes, such as the transition from hunting and gathering to farming in the British Isles, may prove to have been associated with climatic events revealed by tree-rings. Baillie concluded a paper on these events with an optimistic judgement: 'There appears to be unlimited potential for the reconstruction of various aspects of past environmental change from tree-ring records' (1992, 20).

8 Animal remains

8.1 Animal bones

(Davis 1987; Rackham 1994)

The principal task of a zoologist confronted with a collection of ancient bones is to identify the species that are represented. The zoologist must have experience of archaeological samples, and may need to consult reference collections of bones from other excavations. Domesticated animals in particular differ considerably from their modern counterparts, and closely related animals like sheep and goats are difficult to separate from each other. Another important task is to estimate the number of animals involved. It is not sufficient simply to count the bones, for while some animals may be represented by just one bone, there may be many from others. It is customary to count specific bones to estimate the minimum and maximum number of individual animals required to produce the sample; the larger the collection available, the more accurate these estimates will be. The approximate ages of individual animals may be ascertained by examining the state of ossification of particular bone structures, the eruption of teeth in jaw bones, and the amount of wear on teeth. Sex is more difficult to establish, but statistical studies of large samples of bones may help to divide them into groups of different sizes, of which the smaller is likely to represent females (fig. 5.11).

Interpretation (Grayson 1984; Clutton-Brock 1988) It is important to understand the nature of any context from which bones have been recovered. Other finds, such as datable pot-sherds, may indicate whether it formed over a long or short period, and the condition of the bones themselves may also tell something about the circumstances of formation. Weathered, broken bones with signs of damage from rodents or scavenging animals are readily distinguishable from those that were buried immediately, and this information will of course be valuable to the excavator as well as the bone specialist. Obviously, it would be a waste of a specialist's time to interpret bones from a disturbed deposit. It may be necessary to conduct scientific tests to check the consistency of early prehistoric deposits that lack closely datable finds (above, p. 125).

Once reliable deposits have been recognized, and the species and numbers of the animals identified, many further observations are possible (fig. 5.12). A factor that needs to be taken into account is the effect of human selection on the sample of bones that survives. Hunters may well have butchered the carcasses of large animals where they were killed, leaving the majority of bones far from their living sites (Smith 1992, 28–34; 105–7). Furthermore, bones discarded by humans are frequently exploited by scavenging animals, such as wild hyenas or domestic dogs; experimental work has shown that different kinds of bones have varying chances of surviving scavenging (Marian 1992). Bones found on a hunter-gatherer site that was only occupied for part of the year may give a very limited view of the inhabitants' exploitation of animals; other camps may have been associated with the same groups of people at different times according to

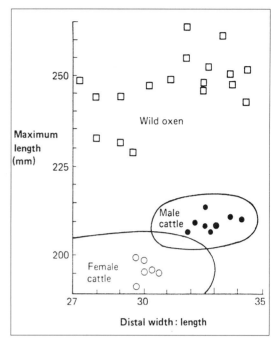

5.11 Detailed measurements of neolithic animal bones from a site at Troldebjerg, Denmark, revealed three distinct groups that probably reflect differences between wild and domesticated cattle, and separate sex groups within the latter. As with the characterization of obsidian (see fig. 5.3) careful statistical analysis of significant measurements, or ratios between measurements, may be required to reveal such differences. *Audio Visual Centre, University of Newcastle, after Evans 1978, fig. 16*

the seasonal availability of animals, fish, molluscs and plants.

Where a site was a permanent human habitation belonging to a period after the introduction of farming, different questions can be asked about food supply and diet. To what extent did the occupants still exploit wild animals along with domesticated species, and how much meat could be obtained from the animals found? The age structure of animal populations is particularly important for the analysis of farming practices. The inhabitants may have enjoyed the luxury of eating succulent young animals, or it may have been necessary to maximize the use of cows and sheep for milk and wool until they were several years old. Bones from towns present additional problems: rubbish associated with houses may

147

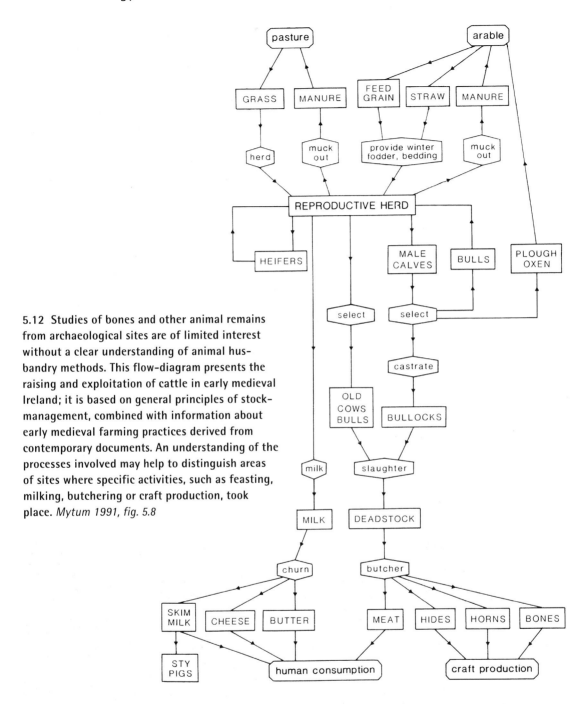

5.12 Studies of bones and other animal remains from archaeological sites are of limited interest without a clear understanding of animal husbandry methods. This flow-diagram presents the raising and exploitation of cattle in early medieval Ireland; it is based on general principles of stock-management, combined with information about early medieval farming practices derived from contemporary documents. An understanding of the processes involved may help to distinguish areas of sites where specific activities, such as feasting, milking, butchering or craft production, took place. *Mytum 1991, fig. 5.8*

offer insights into diet, but care must be taken to distinguish it from waste from butchers' shops or industrial workshops where bone was used as a raw material for making artefacts. Sites occupied over a long period with good stratified collections of bones offer additional possibilities for comparisons between food supply and animal husbandry practices at different times. However, care must be taken to test the validity of any conclusions that are drawn, especially where collections of different scales are concerned; some straightforward statistical probability tests measure the significance of any interesting observations (below, p. 155).

The most important aspect of the study of bones is that the *nature* of an excavated context must always be looked at very closely. Bones found on sites reflect living populations of hunted or domesticated animals in different ways, and a sample recovered from an excavation may not be representative of the whole site. In one enlightening case in North America, the excavated bones could be compared with the documented history of an eighteenth-century British fort. The number of animals represented by bones would only have been sufficient to feed the fort's occupants for a single day, but a garrison of varying strength was in occupation for eight years. The soldiers' diet consisted largely of boneless salt pork brought to the site from elsewhere (Guilday 1970).

Besides identifying species and calculating the numbers of animals represented by a collection of bones, and their sex and age, specialists may be able to glean further information from bones. Hunting techniques may be deduced from injuries, and butchery practices are sometimes revealed by ways that the bones were cut or broken. The exploitation of animals for transport and traction has important social implications. Evidence that horse-riding began around 4000 BC in the Ukraine was found through a study of surface wear on horse teeth, using a scanning electron microscope (Anthony Brown 1991) (fig. 5.13) Signs of rope-marks on the horns of neolithic cattle found at Bronocice in Poland (*c.* 3000 BC) probably indicate that the animals had been used to pull ploughs or vehicles. This interpretation was reinforced by the discovery that many of the cattle bones from the site were from oxen, and that some were aged up to 5 or 10 years – much too old for the production of beef or dairy products (Milisauskas & Kruk 1991).

DNA recovered from animal bones offers great potential for confirming difficult identifications of species or sex, and for studying the processes of domestication by examining the genetic links between wild and domesticated animals

5.13 Photomicrographs taken with a scanning electron microscope (SEM) provide images with a depth of focus that allows artefact surfaces, plant remains, etc., to be studied in almost three-dimensional detail. The technique has been used extensively in use-wear analysis, and is proving valuable in the study of ancient textiles, both for the identification of plant and animal fibres and for detecting signs of wear resulting from manufacture or use. These images show heavily worn woolen leg-bindings from Vindolanda, a Roman fort near Hadrian's Wall, enlarged 50 and 500 times. It is hoped that DNA studies may eventually add further precision to the identification of the plants and animals from which fibres were converted into textiles. *Dr J-P Wild/W D Cooke, Manchester Ancient Textile Unit*

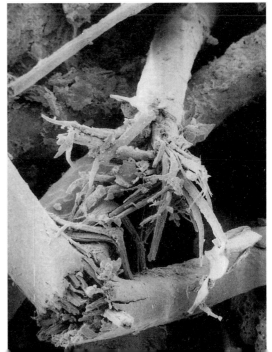

(Brown 1992, 19). Another fascinating line of research is offered by the fact that animal blood and hairs may sometimes be found on prehistoric tools. As with indirect evidence for plants (above, p. 143), DNA study of these traces extends the range of information about animals to the stages of food processing and consumption (Loy & Hardy 1992).

In some cases studies of animal bones merge imperceptibly into dating methods. Bones of pigs and elephants are much more common in East African geological deposits than those of humans, and their evolutionary development is well established. Thus, fieldworkers searching for human fossils make a rough estimation of the age of a deposit without resorting to scientific dating methods, and this will also highlight discrepancies between scientific dates and the **biostratigraphic** date derived from the animals' evolutionary stages (Johanson & Shreeve 1991, 92–101).

The following sections outline the study of fish bones and molluscs; space does not permit the discussion of many other interesting kinds of animal remains, such as insects and parasites. These remains reveal fascinating insights into the environment, living conditions, diet and health of humans in the past (Buckland & Coope 1991; Jones 1988).

8.2 Fish bones
(Brinkhuizen & Clason 1986; Wheeler & Jones 1989)

Sieving and flotation techniques have improved the recovery of bones from small mammals, birds, reptiles, amphibians and fish. Unlike all the others, fish bones appear on archaeological sites on dry land as a direct result of human activity. Unfortunately fish bones have a much lower chance of survival than animal bones because of their small size and cartilaginous consistency. Interesting (if rather distasteful) experiments have been conducted on the survival of modern fish bones that have passed through the digestive systems of pigs, dogs and humans. Less than 10% of the bones of medium-sized fish survived, with the implication that the importance of fish in the diet will be underestimated on many sites, even

when small fragments have been recovered by sieving (Jones 1986). If rats were common on a site, bones that they gnawed and digested could disappear altogether.

Nevertheless, the few bones that do survive allow species to be identified; **otoliths** ('ear stones') survive rather better, and they may be used to estimate the size and age of fish. This information gives insights into food gathering strategies, and the range of habitats reveals the extent of fishing, whether in local ponds and streams or far out to sea. Otoliths also reveal seasonal exploitation of fishing, because they incorporate growth rings similar to those visible in mollusc shells. Otoliths from a mesolithic midden at Cnoc Coig (Inner Hebrides) demonstrated that most saithe (a cod-like fish) were caught in the autumn (Smith 1992, 155–7). An indirect indication of fish and other marine resources may be obtained by examining carbon-12 and carbon-13 isotopes in the bones of humans or animals, for their ratio is influenced by a diet that contains seafood (below, p. 153).

8.3 Shells

Shells found in archaeological deposits fall into two distinct categories. Some were brought to settlements from the sea-shore and discarded after their contents had been eaten, and are informative about diet and the exploitation of marine resources. Others belonged to land molluscs that lived on the site; many of these are extremely small and can only be separated from samples of soil under laboratory conditions, but they provide valuable insights into the local environment.

Marine shells (Stein 1992)
Large mounds of discarded shells (**middens**) are found along many coastlines, providing evidence of extensive marine exploitation in the past. The food potential of shells is fairly simple to calculate, but deeper insights may be gained by more detailed observations. The size and shape of common species, such as the limpet, show whether they were collected at random or whether particularly large examples were chosen at low tide; a limpet shell's shape varies according to how far below the high water mark it lived. Non-random collection would obviously imply planned exploitation, perhaps indicating a

150

greater dependence on shellfish than on other food sources. Measurements of oxygen isotopes present in the edges of shells reveals whether collecting took place all year round or only seasonally (fig. 5.14). Since the proportions of these isotopes vary according to the prevailing temperature, middens associated with summer camps should show uniform proportions, while permanent sites should contain the range found in a whole year. As an alternative to isotopic study, seasonal growth patterns can be seen in cross-sections of the shells of some species (Smith 1992, pl. vi b). Native Americans exploited soft-shell clams on the Atlantic coasts of North America, and the growth patterns found in middens reveal a collection strategy based on intensive autumn harvesting (Lightfoot 1993). Oxygen isotope analysis of samples from deeply stratified sites may also document longer term climatic fluctuations that can be checked against the presence or absence of particular species that are sensitive to temperature conditions. First-order radiocarbon dating provides a useful means of dating shell deposits found during fieldwork, at a fraction of the cost of conventional methods (above, p. 122).

Sea shells are not always evidence of diet, particularly when found inland. Large examples may act as containers, spoons and even tools, while the Mediterranean *murex* provided purple dye. Other exotic uses, such as charms, jewellery and even ceremonial trumpets, have been recorded by archaeologists and ethnographers. Strontium isotope dating has demonstrated that *spondylus* shells found widely throughout neolithic Europe really were modern specimens gathered around the Mediterranean coasts, rather than fossil examples collected from geological deposits (Shackleton & Elderfield 1990). These examples demonstrate again that the scientific skills of marine biologists are needed to identify shell species and subject them to various forms of analysis, but, as with other scientific and technical information, the results require careful interpretation by archaeologists.

Land molluscs (Evans 1973)

Land molluscs (mainly snails: Evans 1973) range from large edible species to forms only visible and identifiable with the help of a microscope.

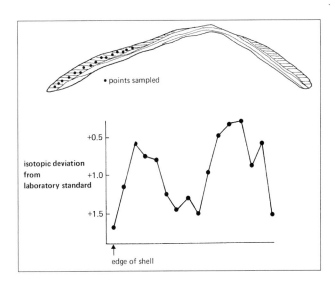

5.14 Analysis of mollusc shells can provide information about sea temperatures. The balance between different oxygen isotopes incorporated into this limpet shell during two years' growth shows fluctuations that reflect the temperature of the sea. Since the peaks of the graph indicate summers, the shell evidently stopped growing in winter. Thus, studies of large numbers of shells from human occupation sites can show whether harvesting took place all year round, or in one particular season. *Audio Visual Centre, University of Newcastle, after Evans 1978, fig. 26*

Species recovered from ancient soils or geological deposits reflect variations in the climate during successive Ice Ages and warmer periods. They mirror changes in temperature in the same way as vegetation (p. 144), and their distributions in the past may be compared with their modern habitats in exactly the same manner. Of more direct relevance to archaeology is that hundreds of small shells may be recovered from layers of soil. Samples are sorted into groups of species that prefer grassland or woodland, open or shaded localities, etc. Thus, the snail species found in a ground surface buried beneath a structure such as a rampart or burial mound will indicate whether it was erected on open heath (if light-loving grassland species are dominant) or in freshly cleared forest (if species that live in dark and damp woodland conditions are more numerous). A particularly gruesome illustration of this technique comes from the Roman city

151

of Cirencester in Gloucestershire, where several human skeletons were found in a roadside ditch within the city. The snail species found inside a skull favoured a damp dark habitat, but not an underground one, implying that the body had not been buried, but had rotted where it lay in the overgrown ditch. This find clearly implies a decline in civic life at the end of the Roman period, and it has been suggested that the bodies were victims of a plague that led to the desertion of the city in the fifth century AD. This example typifies how scientific evidence may be used as the basis for archaeological hypotheses that would be very difficult to develop in any other way (Wacher 1974, 313).

A further advantage of land snails is that they survive well on calcareous soils that do not favour the preservation of pollen. In practice, they reflect a much more local environment, for pollen is scattered over many miles by wind. Ideally, both sources of evidence should be examined together to establish the general and immediate environment of a site.

9 Human remains

(Ortner & Puschan 1985; Zivanovic 1982; Boddington *et al.,* 1987; Price 1989)

The questions asked about human remains tend to be rather different from those asked about animal bones or shells, which were normally disposed of along with domestic rubbish. Evidence for early prehistoric people is very fragmentary, especially the fossil bones from the geological deposits in East Africa that are so important for tracing the emergence of modern species (Leakey 1992). Human remains were regularly treated with more respect 35,000 years ago, and even at this date complete bodies were buried with 'grave goods'. Objects placed in graves help to date burials and may indicate ritual activities or hint at the social status of the deceased. Where soil conditions allow, burials allow complete skeletons to be recovered for study, and this offers the possibility of establishing the cause of death, which demands the expertise of a pathologist. The study of well-preserved bodies is like an excavation itself, involving X-ray examination, dissection and the study of all the materials encountered, whether fibres of clothing, skin tissues, or food remains (fig. 5.15). The most famous examples are of course Egyptian mummies (David 1987), but other notable finds range from the bog bodies that are fairly common in northern Europe, for example the Iron Age Lindow Man from England (Stead 1986), to frozen bodies of medieval Inuit from Greenland (Hansen 1991) or the remarkable late neolithic 'Ice Man' found in the Alps (Spindler 1994). These bodies result from intentional burial, ritual murder and accidental death; each category offers different insights into ancient societies.

Multiple burials are common, where bodies have been jumbled together in collective tombs over long periods, or where cremated bones were emptied into burial chambers in irretrievable confusion. To complicate matters further, incomplete bodies were sometimes buried after the corpse had been exposed to the elements and scavenging birds and mammals. This practice is well known from native American peoples and modern inhabitants of New Guinea, as well as on many excavated prehistoric sites. Expert work on burials at the Anglo-Saxon royal cemetery at Sutton Hoo (Suffolk) has demonstrated that careful excavation of soils of subtly differing colour and texture may reveal outlines of decayed flesh and bones that have been destroyed by the acidic sandy soil (Carver 1992). Burials where the body was cremated, and the surviving fragments of bone were crushed and placed into an urn or other container, are less favourable for scientific study.

Given reasonably well-preserved remains, the techniques employed in the study of human bones are very similar to those applied to animal remains. Age may be estimated from a number of osteological developments, such as the fusion of the skull bones and the growth of teeth. Sex may be determined (with some difficulty) from the sizes of various parts of the skeleton, while stature may be estimated from comparisons with modern people – although discrepancies of several centimetres exist between different systems of measurement. Pathologists examine deformities and evidence of disease ranging from malnutrition, arthritis and dental decay to the erosion of bone

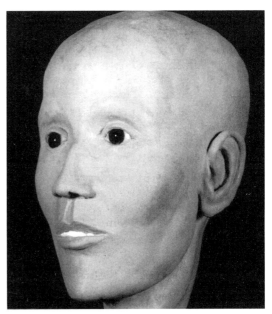

5.15 The ghostly image on the left, a computer generated stacked-image axial scan of an Egyptian mummy, was produced using medical equipment. The scanner records a series of sections through the body in digital form and stores them in a computer. The data may then be manipulated on a screen to present a three-dimensional image (*right*) that can be rotated for viewing from different angles, or modified to show tissues and bone of different densities. This information allowed an expert in facial reconstruction (Brian Hill, Newcastle Dental Hospital) to model the features of the dead woman, last seen by embalmers 3500 years ago. The finished head of Bakt-Hor-Nekht (with appropriate hair, jewellery and clothing) now forms part of an attractive museum display that not only generates public interest in Egyptology, but also demonstrates one way in which modern technology enhances our perception of the past.
Liz Watson, Hancock Museum; Michael Myres, Royal Victoria Infirmary, Newcastle upon Tyne

through leprosy, as well as injuries, whether healed or fatal. Diet may be investigated through the analysis of carbon isotopes, or trace elements such as strontium, contained in bones; their ratios or levels may indicate a preponderance of seafood, maize or rice. Samples derived from bone collagen limit analysis to the last 10,000 years, but studies of tooth enamel may allow these techniques to be extended to early hominids (Van der Merwe 1992).

Archaeologists need to scrutinize evidence provided by the examination of human bones particularly closely. It is very difficult to estimate the age structure and physical well-being (or otherwise) of a population because it is impossible to tell whether burials recovered from a particular culture (if soil conditions allow their preservation) represent the dead of all levels of society, or simply a social élite. Were primitive people tall, healthy, 'noble savages', or diseased, short-lived, stunted individuals for whom life was 'nasty, brutish, and short'? Roman gravestones frequently commemorate persons of advanced age, but memorials were presumably only erected for individuals of high social standing whose lifestyle favoured longevity. Nevertheless, excavated remains and tombstones combine to confirm the general impression that few individuals lived to a great age, while infant mortality was high and many young women died in childbirth or as a result of it (Hedges 1983). Only very rarely do archaeologists uncover a large number of bodies that might represent a true cross-section of society – for example, a community of 486 native Americans massacred around AD 1325 at Crow Creek, South Dakota (Willey 1992), or citizens of Herculaneum and Pompeii, who perished during the eruption of Vesuvius in AD 79. Even then there is always a high chance that young able-bodied individuals had

153

already made their escape.

Ideally, evidence derived from the pathological study of human remains should be integrated with other information. A study of this kind has been conducted in southern California, where sites around the Santa Barbara Channel dating from the eighteenth century AD back to 7200 BC were examined (Lambert & Walker 1991). A decline in tooth disease accompanied by a rise in arthritis seems to reflect a shift from the consumption of vegetables and tubers to fish and sea-mammal meat, while an increase in deaths from infectious diseases and poorer nutrition coincided with the growth of sedentary villages. Evidence for violent conflict existed at most times, represented by head injuries and embedded projectile points, but it showed a notable increase when the bow and arrow were introduced around AD 500. Evidence for social and cultural change deduced from burials and settlement sites was also correlated with periods of temperature change and drought known from tree-ring data.

9.1 Genetics

(Jones 1993)

Work is progressing rapidly on the recovery of DNA and blood proteins from bones or (when preserved) other body tissues (Brown 1992; Cattaneo 1991). At a basic level, DNA indicates the sex of a deceased individual – not always possible from skeletal remains. It also offers the possibility of studying whether bodies found in a cemetery come from related family groups. Like existing studies of blood groups, this information might prove useful on a broader scale in charting ethnic continuity or change-over periods when artefacts seem to indicate the arrival of external influences. Change may result from peaceful contact and trade, or migrations by invaders and settlers (Sokal 1987). Great difficulties are involved, for it will take many years before sufficient samples have been studied to define recognizable groups in historical periods; the situation may be slightly easier in prehistoric populations that have not yet undergone too much confusing interaction. It is now well established that the genetic diversity of all native Americans is so small that the entire population of both continents probably descends from a rel-atively small number of pioneers who crossed the Bering Straits from Russia to Alaska in around 20,000 BC (Jones 1993, 122–3). Arguments about the emergence and spread of early hominids should eventually be settled by means of mitochondrial DNA inherited through the maternal line. At present it suggests that all modern humans originated in a population living in East Africa little more than 100,000 years ago, and that the rest of the world was gradually peopled from this source, replacing earlier species (Leakey 1992, 218–28). Studies of DNA demand extreme care in the selection, preservation and handling of specimens to avoid modern contamination (Hedges and Sykes 1992). Furthermore, 'the interpretation must of course take into account the whole range of archaeological evidence pertaining to the question being asked, and should also consider ancient biomolecules other than DNA' (Brown 1992, 21).

9.2 The study of coprolites

Human coprolites (solid excreta) preserved on arid sites in the south-western United States, Mexico and South America have made a notable contribution to research into the natural resources available to early native American cultures. The arid conditions ensure the preservation of fibrous matter that has passed through the human digestive system, including fragments of bone, skin, scales, hair, feathers and meat, as well as pieces of insects, parasites and their eggs. Plant fibres and seeds are also found, together with microscopic pollen and 'plant opals' (distinctively shaped silica crystals formed by some plants). Even soft tissues from plants and animals can be extracted and identified by careful processing and sieving of rehydrated coprolites. Large collections recovered from latrine deposits allow detailed surveys of the diet of the occupants of a site to be made. If deposits of different dates are recorded from a particular site or area, long-term changes of diet may be charted and related to variations in the availability of foodstuffs.

Coprolites may also contain eggs of parasitic worms that once infested the digestive tract of a living human (Horne 1985). Conversely, where environmental conditions do not favour the survival of coprolites, soil samples can be analysed to detect parasite eggs, whose presence may help to explain the function of latrines or pits. Parasites that infest a specific animal species are valuable indicators; eggs from a nematode associated with horses were found in early military deposits on a Roman site at Carlisle, Cumbria, where some buildings had already been suggested to be stables (Jones 1988).

10 Statistics

(Shennan 1988; Fletcher & Lock 1991)

Archaeology is full of intuitive statements based on experience rather than calculation. Simple statistics are useful for checking almost any statements that involve comparisons, such as claims that the dimensions of a type of artefact change over time, or that settlement sites of a particular period tend to occupy one particular kind of soil. **Probability testing** is appropriate in these circumstances. In the latter case, the number of sites located on each soil type should be counted, and a simple statistical analysis will compare the totals with the numbers that would have occurred if the distribution had been entirely random. The results are expressed as a significance level; most sciences demand a level of at least 0.05, at which the figures observed have only a 1 in 20 probability of occurring by chance. Statistical tests also take account of the size of a sample, and data may have to be rejected if the sample is too small. Similar tests may also be conducted on the distribution patterns of sites or artefacts, and again the basis is a measurement of the difference from a random scatter. An understanding of probability is of growing importance in radiocarbon dating, for the calculation of dates from laboratory samples always involves estimates of error. This has to be taken into account when a calendar date is calculated from a calibration curve, for it has a built-in margin of error.

Correlation is another common statistical measure used by archaeologists. The relationship between any two sets of numerical variables may be tested by plotting them on a scatter diagram, and observing the pattern that results. A simple example might be to plot the length and breadth of Anglo-Saxon timber buildings (see fig. 3.30) to test the uniformity of their ratio. A straight line on the graph would indicate that the builders shared a uniform concept of proportions, irrespective of size, whereas a wide scatter of variables would indicate that buildings were constructed without any such guiding principles. The degree of correlation may be calculated, ranging from a maximum of 1.0 (if all buildings were always exactly twice as long as they were wide) to 0.0 (if there was no relation at all). When the sample size is taken into account, the degree of correlation may also be expressed as a level of significance. Julian Richards used extensive tests of correlations and significance levels to investigate Anglo-Saxon burials, and discovered subtle relationships between grave goods and the sex, age or social standing of the deceased. Various factors, such as the height of pots or their decorative motifs, were found to be significant in ways that would not have been noticed without a careful numerical analysis (Richards 1987).

An awareness of probability and correlation also leads to a better understanding of **sampling**. If a statistical study carried out on the dimensions of a class of 400 axes, for example, found that they could be divided into 3 separate classes according to their length in relation to their breadth, the results would be expressed in terms of levels of probability. This would estimate the likelihood that the 3 divisions had occurred by chance in a sample of 400 items. It would then be possible to work out the *minimum* number of axes that would have to have been measured to give a significant result. This is an important concept in planning research, whether it is related to objects or fieldwork; most modern field survey projects, such as the Dalmatian project described in chapter 2, are designed with a clear sampling strategy in mind (above, p. 54). Sampling is the mathematical expression of what is known colloquially as the law of diminishing returns.

Scientific analyses carried out for purposes such as the characterization of obsidian or clay (above, p. 135) produce bewildering columns of figures that can only be clarified by means of statistical methods. **Multivariate** procedures have been designed to look for significant relationships or contrasts between elements or minerals to define groups that may bring some order into the data (see fig. 5.3). Multivariate statistics, notably cluster analysis, also lie behind some computerized exercises in the typological classification of artefacts or the seriation of assemblages found in stratified contexts or graves. The ready availability of powerful microcomputers facilitates and speeds up statistical analysis, so that a mass of confusing detail can be weighed up absolutely consistently. However, complicated computerized statistical procedures may be dangerous if their results are accepted uncritically, and modern computer software allows sophisticated techniques to be carried out all too easily by archaeologists who lack any understanding of statistics. Results are only as good as the evidence they are based on, and the suitability of the tests that have been employed. Nevertheless, even a very basic awareness of statistical concepts should encourage archaeologists to design research questions in a way that will allow the results to be tested, and enable the outcome to be stated as levels of statistical probability, rather than subjective intuition.

10.1 Computers

(Reilly & Rahtz 1992; Ross 1991)

Computers are so well integrated into archaeology, from prospecting and discovery to storage and publication, that it is no longer necessary to discuss computing as a separate topic. Computers have become so cheap, widely available and 'user friendly' that their use requires no knowledge of electronics or programming. Many processes that demanded the use of 'mainframe' computers from the 1950s to the 1970s are now performed by an individual user's desktop PC. A remarkable combination of flexible software, memory, disk storage, processing speed, graphics and printing capabilities had become available by the 1990s.

Most scientific dating methods, along with techniques used in the analysis of artefacts, employ apparatus linked directly to computers that monitor the operation of the equipment and record and process the results. Computers not only save the time of skilled laboratory staff, but are faster and more reliable. Their importance is obvious in the estimation of the margin of error involved in measurements of radioactivity in samples of ancient carbon, and the subsequent calibration of dates. The 1993 issue of *Radiocarbon* included not only a revised calibration curve, but also a floppy disk with a computer pro-

gram to help with these complex calculations! Computers are also an integral part of the technical equipment involved in processing aerial photographs and readings recorded during geophysical surveys (chapter 2; fig. 2.12). In both cases the principal benefit comes from their ability to 'filter' data by eliminating natural background variations so that archaeological features are enhanced (above, p. 46). The adjustment of oblique aerial photographs to fit an image on to a uniform horizontal scale involves extraordinarily complicated mathematical procedures (Scollar 1990).

Besides their involvement in statistics, laboratory science and cartography, the principal function of computers in archaeology is to record, store and retrieve large quantities of information, such as excavation records or museum archives; this is a question of management rather than science (Jones 1991). However, **geographical information systems** (GIS) are a rather more scientific application of computing that combines maps, environmental and archaeological data with statistical calculations to produce graphic visualizations of relationships between these categories of information. GIS promises to provide major advances in the analysis and interpretation of ancient landscapes (above, p. 56; see fig. 2.15).

11 Experimental archaeology
(Coles 1979; Robinson 1990)

One welcome by-product of a scientific approach to archaeology has been the increasingly frequent use of practical experiments to test hypotheses. Most have been one-off tests of specific ideas, but a few, for example the Butser Ancient Farm Project (fig. 5.16; Reynolds 1979; 1987), have developed into long-term programmes observing a whole range of variables over several decades. The strict definition of an experiment employed in the scientific world is rarely fulfilled in an archaeological context, for many factors are difficult to control or measure, let alone replicate on another occasion. Even when they are demonstrations or simulations rather than true experiments, they may still produce valuable information.

11.1 Artefacts

(Amick & Mauldin 1989)

Experimental archaeology is a useful companion to scientific analysis in the study of artefacts, for their composition and structure may suggest methods of manufacture. Ancient technology has been explored by reconstructions of metal casting procedures, the making and firing of pottery, and various forms of stone working. If one particular manufacturing technique suggested by an archaeologist is found to be successful in practice, the experiment only confirms that it *could* have been used in the past, not that it actually was. For this reason it is important to adopt a more scientific approach; a single demonstration of one method of firing ancient pottery is of limited value without a series of comparative firings carried out using different fuels, kiln structures, methods of arranging the pots in the kiln, etc. Again, it will never be proved that the technique found to be most effective today was the one employed in the past, but the possibility of gross misinterpretation will be reduced if some unsatisfactory techniques are ruled out. It is essential that appropriate techniques, materials and equipment known to have been in use in the relevant society are employed.

Besides experiments concerning manufacture, the functions and efficiency of tools have also been examined. Again, scientific analyses may provide relevant information, and experiments are frequently carried out in association with microscopic **use-wear analysis**. Patterns of wear or damage to working surfaces may suggest how a tool was used; if a replica is used for the same purpose it can be examined afterwards to see if the same effects are observable. One danger inherent in experiments about the functions of artefact is that 'efficiency', measured in terms of time and energy, is a very modern concept. Anthropological studies of pre-industrial societies reveal that ritual and symbolism may override purely practical considerations. In addition, a twentieth-century archaeologist will not possess either the physical fitness or the experience of the original user of an artefact. Anthropology might also help to limit the potential for other blunders contained in modern assumptions about the purpose of artefacts. If a

5.16 The Butser Ancient Farm, Hampshire, is a large-scale, long-term experiment in which prehistoric and Roman agricultural practices and equipment are observed under conditions of careful scientific observation. *Peter Reynolds*

neolithic axe was assessed purely according to its ability to cut through wood, the results would be meaningless if the axe was used as a weapon, rather than a tool; perhaps forests were cleared by burning rather than being cut down.

11.2 Sites and structures

(Morrison & Coates 1986)

Large-scale structures such as ships, buildings or earthworks may also be subjected to experiments and simulation studies, normally by means of reconstructions based on evidence derived from excavations. If possible this evidence should be supplemented with anthropological data, or, in the case of more recent historical reconstructions, contemporary information and illustrations found in archives (see fig. 3.34). At the most basic level, an exercise of this kind tests whether a structure postulated by an archaeologist could have stood up. Once this requirement has been satisfied, other worthwhile questions include estimates of human effort involved in construction, and the quantity and sources of the necessary raw materials.

The chief advantage of simulation studies is that they demand a much closer analysis of excavated traces than might otherwise be carried out.

If the reconstruction of an excavated structure is found to be difficult or even impossible, the excavator will be forced to review the evidence, and to look again for features that may have escaped notice or whose significance was not recognized. In contrast, other excavated traces that have proved difficult to explain may be clarified; a scatter of post-holes around a building may have supported scaffolding or temporary props during construction, for example.

Since archaeologists excavate the decayed remains of structures, the study of decay processes is fundamental to their interpretations, and many experiments have been designed to explore this area. In Denmark, reconstructed timber buildings have been burnt down and then re-excavated to learn how the remains reflect the superstructure, to facilitate the interpretation of ancient burnt remains on other sites. In England, long-term studies of the erosion of earthworks begun in the early 1960s will be monitored well into the next century; at Overton Down, Wilts, a bank and ditch were constructed on a chalk subsoil, and near Wareham, Dorset, a similar structure was created on sand. The earthworks were constructed to exact measurements, and objects and other organic and inorganic samples were buried at precisely recorded locations. Erosion, settlement, decay and the movement of objects by earthworms and other disturbances of the soil can all be charted by periodic excavations of small sections of the earthworks. But because access to the sites is strictly limited, the effects of human erosion that would have affected a real structure in everyday use have been excluded. Furthermore, most structures in the past were probably carefully maintained until obsolete, and not allowed to deteriorate as soon as they were completed. These problems illustrate the greatest weakness of experimental archaeology; experiments require controls, but past human activity was not necessarily rational or consistent.

Many full-size reconstructions of ships have been built and tested since the nineteenth century. Greek and Roman warships have been particularly popular because many accounts of naval battles survive in classical literature. The most recent example is the *Olympias*, an Athenian trireme constructed to test configurations of oarsmen and claims for the speed and manoeuvrability made in Greek historical texts (Morrison & Coates 1986; Welsh 1988). This ship raises a typical problem involved in reconstructions; many warships are illustrated in Greek paintings and carvings, and texts provide details of the size of crews, but no illustration or description gives an unambiguous account of the arrangement of the oars and rowers within the hull. This problem is so serious that the validity of the entire experiment has been questioned by some critics (e.g. Tilley 1992).

12 Conclusion

The scientific methods employed in archaeological research now impinge upon most areas of the subject. The relationship between archaeology and science remains clear, however; science supplies increasingly detailed and precise information upon which improved archaeological interpretations can be based. Furthermore, the use of scientific evidence and an awareness of scientific methods enhance the design and conduct of archaeological research. Archaeologists and historians ignore scientific evidence at their peril if they wish to understand the chronological framework of the past, or the material resources available to ancient societies, and the natural environments where they lived. The development of new techniques, and the inevitable errors that they will contain at the outset, provides an opportunity for interaction between science and archaeology when disagreements arise, for both must re-examine their own particular forms of data and analysis. 'For is it not, these days, a defining characteristic of real science that it is testable? . . . That archaeological science should sometimes give wrong answers, and that these can later be shown to be indeed erroneous, must be counted one of the subject's great strengths' (Renfrew 1992, 292).

Note: a guide to **further reading** that includes topics covered in this chapter begins on p. 185.

6 Making Sense of the Past

Chapters 1–5 have clear subjects because they focus upon specific principles and methods used in archaeology, placed where appropriate into a historical perspective. Some references have been made to changes in interpretation that have modified attitudes to fieldwork, excavation or the collection of scientific data. This final chapter will begin by looking more closely at the philosophy of the subject and examine the importance of **archaeological theory**. I will then comment on a series of aspects of archaeology that seem important in the closing years of the twentieth century. Some of them reflect my own interests, and many may in the future be judged to have been unproductive distractions.

Placing 'theory' into a separate chapter at the end of this book is an attempt to draw attention to its special role. It does not mean that I consider theory to be something separate from practice, any more than I would draw a dividing line between science and dating, or excavation and fieldwork. If the effect is still 'to identify the discipline with its technical instrumentation' – an accusation levelled at the first edition of this book by Shanks & Tilley (1987a, 22) – this should be seen as a failure to devise a better way of organizing the book, rather than an expression of my own point of view.

1 Where is archaeology at the end of the twentieth century?

Chapter 1 explored how 'archaeology' began in Europe after the Renaissance as a harmless distraction for the educated rich. It commonly took the form of collecting, either of curiosities or works of art; alternatively, archaeological sites might be recorded, and even investigated by excavation, as part of an attempt to supplement the exploration of the past through documents. Some aspects of archaeology, notably the study of human origins and early prehistory, developed into a respectable scientific pursuit in the nineteenth century. Archaeology underwent accelerated growth after 1900, so that today virtually every country in the world operates some form of State-financed protection of ancient monuments, as well as supporting research into the subject in public universities and museums.

Archaeology has become a popular part of education at both school and university levels, perhaps because it involves a variety of practical and theoretical work, and a mixture of scientific and aesthetic approaches. It is also concerned with everyday objects and structures, as well as the social élites upon whom history has tended to concentrate. Museum displays are now aimed at general visitors rather than specialists, and well-documented 'designer' displays are displacing dull rows of pots with terse type-written labels. Mobility and leisure have increased to the extent that mass-tourism now regularly includes ancient sites and museums. Archaeology receives extensive publicity through popular writing and journalism; it even contributes to home entertainment through television programmes shown at peak viewing times without causing any surprise. This degree of familiarity makes it particularly important to keep on asking questions about exactly what archaeologists are trying to do, and for whom; the answers are frequently uncomfortable. Are we simply making what we want of the past because we can do nothing about the present, let alone change the future?

1.1 Too much knowledge?

When human antiquity was established in the middle of the nineteenth century, the academic world was small and international, and not confined to universities and museums. John Evans, who visited Boucher de Perthes and witnessed the stratigraphic position of palaeolithic artefacts at Amiens in 1859 (above, p. 13), was a busy paper-mill manager, and published articles and books on geology, pre-Roman coins, bronze implements and flints in his spare time (Evans 1943). As President of the Royal Society in London, he not only rubbed shoulders with most of the prominent geologists, physicists, biologists and other scientists of his day, but was accepted amongst them on equal terms. The rapid exchange of information and ideas between figures such as Evans, Lyell and Darwin that lay behind this exciting phase in the development of archaeological thinking would be more difficult today: cooperation between different disciplines tends to be directed towards specific research projects with less ambitious objectives.

As the amount of information produced by excavation, fieldwork and other forms of research has increased, so too have expectations about its quality and detail. The many supporting techniques and sources of specialist information make it more difficult, rather than easier, to complete a report for publication. The size and complexity of the end-product may be unwieldy, expensive, and impossible for non-specialists to digest. Archaeologists need to think about their duties to taxpayers, and find convincing justifications for yet more analyses of the material remains of the past. Authors of major archaeological reports have an obligation to communicate clearly without oversimplification, and to present the results in a form accessible to the public as well as to specialists. Otherwise, what is the purpose of archaeological research?

Almost every subject in the humanities and sciences has undergone an information explosion in recent decades. Librarians are particularly aware of the increase in the number and thickness of books and periodicals, and of the search for alternatives to the printed page such as CD-ROMs, on-line computer databases and multimedia information storage and retrieval systems. It is difficult for specialists to keep up to date in anything more than their own narrow field of research, and almost impossible for reliable 'overviews' or syntheses to be presented to the public without gross simplification. These factors have led to a fragmentation of academic archaeology into restricted periods of the past, limited geographical areas or arcane philosophies of interpretation.

The difficulties that exist in communicating the results of archaeology have undoubtedly contributed to the flourishing of writers, such as Erich von Däniken, who take a particular delight in deriding the inability of 'experts' to find explanations that seize the imagination of the public. Although Stukeley's obsession with Druids demonstrates that finding supernatural or mystical connotations with antiquities is not new, views of this kind have never been so widely disseminated (Williams 1991). Few archaeologists have sold as many paperbacks as von Däniken; more recently, a meteorologist who linked crop circles to prehistoric ring-ditches or round barrows generated a reaction that no orthodox student of these monuments has ever achieved (Meaden 1991).

2 Archaeological theory
(Trigger 1989; Malina & Vašíček 1990)

The abundance of information available about the past, and the growth of unusual interpretations by people outside the academic archaeological world, require careful thought by archaeologists. The history of the subject illustrates many attempts to establish satisfactory conceptual frameworks into which to slot surviving remains, frequently in ways that seem ludicrous today. However, the building of frameworks, whether deliberately or unconsciously, remains a prerequisite of serious research. Some archaeologists still consider that they examine data objectively, and 'let the facts speak for themselves'. The majority now develop a conscious theoretical approach and gather data or explore existing information with an explicit theoretical framework in mind and a clear problem orientation.

Theoretical frameworks now come and go with frightening rapidity, according to the progress of research or sometimes mere taste. Whereas in the 1960s and 1970s the hottest area of debate was between traditional and 'new' archaeology, discussion now centres upon the applicability of rival theoretical approaches. Regrettably, many archaeologists, notably those who operate in familiar historical periods, still regard archaeological theory as a sub-discipline that may be ignored. Their mistake is to overlook the fact that *all* investigations of the past involve a theoretical perspective. We are products of a social environment that has conditioned our outlook on the world, and our view of the past is inevitably influenced by our perception of the present. It is impossible to disentangle subjectivity from supposedly 'objective' research, for our very choice of research topic probably reflects our personal opinions. Awareness of archaeological theory allows us to acknowledge this problem, even if there is very little that we can do about it. Since most branches of archaeological theory have their roots in philosophy or other disciplines such as sociology or anthropology, they offer the possibility of gaining new and unexpected insights into familiar aspects of the past. Theory does not provide answers, but it suggests a wider range of interesting questions that revitalize existing data and stimulate a search for new and better information.

This chapter will not attempt to explain the current state of archaeological theory, for this could only be an interim report. Indeed, it is a reflection of the maturity of the subject that entire books are beginning to be devoted to a retrospective analysis of archaeological theory as it has developed since the 1950s (Gibbon 1989). I will nevertheless consider the origins of some of the principal ideas involved, and provide some examples of their application.

3 Social evolution
(Friedman & Rowlands 1982; Renfrew 1984)

3.1 Early anthropology
(Kuper 1988)

Before looking at theoretical archaeology, it is necessary to look back at early examples of the use of anthropology or even abstract political philosophy to provide frameworks for the interpretation of the past. At the most basic level, the way that early antiquaries drew analogies between artefacts from the New and Old Worlds is an obvious example of an informative interaction between the observation of existing 'primitive' cultures and deductions about the

past (see fig. 1.10). It was not necessary for antiquarians to make systematic investigations into anthropology, for classical Greek philosophy contains extensive speculation about the development of human societies and their technologies (Blundell 1986). These writers influenced the sociological approach of some French and Scottish thinkers of the eighteenth century (Rousseau is the most widely known) who proposed schemes for stages of development in human society through hunting and fishing, pasturage, agriculture and commerce (Piggott 1976, 153). Any well-read antiquarian of the late eighteenth or nineteenth century who encountered ancient objects and sites would probably approach their interpretation with a mixture of historical and biblical knowledge, and some theoretical concept of human development and progress. It is interesting to view John Frere and Boucher de Perthes in this light (above, p. 11)

3.2 The impact of Darwin
(Bowler 1989)

The Darwinian concept of evolution became universally known in learned circles in the 1860s, even amongst those who rejected both its basis and implications. The great antiquity of human ancestors was established by geologists and archaeologists at around the same time (above, p. 15). As might be expected, Darwin's biological concepts were particularly welcomed by writers who combined the evolutionary approach to past societies with new anthropological and archaeological observations. An American anthropologist, Lewis Morgan, used his knowledge of native Americans to define an elaborate series of stages of development in a very influential book, *Ancient Society* (1877). This book took on wider significance when it was used as a source by Karl Marx; Friedrich Engels subsequently summarized Marx's interpretation of Morgan's developmental stages:

Savagery – the period in which man's appropriation of products in their natural states predominates; the products of human art are chiefly instruments that assist this appropriation. Barbarism – the period during which man learns to breed domestic animals and to practise agriculture, and acquires methods of increasing the supply of natural products by human agency. Civilization – the period in which man learns a more advanced application of work to the products of nature, the period of industry proper and art. (1884, quoted in Daniel 1967, 139–40)

3.3 'Culture history'
(Trigger 1980)

It has been stressed in chapter 1 that the 'evolutionary' approach to the typology of artefacts that led to the acceptance of the Three-Age System in early nineteenth-century Scandinavia was quite separate from Darwin's, although both incorporated assumptions of linear progress and improvement (above, p.28). Nevertheless, the combination of evolutionary concepts related to animals (including humans), artefacts, economic systems and societies made a substantial contribution to twentieth-century archaeology. For

example, in a popular work entitled *What Happened in History* published in 1942, the Australian Marxist prehistorian V. Gordon Childe employed chapter headings such as 'Palaeolithic Savagery' and 'The Higher Barbarism of the Copper Age'. Childe was also influenced by historical accounts of the past; he classified recurrent groups of related prehistoric artefacts and settlements into 'cultures', and proposed that they represented distinct ethnic or social groupings of people. Support for this view could be obtained from the work of archaeologists such as the Swede, Nils Åberg, who had studied some of the peoples (Goths, Franks, Saxons, etc.) involved in complex folkmovements in Europe in the late Roman and early medieval periods. Distinctive artefacts such as decorated brooches, buckles or pottery found in cemeteries could be matched with historical records of migrants or settlers in the areas where they were found. This culture-historical approach will be examined further below because of its contribution to nationalist and racist archaeology (p. 167).

4 Diffusionism
(Renfrew 1973)

The idea of **diffusion** supplied a critical connecting thread in earlier prehistoric periods where documents were not available. Because of the geographical focus of the Bible and Greek and Roman literature, European scholarship had been haunted by the civilizations of the Mediterranean and Near East ever since the medieval period. Childe, like Montelius and others before him, made an assumption that all innovations or improvements observed in European prehistory must have originated in those areas where civilizations flourished at the earliest date (fig. 6.1). It must be emphasized that there was no logical inconsistency in asserting that all impulses towards progress should have emanated from those areas, particularly when Mesopotamia and Egypt became better known in the nineteenth century. Diffusionism gained support from the concept of evolution, because it provided a powerful metaphorical explanation of 'progress' and the inevitable

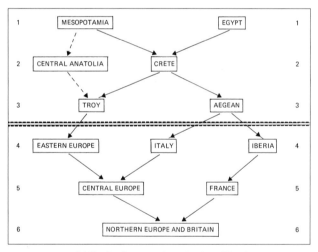

6.1 Diffusionism: archaeologists like Oscar Montelius or Gordon Childe envisaged a spread of cultural influences and innovations from the civilizations of the Near East into prehistoric Europe. This view was based on apparent connections between the typologies of artefacts found in these regions, but, by the 1970s, radiocarbon dates had broken the chronological sequence of links between stages 3 and 4. A complete reconsideration of phenomena such as the use of metals and the building of megalithic tombs was required when their origins and spread could no longer be attributed simply to diffusion. *Audio Visual Centre, University of Newcastle, after Renfrew*

spread of 'improvements' from advanced to less developed areas. This assumption became firmly rooted in twentieth-century archaeology, whether in a rational manner amongst scholars like Montelius or Childe, or in the extreme views of Eliot Smith, who claimed that the influence of Egyptian pyramids and embalming techniques extended to similar phenomena found in South America at a much later date (Daniel 1981, 115).

The idea of diffusion illustrates the virtues of examining all aspects of archaeological explanation from a theoretical standpoint. The problem lay not in the *idea* of diffusion, for the history of technology provides many well-documented examples of invention followed by diffusion, but in the way that it was accepted as a fundamental fact, rather than as a theoretical proposition that might be supported or refuted by further evidence. In consequence, it was eventually rejected altogether. By the 1960s British archaeology was placed into a curious state, for many prehistorians considered that the major technological and social changes had resulted from independent development and internal evolution, rather than having been introduced by immigrants or invaders. Ironically, the invasion-free centuries of later prehistory were followed by periods marked by well-documented raids, invasions and colonization by foreign settlers: the Roman conquest in AD 43; Anglo-Saxons in the fourth to fifth centuries; Vikings in the eighth to ninth centuries; and of course the Norman Conquest in 1066. However, major changes in settlement sites, architecture and artefacts also took place in areas such as Ireland that were not occupied by Roman invasion or Anglo-

Saxon settlement. Many of these changes happened as a result of the arrival of Christianity, a phenomenon of Near-Eastern origin that spread throughout western Britain as a result of direct links with western Europe and the Mediterranean. This is a clear example of diffusion.

4.1 Diffusionism in disrepute: megalithic tombs
(Renfrew 1983)

These large stone constructions are found in many parts of western Europe, Scandinavia and Germany (see fig. 6.3), and they usually contain stone-lined chambers, some with long entrance passageways. Some are architecturally sophisticated, with enormous stones or elaborate vaulting, and they may be decorated with geometric or curvilinear carving. The original covering mound of earth or stones has frequently disappeared, leaving distinctive uprights and capstones that feature in many illustrations by early antiquarians (fig. 6.2). Where the contents of the chambers survive, excavation usually reveals collective burials of large numbers of individuals.

Monumental stone architecture appeared in Egypt early in the second millennium BC and

6.2 This characteristic view of a megalithic tomb (Kits Coty House, Kent) makes it clear why they were among the first antiquities to attract attention and illustration, and why their size gave rise to tales of construction by mythological heroes or giants. The burial chamber has been exposed by erosion of an earth mound that originally covered the stonework. *Stukeley 1776, II, pl. 32*

reached remarkable sophistication in monuments such as Zoser's step pyramid at Saqqara, c. 2650 BC. Tombs with stone passageways and vaulted chambers exist in the Aegean area around 1600 BC, and it was natural to assume that these must have inspired the megalithic tombs that they resemble. Stuart Piggott summarized the diffusionist interpretation in 1965:

> Their distribution poses a problem: what likely set of circumstances in antiquity can cause a group of specialized ritual structures to be built over such a sweep of territory? It is not, I think, inapposite to consider these monuments in the same terms as one would the churches of Christendom or the mosques of Islam . . . Creeds and beliefs can be transmitted in many ways; conquest or evangelism, fanaticism or fashion, by saints or merchants . . . An eastern Mediterranean origin seems inherently likely, but is difficult to document with any precision. (Piggott 1965, 60)

However, the newly developed radiocarbon dating technique was already beginning to cause problems for this kind of interpretation, because samples from megalithic tombs produced dates around 3000 BC. Not only was this embarrassingly early in relation to supposed prototypes in the Aegean, but it was even earlier than the first stone architecture in Egypt! It was suggested initially that there must be errors in the dates from France. The diffusionist view survived into the second edition of Grahame Clark's authoritative *World Prehistory* (1969), but a new categorical statement appeared in its third edition (1977):

> Despite . . . variations which were commonly favoured in particular regions, the occurrence of collective tombs in most cases of megalithic construction over so great an extent of the Atlantic seaboard has often been attributed exclusively to seaborne diffusion. On the other hand the notion that burial in collective tombs of monumental construction originated in the east Mediterranean has recently been disproved by radiocarbon dating. (op. cit. 135)

Clark suggested that these tombs spread around the coastal fringes by means of fishermen following hake and mackerel, rather than the priests or trader/prospectors favoured by earlier writers. More fundamental reinterpretation was made necessary by calibration of radiocarbon dates according to the tree-ring curve (above, p.117; see fig. 4.14). Many new dates for megaliths were now available, including several from Britanny earlier than 4000 BC. Colin Renfrew stated the new position forcefully in *Before Civilization*, a particularly stimulating book on the impact of radiocarbon dating upon European prehistory:

> The implications are altogether clear: passage graves, some with corbelled vaults, were already being built in these regions before 2500 b.c. in radiocarbon years, and thus by 3300 BC in calendar years. Quite obviously, if they have their ultimate origin in the Aegean, this must have been a long time before 3000 BC. Yet there are no collective built tombs in the Aegean until after this date. The Breton dates, even without calibration, make nonsense of the diffusionist case. (1973, 89–90)

Scientific dating now shows that megalithic tombs were established in north-western France by 4700 BC (see fig. 6.4; Scarre 1993). Calibrated radiocarbon dates have also severed many other diffusionist links between the Aegean and the Balkans, western and northern Europe.

4.2 New interpretations of megalithic tombs
(Renfrew 1979)

The diffusionist account had been both intellectually satisfying and methodologically sound. Renfrew now proposed an alternative:

> . . . we are no longer obliged to see the tombs as the result of a single movement, whether it originated in Iberia or in Brittany (as one could now argue, on the basis of the new dates). Instead our task is to create some social model, some simple picture of how it all came about. (1973, 124)

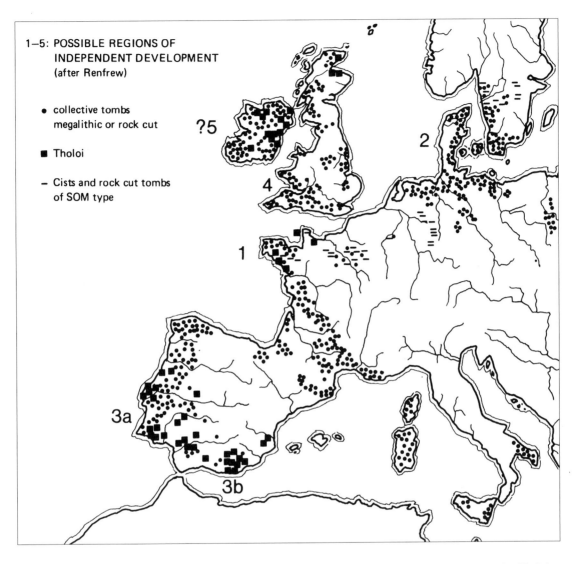

1–5: **POSSIBLE REGIONS OF INDEPENDENT DEVELOPMENT** (after Renfrew)

● collective tombs
   megalithic or rock cut

■ Tholoi

– Cists and rock cut tombs
   of SOM type

6.3 Distribution map of megalithic tombs. Tholoi are tomb chambers with corbelled roofs originally thought to have been derived from examples around the Aegean, but they are now known to be much earlier. Radiocarbon dates suggest that the earliest megalithic tombs are in Britanny, but rather than simply proposing that their diffusion originated there, Renfrew has proposed five possible regions where they might have developed independently. *Audio Visual Centre, University of Newcastle, after Fox 1959, fig. 7*

He divided the area where megaliths are found into four or possibly five regions where an independent local origin could be claimed, and stressed that the tombs might be the only thing that they had in common (fig. 6.3). The hypothesis that such tombs could be the products of small farming groups was developed and then tested against the geography of two Scottish islands where suitable tombs occurred; information about social structures and community burial practices was supplied by studies of a modern 'megalithic' culture in Borneo. Although Renfrew's fieldwork and anthropological analogies demonstrated that his explanation was possible, it was always accepted that further analogies, new fieldwork or excavation might

generate alternative hypotheses.

Renfrew also tackled the problem of *general* explanation – why should similar monuments develop in as many as five different parts of the

165

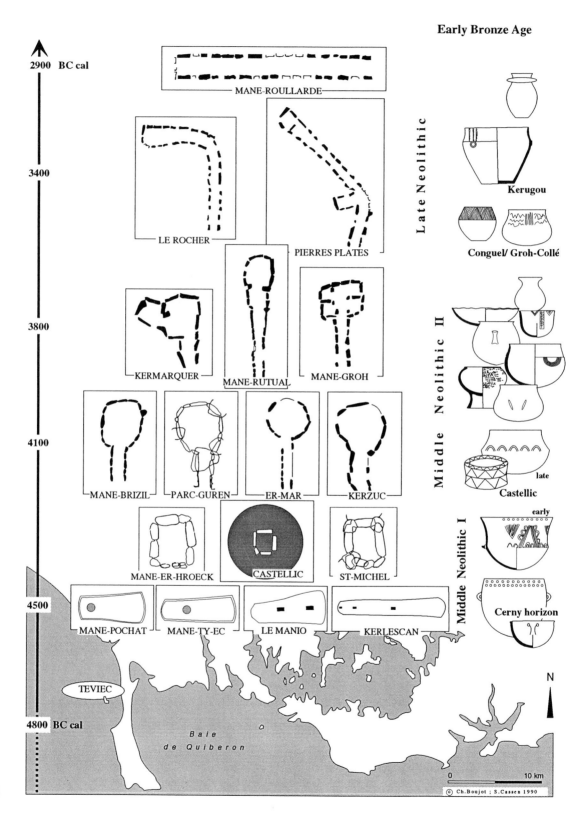

Early Bronze Age

Late Neolithic

Middle Neolithic II

Middle Neolithic I

2900 BC cal

3400

3800

4100

4500

4800 BC cal

MANE-ROULLARDE

LE ROCHER

PIERRES PLATES

KERMARQUER

MANE-RUTUAL

MANE-GROH

MANE-BRIZIL

PARC-GUREN

ER-MAR

KERZUC

MANE-ER-HROECK

CASTELLIC

ST-MICHEL

MANE-POCHAT

MANE-TY-EC

LE MANIO

KERLESCAN

TEVIEC

Baie de Quiberon

Kerugou

Conguel/ Groh-Collé

Castellic

late

early

Cerny horizon

N

0   10 km

© Ch.Boujot ; S.Cassen 1990

6.4 This diagram illustrates the stages of typological development of megalithic tombs in Brittany, along with radiocarbon dates expressed in calibrated years BC. It is superimposed upon a map of Quiberon Bay, where some of the best examples are found, and accompanied by a typology of local pottery forms that would help to relate undated tombs or settlement sites to the dated sequence.
Boujot & Cassen 1993, fig. 3

fringes of Europe (but nowhere else) at around the same time? He proposed (very tentatively) that population pressures developed as farming communities reached the coastal limits of Europe, where they were influenced by indigenous hunter-fisher peoples; in other words, similar circumstances produced similar results in separate, but comparable, areas:

> To make the coincidence understandable, all we have to do is show that the development of monumental building in this way was, in the special circumstances of each individual area, the natural result of intelligible processes operating more generally.... we can now begin to talk about these monuments in human terms, as a product of living communities, and to give full credit to their builders, the world's first architects in stone, without any longer appealing by way of explanation to the convenient arrival of wise men from the east. (op. cit. 142; 146)

I have discussed megaliths in some detail, because they demonstrate many of the problems involved in making sense of the past. First, the impact of radiocarbon dates and their calibration into earlier calendar years show just how quickly accepted interpretations may come crashing down in ruins when one prop is removed (fig. 6.4). Second, this happened at a time when new approaches and preoccupations were emerging amongst anthropologists and archaeologists in the United States. Renfrew's reinterpretation of megalithic tombs shows how a theory is tested in a real situation, and illustrates the continuing importance of anthropological analogies. His ideas are not a *replacement* for the diffusionist explanation, for any hypothesis is liable to be re-examined, and, if necessary, rejected. This constant uncertainty, although very good for

archaeology itself, increases the difficulty of communicating comprehensible results to the public:

> Diffusionist explanations may have been in error, but they may also have been necessary, an inescapable stage in the progress of the discipline that enabled it to advance from the 1920s to the 1950s and 1960s when independent chronologies at last liberated European prehistory from dependence on an axiom that had been untested because it had been untestable. (Chippindale 1989, 24)

5 Nationalism and racism
(Gathercole & Lowenthal 1990; MacDougall 1982)

Concepts of social evolution and diffusion did not always bring positive changes to archaeological interpretation. Although Darwinism reinforced rather than initiated racist interpretations of the past, evolution and diffusion influenced the political outlook of the leading European governments. The situation in England in Pitt Rivers' time has been summarized forcefully by Donald Johanson:

> For a society bursting with the self-congratulatory fervor of a colonial power and the potency of an industrial revolution, it took very little effort to prop this biological premise under a social construct and extend the ladder just a bit to justify the white man's inherent superiority over the 'lesser' peoples of the earth. (Johanson & Shreeve 1991, 45–6)

Pitt Rivers did not devote his extensive intellectual energy and financial resources to excavation and the typological study of artefacts for purely academic reasons. He considered that evidence for the gradual evolution of artefacts should be impressed upon museum visitors to counteract revolutionary tendencies in nineteenth-century politics (Bowden 1991, 141–2). John Lubbock, a close associate of Darwin, combined archaeology, anthropology and rigid evolutionary theory in his influential book *Prehistoric Times* (1865), and concluded that non-European cultures were biologically inferior, and that the most primitive peoples were doomed to inevitable extinction through natural selection. Thus, no moral responsibility need be felt for their decline or loss of identity through colonization, since they resulted from innate biological differences (Trigger 1989, 110–18). Interestingly, Alfred Wallace, the co-discoverer with Darwin of natural selection, had first-hand knowledge of tribal peoples in South America and Asia, and considered that their mental abilities matched those of Europeans (ibid. 113). Pitt Rivers was more typical in his view that savages were not capable of benefiting from the civilizing influence of superior races by any means other than slavery (Bradley 1983, 5–6). More recent uses of images of the past that reflect or justify the political preoccupations and actions of the present will be explored in more detail below (p. 175).

The failing grip of the Ottoman Empire in the nineteenth century stimulated the exploration of Greek civilization. Greece gained its independence in 1831 and foreign excavators rapidly cleared the Acropolis of Athens, releasing the remains of such buildings as the Erechtheum and Parthenon from the encumbrances of a harem and mosque respectively (see fig. 1.13). This action illustrates the fact that archaeological research is highly selective when combined with nationalism. Societies select the past that they wish to emphasize; the removal of physical reminders of Turkish rule and its religion, Islam, allowed the new Greek nation to underline its connections with the European roots of classical culture (McNeal 1991). Ironically, 150 years later, Bernal has taken an opposite view in stressing the non-European contribution to ancient Greek culture, in a major work of scholarship with the arresting title *Black Athena: The Afroasiatic roots of Classical civilization* (1987; 1991).

North European archaeologists, notably Gustav Kossina (1858–1931), used recurrent groups of distinctive prehistoric artefacts in an innovative manner to define *cultures* of the kind observed by ethnographers amongst living societies. It was a small step from classifying cultures in material terms to equating them with social or political units and calling them tribes or peoples (Trigger 1989, 148–206). Since most of the historically attested nations and linguistic groups of Europe clearly originated in an undocumented prehistoric period, nineteenth-century concepts of nationalism were soon projected back into earlier times. Thus, a novel variant of diffusionism from the East was propounded by Kossina, who traced all major European developments back to origins in prehistoric Germany, credited to a pure Nordic ('Aryan') race (Trigger 1989, 163–7). His views were developed with enthusiasm after his death because they gave welcome support to Nazi claims for the superiority of the Aryan race. The outcome of this enthusiasm was of course the invasion of neighbouring countries to restore their rightful Teutonic ownership, and the attempt to enslave or exterminate inferior peoples, notably Slavs, Jews and gypsies.

The extreme nature of this example should not blind us to the lesser prejudices contained in most research; how many archaeologists considered the feelings of native Americans or Australians when excavating the bones of their ancestors and placing them on public exhibition in museums? Why do pictorial reconstructions of prehistoric life always seem to show men hunting or using tools while women cook and weave? The protests of native peoples and feminists have only very recently begun to force archaeologists to review their perspectives on these aspects of the past, even though most had already done so in relation to nationalism and racism. The past is indeed pliable and potent.

6 Towards processualist archaeology
(Willey & Sabloff 1980; Lamberg-Karlovsky 1991)

The development of functional and then processual approaches to archaeological data represented a replacement of the increasingly sterile preoccupation of culture-historical archaeology with ethnicity by a vital new interest in how prehistoric cultures operated and changed. (Trigger 1989, 288)

This quotation demonstrates simultaneously two important facets of the study of theoretical archaeology in the late twentieth century. First, it underlines the continued importance of taking a historical view of the development of the subject to place it into context, both in terms of its own content and its relationship to other subjects. Second, it underlines that it is necessary to acquire an extensive new vocabulary to participate in the subject, for much of the discussion is conducted at a philosophical level, and is full of scientific or sociological terminology that makes it inaccessible to outsiders.

The point that Trigger makes in this quotation is that much of the archaeology of the nineteenth and early twentieth centuries was dedicated to description rather than exploration or explanation. This was of course inevitable in the early stages, because little or no meaningful explanation could take place until questions about dating had been sorted out. However, once the main sequences of artefacts and cultures had been established, and after they had been placed into a chronological framework through documentary evidence or radiocarbon dating, they could be studied in much more imaginative ways. In the ethnic approach, the relationships between cultures were discussed in terms derived from historical archaeology: invasion, colonization, trade, etc. Alternatively, the development of cultures through time could be seen in evolutionary terms, from a biological, ecological, social, political or economic point of view. Thus, strict Marxist archaeologists saw in sites and artefacts the physical evidence for a progression that they already believed in on philosophical grounds.

6.1 Social evolution and Marxism
(Bintliff 1984; McGuire 1992)

Abstract concepts such as evolution (whether biological or social) and Marxism could be very comforting for prehistoric archaeologists faced with complicated typologies or sequences of cultures. Evolution explained change in terms of competition between humans and other animals, accompanied by a need to adapt to the natural environment. Marxism placed more emphasis on the economy, and its influence upon ritual and social systems; it was the stresses between conservative and progressive social forces that provoked change, and the experiences of the Russian Revolution in 1917 demonstrated that these could be rapid and dramatic. It is no coincidence that V G Childe talked of a Neolithic revolution (the adoption of food production) and an urban revolution (settlement in towns rather than villages) in prehistory, both involving technological and social change.

The adoption of abstract evolutionary and political concepts did have practical implications for archaeology, however, for both emphasized the importance of material evidence. After all, excavated sites could provide evidence for economic activities such as farming, crafts and trade. Social systems should also be reflected in the disposition and form of houses, and in the diversity of objects found in settlements or graves that indicated differences in status or wealth. Evolutionary interests stimulated the study of aspects of sites and their surroundings that could reveal the relationship of the inhabitants to their natural environment; pollen analysis, soil science and the identification of seeds from food plants all gained enhanced interest in the context of ecology and adaptation. Broader climatic and environmental factors could also help to explain changes in human societies and economies.

Thus, the middle decades of the twentieth century witnessed many overlapping schools of thought about anthropology, archaeology and the goals of these subjects. However, most of these approaches demanded closer attention to the excavation and recording of sites and artefacts to fit them into broader 'functionalist' views of the past (Trigger 1989, 264–88). American archaeologists were at an advantage, for they were concerned with indigenous peoples unconnected with the Old World, some still following non-European lifestyles well into the twentieth century. New World agriculture and civilization had developed independently (except in the minds of a few 'hyperdiffusionists' who claimed contacts with ancient Egypt or other exotic cultures), but their study had been ignored by most European archaeologists. It is not surprising to find that North America in particular became a vigorous debating ground for new approaches to archaeological study that influenced the thinking of the rest of the world.

6.2 The 'new' archaeology
(Clarke 1978; Binford 1972; 1989)

The 'new' archaeology has to be examined (with the benefit of hindsight) in the light of post-processualism, which had become well established by the 1990s. Just as Wagner's 'new' music resembles that of other late Romantic composers when compared with what Schoenberg or Stravinsky composed soon afterwards, processual archaeology blends into the ecological and functional approaches that preceded it. It also bears similarities to some of the objectives of Russian archaeology that developed quite independently in the 1930s (Trigger 1989, 326). Perhaps the most important key-words of the 'new' archaeology are 'system', 'hypothesis-testing', 'laws', 'process' and 'explanation'.

Systems theory (originally developed in the 1940s) was used to study interactions between a society and its environment, and they were frequently presented in the graphic form used for electrical circuit diagrams. The details of the diagram would be constructed from precise observations of archaeological and environmental evidence, and the result might use the concept of 'feedback' to assess how an interaction might cause changes in the system. Interpretations of change based upon systems theory favoured modifications *within* societies, and helped to discourage 'historical' explanations that invoked diffusion, invasion or migration. The formulation and testing of **hypotheses** reflect the growing interest in scientific methodology, combined with the use of statistics, that characterized most of the social sciences in the 1960s. This approach contrasted with the traditional method of reaching conclusions intuitively after looking at the data; in the words of Lewis Binford, a leading light of the 'new' archaeology:

> What is argued ... is that the generation of inferences regarding the fact should not be the end product of the archaeologist's work ... once a proposition has been advanced no matter by what means it was reached the next task is to deduce a series of testable hypotheses that, if verified against independent empirical data, would tend to verify the proposition. (1972, 90).

Furthermore, just as in experimental science, the purpose of hypothesis-testing was the establishment of generally applicable laws:

> In our search for explanations of differences

and similarities in the archaeological record, our ultimate goal is the formulation of laws of cultural dynamics.(ibid. 100)

Doubts about the two-fold assumption that laws of this kind not only existed, but could be detected archaeologically, prevented many 'old' archaeologists from embracing 'new' archaeology. Subsequently, doubt has also been cast on the empirical nature of the archaeological record and our ability to interpret it.

Binford's writings reflect an almost evangelical desire to propagate better modes of thought, because archaeology could provide a depth of information about the past that anthropologists could never achieve, for the simple reason that they did not live long enough to witness the unfolding of a major **process**. He expressed dissatisfaction with the chosen restrictions of traditional archaeology and anthropology, and emphasized the role of 'theory' as a conscious working process that should be combined with precise scientific thinking. The sequence of the essential components of his approach are condensed into the following paragraph, which is, incidentally, typical of his difficult written style:

> Process, as I understand it, refers to the dynamic relationships (causes and effects) operative among the components of a system or between systematic components and the environment. In order to deal with process we must seek explanations for observed phenomena, and it is only through explanations of our observations that we gain any knowledge of the past. *Explanation begins for the archaeologist when observations made of the archaeological record are linked through laws of cultural or behavioural functioning to past conditions or events* [my italics]. (1972, 117)

Sceptics disagreed; Glyn Daniel predicted that the 'new' archaeologists of the 1960s would become the disillusioned men of the 1980s and 1990s, principally because the pursuit of laws of cultural dynamics was doomed to failure. However, most archaeologists would give the 'new' archaeology credit for improving the recording and description of archaeological information, because any attempt to reconstruct social and ecological systems demanded high-quality data. One result was rigorous analysis of archaeological sites, partly through better techniques of excavation but principally through an improved understanding of how sites were formed. The study of **formation processes** (taphonomy) applies not only to the understanding of artefacts and structures, but also the contexts where economic and environmental data, such as bones or plant remains, are found. Michael B Schiffer was a prominent early writer on taphonomy (1976; 1987), and has subsequently edited a long series of volumes devoted to bringing together critical studies of archaeological method and theory. Studies of formation processes are taken further by archaeological experiments involving reconstructions of ancient buildings, or replications of crafts and food preparation methods. Scientific observation of the processes involved and the residues that they leave behind may help to illuminate remains encountered on an archaelogical site (above, p. 157).

Processualism did not only look towards anthropology and prehistory. Stanley South pioneered the search for pattern recognition in artefacts from historical sites in North America, using rigorous data collection and statistical analysis (1977). He studied the changing nature of historical archaeology itself by drawing a seriation diagram of the gradual emergence of publications on theory and method, and the consequent reduction of purely narrative site reports, in historical archaeology publications from 1960 to 1975 (ibid. 20, fig. 3). His diagram is enhanced by the addition of a snail, whose somewhat bemused expression parodies the reaction of many historians to the move from a 'traditional particularistic paradigm' to an 'emerging nomothetic paradigm'. Binford recognized the great interest of South's book to anthropologists concerned with other time periods, and concluded his foreword with the words 'Welcome historic sites archaeology to the science of archaeology' (xii).

7 Ethnoarchaeology
(Hodder 1982a; 1982b;
Gould 1990)

One of the disadvantages of experimental archaeology is that it is conducted by people with modern ideas about work and efficiency. An alternative approach is to study living peoples, and to incorporate additional information made

6.5 Ethnoarchaeology: postgraduate students from Cambridge University observing a smith of the Tugen tribe (Barengo district, Kenya) making an iron spear. Studies of the physical traces left by such activities may help to elucidate Iron Age sites in other parts of the world, while an understanding of social and ritual aspects of craft production may broaden our concepts of economic activities in pre-industrial, non-western societies.
Ian Hodder

available by the possibilities of discussing artefacts, structures and processes with the people involved. Anthropological observation aimed at the understanding of the nature of archaeological evidence is often called **ethnoarchaeology**. The demand for better understanding of archaeological sites and societies caused Lewis Binford

171

and Ian Hodder to conduct ethnoarchaeological investigations amongst the Inuit (Eskimos) in Canada (Binford 1978) and in several parts of Africa (fig. 6.5; Hodder 1982b). Such studies are a matter of urgency, of course, for the number and range of 'primitive' lifestyles still available for observation are diminishing rapidly. The implications of ethnoarchaeology for taphonomy are not always encouraging, for they underline that many important social and economic activities take place without leaving any helpful physical traces; such difficulties must be recognized and faced if archaeology is to progress.

Middle Range Theory involves the study of site formation processes together with the identification, through ethnoarchaeology, of physical evidence that reflects human behaviour (Trigger 1989, 361–7). This approach has had a considerable impact on the study of early hominids in East Africa. Donald Johanson witnessed at first hand Binford's intrusion into the small group of specialists who had been working in East Africa for many decades '. . . with the sweeping bravado of a Broadway veteran come to show the yokels how to act. "It's clear from the bone distributions and the way the limbs had been busted up," Lew told me on the site. "The Olduvai toolmaker was no mighty hunter of beasts. He was the most marginal of scavengers." So much for romance' (Johanson & Shreeve 1991, 233; 235).

Thus, one side effect of the 'new' archaeology was a revitalization of the relationship that had existed between archaeology and anthropology since the nineteenth century. Anthropology is an ideal source of information for generating hypotheses and for offering explanations, for it may provide a comparative approach to activities such as trade, agriculture, or burial, and the ways that they are carried out in societies with different hierarchies, religions and resources. Thus, Renfrew's propositions about the construction of megalithic tombs in neolithic Europe incorporated observations about modern communities in Borneo (above, p. 165). However, most 'primitive' peoples who survived into the twentieth century had undoubtedly been affected by contact with Europeans, even if indirectly. For this reason explanations based upon modern anthropological research that are applied to prehistory should only be regarded as hypotheses to be refuted or falsified.

8 Post-processualism
(Hodder 1991; Hodder & Shanks 1993)

Archaeology has come under many influences since the 1970s, including structuralism, post-structuralism and forms of post-modernist criticism that, if taken to extreme lengths, reject not only those values and judgements that have been made in the past, but even the possibility of making any meaningful judgements at all today. It is hardly surprising that processualism, based on systems deduced from detailed observations of sites and artefacts, came under forceful attack from many directions. As has happened in so many political and intellectual movements in the past, yesterday's revolutionaries have become today's conservatives. However, the 'new' archaeologists of the 1960s and later did not maintain an unaltered set of theory; the pursuit of general laws soon appeared unattainable, but many interesting ideas were generated along the way. However, some of those who benefited from the advances in theory and methods now consider that their achievements, and indeed those of their predecessors, are under threat.

The lack of consensus is reflected by the proliferation of publications about archaeological theory itself, rather than 'real' archaeology set into a theoretical context, and also by the passions generated by disputes about the validity of different theoretical approaches. New theoretical approaches continue to rely upon 'mining-and-bridging' exercises that borrow (mine) useful theories from other disciplines, and modify them to provide explanations (bridges) in archaeological situations; 'new' archaeology had itself benefited from precisely this kind of activity in the 1960s (Yoffee & Sherratt 1993, 3–4). One problem is that post-processual archaeology presents a rapidly moving target, far harder to criticize than its processual predecessor. It thrives on contradictions, oppositions and confrontations with traditional approaches:

Post-processual archaeology, then, involves the breaking down of established, taken-for-granted dichotomies, and opens up study of the relationships between norm and individual, process and structure, material and ideal, object and subject. Unlike processual archaeology it does not espouse one approach or argue that archaeology should develop an agreed methodology. That is why post-processual archaeology is simply 'post-'. It develops from a criticism of that which went before, building on yet diverging from that path. It involves diversity and lack of consensus. It is characterized by debate and uncertainty about fundamental issues that may have been rarely questioned before in archaeology. It is more an asking of questions than a provision of answers. (Hodder 1991, 181)

8.1 Context, structure, mind …

(Renfrew 1982; Shanks 1991)

One major drawback of a strictly processual view of the past is its failure to address some of the most profound aspects of human life related to thought and belief. Renfrew had confronted this issue in 1982 by discussing 'an archaeology of mind', and deploring the traditional division between mind and matter:

> The gap cannot be bridged, nor can 'mind' usefully be considered when taken in isolation from its 'thoughts'. These 'thoughts', I assert, or some of them do find effective expression in the material record. (1982, 27)

He identified some of these expressions, such as systems of weights that indicate concepts of mass and measurement, religious objects and structures that imply ritual or ideology, deliberate designs of artefacts, and most forms of artistic depiction.

This kind of thinking accords well with the **contextual archaeology** developed by Ian Hodder as a result of his ethnographic research in Kenya and elsewhere (Hodder 1982b; 1991). He generated a much more sophisticated view of the role of material culture, in which artefacts and their ornamentation possessed a powerful role in societies, and were used in an active manner to display, in symbolic form, feelings of allegiance, defiance, etc. Attention to symbols is also an

important element in **structuralism**, an approach more commonly found in anthropology and linguistics, where words, ideas or artefacts are linked into subtle patterns of meaning. A positive feature of philosophies of archaeology that seek meaning in psychological terms is that they are unlikely to neglect the active role of the individual in society, whereas an excessively processual point of view may lead to a mechanical notion of human societies shaped entirely by environmental forces.

9 Reconstructing archaeology …
(Shanks & Tilley 1987; 1992)

Glyn Daniel stated that 'man's past is something to be recorded, described, appreciated and understood' (1981, 192), as if there were no important problems in gaining understanding, once 'something' had been recorded and described properly. Readers of the editorials he wrote for *Antiquity* from the 1950s to the 1980s (published in book form in 1992) were left in no doubt that the past was to be appreciated by connoisseurs in the same manner as a good French wine. It should certainly be protected from the 'lager-louts' of theoretical archaeology, and kept out of the hands of those who placed themselves beyond the pale by showing an interest in treasure hunting or UFOs.

The title of this section is taken from a fascinating book, *Re-constructing Archaeology: Theory and practice* by Michael Shanks and Christopher Tilley, first published in 1987. An updated edition appeared in 1992 with an appendix that restated the authors' central views with the benefit of five years' hindsight, and in the light of criticisms that they had received. *Re-constructing Archaeology* was accompanied by a separate book, *Social Theory and Archaeology* (1987). Despite their assertion that a simplified textbook version of complex ideas 'is merely a valorization of anti-intellectualism' (1992, 262), I will take this risk if only to encourage readers to look up these books for themselves. Few authors of books on archaeology rival Shanks & Tilley's ability to stimulate and depress, fascinate and irritate, excite and repel their readers.

Shanks & Tilley's principal objection to the 'new' archaeology was the separation between the development of theories and the case-studies carried out to test them:

> We attempted to emphasise theory as a practice, as a process indelibly linking the archaeologist and that which he or she constructs and re-constructs. Such a position puts an end to theory viewed as something essentially divorced from and standing beyond the practice of actually doing archaeology. What we were working towards was a theory of and in practice, the notion that all archaeology is theoretical practice. (248)

The rejection of 'scientism' may have struck at the heart of many archaeologists, but more shocks were in store. In answering their critics over accusations of '... relativist pluralism, for apparently arguing that validity depends simply on the present, for being nihilistic, negative and political', Shanks & Tilley observed that the strongest objections came from the most imperialist capitalist nation-states (the USA and Canada) and Britain, 'riddled with deep-rooted class division' (257). This underlined the political dimensions of their work:

> Archaeology is a making of a past in a present. ... Taking the past seriously involves recognizing its otherness not as a matter of exoticism but as a means of undercutting and relativizing the legitimacy of the present (260).

> ... We are seeking ... to disrupt and to render dishevelled prevailing contemporary archaeological discourses in order to foster fresh discourses and new pasts, socially and politically relevant pasts. (262–3)

So where does all this lead?

> We intend to develop further a critical sociology of archaeology ... Central questions to be asked here are: who produces the past and why? For whom exactly is this production taking place? In what circumstances? Who has the right to speak and expect to have their statements considered as worthy of attention and comment? (263)

Shanks & Tilley end on an upbeat note, expressing a sentiment with which I agree, for it summarizes my perception of the value of archaeology as an academic discipline worthy of a place in education: 'We embrace a contradictory and fluid past which, even if not simple, will be intelligible' (265). Others disagree, finding little comfort in Shanks & Tilley's denial of relativism, and disliking a political agenda that threatens their own established position:

> Indeed, the post-processual school is no school at all ... in that it does not attempt to formulate a constructive archaeological agenda, launches no coherent body of theory and method for interpreting the past, and sets out deliberately to obfuscate the genuine gains made in over a century of systematic research. The ideological danger posed by the grimmest processual scientism pales in comparison to the threat of those who seek to undermine the framework of traditional archaeological practice and who, at their most systematically critical, are indeed nihilists. (Yoffee & Sherratt 1993, 8)

10 Current issues in archaeology

I hope that this extended discussion of the role of theoretical archaeology has shown that its importance is not restricted to understanding the past. It also helps us to perceive our own points of view more clearly, and to guard against an unthinking imposition of our own values and preoccupations on ancient societies. Although there is nothing new in recognizing that our opinions about the past tend to reflect our views on the present, it is not always easy to bear it in mind.

One distinctive aspect of western society in the late twentieth century is a reaction against modernism. It ranges from concern about environmental problems, such as global warming, that are seen as a result of industrialization, to the romantic appeal of primitive lifestyles, whether those of modern peoples such as the Yanamamo Indians or supposedly egalitarian and peaceful prehistoric societies. The confidence that allowed Victorian England to rule and exploit colonies abroad while young women and children worked in factories at home has almost entirely disappeared. Prosperity and education have subsequently raised awareness of the rights of individuals to a very high degree, and the social background of people who participate in archaeology is now very diverse. As a result, sites are studied and preserved by professional academics and civil servants rather than the leisured churchmen and indulgent landowners of the eighteenth century. Archaeology has also become involved in broader issues, such as the market-led deregulated economics of Thatcher and Reagan, multiculturalism, 'green politics', feminism, the rights of indigenous peoples, and ethical questions over the ownership of 'cultural property' ranging from classical Greek sculptures to relatively modern 'tribal' artefacts from the Third World. Again, it is important to stress that a subject that involves so many current issues has great educational potential, and its exponents are increasingly unlikely to operate in 'ivory towers' isolated from modern pressures.

11 Managing our heritage
(Cleere 1989)

One context where it is particularly difficult to evade broad ethical and political issues is sometimes known as the heritage movement (or even the heritage industry). This term embraces many different approaches to presenting the past to the public, and provokes strong reactions and hot debate. A less emotive description of the conservation and presentation of sites, landscapes and artefacts is **cultural resource management** (CRM). Heritage management has become an important source of employment for archaeologists in the 1980s and 1990s, and it has absorbed a large number of specialists who, in previous decades, would have made their careers in universities or academic museums.

This expansion of employment opportunities (in a time of general economic recession) is intimately bound up with the move towards a post-industrial society, with its emphasis on leisure and the service sector. Many private industries have opened their own museums, covering the industrial histories of anything from pencils (Keswick, Cumbria) to whisky (Edinburgh) and even fishing-tackle (Alnwick, Northumberland). Furthermore, while some 'heritage' projects have been financed by property developers whose activities tend to destroy archaeological sites, a significant proportion has benefited from the injection of government funds into areas that have suffered most from the decline of heavy industries such as mining or ship-building. At the same time, governments committed (in theory) to efficiency, deregulation and lower public expenditure have had to establish an extensive bureaucracy at national and local levels to cope with new legislation about ancient sites and with tighter guidelines to the authorities who grant planning permission for developments affecting historic buildings or archaeological sites.

11.1 Archaeology and the State

It is interesting to observe changes in the names of state bodies that have looked after ancient monuments over the years in Britain. When Pitt Rivers initiated the process of guardianship of scheduled sites in 1882, he acted (largely at his own expense) on behalf of His Majesty's Office of Works. By the 1950s this had been replaced by the rather more democratic-sounding Ministry of Public Building and Works, and the trend towards image-projection continued in the 1970s with the invention of the Department of the Environment. Even more dramatic changes took place during the Thatcher years, first with the creation of an impressively named committee, the Historic Buildings and Monuments Commission, and the removal of responsibility for ancient monuments from the Department of the Environment in 1984 into the hands of English Heritage. This organization was (theoretically) independent of the government, but overall control of the purse-strings remained in the hands of the Department of the Environment.

Management of sites by English Heritage brought visible changes: visitors to ruined castles were now greeted by enthusiastic custodians, some of them young graduates, wearing sweatshirts adorned with the logo of EH's new corporate image, in place of the dark uniforms and peaked caps of their dour predecessors. Most sites open to the public received bright new ticket offices, shops containing an attractive range of souvenirs and information, and, in some cases, cafés as well. The new atmosphere of customer orientation was even enhanced by a period of sponsorship by a supermarket chain. Similar developments took place beyond England with the creation of Historic Scotland, and its Welsh counterpart, CADW. English Heritage now offers a range of educational, cultural and historical events at major sites, provides subscribing members with a glossy magazine, and publishes popular books about its sites and archaeology in general in a joint venture with a commercial publisher. The result is that it is difficult for a visitor to distinguish between a site in the care of the State and one owned by an entirely private organization such as the National Trust.

English Heritage still retains responsibility for enforcing the legal protection of sites and historic buildings, and it funds a large number of rescue excavations and the publication of a backlog of sites excavated over recent decades. However, in tune with the vogue in the 1980s and 1990s for privatization and competitive tendering, much of this work is carried out indirectly by teams of contract archaeologists and self-employed consultants. In the same spirit, English Heritage also attempts to place most of the financial burden for excavation and publication on the shoulders of developers, who, as part of the process of applying for planning permission, must commission reports on the impact of their proposals upon the environment (including archaeology). The production of impact reports offers yet another opportunity for independent consultants, who may then bid for the contract to carry out whatever work is required. Obviously, ethics intrude here, for competition drives down prices, and a developer has a vested interest in obtaining an impact report that minimizes the harmful effects of whatever project is proposed. Fortunately, archaeology attracts publicity in the press, and few respectable developers wish to incur the cost of damaging their public image when a few thousand pounds devoted to an excavation might enhance it.

Thus, in little over a century, State involvement in British archaeology has progressed from informal supervision of a small number of sites, through cooperation with sympathetic landowners, to the provision of a major focus of leisure and tourism. Furthermore, visitors to sites are now encouraged to feel that they are participating in their heritage, rather than being

allowed the privilege of access to Crown property. However, we must not forget that Pitt Rivers saw museums as a means of discouraging popular desires for radical political change (above, p. 167); what message lies behind the current style of English Heritage's presentation? I feel that the answer lies in conservative Britain's fears that European integration through the EEC threatens national sovereignty; thus, the united kingdoms of England and Scotland, along with the Principality of Wales, all have a heritage administration bearing their own name. Is it cynical to see in the title *English* Heritage an exclusive label that not only counters pro-European sentiments, but discourages multiculturalism? Did the Secretary of State for the Environment who chose this title in 1984 wish to promote the heritage of people who consider themselves English rather than British, or all the inhabitants of a country called England?

11.2 Museums: from art gallery to 'experience'
(Hudson 1987; Lumley 1988)

The fears that I have voiced over the 'ownership' of the past find much stronger expression in the context of museums. Unlike an ancient site or historic building, a museum is a modern creation whose very form embodies the ideas of a designer. These ideas are then enhanced by the selection of particular items for display, and by the kind of information offered in the form of labels and other documentation. Older museums are inseparable from art galleries in that the artefacts they display are grouped by period, and presented as beautiful objects to be contemplated with minimal documentation. A connoisseur of art is expected to be well-informed about the significance and history of a painting, and needs only to be given that the name of the artist, and the place and year it was painted. Likewise, archaeological museums assumed for many centuries that all a visitor needed to know were the origin, date and function of an artefact on display. In the twentieth century museums gradually began to make fewer assumptions about their visitors, and attempted to provide more information about objects on view, normally by providing commentaries in the form of pictures of contemporary sites and extended text and labels. Understanding was enhanced by placing objects into context with the help of models and reconstructions, and might extend to establishing a display including human figures as well as objects.

York

This trend has culminated in a few remarkable 'museums' (this term is no longer the obvious description) such as the **Jorvik Viking Centre**; in the words of an advertisement:

> Visit the Jorvik Viking Centre in York and a time car will whisk you back 1000 years to a reconstruction of an actual street in Viking Age Jorvik. Complete with sights, sounds and smells, it's an unforgettable experience.

The success of this approach may be measured by the length of the queue of people who are prepared to wait several hours for this short, expensive experience. On the surface, there is little difference between Jorvik and other tourist attractions in the city. The Friargate Museum uses wax figures to mix history (kings and queens, Thatcher and Major) with sensation (Dracula and unexpected jets of water in the dark), while the York Dungeon presents lurid scenes of life-size figures undergoing horrific medieval tortures. The Friargate Museum leads into a shop full of exploding pens, plastic skeletons and other familiar joke-shop toys. In contrast, Jorvik ends with a conventional museum gallery full of artefacts, followed by a shop full of rather expensive but tasteful gifts, games and books, mostly with a clear historical relevance or educational purpose. Jorvik was set up in 1984 by the York Archaeological Trust, a team of archaeologists that deals with rescue archaeology in the city. The Trust formed a company to invest in this project in the expectation of making a profit that could be ploughed back into supporting its principal archaeological activities, whose funding was always unpredictable and liable to be cut back during times of financial difficulties for English Heritage or the local council (Addyman 1990).

Jorvik maintains a clear separation between reconstructed scenes and authentic artefacts displayed in glass cases, and it presents archaeological methods by means of 'frozen' scenes of the archae-ological excavation upon which the reconstruction is based, and the laboratory where the finds were classified and conserved in 1980. It is interesting that these displays have already become historical in themselves, for there have been technical advances in both surveying methods and computerized cataloguing of finds since they were prepared to provide a 'state of the art' picture of archaeological methods. A solution to this problem is to be found in the **ARC** (**Archaeological Resource Centre**: fig. 6.6), a separate 'museum' (it consciously avoids that name), also created by the York Archaeological Trust.

The ARC breaks two major conventions in museum display. First, there are no glass cases, and no permanent collections of specimens of any kind. Second, it is an integral part of the process of interpreting the past, for visitors handle and sort actual finds from excavations, and they see 'real' archaeologists at work through the glass doors and walls of offices in the same building. ARC invites visitors to learn by taking part, once they have watched an introductory video about the process of excavation. They are encouraged to handle artefacts or bones and to discuss them with ARC staff; they may also try sewing leather shoes, or weaving on a replica of an early medieval loom. An assortment of computers allows visitors to catalogue objects, to analyse the distributions of finds in relation to the plan of an excavated building, or to use an interactive videodisk to study the details of photographs of a site. There is no narrative, no heavy-handed educational message, simply an open invitation to participate; it appeals to children, adults, and even professional archaeologists who manage to join in without standing on their dignity. Two clear messages are communicated: that archaeologists do not dig to discover spectacular finds, and that the ordinary scraps of pottery and bone they find really are interesting and informative.

The purpose of the ARC is not purely altruistic, of course. The citizens of York, and tourists from elsewhere, pay taxes to support rescue archaeology and finds processing, but they would not value these activities highly in a time of government spending cuts. A pleasant outing to York is enhanced by a visit to the Jorvik Viking Centre, and the ARC demonstrates the kinds of archae-

6.6 The Archaeological Resource Centre, York, introduces the work of archaeologists through practical activities, rather than static displays and glass cases. Visitors may handle and classify genuine artefacts and bones, try out ancient weaving and leather-working techniques, and make use of computers that allow them to explore aspects of excavation and finds-processing in their own way. The upper floor of this modified church building accommodates archaeologists who may be observed at work through glass walls by visitors.
York Archaeological Trust

ological methods that were employed to interpret the remains that have been reconstructed in Jorvik's Viking street scene. An understanding of the kind of work that archaeologists actually do, gained by participation, is likely to give visitors a more positive attitude towards funding it. Ironically, the ARC is located in a redundant church, whose owners are delighted that it has found a use. Does this suggest that the materialist society of the late twentieth century gains greater comfort from handling the physical remains of the past than from contemplating the spiritual promise of life after death?

11.3 Controlling the present by means of the past?
(Hewison 1987; McBryde 1985)

Post-processual archaeology has heightened our awareness of the importance of symbolism in the past, and the political implications of the interpretations we make today. The 'heritage movement' has not escaped scrutiny, and museums have come in for particularly trenchant criticism. Some of the most severe opprobrium is directed towards museums that present the recent industrial past, such as the collection of buildings re-erected at the North of England Open Air Museum at Beamish, in County Durham. A publicity leaflet described it as '. . . a working example of what life in the North of England was really like in the early 1900s . . . Beamish leaves little to the imagination. The experience is authentic.' This celebration of coal-mining and other heavy industries emphasizes cheerful communities based around terraced houses and busy local shops. It makes a poignant contrast with the realities of life in contemporary north-eastern England, and evokes nostalgia and a sense of the loss. Yet it was the horrors of nineteenth-century industrial towns that stimulated most of the reforms of government, health and social administration that came to be valued in the twentieth century. Does a museum like Beamish simply reinforce the politics of the New Right, by idealizing 'Victorian values', and glorifying a world where trade unions and socialism had not yet challenged the comfortable class-values of landowners and industrialists? It will be very interesting to observe how the Berlin Wall is exploited in the twenty-first century to tell visitors about the division and reunification of Germany (Baker 1993).

11.4 Stonehenge

Political issues of this kind are less obvious in relation to sites or museums that belong to earlier periods, but they always lurk beneath the surface. Beamish relates to the memories of local families (reinforced by the novels of Catherine Cookson), and Jorvik may be conceptualized as an analogy for the shopping streets that surround it. What should be made of older monuments such as Stonehenge? Why should we feel any interest in, or responsibility towards, this accidental survival from a distant, forgotten past?

A deserving winner of an archaeological 'book of the year' award was *Stonehenge Complete*, by Christopher Chippindale (1983). It required an introduction of only ten pages of text and photographs to describe Stonehenge, supplemented by a further eight at the end ('Stonehenge: what is known', 264–72). Between these two sections are 16 chapters that follow the site from its first surviving written record (AD 1130) up to the Druidic and 'hippie' festivals of the 1970s and 1980s. Archaeological study began in the sixteenth century, accelerated in the seventeenth and eighteenth with Aubrey and Stukeley (above, p.20–1), and culminated in serious excavation only after 1900. Stukeley dated Stonehenge to the pre-Roman period by means of various ingenious field observations (Chippindale 1983, 77–82). This was refined to the Bronze Age in the nineteenth century, but an age in years was only achieved in the twentieth century, first by cross-dating and finally by radiocarbon. Excavations between 1900 and the 1950s revealed that the site had a long sequence of phases that began, according to the current calibration of radiocarbon years, around 3100 BC. Construction of what *we* recognize as Stonehenge, with its massive sarsen trilithons, began a thousand years later, and was modified several times over the next thousand years.

Thus, unlike Beamish, Jorvik or a medieval cathedral, everything that is currently known or believed about Stonehenge is the cumulative result of almost nine centuries of speculation, observation and excavation. Since nothing about its builders or its original purpose links it directly to the present, its popular attraction stems more from ignorance than knowledge, and provides an interesting example of the problems of cultural resource management. Christopher Chippindale edited a further book about the site in 1990, this time entitled *Who Owns Stonehenge?* It contains chapters by an extraordinarily diverse range of people: there are three archaeologists, two English (an editor/museum curator and a university professor) and one Welsh (working in Australia); the director of the Centre for Earth Mysteries; and the Secular Arch-Druid. Chippindale summarized the issues in an elegant sentence that contains reminders of post-processual concerns, and a hint of the relativism so despised by opponents of post-modernism in general:

> Beneath its weathered old surface, a superficially straightforward site is just one item in a compound of powerful ingredients: archaeology, yes, and landscape history, but, overpowering the delicacies of scholarship, a stronger and bubbling brew of issues concerning intellectual freedom, rational and intuitive knowledge, preservation, presentation and access, the place and role of religious beliefs, the State and its dissidents, the rights of dispossessed ethnic minorities, and even the concept of ownership. (1990, 9)

The preparation of Chippindale's book coincided with a violent confrontation between police and people (sometimes described as 'New Age travellers') who had held a free festival near Stonehenge from 1974 to 1984. The police sealed off all approaches to the site over the midsummer period because English Heritage and the National Trust had banned not only the festival, but the annual rituals performed by modern Druids within the stone circles (fig. 6.7). The 1980s closed with Stonehenge in the summer '. . . festooned in barbed-wire, surrounded by police, and patrolled by privately employed security guards. It has looked like a concentration camp, the unacceptable face of militarism in a democracy' (ibid. 33). In 1993, English Heritage scrapped all existing plans for improving visitor access, parking and information, and called for a wide discussion of the possibilities. Stonehenge became public property in 1918, long after the number of visitors had begun to pose problems of conservation and management. Archaeology may have achieved many things in the twentieth century, but it will not be surprising if the centenary of public management at Stonehenge has to be celebrated in visitor facilities that fall a long way short of the dignity of the site.

Who Owns Stonehenge? does an important job by bringing together many opinions in one book, and makes proposals for the future. Whether you believe them or not, the chapters by exponents of earth mysteries and Druidism are just as serious as those by the archaeologists, and make it clear that such views will have to be taken into account if plans for the management of the site are to

6.7 In the 1980s and 1990s, Druids and New Age travellers wanting to celebrate the summer solstice at Stonehenge came into increasingly violent conflict with police who were attempting to enforce measures introduced by English Heritage and the National Trust for the protection of the ancient monument. This print, which accompanied a newspaper feature about the difficult issues involved, encapsulates the transformation of an ancient site into a modern symbol of state power by echoing the form of the stones in 'trilithons' made from traffic cones and barriers that exclude Druids from the focus of their rituals. Post-processual archaeology has done much to create a wider awareness of the power of symbols, and to underline ways in which the management of the past is influenced by modern judgements of a political or philosophical nature. *David Bromley; Guardian, 15/6/1992*

succeed. Meanwhile, we must reflect upon the irony that Stonehenge, of all sites, should have come to symbolize authoritarian repression and exclusive ownership (in the names of English Heritage and the National Trust) to those few individuals who value it as a symbol of 'otherness' in cosmic or ritual terms today.

12 Ethical issues

12.1 The antiquities trade

(Greenfield 1989; Wilson 1989)

It does not take much imagination to realize that the raw materials of archaeology are finite. Destruction of sites escalated rapidly from the eighteenth century onwards, as agriculture expanded to match population growth, and by the end of the nineteenth century a serious conservation ethic had begun to develop in several European countries. Nevertheless, many archaeologists and museums regarded sites and artefacts from around the Mediterranean, the Near East and other parts of the world as yet another resource to be exploited for the benefit of their own countries. This is no longer official policy, but it has left a powerful legacy, in the form of a vast international market for works of art, antiquities and 'tribal' material from the Third World. Public museums have a reasonably good record in refusing to purchase items that lack proper documentation about their origins and ownership, but private collectors are not always so scrupulous.

The result is that ancient sites and cemeteries all over the world are systematically plundered in the search for pots, jewellery, carvings or anything else that may be sold. This problem is most serious in the Third World, where antiquities form a valuable supplement to low incomes, along with other sought-after materials such as drugs or ivory. The treasure-hunters of Africa and South America receive pitifully small rewards in comparison with the high prices that antiquities command in London or New York. The problem is not restricted to the Third World: architectural sculptures, mosaics and wall paintings removed from European churches have turned up in salerooms and museums in the United States, and protected sites in Britain are regularly raided by illegal commercial metal-detector operators.

It is difficult for archaeologists based in the former colonial powers to denounce the antiquities trade when museums in their own countries are full of items from overseas possessions. The British Museum is perhaps the greatest example of a global collection, and many of its most famous items (not just the Elgin marbles from the Parthenon in Athens) were removed with the permission of their owners in the past. But why should modern Greece or Egypt recognize legal agreements made before they gained independence from Turkish rulers? And were 'gifts' and purchases from Africa or India really made between equals, without political or military pressure? The relativism for which post-processual archaeology is frequently criticized certainly helps to force archaeologists and museums to confront not only the politics of their activities, but the ethics of their approach.

12.2 Indigenous peoples

(Layton 1989a; 1989b)

Prehistory is a Western concept according to which those societies which have not developed writing – or an equivalent system of graphic representation – have no history. This fits perfectly into the framework of evolutionist thought typical of Western cultures.... Archaeology has been up until now a means of domination and the colonial dispossession of our identity. If it were to be taken back by the Indians themselves it could provide us with new tools to understand our historical development, and so strengthen our present demands and our projects for the future. (Mamami Condori 1989, 51, 58)

This observation by a Bolivian Indian archaeolo-

gist emphasizes how worries over the ethics of collecting antiquities or 'tribal' art from the Third World are closely linked to growing sensitivities about the rights of indigenous peoples. The general issues were made more apparent during celebrations of the bicentenary of the colonization of Australia in 1988, and in the 500th anniversary in 1992 of the 'discovery' of America by Columbus: in the words of one poster, 'Native Americans are not celebrating'. Arguments about the ownership of 'cultural property' in the form of antiquities and works of art take on an interesting additional dimension when they are focused on the question of the treatment of human remains. In both North America and Australia, there have been demands for the reburial of remains excavated by archaeologists – whatever their age. Furthermore, there have been requests to return material taken as specimens by nineteenth-century anthropologists and anatomists.

Archaeologists sometimes justify the disturbance of indigenous sites and burials on the grounds that they benefit native populations today by illustrating their origins and early history. It is true that this kind of evidence may support claims for the ownership of land, but it assumes a very 'western' view of the past, involving linear (rather than cyclical) time, and a notion of death as final: '... to most Aborigines this would be meaningless sophistry. Human bones are the remains of their ancestors, the landscape itself the remains of ancestral beings and creators' (Haglund, quoted in Hubert 1989, 156). By the 1990s, agreements about the treatment of burials had been reached between indigenous peoples and archaeologists in many parts of the world (e.g. Kucera 1991). The process has been stressful for many archaeologists, forced to confront the prejudices that lurked behind their 'liberal' self-image, but the recognition of the validity of other views of the world is likely to be beneficial in the long term (Zimmerman 1989).

12.3 Gender

(Gero & Conkey 1991; Claasen 1992)

A parallel issue to that of indigenous rights is gender, for it also confronts prejudices that may lie so deep that they are unconscious (figs 6.

8–9). The first blunder that male archaeologists make is to assume that an interest in gender is equivalent to feminism. After all, one approach to gender (or race) is to promote equality, and to ignore genuine differences; an emphasis on 'engendering' archaeology demands that it should be a serious aspect of any inquiry. The feminist dimension arises from the problem that while females do tend to see gender as a perspective, males frequently ignore it:

> Women archaeologists who study gender relations, either women in prehistory or women in archaeology, expressly state their perspective, which is in fact often considered to be only a perspective by mainstream male archaeologists, and they acknowledge that their view is partial. ... Feminist theorists admit their position, the context and perspective of their research/writing. ... In addition, post-processualists often show a total lack of an understanding of themselves as gendered individuals, as well as of gender's part in the structuring of individuals, culture and society. (Engelstad 1991, 512)

The absurdity of some male attitudes to archaeological studies is illustrated by two interpretations of early Stone Age art. Carved objects bearing two rounded protrusions were classified as 'breast pendants' for many years, but when rotated through 90°, they could equally represent penises and testicles, which were very frequently featured on pendants in the Roman period (Kehoe 1991). The second example concerns 'Venus' figurines that were supposedly carved to exaggerate the female body in a religious symbolism of fertility around 25,000 BC. While this ritual interpretation cannot be tested, a study of the physical proportions of modern women shows that the figurines fit into the normal range of obesity (Duhard 1991). The basis of their interpretation as 'cult-figurines' rests upon an idealized (predominantly male) image of the shape of women, rather than an observation of reality.

One reaction to the male dominance of the modern world is to propose that a different kind of society existed in the past. The concept of a Great Goddess has been given progressively greater emphasis over recent decades by Marije Gimbutas, a major expert on European prehistory. She has welcomed the shift away from the interpretation of megalithic stone monuments that dominated the 1960s and 1970s, when they were seen as expressions of societies who possessed sophisticated mathematical and astronomical skills (very much associated with male practitioners today). Instead, emphasis has been placed upon the purpose of their alignments with the solar and lunar calendar: 'An ideology based on belief in an unending and returning cycle is disclosed – birth, life, death, rebirth. The tombs and sanctuaries are permeated with the idea of regeneration of life powers that depend on the Cosmic Mother' (Gimbutas, in Meaden 1991, 10). The feminine attributes of the Goddess are contrasted with the less attractive associations of machismo:

> ... She was Provider throughout the immense period of time which was the Neolithic and Bronze Ages, an era which for Britain, Ireland and Brittany was largely a time of tranquillity. She ruled over a classless, balanced society, until the convulsions of the Iron Age brought widespread fortifications to hilltops following invasions by male-ruling, God-dominated warrior groups – the so-called 'heroic' societies. Thus ended the serenity of the Age of the Goddess. So began the Age of Wars which has lasted to this day. (Meaden 1991, 214)

Echoes of the 'New Age' philosophies of California (where Gimbutas was based) are evident in this kind of writing; utopian evocations of lost Golden Ages have a much longer history, stretching back to ancient Greece.

General problems of sexual inequality affect archaeology in much the same way as other professions, for the same underlying reasons. Competition for careers in museums, universities or field archaeology does not favour people who have stepped off the promotions ladder to raise families; this is where feminism must stimulate changes in attitudes. The transition from feminism and the archaeology of women to an archaeology of gender remains a goal that '... will be partly realized when gender is considered not as an optional issue, but as another structuring principle fundamental to interpreting past societies' (Gilchrist 1991, 499).

6.8–9 The 1951 Festival of Britain celebrated an optimistic beginning to a new era, after a half-century that had included two world wars and the Great Depression. It is interesting to see that while the South Bank Exhibition site in London looked forward through 'contemporary' architecture, it also involved 'the people giving themselves a pat on the back'. It is interesting to reassess a series of models showing the British family through the ages (now at the Jewry Wall Museum, Leicester, and still very popular with visitors) from the perspective of the 1990s. Were they intended to reassure people who feared that the recently re-elected Labour government threatened social upheavals? They imply that the nuclear family unit had remained a constant feature of British society throughout millennia of progress and change; the same kinds of family images also featured heavily in advertisements at the time. The Anglo-Saxon family is particularly intriguing, for despite two recent wars, it seems to underline the Germanic origins of military and cultural achievements in British history. The mother and daughter on the left also bear uncomfortable similarities to propaganda images of blond Aryan families produced in Hitler's Germany. Both families wear the full, billowing clothes introduced by Dior's 'New Look' in 1947, despite its condemnation for wastefulness by government ministers; the Iron Age woman even echoes the facial expression and hairstyle of Dior's models.

Most of the artefacts and costume accessories included in these groups are derived from a social élite, not ordinary families. The figures also provoke mixed reactions today because of the manner in which they present gender roles. *Jewry Wall Museum, Leicester*

12.4 The Green movement

(MacInnes & Wickham-Jones 1992)

Samples of tree-rings taken from oak trunks preserved in the peat bogs of Ireland include a series of exceptionally narrow rings that indicate an episode of cold, wet weather beginning in 1159 BC and lasting around twenty years. It was almost certainly the result of a volcanic eruption detected by a layer of acidity found in ice-sheet cores at 1100 ± 50 BC. Minute particles of volcanic glass have been discovered in peat bogs from northern Britain sampled for their pollen content, and the chemical composition of the volcanic minerals matches material from a massive eruption of Hekla in Iceland. We know from recent experience that volcanic eruptions send enormous quantities of volcanic dust and ash into the upper atmosphere. Mount St Helens in the United States and Mount Pinutabo in the Philippines provided vivid examples of this phenomenon in recent years; they were modest in comparison with Hekla, however.

The quantities of dust that Hekla poured into the atmosphere were sufficient to shield the Earth's surface from solar radiation to such an extent that the climate was disrupted for the twenty-year period revealed by tree-rings. The effect upon humans was even more dramatic, for it seems that settlement patterns and farming practices were disrupted for long enough to cause the abandonment of most upland areas of northern Britain. An archaeologist, Colin Burgess, had already observed a rupture in the archaeological evidence for settlements and artefact types from this late Bronze Age period, and even went as far as suggesting that it might have been the result of a natural catastrophe such as a volcano. Baillie's work on tree-rings provided independent confirmation of the proposition that an environmental catastrophe had been responsible for these profound changes in human behaviour.

There are clear lessons to be drawn from the eruption of 1159 BC. It is a timely reminder that we live in a fragile ecosystem, under constant threat from natural disasters that may strike from any quarter. It also underlines the seriousness of current concern about global warming, for if a temporary disturbance of the atmosphere by a single volcano may put large tracts of land out of use for a generation, what will the continuing build-up of greenhouse gases do over the next century?

Archaeology also demonstrates the effects of human changes to the landscape. Irrigation in Mesopotamia raised the salinity of soils too far for crops to grow successfully; forest clearance in the Apennines led to erosion that filled Mediterranean valleys with metres of silt, and turned the low-lying areas of Rome into an unhealthy swamp. Mayan civilization may have collapsed as a result of an excessive population's demands on the limited fertility of its land; Easter Island's forest was destroyed by rival populations involved in competition to quarry, transport and erect huge stone statues (Bahn & Flenley 1992). In other words, human societies in the past did not live in harmony with their environments; they frequently exploited and destroyed them. This knowledge does not give us an excuse for doing the same thing; rather, it adds to our responsibility to explore non-destructive agriculture, to utilize materials less wastefully, and to avoid non-productive competitive activities – notably warfare.

13 Conclusion

The interpretation of the past from archaeological remains has come a long way since antiquarians first managed to disprove Samuel Johnson's depressing contention that 'We can know no more than what old writers have told us'. The terminology and preoccupations change, but the objectives and attitudes to the evidence (not to mention the disputes with opponents) have a familiar ring. One of the great benefits of a retrospective study of archaeology is to appreciate this point, and to take a more detached view of any school of thought that claims to be 'new', or to have exclusive possession of the truth.

An open-minded attitude is required not only to changing fashions in archaeological interpretation, but to the subject as a whole. The lesson to be learnt from the rapid advance of scientific techniques in recent decades is that new and revolutionary evidence may appear at any moment from a completely unsuspected source. My personal commitment to the subject is greatly enhanced by this aspect: a discipline that incorporates so much uncertainty and so many different academic approaches, while it ignores conventional boundaries between the sciences and the humanities, is well worth studying at school, university or as a leisure pursuit. If my book has conveyed any of this feeling to its readers, I will consider it to have been a success.

Note: a guide to **further reading** that includes topics covered in this chapter begins on p. 185.

Guide to Further Reading

Note: Many fundamental works are cited in headings within each chapter; these should be consulted first. References to publications that *only* appear in this section are given in full; those that are described more briefly are included in the detailed bibliography below.

General Works

Reference works

Concise accounts of many methods, sites and cultures may be found in the *Collins Dictionary of Archaeology* (Bahn P (ed), Glasgow; HarperCollins, 1992) or *The Penguin Dictionary of Archaeology* (Bray W and Trump D (ed), 1970); S Champion's *Dictionary of Terms and Techniques in Archaeology* (Oxford, Phaidon, 1980) is still worth pursuing. Lavishly illustrated works that cover prehistoric and historical cultures and civilizations, as well as explaining archaeological methods, are *The Cambridge Encyclopedia of Archaeology* (Sherratt 1980) and *Past Worlds: The Times Atlas of Archaeology* (London, Times Books Ltd, 1989).

Period outlines

Brian Fagan has written several readable overviews of prehistory, including *World Prehistory: A brief introduction* (2nd ed, HarperCollins, 1993) and *The Journey from Eden* (1990). The 'feel' of the search for the earliest humans is conveyed by Leakey & Lewin's *Origins Reconsidered* (1992), while Maisels covers *The Emergence of Civilisation in the Near East* (1993). The role of archaeology in historical periods is clearly illustrated in M Grant's *The Visible Past: Greek and Roman history from archaeology* (London, Weidenfeld and Nicolson, 1990). *Archaeology in Britain since 1945* (Longworth H and Cherry J (ed), London, British Museum, 1986) shows how much archaeology has enlarged the perception of the British past, while Fagan's *New Treasures of the Past* (London, Quarto, 1988) takes a world-wide approach.

Other introductions

John Gowlett's *Ascent to Civilization* (2nd ed, New York, McGraw-Hill, 1993) manages to explain techniques and results in an exemplary manner, supported by superb illustrations. Renfrew & Bahn's *Archaeology: Theories, methods, and practice* (1991) and Fagan's *In the Beginning* (1993) are 'heavy-weight' textbooks that are more effective as reference works than introductory reading. A lighter note is struck by P Rahtz in *Invitation to Archaeology* (Oxford, Blackwell, 1991) and Paul Bahn's *Bluff your Way in Archaeology* (London, Ravette, 1989), while a book written by one amateur for others is *Amateur Archaeologist* by S Wass (London, Batsford, 1992).

Periodicals and magazines

News of new discoveries and techniques, discussions of theories, book reviews and comments on political issues feature in the British quarterly periodical *Antiquity*. A more popular approach is taken by *Archaeology* in America, *Dossiers de l'archèologie et d'histoire* in France, *Archäologie der Welt* in Germany, and *Current Archaeology* in Britain. The National Geographical Magazine includes archaeological articles; a selection has been edited by C Lutyck (*The Adventure of Archaeology*, Washington, 1992)

Chapter 1: The idea of the past

Glyn Daniel's *A Short History of Archaeology* (1981) is a well-illustrated introduction, although less detailed than *150 Years of Archaeology* (1975). *The Idea of Prehistory* was reissued in 1988 (with additional chapters by Renfrew), and further insights may be gained from *Antiquity and Man: Essays in honour of Glyn Daniel* (Evans J D Cunliffe B and Renfrew C (ed), London, Thames & Hudson, 1982). A wider range of issues is raised in *Tracing Archaeology's Past*, edited by A L Christensen (Southern Illinois Univ Press, 1989).

Avenues of investigation

Grayson's *The Establishment of Human Antiquity* (1983) remains the authoritative work on the conceptual breakthrough that took place in the nineteenth century, while Gould's *Time's Arrow, Time's Cycle* (1987) explores the intellectual context of the discovery of geological time; see also A Hallam's *Great Geological Controversies* (2nd ed, Oxford Univ Press, 1989). Joan Evans' *Time and Chance* (1943) explains how John Evans (her grandfather) became involved in the momentous events of 1859.

Trigger's *A History of Archaeological Thought* (1989) is a comprehensive guide, supplemented by Malina & Vasicek's *Archaeology Yesterday and Today* (1990). Stuart Piggott places British archaeology into the context of European thought in *Ancient Britons and the Antiquarian Imagination* (1989), and this background is covered by Sklenar in *Archaeology in Central Europe* (1983).

Antiquarian fieldwork in Britain

Stuart Piggott has written a full biography of William Stukeley (1985). Various editions of Richard Gough's 1789 translation of Camden's *Britannia* may be found in reference libraries, while facsimiles of John Aubrey's *Monumenta Britannica or A Miscellany of British Antiquities* (Parts 1 & 2) have been published with editorial comments from Fowles J & Legg R (Boston, Little, Brown & Co, 1980–82). *Avebury Reconsidered: From the 1660s to the 1990s* by Ucko P, Hunter M and Clark A (London, Unwin Hyman, 1990) is a case-study of the continuing importance of antiquarian records.

Touring and collecting

The northern European passion for Greek and Roman antiquities is illuminated in Haskell F and Penny N, *Taste and the Antique: The lure of classical sculpture, 1500–1900* (Yale Univ Press, 1981), and Penny's study of an important collector, *Thomas Howard, Earl of Arundel* (Oxford, Ashmolean Museum, 1985). The transformation of private collections into public museums is explained in *Museums and the Shaping of Knowledge* by Hooper-Greenhill (1992) and Impey & MacGregor's *The Origins of Museums* (1985). One case is presented in detail in M Caygill's *The Story of the British Museum* (London, 1992), while *Archaeologists and Aesthetes: The sculpture galleries of the British Museum in the 19th century* by I Jenkins (London, British Museum, 1992) discusses a major disagreement about how things should be displayed. Collecting was particularly important to the development of the Three-Age System; the background is presented in O Klindt-Jensen's *A History of Scandinavian Archaeology* (London, Thames and Hudson, 1975).

The discovery of civilizations

Contemporary reports from the *Illustrated London News* recapture the excitement of nineteenth-century discoveries (Bacon E, *The Great Archaeologists*, London, Secker and Warburg, 1976); *Great Adventures in Archaeology*, edited by R Silverberg (Penguin, 1985) is an anthology of writings by discoverers. H Winstone's general account, *Uncovering the Ancient World* (London, Constable, 1986) is supplemented by his biographies of *Woolley of Ur* (London, Secker and Warburg, 1990) and *Howard Carter and the discovery of the Tomb of Tutankhamun* (London, Constable, 1991). Other interesting biographies include *Flinders Petrie* (Drower 1985) and *The Find of a Lifetime: Sir Arthur Evans and the discovery of Knossos* (S Horwitz, London, Weidenfeld & Nicolson, 1981). The interaction between discoverers and collecting institutions is illuminated by J L Fitton's *Heinrich Schliemann and the British Museum* (London, British Museum Occ Pap 83, 1991).

Analytical approaches to discoveries include McDonald & Thomas' *Progress into the Past: The rediscovery of Mycenean civilization* (1990) and R T Ridley's *The Eagle and the Spade: Archaeology in Rome* during the Napoleonic era (Cambridge Univ Press, 1992). Discoveries outside Europe and the Near East are featured in Fagan's *Elusive Treasure* (1977) and Willey & Sabloff's *A History of American Archaeology* (1980). D K Chakrabarti has written *A History of Indian Archaeology: From the beginning to 1947* (New Delhi, Munshiram Manoharlal, 1988), while *A History of African Archaeology* has been edited by P Robertshaw (London, James Currey, 1990).

Chapter 2:
Discovery, fieldwork and recording

The discovery and recording of sites

Traditional methods are described in Brown's *Fieldwork for Archaeologists and Local Historians* (1987) and C Taylor's *Fieldwork in Medieval Archaeology* (London, Batsford, 1974). For interpretation see *Interpreting Artefact Scatters: Contributions to ploughzone Archaeology*, edited by J Schofield (Oxford, Oxbow, 1990), or Shennan's *Experiments in the Collection and Analysis of Archaeological Survey Data* (1985). Basic recording is covered in *Surveying for Archaeologists* by F Bettess (Univ of Durham, 1992). The problem of maintaining systematic catalogues of sites is the subject of *County Archaeological Records: Progress and Potential*, edited by Ian Burrow (Assoc County Archaeol Officers, 1985), and a Danish volume, *Sites and Monuments: National archaeological records*, edited by Larsen (1992). A brief case-study of an interesting fieldwork exercise that rediscovered a port in northern France is David Hill's 'Quentovic defined' and 'The definition of the early medieval site of Quentovic', *Antiquity* 64 (1990) 51–8 and 66(1992) 965–9.

Aerial photography and geophysical surveying

The best introductions are Riley's *Air Photography and Archaeology* (1987) and Wilson's *Air Photo Interpretation for Archaeologists* (1982). Informative case studies are included in *The Impact of Aerial Reconnaissance on Archaeology* (Maxwell G S (ed), London, Coun Brit Archaeol Res Rep 49, 1983), and *Into the Sun*, edited by D Kennedy (Sheffield, J Collis, 1989). Important aspects of interpretation and recording are discussed in *The Emerging Past: Air photography and the buried landscape* by Whimster (1989). Specific projects are described in *Rome's Desert Frontier from the Air* by D Kennedy & D Riley (London, Batsford, 1990), *The Archaeology of Dartmoor from the Air* (Greeves T (ed), Exeter, Devon Books, 1985) and R Palmer's *Danebury: An aerial photographic interpretation of its environs* (London, HMSO, 1984).

Geophysical surveying is explained clearly in Clark's *Seeing Beneath the Soil* (1990), and the detailed electronic and mathematical background is presented in Scollar's *Archaeological Prospecting and Remote Sensing* (1990). Many case studies can be found in *Geoprospection in the Archaeological Landscape*, edited by Spoerry (1992). An excellent case-study of soil analysis in a fieldwork project has been published by Prosch-Danielson L and Simonsen A: 'PCA of pollen, charcoal & soil phosphate data as a tool in prehistoric land-use investigation at Forsandmoen, SW Norway', *Norwegian Archaeological Review* 21.2 (1988) 85–102.

Landscape archaeology

Aston's *Interpreting the Landscape* (1985) concentrates on British fieldwork, and the results can be seen in interpretations such as C Taylor's *Village and Farmstead: A history of rural settlement in England* (London, Chapman and Hall, 1983). Oliver Rackham's *The History of the Countryside* (London, Dent, 1993) includes fascinating studies of woodlands. The role of environmental sciences is underlined by *Alluvial Archaeology in Britain*, edited by Needham S and Macklin M (Oxford, Oxbow Monog 27, 1992), and by a 'state of the art' paper ('An environmental history of the upper Kennet valley, Wiltshire, for the last 10,000 years') by John Evans, in *Proceedings of the Prehistoric Society* 59 (1993) 139–95. Theoretical issues are debated in *Space, Time, and Archaeological Landscapes*, edited by Rossignol J and Wandsnider L (New York, Plenum, 1992).

Regional field survey projects

Some British projects deserve study for their methods as well as their results. Andrew Fleming's *The Dartmoor Reaves: Investigating prehistoric land divisions* (London, Batsford, 1988) examines uplands, while *The Maddle Farm Project: An integrated survey of prehistoric and Roman landscapes on the Berkshire Downs* by Gaffney V and Tingle M (Oxford, Brit Archaol Rep 200, 1989) includes intensively cultivated land. The context of an individual site is emphasized in *The Stonehenge Environs Project* (Richards 1990). The extent of work around the Mediterranean and elsewhere is apparent in *Archaeological Field Survey: Britain and abroad* edited by Macready S and Thompson F H (London, Soc of Antiq, 1985), and *Roman Landscapes* (Barker & Lloyd 1991). Renfrew & Wagstaff's *An Island Polity: The archaeology of exploitation in Melos* (1982) contains valuable discussions of methodology focused on an Aegean island.

Examples of a significant new development are contained in *Interpreting Space: GIS and archaeology* (Allen 1990), while Gaffney V and Stancic Z have made a study of one Croatian island, Hvar, in GIS *Approaches to Regional Analysis* (Ljubljana, Faculty of Arts, 1991). Many geographical and mathematical approaches are contained in *The Interpretation of Archaeological Spatial Patterning* (Kroll E M and Price T D (ed), New York, Plenum, 1991).

Chapter 3: Excavation

The development of excavation techniques

Several books by Glyn Daniel cited above (Chapter 1) chart the beginnings of methodical excavation. The early chapters of Harris's *Principles of Archaeological Stratigraphy* (1989) explain how geological concepts were adopted by early excavators. The disappearance of evidence through careless clearance and 'excavation' was documented by R Lanciani as early as 1899 in *The Destruction of Ancient Rome* (London, Macmillan).

M W Thompson's *General Pitt-Rivers* (1977) has been followed by a further biography by Bowden (1991); unfortunately, the four massive volumes that Pitt Rivers distributed privately (*Excavations in Cranborne Chase*, London, 1887–1898) are not easy to find in libraries. Mortimer Wheeler summarized his own techniques in *Archaeology from the Earth*, first published in 1954. His racy autobiography *Still*

Digging (London, Michael Joseph, 1955) traces much of his professional career, but Jacquetta Hawkes' biography (1982) leaves many questions unanswered.

Excavation procedure

The 'classic' work is Philip Barker's *Techniques of Excavation* (1993), but his earlier *Understanding Archaeological Excavation* (1986) may be easier for beginners. Harris's *Principles of Archaeological Stratigraphy* (1989) remains the best account of this difficult aspect. Taphonomy is explored in Schiffer's *Formation Processes of the Archaeological Record* (1987), and further relevant papers are contained in Natural *Formation Processes and the Archaeological Record*, edited by Nash D T & Petraglia M D (Oxford; Brit Archaeol Rep, 1987), and *Archaeological Formation Processes*, edited by K Kristiansen (Copenhagen, National Mus, 1988).

Popular syntheses of work on individual sites help to explain the selection of a site, excavation strategy, and interpretation. The English Heritage/Batsford series contains a growing number of these, including *Wharram Percy: Deserted medieval village* (Beresford M and Hurst J 1990); two Iron Age hillforts, *Danebury: The anatomy of an Iron Age hillfort* (B W Cunliffe 1993) and *Maiden Castle* (Sharples 1991); and *Flag Fen: Prehistoric fenland centre* (Pryor 1993). Two medieval sites featuring an interesting combination of excavation, documentary history and architectural analysis are *Norton Priory* by J P Greene (1989) and *A Temple for Byzantium: The discovery and excavation of a palace church in Istanbul* (R M Harrison, London, Harvey Miller, 1989). Dealing with developers and the public in a busy urban setting are aspects of Richard Hall's *The Viking Dig: Excavations at York* (London, Bodley Head, 1984). Ian Hodder's article 'Writing archaeology: site reports in context' (*Antiquity* 63 (1989) 268–74) provides an interesting perspective on the excavator's creative role, while technicalities of publishing a site are outlined in the Council for British Archaeology's *Signposts for Archaeological Publication* (London, 1991). For some long-term problems that might easily be overlooked see *Preserving Field Records: Archival techniques for archaeologists and anthropologists*, edited by Kenworthy M A (Philadelphia, Univ Pennsylvania Museum, 1985). The continuing interaction of excavation and destruction by modern development is featured in *Rescue Archaeology: What's next?*, edited by Mytum H and Waugh K (York Univ, Archaeol Monog 6, 1987); it follows on from Barri Jones' *Past Imperfect: The story of rescue* (London, Heinemann, 1984).

Excavation: special cases

For town sites see M Carver's *Underneath English Towns: Interpreting urban archaeology* (London, Batsford, 1987) and *Arguments in Stone: Archaeological research and the European town in the first millennium* (Oxford, Oxbow Monog 29, 1993), also P Ottaway's *Archaeology in British Towns from the Emperor Claudius to the Black Death* (London, Routledge, 1992). Waterlogged sites are the subject of B & J Coles's *Peoples of the Wetlands: Bogs, bodies and lake dwellings: a world survey* (London, Thames and Hudson, 1989), while *The sea Remembers: Shipwrecks and archaeology* by P Throckmorton (London, Weidenfeld and Nicolson, 1987) illustrates many marine sites. All aspects of marine 'fieldwork', excavation and recording are contained in the Nautical Archaeology Society's *Archaeology Underwater*, edited by Dean (1992). At the opposite extreme, A M Rosen's *Cities of Clay: The geoarchaeology of tells* (Chicago Univ Press, 1986) concerns mud-brick sites. Rodwell's *Church Archaeology* (1989) discusses cemeteries as well as church buildings, and an interesting burial site is explored in A Boddington's *Raunds: Furnells church and cemetery* (London, English Heritage, 1989). A volume of studies on *Burial archaeology* has been edited by Roberts (1989). *Retrieval of Objects from Archaeological Sites* (Payton R (ed), Denbigh, Archetype, 1992) is a collection of case-studies about the conservation of structures and artefacts revealed by excavation. Many interesting discussions of stone and timber structures are included in *Structural Reconstruction*, edited by Drury (1982).

Chapter 4:
Dating the past

Dating methods are also included in the historical surveys and general books cited at the beginning of this section and in relation to chapter 1 (above, p. 185).

Historical dating

South's *Method and Theory in Historical Archaeology* (1977) is a complex but rewarding work, and theoretical dimensions can also be appreciated in *Archaeology as long-term History*, edited by Ian Hodder (Cambridge Univ Press, 1987). M Baillie's *A Slice Through Time: Dendrochronology and precision dating* (London, Batsford 1995) shows how scientific methods are reducing the difference between prehistory and history. A controversial discussion of historical dating in Mediterranean, Egyptian and Near-eastern archaeology is *Centuries of*

Darkness, edited by P James (London, Jonathan Cape, 1991); an orthodox view is set out in Warren P M and Hankey V, *The Absolute Chronology of the Aegean Bronze Age* (Bristol, Classical Press, 1989). Greek and Roman archaeology features in W R Biers' *Art, Artefacts and Chronology in Classical Archaeology* (London, Routledge, 1992). Pèrin's *La datation des tombes mèrovingiennes* (Geneva, Librairie Droz, 1980) uses burials, typology, and historical texts to chart early medieval settlement in France. My own book *Interpreting the Past: Roman pottery* (London, British Museum, 1992) includes a chapter on dating methods, while A Burnett's *Interpreting the Past: Coins* (London, British Museum, 1991) outlines the potential of numismatics.

Typology

Graslund's *The Birth of Prehistoric Chronology* (1987) is the fundamental work on nineteenth-century developments, and Montelius's *Dating in the Bronze Age with Special Reference to Scandinavia* (Stockholm, Royal Academy of Letters, History and Antiquities, 1885) is available in a translation by H Clarke. Pitt Rivers' contribution is discussed in biographies by Bowden (1991) and Thompson (1977). Modern theoretical discussions include *Archaeological Typology* by L S Klejn (Oxford, Brit Archaeol Rep S153, 1982), *Archaeological Typology and Practical Reality* by Adams W and Adams E (Cambridge Univ Press, 1991), and *Essays on Archaeological Typology* edited by Whallon R and Brown J A (Evanston, Kampsville Seminars in Archaeology 1, 1982).

Scientific dating techniques

Martin Aitken's *Science-based Dating in Archaeology* (1990) is essential reading. Its structure prevents complexities of the background science from getting in the way of general principles, and it contains comprehensive scientific and archaeological references. Clear accounts of scientific dating may also be found in Gowlett's *Ascent to Civilization* (1993) and in *Science and the Past*, edited by Bowman (1991). Useful information can also be gained from *Current Scientific Techniques in Archaeology*, edited by Parkes (1986), *New Developments in Archaeological Science*, edited by Pollard (1992), and *Dating and Age Determination of Biological Materials*, edited by Zimmerman M R and Angel J L (Beckenham, Croom Helm, 1986).

Dating and interpretation are inseparable in the study of early human evolution. Johanson's *Lucy's Child* (1991) or Leakey & Lewin's *Origins Reconsidered* (1992)

introduce issues that are explored further in *The Origin of Modern Humans and the Impact of Chronometric Dating*, edited by Aitken M, Stringer M and Mellars P (Princeton Univ Press, 1993). For the conflict between traditional and scientific dating over Akrotiri, a Bronze Age town destroyed by a volcano, see *Thera and the Aegean World III*, edited by Hardy and Renfrew (1990). Spindler's *The Man in the Ice* (1994) is another example of the role of scientific dating, while its use in testing authenticity is included in Spencer's *Piltdown: A scientific forgery* (1990).

Tree-ring dating

M G Baillie's *Tree-ring Dating and Archaeology* (London, Routledge, 1981) remains an excellent account; see also D Eckstein's *Dendrochronological Dating* (Strasbourg, European Science Foudation, 1984), *Tree rings* by Schweingruber (1987) and *Applications of Tree-ring Studies: Current research in dendrochronology and related subjects*, edited by R Ward (Oxford, Brit Archaeol Rep S33, 1987). All studies of radiocarbon dating (see below) also discuss dendrochronology in relation to calibration. Varves, pollen analysis, sea-bed deposits and ice-sheet cores feature in books on environmental archaeology and climatology – and of course in Aitken's *Science-based Dating*.

Radiocarbon dating

Radiocarbon dating by Bowman (1990) is an ideal introduction. Advances in high-precision measurement are discussed in *Archaeological Aspects of Accelerator Dating*, edited by Gowlett J and Hedges R (Oxford, OUCA Monog 11, 1986); see also *Radiocarbon Dating: Recent applications and future potential*, edited by J J Lowe (Quaternary Research Assoc, 1991). The technique's dramatic impact on European prehistory is explained in Renfrew's *Before Civilization* (1973). Taylor's *Radiocarbon Dating: An archaeological perspective* (1987) contains a comprehensive assessment, including its history, and Taylor has also edited *Radiocarbon after Four Decades* (with Long & Kra, 1992).

Archaeology, Dendrochronology and the Radiocarbon Calibration Curve, edited by B Ottaway (Edinburgh Univ Press, 1984), contains papers of enduring interest, as does the special radiocarbon section in *Antiquity* 61 (1987), which includes Pearson's important paper 'How to cope with calibration'. Finally, full details of calibration methods, including a computer program, can be found in a *Radiocarbon* 35.1, edited by Stuiver, Long & Kra (1993).

Other scientific dating methods

There are monographs on *Thermoluminescence Dating* by G A Wagner (Strasbourg, European Science Foundation, 1983) and Aitken (1985), while Tarling's *Palaeomagnetism* (1983) remains the fundamental work on magnetic dating. Reports on refinements in dating techniques appear in the periodicals *Archaeometry* or *Journal of Archaeological Science*, and less technical accounts are likely to be included in *Antiquity*, or magazines such as *Nature* or *Scientific American*.

Chapter 5:
Science and archaeology

Note: scientific aspects of archaeological fieldwork are cited in relation to chapter 2 above.

General works

Important articles appear in the journals *Archaeometry* and *Journal of Archaeological Science*, and many developments are reported in Antiquity. A historical perspective can be gained from M S Tite's article 'Archaeological science – past achievements and future prospects' in *Archaeometry* 32.3 (1991) 139–51.

Archaeological science has become very specialized, and it is scarcely possible for any individual author to cover it. The most readable general survey is *Science and the Past*, edited by Bowman (1991); Parkes' *Current Scientific Techniques in Archaeology* (1986) is much more detailed. An outstanding exhibition catalogue is *Les mystères de l'archéologie: les sciences à la recherche du passé* (Presses Universitaires, Lyon, 1990). Many books contain collections of papers (frequently generated by conferences) that tend to be overtaken by newer work, but of lasting interest are *New Developments in Archaeological Science*, edited by Pollard (1992) and *Scientific Analysis in Archaeology*, edited by Henderson (1989). Volumes with a more specific area of interest are Jones & Catling's *Science in archaeology* (1986), mainly relevant to Greece, and *Science in Egyptology* by David (1987). For the overall context of scientific work see *Research Priorities in Archaeological Science*, edited by P Mellars (London, Council Brit Archaeol, 1987).

The examination of objects and raw materials

Scanning Electron Microscopy in Archaeology, edited by Olsen (1988), demonstrates the wide application of microscopic examination. The study of artefacts has generated many publications, including L Hurcombe's *Use Wear Analysis: Theory, experiments and results*

(Sheffield Archaeol Monog 4, 1992), R Grace's *Interpreting the Function of Stone Tools* (Oxford, Brit Archaol Rep S474, 1989) and *The Interpretative Possibilities of Microwear Studies*, edited by B Graslund (Uppsala, Societas Archaeologica, 1990).

Studies of **stone** include *The Scientific Study of Flint*, edited by Sieveking G and Hart M (Cambridge Univ Press, 1986), *Marble: Art historical and scientific perspectives on ancient sculpture* (Malibu, Getty Museum, 1990) and Clough's *Stone Axe Studies* (1988). The broader context of analytical results is examined in R Torrence's *Production and Exchange of Stone Tools: Prehistoric obsidian in the Aegean* (Cambridge Univ Press, 1986) and Bradley & Edmonds' *Interpreting the Axe Trade* (1993). For pottery see *Recent Developments in Ceramic Petrology*, edited by Middleton A and Freestone I (London, British Museum Occ Pap 81, 1991) and *Greek and Cypriot Pottery: A review of scientific studies* by R E Jones (British School at Athens, 1985).

A range of spectrographic techniques is presented in *Neutron Activation and Plasma Emission Spectrometric Analysis in Archaeology*, edited by Hughes (1991). Analysis and characterization of metals feature in *Aspects of Early Metallurgy*, edited by Oddy (1991) and *Bronze Age Trade in the Mediterranean*, edited by Gale (1991). These studies are also important for ancient coinage – see *Scientific Studies in Numismatics*, edited by Oddy (1980) and *Metallurgy in Numismatics*, edited by Archibald & Cowell (London, Spink/Royal Numismatic Soc, 1993).

Conservation is an important area of archaeological science, and recent books include Cronyn's *Elements of Archaeological Conservation* (1989) and Sease's *A Conservation Manual for the Field Archaeologist* (Los Angeles, UCLA Inst Archaeol, 1992). Several case-studies are described in *The Art of the Conservator*, edited by Oddy (1992). The role of analysis in detecting forgeries should not be overlooked; see *Fake? The art of deception*, edited by Jones (1990).

The environment

This subject has become so large and diverse that introductory books are scarce. Shackley's *Environmental Archaeology* (1982) and *Using Environmental Archaeology* (London, Batsford, 1985) remain useful, as does John Evans' *An Introduction to Environmental Archaeology* (1978). Environmental archaeology is integrated with a wider geographical picture in *Changing the Face of the Earth* by Simmons (1989) and *Late Quaternary Environmental change* by Bell & Walker (1992). The many general collections of papers include *Issues in Environmental Archaeology*, edited by N Balaam and J Rackham (London, Institute of Archaeolgy, 1992); *Conceptual Issues in Environmental Archaeology*, edited by J Bintliff (Edinburgh Univ Press, 1988); *Palaeo-environmental Investigations*, edited by N Fieller (Oxford, Brit Archaeol Rep S258 and S266, 1985); and *Recent Developments in Environmental analysis*, edited by E Webb (Oxford, Brit Archaeol Rep S416, 1988). Theoretical perspectives are included in *Modelling Ecological Change*, edited by D Harris and K Thomas (London, Institute of Archaeology, 1991).

Informative studies about Britain include *Environmental Archaeology: A regional review*, edited by H Keeley (London, English Heritage, 1984 and 1987) and Martin Jones' *England before Domesday* (London, Batsford, 1986). Work that complements fieldwork projects abroad (chapter 2) can be found in *Man's Role in the Shaping of the Eastern Mediterranean Landscape*, edited by S Bottema (Rotterdam, Balkema, 1990) or P Horden and N Purcell, *The Mediterranean World: Man and environment in antiquity and the middle ages* (Oxford, Basil Blackwell, 1991). The role of climatology may be examined in *Climatic Change in Later Prehistory*, edited by A F Harding (Edinburgh Univ Press, 1982) or *Climate and History*, edited by Wigley (1981).

Soil science

Soils add an important dimension to environmental archaeology; three books of collected papers on this topic are *Man-made Soils*, edited by W Groeneman-van Waateringe & M Robinson (Oxford, Brit Archaeol Rep S410, 1988); *Soils and Micromorphology in Archaeology*, edited by Courty (1989); and *Soils in Archaeology*, edited by Holliday (1992).

Plant remains

G W Dimbleby's *Plants and Archaeology* (London, J Baker, 1978) remains a useful introduction. Detailed books include Pearsall's *Paleoethnobotany* (1989), J Greig's *Archaeobotany* (Strasbourg, European Sci Foundation, 1989) or R Brookes' *Phytoarchaeology* (Leicester Univ Press, 1991). Useful collections of studies include *Current Paleoethnobotany*, edited by C Hastorf & V Popper (Chicago, Prehist Archaeol & Ecology Series, 1988), *Phytolith Systematics: Emerging issues*, edited by G Rapp & S Mulholland (New York, Plenum, 1992) and *Progress in Old World Palaeoethnobotany*, edited by W van Zeist (Rotterdam, Balkema, 1991).

Detailed British studies are contained in *Archaeology and the Flora of the British Isles*, edited by M Jones (1988), while M Van der Veen's *Crop Husbandry Regimes* (1992) includes very interesting methods and interpretations. Wider questions of human exploitation of plants are addressed in *Foraging and Farming*, edited by D Harris and G Hillman (London, Unwin Hyman, One World Archaeology 13, 1989) and *New Light on Early Farming: Recent developments in palaeoethnobotany*, edited by Jane Renfrew (Edinburgh Univ Press, 1991); see also D Zohary & M Hopf's *Domestication of Plants in the Old World: The origin and spread of cultivated plants in west Asia, Europe and the Nile valley* (Oxford, Clarendon, 1993). Two interesting case-studies are *Corn and Culture in the Prehistoric New World*, edited by S Johannessen & C Hastorf (Oxford, Westview Press, 1993), and *Pharaoh's Flowers*, a study of plants from Tutankhamun's tomb by F Hepper (London, Royal Botanic Gardens Kew/HMSO, 1990).

Pollen analysis is explained thoroughly in Dimbleby's *The Palynology of Archaeological Sites* (1985) and in a more general text, *Pollen Analysis* by Moore, Webb & Collinson (1991).

Animal remains

The Archaeology of Animals by Davis (1987) is very readable, and is complemented by Rackham's *Interpreting the Past: Animal bones* (1994). Technical aspects are covered in *Ageing and Sexing Animal Bones from Archaeological Sites*, edited by B Wilson (Oxford, Brit Archaeol Rep 109, 1982), R Lyman's *Vertebrate Taphonomy* (Cambridge Univ Press, 1994) and S Hillson's *Teeth* (Cambridge Univ Press, 1986). Clutton-Brock has written *A natural History of Domesticated Animals* (1988), and edited *The Walking Larder: Patterns of domestication, pastoralism and predation* (1988).

L Binford challenged traditional **interpretations** of animal remains in *Bones: Ancient man and modern myths* (New York, Academic Press, 1981). Other examples of interpretation can be found in excavation reports; an early hunter-gatherer site is *Starr Carr Revisited: A re-analysis of the large mammals* by A Legge & P Rowley-Conwy (Univ of London, Dept of Extra-Mural Studies, 1988), while a historical example from York is *Bones from Anglo-Scandinavian Levels at 16–22 Coppergate* by T O'Connor (London, CBA, Archaeol of York 15.3, 1989). The contrast between rural and urban assemblages may be pursued further in Groeneman-van Waateringe & Wijngaarden-Bakker's *Farm Life in a Carolingian Village* (1987) and *Diet and Craft in Towns:*

191

The evidence of animal remains from the Roman to the post-medieval periods, edited by D Searjeantson & T Waldron (Oxford, Brit Archaol Rep 199, 1989).

Birds, fish, shells and insects

Cohen A and Searjentson D have produced *A Manual for the Identification of Bird Bones from Archaeological sites* (Univ of London, Dept of Extra-Mural Studies, 1987). Wheeler & Jones have written an overview of *Fishes* (1989), and many further studies are included *Fish and Archaeology*, edited by Brinkhuizen & Clason (1986). Studies of marine molluscs feature in *Deciphering a Shell Midden*, edited by Stein (1992) and W F Buchanan's *Shellfish in Prehistoric Diet: Elands Bay, S W Cape coast, S Africa* (Oxford, Brit Archaol Rep S455, 1988). *Land Snails in Archaeology* by J G Evans (1973) remains an important source. In addition to H Kenward's pioneering *The Analysis of Archaeological Insect Assemblages* (London, CBA, The Archaeology of York 19.1, 1978), see Buckland & Coope's *A Bibliography and Literature Review of Quaternary Entomology* (1991). Insect remains are integrated into a full review of site finds at York in R Hall & H Kenward's *Environmental Evidence from the Colonia: Tanner Row and Rougier Street* (London, CBA, Archaeology of York 14.6, 1990).

Human remains

An excellent introduction is A Chamberlain's *Interpreting the Past: Human remains* (London, British Museum, 1994), followed up with studies of individual finds such as Spindler's *The Man in the Ice* (1994) or Brothwell's *The Bog Man and the Archaeology of People* (London, British Museum, 1986) and *Lindow Man*, edited by Stead (1986). An Egyptian example is *The Mummy's Tale: The scientific and medical investigation of Natsef-Amun*, edited by A R David & E Tapp (London, O'Mara Books, 1992), and an unusual group of medieval Inuit (Eskimos), accompanied by clothing, is beautifully illustrated in *The Greenland Mummies*, edited by Hansen (1991). Forensic science and the pathology of **diseases and injuries** are important; see Boddington's *Death, Decay and reconstruction* (1987), K Manchester's *The Archaeology of Disease* (Univ of Bradford, 1983), Ortner & Puschan's *Identification of Pathological Conditions in Human Skeletal Remains* (1985) or *Health in Past Societies*, edited by H Bush & M Zvelebil (Oxford, Brit Archaol Rep S567, 1991). Particularly interesting deductions from site finds are to be found in T White's *Prehistoric Cannibalism at Mancos 5MTUMR-234-6* (Princeton Univ Press, 1992) and J Hedges' *Tomb of the Eagles: A window on Stone Age tribal Britain* (1984), which analyses a community found in a Scottish megalithic burial.

Bones in particular are the subject of D Ubelaker's *Human Skeletal Remains* (Washington, Taraxacum, 1984), T White's *Human Osteology* (London, Academic Press, 1990) and *Histology of Ancient Human Bone*, edited by G Grupe & A Garland (Berlin, Springer Verlag, 1992). Analyses are presented in *The Chemistry of Prehistoric Human Bone*, edited by Price (1989) and *Prehistoric Human Bone: Archaeology at the molecular level*, edited by J Lambert & G Grupe (Berlin, Springer Verlag, 1993). The investigation of evolution through genetics is examined in *The Human Revolution: Behavioural and biological perspectives on the origins of modern humans*, edited by P Mellars & C Stringer (Edinburgh Univ Press, 1989) and Fagan's *The Journey from Eden* (1990). Technical aspects can be found in *Ancient DNA: Recovery and analysis of genetic material*, edited by B Herrmann & S Hummel (Berlin, Springer Verlag, 1993).

Statistics and computing

Good introductions are Orton's *Mathematics in Archaeology* (Cambridge Univ Press, 1982) and Fletcher & Lock's *Digging Numbers* (1991). Shennan's *Quantifying Archaeology* (1988) and *Quantitative Research in Archaeology: Progress and prospects*, edited by M Aldenderfer (London, Sage, 1987), are more detailed, while full complexities are displayed in *To Pattern the Past: Proceedings of the symposium on mathematical methods in archaeology*, Amsterdam, 1984, edited by B Voorrips & S Loving (PACT 11, Strasbourg, Council of Europe, 1985). Mathematical approaches to artefacts and site distributions were very popular during the 1970s: see Hodder & Orton's *Spatial Analysis in Archaeology* (1976) and parts of the influential *Analytical Archaeology* by David Clarke (revised by Chapman, 1978). A particularly interesting combination of statistics and typology is Richards' *The Significance of Form and Decoration of Anglo-Saxon Cremation Urns* (1987), which shows what subtleties may be revealed by these methods.

Books on **computing** become obsolete very quickly; samples of current work are found in conference proceedings such as *Computing the Past: CAA 92*, edited by Andresen J, Madsen T and Scollar I (Aarhus Univ Press, 1993) or *Computer Applications and Quantitative Methods in Archaeology*, 1991, edited by G Lock & J

Moffett (Oxford, Brit Archaol Rep S577, 1992). Rather more general are *Computing for Archaeologists*, edited by Ross (1991) and *Archaeology and the Information Age*, edited by Reilly & Rahtz (1992).

Experimental archaeology

John Coles's book *Experimental Archaeology* (1979) still provides a thorough introduction to the potential and pitfalls of the experimental approach, which continues to flourish, and may involve anything from Shennan's *Experiments in the Collection and Analysis of Archaeological Survey Data* (1985) to the reconstruction of a Greek warship (Welsh, *Building the Trireme*, 1988). The latter project has been comprehensively documented: see *An Athenian Trireme Reconstructed: The British sea trials of Olympias*, 1987, edited by J Morrison & J Coates (Oxford, Brit Archaol Rep S486, 1989). Another important area is illustrated by C Sussman's *A Microscopic Analysis of Use-wear and Polish Formation on Experimental Quartz Tools* (Oxford, Brit Archaol Rep S395, 1988). Nothing available in English approaches the superbly illustrated *Experimentelle Archäologie in Deutschland*, edited by M Fansa (1990).

Chapter 6: Making sense of the past

Archaeological theory

It will only become apparent in future decades which current themes are of enduring significance. The influence of evolution and anthropology began in the nineteenth century, and their impact can be studied in some of the books cited in Chapter 1, but the historical overviews by Piggott and Daniel do not do justice to the rapid changes of the later twentieth century. Fortunately there is now a wide choice of books: Trigger's *A history of Archaeological Thought* (1989) covers the entire history of the subject, while Malina & Vašíček's *Archaeology Yesterday and Today* (1990) is almost as comprehensive. Theory also receives extensive treatment in two textbooks: Renfrew & Bahn's *Archaeology: Theories, methods, and practice* (1991) and Fagan's *In the Beginning* (1993). Willey & Sabloff's *A History of American Archaeology* (1980) is also useful in outlining the background of modern American theory.

Modern developments are followed in Ian Hodder's *Reading the Past* (1991) and a collection of regional studies that he edited: *Archaeological Theory in Europe: The last three decades* (London, Routledge, 1991); Gibbon's *Explanation in Archaeology* (1989) is also use-

ful. The development of Binford's thinking can be followed in two collections of his papers, *In Pursuit of the Past: Decoding the archaeological record* (London, Thames and Hudson, 1983) and *Debating Archaeology* (1989).

Post-processualism

The route from processualism through ethnoarchaeology to post-processualism is outlined in Hodder's *Reading the Past* (1991), and typical papers are contained in *The Meaning of Things: Material culture and symbolic expression*, edited by I Hodder (London, Unwin Hyman, *One World Archaeology* 6, 1988). Other elements are represented in *Critical Traditions in Contemporary Archaeology*, edited by V Pinsky & A Wylie (Cambridge Univ Press, 1989), *Archaeology After Structuralism*, edited by I Bapty & I Yates (London, Routledge, 1991) and *The Ancient Mind: Elements of cognitive archaeology*, edited by C Renfrew & A Zubrow (Cambridge Univ Press, 1994). Further insights may be gained from *Interpretive Archaeologies*, edited by Hodder & Shanks (1993) or C Tilley's *Reading Material Culture: Structuralism, hermeneutics and post-structuralism* (Oxford, Basil Blackwell, 1990). A collection of backlashes is *Archaeological Theory: Who sets the agenda?*, edited by Yoffee & Sherratt (1993), while Hodder's *Theory and Practice in Archaeology* (1992) is an attempt to reconcile abstract thoughts and practical action.

One work by a historian that has provoked interest amongst archaeologists is *The Sources of Social Power 1: A history of power from the beginning to AD 1760*, by M Mann (Cambridge Univ Press, 1986). A European school of historical thought has influenced many writers on later prehistory and historical archaeology: see *The Annales School and Archaeology*, edited by J Bintliff (Leicester Univ Press, 1991) or *Archaeology, Annales, and Ethnohistory*, edited by A Knapp (Cambridge Univ Press, 1992).

Heritage, archaeology, the public and the State

D Lowenthal's *The Past is a Foreign Country* (Cambridge Univ Press, 1985) and Hewison's *The Heritage Industry* (1987) set a pessimistic critical tone for public presentations of the past. However, this has not deterred practical approaches such as G Binks' *Visitors Welcome* (London, HMSO/English Heritage 1988) or the Institute of Field Archaeology's *Archaeological Resource Management in the UK*, edited by J Hunter & I Ralston (Stroud, Alan Sutton, 1993). Among dozens of books that examine museums are Hudson's *Museums of*

Influence (1987) and Hooper-Greenhill's *Museums and the Shaping of Knowledge* (1992), while their future is discussed in *Museums 2000: Politics, people, professionals and profit*, edited by P Boylan (1993). Ethical aspects are the concern of Greenfield's *The Return of Cultural Treasures* (1989) and *The Elgin Marbles: Should they be returned to Greece?* by Hitchens C, Browning R and Binns G (London, Chatto and Windus, 1987).

Political issues

Shanks & Tilley demand that archaeologists should develop a politically aware attitude in *Re-constructing Archaeology* (1992), and many individuals involved in ethnoarchaeology have become supporters of the rights of indigenous peoples. Two books edited by Layton contain papers on these themes: *Who needs the past?* and *Conflict in the Archaeology of Living Traditions* (both 1989). They resulted from sessions at the World Archaeological Congress of 1986, which was riven by political disputes about the participation of South African archaeologists; see Ucko's *Academic freedom and Apartheid: The story of the World Archaeological Congress* (Gloucester, Duckworth, 19). Another contemporary concern, gender, is explored in H Moore's *Feminism and Anthropology* (Cambridge, Polity Press, 1987), *Engendering Archaeology*, edited by Gero & Conkey (1991) and *Exploring Gender through Archaeology*, edited by Claasen (1992). A biography of one pioneering woman who made a career in archaeology is *Born to Rebel: The life of Harriet Boyd Hawes* by M Allsebrook (Oxford, Oxbow, 1992).

Bibliography

Note: items cited in the Further Reading section above are not repeated here.

Adam J-P 1994, *Roman Building: Materials and Techniques*, London, Batsford

Addyman P V 1990, 'Reconstruction as interpretation: the example of the Jorvik Viking Centre, York', in Gathercole P & Lowenthal D, *The Politics of the Past*. London, Unwin Hyman One World Archaeology 12 257–64

Addyman P V 1992, *York Archaeological Trust: 21 years of archaeology in York*, reprinted from Yorks Philos Soc *Ann Rep*

Aitchison T Ottaway B & Al-Ruzaiza A S 1991, 'Summarizing a group of 14C dates on the historical time scale: with a worked example from the Late Neolithic of Bavaria', *Antiquity* 65 108–16

Aitken M J 1985, *Thermoluminescence Dating*, London, Academic Press

Aitken M J 1990, *Science-based Dating in Archaeology*, London, Longman

Alcock L 1972, *'By South Cadbury is that Camelot': the excavation of Cadbury Castle 1966–1970*, London, Thames and Hudson

Allaby R Jones M & Brown T 1994, 'DNA in charred wheat grains from the Iron Age hillfort at Danebury, England', *Antiquity* 68 126–32

Allason-Jones L & Bishop M C 1988, *Excavations at Roman Corbridge: The hoard*, HBMC London, English Heritage Archaeol Rep 7

Allen K *et al* (ed) 1990, *Interpreting Space: GIS and archaeology*, London/New York Taylor and Francis

Amick D S & Mauldin R P (eds) 1989, *Experiments in Lithic Technology*, Oxford, Brit Archaeol Rep S528

Anderson A 1991, 'The chronology of colonization in New Zealand', *Antiquity* 65 767–95

Andrew C 1992, *The Rosetta Stone*, London, British Museum

Anthony D W & Brown D R 1991, 'The origins of horseback riding', *Antiquity* 65 22–38

Arensberg C 1968, *The Irish Countryman: An anthropological study*, New York, Peter Smith

Aries P 1985, *Images of Man and Death*, Harvard Univ Press

Aston M 1985, *Interpreting the Landscape*, London, Batsford

Aston M & Rowley T 1974, *Landscape Archaeology: An introduction to fieldwork techniques on post-Roman landscapes*, Newton Abbot, David and Charles

Bacon E 1976, *The Great Archaeologists*, London, Secker and Warburg

Bahn P & Flenley J 1992, *Easter Island, Earth Island*, London, Thames and Hudson

Bailey R N Cambridge E & Briggs H D 1988, *Dowsing and Church Archaeology*, Wimborne Intercept

Baillie M G 1989, 'Do Irish bog oaks date the Shang dynasty?', *Current Archaeol* 117 310–13

Baillie M G 1992, 'Dendrochronology and environmental change', in Pollard A M, *New Developments in Archaeological Science*, Oxford, Clarendon 5–23

Baker F 1993, 'The Berlin Wall: production, conservation and consumption of a 20th-century monument', *Antiquity* 67 709–33

Barfield L 1994, 'The iceman reviewed', *Antiquity* 68 10–26

Barker G & Lloyd J (ed) 1991, *Roman Landscapes: Archaeological survey in the Mediterranean region*, British School at Rome Monog 2

Barker P A 1986, *Understanding Archaeological Excavation*, London, Batsford

Barker P A 1993, *Techniques of Archaeological Excavation*, London, Batsford, 3rd edition

Basalla G 1988, *The Evolution of Technology*, Cambridge Univ Press

Becker B 1993, 'An 11,000-year German oak and pine dendrochronology for radiocarbon calibration', *Radiocarbon* 35.1 201–13

Bell M & Walker M 1992, *Late Quaternary Environmental Change: Physical and human perspectives*, London, Longman

Berghaus P (ed) 1983, *Der Archäologe: Graphische Bildnisse aus dem Porträtarchiv Diepenbroick*, Münster, Westfälischen Mus für Kunst und Kulturgesch

Bernal M 1987, *Black Athena: The Afroasiatic roots of Classical civilization 1: The fabrication of ancient Greece 1785–1985*, London, Free Association Press

Bernal M 1991, *Black Athena: The Afroasiatic roots of classical civilisation 2: The archaeological and documentary evidence*, London, Free Association Press

Bersu G 1940, 'Excavations at Little Woodbury, Wiltshire', *Proc Prehist Soc* 6 30–111

Bethell P & Maté I 1989, 'The use of soil-phosphate analysis in archaeology: a critique', in Henderson J, *Scientific Analysis in Archaeology*, Oxford, Oxford Univ Committee Archaeol Monog 19, 1–29

Bidwell P *et al* (ed) 1988, *Portae Cum Turribus*, Oxford, Brit Archaeol Rep S206

Binford L R 1972, *An Archaeological Perspective*, New York Seminar Press

Binford L R 1989, *Debating Archaeology*, London, Academic Press

Binford L R 1992, 'Seeing the present and interpreting the past – and keeping things straight', in Rossignol J & Wandsnider L, *Space, Time, and Archaeological Landscapes*, New York, Plenum 43–59

Bintliff J L (ed) 1984, *European Social Evolution: Archaeological Perspectives*, University of Bradford Press

Bintliff J L *et al* 1990, 'Trace metal accumulation in soils on and around ancient settlements in Greece', in Bottema S *et al*, *Man's Role in the Shaping of the Eastern Mediterranean Landscape*, Rotterdam, Balkema 159–72

Birley E 1959, 'Excavations at Corstopitum,1906-58', *Archaeologia Aeliana* 37 1–32

Birley E & Richmond I 1938, 'Excavations at Corbridge, 1936-1938', *Archaeologia Aeliana* 15 243–94

Bishop M C & Dore J N 1989, *Corbridge: Excavations of the Roman fort and town, 1947–80*, HBMC London, English Heritage Archaeol Rep 8

Black J (ed) 1987, *Recent Advances in the Conservation and Analysis of Artefacts*, London, Inst of Archaeology

Blatherwick S & Gurr A 1992, 'Shakespeare's factory: archaeological evaluations on the site of the Globe Theatre, Southwark', *Antiquity* 66 315–88

Blundell S 1986, *The Origins of Civilization in Greek and Roman Thought*, London, Routledge

Boddington A *et al* 1987, *Death, Decay and Reconstruction: Approaches to archaeology and forensic science,* Manchester Univ Press

Bogucki P 1993, 'Animal traction and household economies in Neolithic Europe', *Antiquity* 67 492–503

Bonde N & Christiansen A E 1993, 'Dendrochronological dating of the Viking Age ship burials at Oseberg, Gokstad and Tune, Norway', *Antiquity* 67 575–83

Booth W Ipson S & Haigh B 1992, 'An inexpensive PC-based imaging system for applications in archaeology', in Lock G and Moffett J, *Computer Applications and Quantitative Methods in Archaeology 1991*, Oxford, Brit Archaeol Rep S577 197–204

Boucher de Perthes J de C 1847–57, *Antiquités celtiques et antediluviennes*, 2 vols, Paris

Boujot C & Cassen S 1993, 'A pattern of evolution for the Neolithic funerary structures of the west of France', *Antiquity* 67 477–92

Bowden M 1991, *Pitt Rivers: The life and archaeological work of Lt-Gen. Augustus Henry Lane Fox Pitt Rivers*, Cambridge Univ Press

Bowler P J 1989, *The Invention of Progress: The Victorians and the past*, Oxford, Basil Blackwell

Bowman S (ed) 1991, *Science and the Past*, London, British Museum

Bowman S 1990, *Radiocarbon Dating,* London, British Museum

Bradley B & Small C 1985, 'Looking for circular structures in post hole distributions: quantitative analysis of two settlements from bronze age England', *J Archaeol Sci* 12 285–98

Bradley R 1993, *Altering the Earth: The origins of monuments in Britain and continental Europe*, Edinburgh, Soc of Antiqs of Scotland Monog 8

Bradley R & Edmonds M 1993, *Interpreting the Axe Trade: Production and exchange in neolithic Britain*, Cambridge University Press

Brinkhuizen D C & Clason A T (ed) 1986, *Fish and Archaeology: Studies in osteometry, taphonomy, seasonality and fishing methods,* Oxford, Brit Archaeol Rep S294

Brown A E 1987, *Fieldwork for Archaeologists and Local Historians*, London, Batsford

Brown T A & K A 1992, 'Ancient DNA and the archaeologist', *Antiquity* 66 10–23

Brunskill R W 1985, *Timber Building in Britain*, London, Gollancz

Buckland P & Coope G R 1991, *A Bibliography and Literature Review of Quaternary Entomology*, Sheffield, J R Collis

Cann J R *et al* 1969, 'Obsidian analysis and the obsidian trade', in Brothwell D and Higgs E, *Science in Archaeology*, London, Thames and Hudson, 78–91

Carver M (ed) 1992, *The Age of Sutton Hoo: The seventh century in north-western Europe,* Woodbridge, Boydell and Brewer

Casson S 1939, *The Discovery of Man*, London, Hamish Hamilton

Cattaneo C *et al* 1991, 'Identification of ancient blood and tissue – ELISA and DNA analysis', *Antiquity* 65 878–81

Caygill M 1992, *The Story of the*

British Museum, London, British Museum

Chapman J C & Shiel R 1991, 'Settlement, soils and societies in Dalmatia', in Barker G & Lloyd J, *Roman Landscapes: Archaeological survey in the Mediterranean region*, Brit School Rome Monog 2 62–75

Chapman J C & Shiel R 1993, 'Social change and land use in prehistoric Dalmatia', *Proc Prehist Soc* 59 61–104

Chapman J C *et al* 1987, 'Settlement patterns and land use in neothermal Dalmatia, Yugoslavia: 1983–1984 seasons', *J Field Archaeol* 14 123–146

Childe V G 1942, *What Happened in History*, Harmondsworth, Penguin

Chippindale C 1983, *Stonehenge Complete*, London, Thames & Hudson

Chippindale C 1988, 'The invention of words for the idea of prehistory', *Proc Prehist Soc* 54 303–14

Chippindale C 1989, ' "Social archaeology" in the nineteenth century: is it right to look for modern ideas in old places?', in Christensen A L, *Tracing Archaeology's Past: The historiography of archaeology*, Southern Illinois Univ Press 21–33

Chippindale C *et al*, 1990, *Who Owns Stonehenge?*, London, Batsford

Claasen C (ed) 1992, *Exploring Gender Through Archaeology: Selected papers from the 1991 Boone Conference*, Madison, Wisconsin, Monogs in World Archaeology 11, Prehistory Press

Clark A J 1990, *Seeing Beneath the Soil*, London, Batsford

Clark J G D 1977, *World Prehistory in New Perspective*, Cambridge Univ Press

Clarke D L (revised Chapman R)

1978, *Analytical Archaeology*, London, 2nd ed. Methuen

Cleere H (ed) 1989, *Archaeological Heritage Management in the Modern World*, London, Unwin Hyman, One World Archaeology 9

Clough T H McK 1988, *Stone Axe Studies 2*, London, Council Brit Archaeol Res Rep 67

Clutton-Brock J (ed) 1988, *The Walking Larder: Patterns of domestication, pastoralism and predation*, London, Unwin Hyman, One World Archaeology 2

Clutton-Brock J 1988, *A Natural History of Domesticated Animals*, Cambridge Univ Press

Coates J F *et al* 1990, *The Trireme Trials 1988*, Oxford, Oxbow Books

Coe M 1992, *Breaking the Maya Code*, London, Thames and Hudson

Coles B (ed) 1992, *The Wetland Revolution in Prehistory*, WARP, Prehistoric Society

Coles B & Coles J M 1986, *Sweet Track to Glastonbury: The Somerset Levels in prehistory*, London, Thames and Hudson

Coles J M 1979, *Experimental Archaeology*, London, Academic Press

Coles J M 1984, *The Archaeology of Wetlands*, Edinburgh Univ Press

Coles J M & Lawson A J (ed) 1987, *European Wetlands in Prehistory*, Oxford, Clarendon

Collingwood R G & Wright R P 1965, *The Roman Inscriptions of Britain*, Oxford, Clarendon

Courty M-A *et al* (ed) 1989, *Soils and Micromorphology in Archaeology*, Cambridge Univ Press

Cowell M & La Niece S 1991, 'Metalwork: artifice and artistry', in Bowman S, *Science and the Past*, London, British Museum 74–98

Craddock P 1991, 'Mining and smelting in antiquity', in Bowman

S, *Science and the Past*, London, British Museum 57–73

Craster H 1914, *A History of Northumberland, 10: The parish of Corbridge*, Newcastle upon Tyne, A Reid

Crawford O G S 1929, *Air-photography for Archaeologists*, London Ordnance Survey

Cronyn J M 1989, *Elements of Archaeological Conservation*, London, Longman

Cunliffe B W (ed) 1982, *The Publication of Archaeological Excavations*, London, Council Brit Archaeol

Cunliffe B W 1971, *Excavations at Fishbourne 1961–1969*, 2 vols, Rep Res Comm Soc Antiq, London 26

Daniel G 1967, *The Origins and Growth of Archaeology*, Harmondsworth, Penguin

Daniel G 1975, *150 Years of Archaeology*, London, Duckworth

Daniel G 1981, *A Short History of Archaeology*, London, Thames and Hudson

Daniel G 1992, *Writing for Antiquity*, London, Thames and Hudson

Daniel G & Renfrew C 1988, *The Idea of Prehistory*, Edinburgh Univ Press

David A R 1987, *Science in Egyptology*, Manchester Univ Press

Davidson D A & Shackley M L (eds) 1976, *Geoarchaeology*, London, Duckworth

Davis S J M 1987, *The Archaeology of Animals*, London, Batsford

Dean M *et al* (ed) 1992, *Archaeology Underwater: The NAS guide to principles and practice*, London, Nautical Archaeol Soc/Archetype

Dearden B & Clark A 1990, 'Pont-de-l'Arche or Pitres? A location and archaeomagnetic dating for Charles the Bald's fortifications on the Seine', *Antiquity*

64 567–619

Dimbleby G W 1985, *The Palynology of Archaeological Sites*, New York/London, Acad Press

Dixon P 1988, *Recording Timber Buildings*, London, Council Brit Archaeol, *Practical Handbooks in Archaeology* 5

Dorn R I *et al* 1988, 'Cation-ratio dating of rock engravings from the Olary Province of arid South Australia', *Antiquity* 62 681–689

Drower M S 1985, *Flinders Petrie: A life in Archaeology*, London, Gollancz

Drury P J (ed) 1982, *Structural Reconstruction: Approaches to the interpretation of the excavated remains of buildings*, Oxford, Brit Archaeol Rep 110

Duhard J-P 1991, 'The shape of Pleistocene women', *Antiquity* 65 552–61

Dunnell R C 1992, 'The notion site', in Rossignol J and Wandsnider L, *Space, Time, and Archaeological Landscapes*, New York, Plenum 21–41

Edis J MacLeod D & Bewley R 1989, 'An archaeologist's guide to classification of cropmarks and soilmarks', *Antiquity* 63 112–146

Edwards N 1990, *The Archaeology of Early Medieval Ireland*, London, Batsford

Engelstad E 1991, 'Images of power and contradiction: feminist theory and post-processual archaeology', *Antiquity* 65 502–14

English Heritage 1989, *The Management of Archaeological Projects*, London

Evans A 1921, *The Palace of Minos at Knossos, I: The neolithic and early middle Minoan ages*, London, Macmillan

Evans A C 1986, *The Sutton Hoo Ship Burial*, London, British Museum

Evans A J 1899–1900, 'Knossos I: the palace', *Ann Brit School Athens* 63–70

Evans C 1989, 'Archaeology and modern times: Bersu's Woodbury 1938 and 1939', *Antiquity* 63 436–50

Evans J 1860, 'On the occurrence of flint implements in undisturbed beds of gravel, sand and clay', *Archaeologia* 38 280–307

Evans J 1943, *Time and Chance: The story of Arthur Evans and his forebears*, London, Longmans Green

Evans J 1956, *A History of the Society of Antiquaries*, Oxford

Evans J D 1982, 'Introduction: on the prehistory of archaeology', in Evans J D, Cunliffe B & Renfrew C, *Antiquity and Man: Essays in honour of Glyn Daniel*, London, Thames and Hudson 12–18

Evans J G 1973, *Land Snails in Archaeology*, London, Seminar Press

Evans J G 1978, *An Introduction to Environmental Archaeology*, London, Elek

Evershed P *et al* 1992, 'The survival of food residues: new methods of analysis, interpretation and application', in Pollard A M, *New Developments in Archaeological Science*, Oxford, Clarendon 187–208

Exploring ... 1991, *Exploring Our Past: Strategies for the archaeology of England*, London, English Heritage

Fagan B 1977, *Elusive Treasure: The story of early archaeologists in the Americas*, New York, Scribner

Fagan B 1990, *The Journey from Eden*, London, Thames and Hudson

Fagan B 1993, *In the Beginning: An introduction to archaeology*, 7th ed, HarperCollins

Fairclough G 1992, 'Meaningful constructions: spatial and functional analysis of medieval

buildings', *Antiquity* 66 348–66

Fairweather A & Ralston I 1993, 'The Neolithic timber hall at Balbridie, Grampian Region, Scotland: the building, the date, the plant macrofossils', *Antiquity* 67 313–23

Feyler G 1987, 'Contribution à l'histoire des origines de la photographie archéologique: 1839–1880', *Mel École Française Rome* 99.2 1019–47

Fieller N R J *et al* (ed) 1985, *Palaeoenvironmental Investigations: Research design, methods and data analysis*, 2 vols: Oxford, Brit Archaeol Rep S258, S266

Flannery K 1976, *The Early Mesoamerican Village*, New York, Academic Press

Fletcher M & Lock G 1991, *Digging Numbers: Elementary statistics for archaeologists*, Oxford, Oxford Univ Committee Archaeol Monog 33

Fox C 1959, *The Personality of Britain*, 4th ed, Cardiff, Nat Mus of Wales

Frere J 1800, 'Account of flint weapons discovered at Hoxne in Suffolk', *Archaeologia* 13 204–5

Friedman J & Rowland M J (ed) 1982, *The Evolution of Social Systems*, London, Duckworth

Gale N H (ed) 1991, *Bronze Age Trade in the Mediterranean*, Studies in Medit Archaeol 90, Paul Astroms Forlag

Gale N H & Stos-Gale Z A 1992, 'Lead isotope studies in the Aegean (the British Academy project)', in Pollard A M, *New Developments in Archaeological Science*, Oxford, Clarendon 63–108

Gamble C 1986, *The Palaeolithic Settlement of Europe*, Cambridge University Press

Gathercole P & Lowenthal D (eds) 1990, *The Politics of the Past*, London, Unwin Hyman One

World Archaeology 12

Gero J M & Conkey M W (eds) 1991, *Engendering Archaeology: Women and prehistory*, Oxford, Basil Blackwell

Gibbon G 1989, *Explanation in Archaeology*, Oxford, Blackwell

Gilchrist R 1991, 'Women's archaeology? Political feminism, gender theory and historical revision', *Antiquity* 65 495–501

Gillam J P 1957, 'Types of Roman coarse pottery vessels in northern Britain', *Archaeol Aeliana* 35 180–251

Gingell C 1982, 'Excavation of an Iron Age enclosure at Groundwell Farm, Blunsdon St Andrew, 1976–7', *Wilts Archaeol Mag* 76 33–75

Glover E Glover I & Vita-Finzi C 1990, 'First-order 14C dating of marine molluscs in archaeology', *Antiquity* 64 562–6

Gough R (trans and ed) 1789, Camden W, *Britannia*, London

Gould R A 1990, *Recovering the Past*, Albuquerque, Univ of New Mexico Press

Gould S J 1987, *Time's Arrow, Time's Cycle; Myth and metaphor in the discovery of geological time*, Harmondsworth, Penguin

Gowlett J 1984, *Ascent to Civilization: The archaeology of early man*, New York, McGraw-Hill

Graslund B 1987, *The Birth of Prehistoric Chronology: Dating methods and dating systems in nineteenth-century Scandinavian archaeology*, Cambridge Univ Press

Grayson D K 1983, *The Establishment of Human Antiquity*, London Academic Press

Grayson D K 1984, *Quantitative Zooarchaeology: Topics in the analysis of archaeological faunas*, London, Acad Press

Green J 1990, *Maritime Archaeology: A technical handbook*, London,

Academic Press

Greene J P 1989, *Norton Priory: The archaeology of a medieval religious house*, Cambridge Univ Press

Greene J P & Greene K 1970, 'A trial excavation on a Romano-British site at Clanacombe, Thurlestone', *Proc Devon Archaeol Soc* 28 130–6

Greene K 1978, 'Apperley Dene Roman fortlet: a re-examination 1974–5', *Archaeol Aeliana* 6 29–59

Greene K 1986, *The Archaeology of the Roman Economy*, London, Batsford

Greene K 1987, 'Gothic material culture', in Hodder I, *Archaeology as Long Term History*, Cambridge Univ Press, 117–31

Greenfield J 1989, *The Return of Cultural Treasures*, Cambridge Univ Press

Greeves T 1989, 'Archaeology and the Green Movement: A case for perestroika', *Antiquity* 63 659–65

Griffith F M 1990, 'Aerial reconnaissance in mainland Britain in the summer of 1989', *Antiquity* 64 14–33

Grimm J L 1970, *Archaeological Investigation of Fort Ligonier 1960–1965*, Pittsburgh, Annals of Carnegie Museum 42

Groeneman-van Waateringe W & Wijngaarden-Bakker L 1987, *Farm Life in a Carolingian Village: A model based on botanical and zoological data from an excavated site*, Assen, Van Gorcum/Univ Amsterdam

Guilday J E 1970, 'Animal remains from archaeological excavations at Fort Ligonier', *Ann Carnegie Mus* 42 177–86

Hallam A 1989, *Great Geological Controversies*, 2nd ed, Oxford Univ Press

Hamerow H 1993, *Excavations at Mucking 2: The Anglo-Saxon settlement*, London, English Heritage

Archaeol Rep 21

Hansen J P H *et al* (ed) 1991, *The Greenland Mummies*, London, British Museum

Hanson W S & Rahtz P A 1988, 'Video recording on excavations', *Antiquity* 62 106–11

Hanson W S *et al* 1979, 'The Agricolan supply base at Red House, Corbridge', *Archaeol Aeliana* 7 1–97

Harris D & Thomas K (eds) 1991, *Modelling Ecological Change*, London, Institute of Archaeology

Harris E C 1977, 'Units of archaeological stratification', *Norweg Archaeol Rev* 10 84–94

Harris E C 1989, *Principles of Archaeological Stratigraphy*, 2nd ed, London, Academic Press

Harris E C Brown M R & Brown G J (eds) 1993, *Practices of Archaeological Stratigraphy*, London, Academic Press

Haselgrove C *et al* 1990, 'Stanwick, North Yorkshire, part 3: excavations on earthwork sites 1981–86', *Archaeol J* 147 37–90

Hatt G 1957, 'Nørre Fjand, an early Iron Age village in west Jutland', *Arkaeol Kunsthist Skr Dan Vid Selsk* 2.2

Hawkes J 1982, *Mortimer Wheeler: Adventurer in archaeology*, London, Weidenfeld & Nicolson

Hedeager L 1992, *Iron-age Societies: From tribe to state in northern Europe, 500 BC to AD 700*, Oxford, Blackwell

Hedges J W 1983, *Isbister: A chambered tomb in Orkney*, Oxford, Brit Archaeol Rep 115

Hedges R E M & Sykes B C 1992, 'Biomolecular archaeology: past, present and future', in Pollard A M, *New Developments in Archaeological Science*, Oxford, Clarendon 267–83

Henderson J (ed) 1989, *Scientific Analysis in Archaeology*, Oxford,

Bibliography

Oxford Univ Committee Archaeol

Hewison R 1987, *The Heritage Industry: Britain in a climate of decline*, London, Methuen

Hillam J *et al* 1990, 'Dendrochronology of the English Neolithic', *Antiquity* 64 210–20

Hind J G F 1980, 'The Romano-British name for Corbridge', *Britannia* 11 165–71

Hodder I 1982, *The Present Past: An introduction to anthropology for archaeologists*, London, Batsford

Hodder I 1982, *Symbols in Action: Ethnoarchaeological studies of material culture*, Cambridge Univ Press

Hodder I 1991, *Reading the Past: Current approaches to interpretation in archaeology*, 2nd edition, Cambridge Univ Press

Hodder I 1992, *Theory and Practice in Archaeology*, London, Routledge

Hodder I & Orton C 1976, *Spatial Analysis in Archaeology*, Cambridge Univ Press

Hodder I & Shanks M (eds) 1993, *Interpretive Archaeologies: Finding meaning in the past*, London, Routledge

Hodges H (ed) 1987, *In Situ Archaeological Conservation*, Santa Monica, J Paul Getty Mus

Hodges R 1991, *Wall-to-wall History: The story of Royston Grange*, London, Duckworth

Hole F *et al* 1969, *Prehistory and Human Ecology of the Deh Luran Plain*, Ann Arbor, Univ of Michigan Mus of Anthropology

Holliday V T (ed) 1992, *Soils in Archaeology: Landscape evolution and human occupation*, Washington, Smithsonian Inst

Hooper-Greenhill E 1992, *Museums and the Shaping of Knowledge*, London, Routledge

Horne P D 1985, 'A review of the evidence of human endoparasitism in the pre-Columbian new world through the study of coprolites', *J Archaeol Sci* 12 299–310

Horsley J 1732, *Britannia Romana*, London, Osborne & Longman

Hoskins W G 1988, *The Making of the English Landscape*, London, Hodder and Stoughton

Hubert J 1989, 'A proper place for the dead: a critical review of the reburial issue', in Layton R, *Conflict in the Archaeology of Living Traditions*, London, Unwin Hyman, One World Archaeology 8 131–66

Hudson K 1987, *Museums of Influence*, Cambridge Univ Press

Hughes M 1991, 'Tracing to source', in Bowman S, *Science and the Past*, London, British Museum 99–116

Hughes M J *et al* (ed) 1991, *Neutron Activation and Plasma Emission Spectrometric Analysis in Archaeology: Techniques and applications*, London, British Museum Occ Pap 82

Humphreys S C & King H (ed) 1981, *Mortality and Immortality: The anthropology and archaeology of death*, London, Academic Press

Impey O & MacGregor A (ed) 1985, *The Origins of Museums: The cabinet of curiosities in sixteenth- and seventeenth-century Europe*, Oxford, Clarendon

Jashemski W F 1979, *The Gardens of Pompeii*, New York, Caratras Bros

Jenkins 1980, *The Boat Beneath the Pyramid: King Cheops' royal ship*, London, Thames & Hudson

Johanson D & Shreeve J 1991, *Lucy's Child: The discovery of a human ancestor*, London, Penguin

Jones A 1986, 'Fish bone survival in the digestive systems of the pig, dog and man: some experiments', in Brinkhuizen D C and Clason A T, *Fish and Archaeology: Studies in osteometry, taphonomy, seasonality and fishing methods*. Oxford, Brit Archaeol Rep S294 53–61

Jones A *et al* 1988, 'The worms of Roman horses and other finds of intestinal parasite eggs from unpromising deposits', *Antiquity* 62 275–6

Jones M (ed) 1990, *Fake? The Art of Deception*, London, British Mus

Jones M K (ed) 1988, *Archaeology and the Flora of the British Isles: Human influence on the evolution of plant communities*, Oxford, Oxford Univ Committee Archaeol Monog 14

Jones M K 1992, 'Food remains, food webs and ecosystems', in Pollard A M, *New Developments in archaeological science*, Oxford, Clarendon 209–219

Jones R E & Catling H W (eds) 1986, *Science in Archaeology*, British School of Athens

Jones S 1993, *The Language of the Genes*, London, HarperCollins

Judd N M 1964, *The Architecture of Pueblo Bonito*, Washington, Smithsonian Misc Coll 147.1

Keeley H C M (ed) 1987, *Environmental Archaeology: A regional view 2*, London, English Heritage

Kehoe A B 1989, 'Contextualizing archaeology', in Christensen A L, *Tracing Archaeology's Past: The historiography of archaeology*, Southern Illinois Univ Press 97–106

Kehoe A B 1991, 'No possible, probable shadow of doubt', *Antiquity* 65 129–31

Kempe D R C & Harvey A P (eds) 1983, *The Petrology of Archaeological Artefacts*, London, Clarendon

King A C & Potter T W 1990, 'A new domestic building-façade from Roman Britain', *J Rom Archaeol* 3 195–204

Klein R G & Cruz-Uribe K 1984, *The Analysis of Animal Bones from Archaeological Sites*, Chicago

Univ Press

Knowles W & Forster R 1910, *The Romano-British Site at Corstopitum: An account of the excavations during 1909*, London and Newcastle upon Tyne

Kucera V *et al* 1991, ' "Shared Principles": a cooperation agreement between a Native American group and archaeologists', *Antiquity* 65 917

Kuper A 1988, *The Invention of Primitive Society: Transformations of an illusion*, London, Routledge

Lamberg-Karlovsky C C (ed) 1991, *Archaeological Thought in America*, Cambridge Univ Press

Lambert P M & Walker P L 1991, 'Physical anthropological evidence for the evolution of social complexity in coastal southern California', *Antiquity* 65 870–8

Lane-Fox A 1875, 'On the evolution of culture', *Notices Proc Roy Inst Grt Brit* 7 496–520

Lanteigne M P 1991, 'Cation-ratio dating of rock-engravings: a critical appraisal', *Antiquity* 65 292–4

Larsen C U (ed) 1992, *Sites and Monuments: National archaeological records*, Copenhagen, National Museum of Denmark

Layton R (ed) 1989, *Who needs the Past? Indigenous values and archaeology*, London, Unwin Hyman, One World Archaeology 5

Layton R (ed) 1989, *Conflict in the Archaeology of Living Traditions*, London, Unwin Hyman, One World Archaeology 8

Lazreg N Ben & Mattingly D 1992, *Leptiminus (Lamta): A Roman port in Tunisia*, Michigan, J Rom Archaeol Suppl Ser 4

Leakey R & Lewin R 1992, *Origins Reconsidered*, Little, Brown

Lightfoot K G *et al* 1993, 'Prehistoric shelfish-harvesting strategies: implications from the growth patterns of soft-shell

clams (*Mya arenaria*)', *Antiquity* 67 358–69

Lloyd Seton 1980, *Foundations in the Dust: The Story of Mesopotamian Exploration*, London, Thames and Hudson

Loendorf L L 1991, 'Cation-ratio varnish dating and petroglyph chronology in southeastern Colorado', *Antiquity* 65 246–55

Longworth H & Cherry J (eds) 1986, *Archaeology in Britain since 1945*, London, British Museum

Loy T H & Hardy B L 1992, 'Blood residue analysis of 90,000-year-old stone tools from Tabun Cave, Israel', *Antiquity* 66 24–36

Loy T H *et al* 1992, 'Direct evidence for human use of plants 28,000 years ago: starch residues on stone artefacts from the northern Solomon Islands', *Antiquity* 66 898–912

Lynn C J 1989, 'Deer Park farms', *Current Archaeol* 113 193–8

MacDougall H A 1982, *Racial Myth in English History*, Montreal, Harvest House

MacInnes L & Wickham-Jones C (ed) 1992, *All Natural Things: Archaeology and the green debate*, Oxford, Oxbow Monog 21

Maisels C K 1993, *The Near East: Archaeology in the 'Cradle of civilization'*, London, Routledge

Maisels C K 1993, *The Emergence of Civilisation from Hunting and Gathering to Agriculture, Cities and the State of the Near East*, London, Routledge

Malina J & Vašíček Z 1990, *Archaeology Yesterday and Today: The development of archaeology in the sciences and humanities*, Cambridge Univ Press

Mamami Condori C 1989, 'History and prehistory in Bolivia: what about the Indians?', in Layton R, *Conflict in the Archaeology of Living Traditions*, London, Unwin

Hyman, One World Archaeology 8 46–59

Manning S W 1991, 'Approximate calendar date for the first human settlement of Cyprus?', *Antiquity* 65 870–8

Manning S W & Weninger B 1992, 'A light in the dark: archaeological wiggle matching and the absolute chronology of the close of the Aegean Late Bronze Age', *Antiquity* 66 636–63

Manning W H 1981, *Report on the Excavations at Usk 1965–1976: The fortress excavations 1968–71*, Cardiff, Univ Wales Press

MAP 1991, *Management of Archaeological Projects*, London, English Heritage

Marian C W *et al* 1992, 'Hyaenas and bones. ...', *J Archaeol Sci* 19 101–21

Mattingly D J 1992, 'The field survey: strategy, methodology, and preliminary results', in Lazreg N Ben & Mattingly D, *Leptiminus (Lamta): A Roman port in Tunisia*, Michigan, J Rom Archaeol Suppl Ser 4 89–112

McBryde I (ed) 1985, *Who Owns the Past?*, Oxford Univ Press Australia

McDonald W A & Thomas C G 1990, *Progress into the Past: The rediscovery of Mycenean civilization*, 2nd ed, Bloomington, Indiana Univ Press

McGuire R H 1992, *A Marxist Archaeology*, London, Academic Press

McNeal R A 1991, 'Archaeology and the destruction of the later Athenian acropolis', *Antiquity* 65 49–63

Meaden T 1991, *The Goddess of the Stones: The language of the megaliths*, London, Souvenir Press

Milisauskas S & Kruk J 1991, 'Utilization of cattle for traction during the Neolithic in south eastern Poland', *Antiquity* 65 562–6

Millett M & James S 1983, 'Excavations at Cowdery's Down, Basingstoke, Hampshire 1979–81', *Archaeol J* 140 151–279

Millon R 1967, 'Teotihuacan', *Scientific American* June 38–48

Mitchell J G *et al* 1984, 'Potassium-argon ages of schist honestones from the Viking age sites at Kaupang, Aggersborg, and Hedeby', *J Archaeol Sci* 11 171–6

Modderman P 1975, 'Elsloo, a neolithic farming community in the Netherlands', in Bruce-Mitford R L S, *Recent Archaeological Excavations in Europe*, London, 260–86

Montelius O 1903, *Die typologische Methode: Die altere Kulturperioden im Orient und in Europe*, Stockholm, Selbstverlag

Moore P D Webb J A & Collinson M E 1991, *Pollen Analysis*, Oxford, Blackwell Scientific

Morrison J S & Coates J F (eds) 1989, *An Athenian Trireme Reconstructed: The British sea trials of Olympias*, 1987, Oxford, Brit Archaeol Rep S486

Mytum H 1991, *The Origins of Early Christian Ireland*, London, Routledge

Needham S P 1986, 'Radiocarbon: a means to understanding the role of Bronze Age metal work', in Gowlett J & Hedges R, *Archaeological Results from Accelerator Dating*, Oxford, Oxford Univ Committee Archaeol Monog 11 143–50

Northover J P 1989, 'Non-ferrous metallurgy in British archaeology', in Henderson J, *Scientific Analysis in Archaeology*, Oxford, Oxford Univ Committee Archaeol Monog 19, 213–36

Oates D J 1976, *The Rise of Civilisation*, Oxford, Elsevier/Phaidon

Oddy W A (ed) 1980, *Scientific Studies in Numismatics*, London, British Museum

Oddy W A (ed) 1991, *Aspects of Early Metallurgy*, 2nd ed, London, British Museum Occ Pap 17

Oddy W A (ed) 1992, *The Art of the Conservator,* London, British Museum

Olsen S L (ed) 1988, *Scanning Electron Microscopy in Archaeology*, Oxford, Brit Archaeol Rep S452

Ortner D J & Puschan W G J 1985, *Identification of Pathological Conditions in Human Skeletal Remains*, Smithsonian Inst Press

Ottaway B S (ed) 1984, *Archaeology, Dendrochronology and the Radiocarbon Calibration Curve*, Edinburgh Univ Press

Pader E J 1981, *An Analysis of Symbolic and SocialRelations from Mortuary Remains*, Sheffield, Dept Archaeol and Prehist

Parker A J 1992, *Ancient Shipwrecks of the Mediterranean and the Roman Provinces*, Oxford, Brit Archaeol Rep S580

Parkes P A 1986, *Current Scientific Techniques in Archaeology*, London, Routledge

Pearsall D M 1989, *Paleoethnobotany: A handbook of procedures*, London, Academic Press

Pearson G W 1987, 'How to cope with calibration', *Antiquity* 61 98–103

Petrie W F 1899, 'Sequences in prehistoric remains', *J Royal Anthr Inst* 29 295–301

Petrie W F 1920, *Prehistoric Egypt*, London, British School of Archaeology in Egypt

Piggott S 1965, *Ancient Europe from the Beginnings of Agriculture to Classical Antiquity*, Edinburgh Univ Press

Piggott S 1976, *Ruins in a Landscape: Essays in antiquarianism*, Edinburgh, Univ Press

Piggott S 1979, *Antiquity Depicted: Aspects of archaeological illustra-*

tion, London, Thames and Hudson

Piggott S 1982, ' "Vast perennial memorials": the first antiquaries look at megaliths', in Evans J D, Cunliffe B & Renfrew C, *Antiquity and Man: Essays in honour of Glyn Daniel*, London, Thames and Hudson 19–25

Piggott S 1985, *William Stukeley, an 18th century Antiquary*, London, Thames and Hudson

Piggott S 1989, *Ancient Britons and the Antiquarian Imagination: Ideas from the Renaissance to the Regency*, London, Thames and Hudson

Pitt Rivers A 1887–98, *Excavations in Cranborne Chase*, 1887, 1888, 1892, 1898, London, privately published

Pollard A M (ed) 1992, *New Developments in Archaeological Science: A joint symposium of the Royal Society and the British Academy,* February 1991, Oxford Univ Press (= Proc Brit Acad 77)

Popham M R 1970, *The Destruction of the Palace at Knossos: Pottery of the Late Minoan IIIA Period*, Gothenburg, Stud Medit Archaeol 12

Prestwich J 1860, 'On the occurence of flint implements, associated with the remains of extinct mammalia, in beds of a late geological period', *Proc Royal Soc London* 10 50–9

Price T Douglas (ed) 1989, *The Chemistry of Prehistoric Human Bone*, Cambridge Univ Press

Pryor F 1993, *Flag Fen: Prehistoric fenland centre*, London, English Heritage/Batsford

Rackham J 1994, *Interpreting the Past: Animal bones*, London, British Museum

Rackham O 1987, *The History of the Countryside*, London, Dent

Reilly P & Rahtz S (ed) 1992, *Archaeology and the Information*

Age: A global perspective, London, Routledge, One World Archaeology 21

Renfrew C (ed) 1983, *The Megalithic Monuments of Western Europe: The latest evidence*, London, Thames and Hudson

Renfrew C 1973, *Before Civilization: The radio-carbon revolution and prehistoric Europe*, London, Cape

Renfrew C 1979, *Investigations in Orkney*, London, Soc of Antiqs Res Rep 38

Renfrew C 1982, *Towards an Archaeology of Mind*, Cambridge Univ Press

Renfrew C 1984, *Approaches to Social Archaeology*, Edinburgh, Univ Press

Renfrew C 1992, 'The identity and future of archaeological science', in Pollard A M, *New Developments in Archaeological Science*, Oxford, Clarendon 285–93

Renfrew C & Bahn P 1991, *Archaeology: Theories, methods, and practice*, London, Thames and Hudson

Renfrew C & Wagstaff J M (ed) 1982, *An Island Polity: The archaeology of exploitation in Melos*, Cambridge, Univ Press

Reynolds P J 1979, *Iron Age Farm: The Butser experiment*, London, British Museum

Reynolds P J 1987, *Ancient Farming*, Princes Risborough, Shire Archaeology 50

Richards J 1990, *The Stonehenge Environs Project*, London, HBMC Archaeol Rep 16

Richards J D 1987, *The Significance of Form and Decoration of Anglo-Saxon Cremation Urns*, Oxford, Brit Archaeol Rep 166

Riley D N 1987, *Air Photography and Archaeology*, London, Duckworth

Roberts C A *et al* (ed) 1989, *Burial Archaeology: Current research,*

methods and developments, Oxford, Brit Arch Rep 211

Roberts N 1989, *The Holocene: An environmental history*, Oxford, Blackwell

Robinson D E (ed) 1990, *Experimentation and Reconstruction in Environmental Archaeology*, Oxford, Oxbow Monograph

Rodwell K & W 1981, 'Barton on Humber', *Current Archaeol* 78 208–15

Rodwell W 1989, *Church Archaeology*, London, Batsford/English Heritage

Rodwell W & K 1985, *Rivenhall: Investigation of a villa, church, and village, 1950–1977,* London, Council Brit Archaeol Res Rep 55

Ross S *et al* (ed) 1991, *Computing for Archaeologists*, Oxford, Oxford Univ Comm Arch Monog 18

Rossi P 1984, *The Dark Abyss of Time: The history of the earth and the history of nations from Hooke to Vico*, Chicago Univ Press

Rule M 1982, *The Mary Rose: The excavation and raising of Henry VIII's flagship*, London, Conway Press

Scarre C *et al* 1993, 'New radiocarbon dates from Bougon and the chronology of French passage-graves', *Antiquity* 67 856–9

Schiffer M B 1976, *Behavioral Archaeology*, New York, Academic Press

Schiffer M B 1987, *Formation Processes of the Archaeological Record*, Albuquerque, Univ of New Mexico Press

Schliemann H 1880, *Ilios: The city and country of the Trojans*, London, John Murray

Schweingruber F H 1987, *Tree Rings: Basics and applications of dendrochronology*, Dordrecht, Reidel

Scollar I *et al* (eds) 1990, *Archaeological Prospecting and Remote*

Sensing, Cambridge Univ Press

Sealy J 1986, *Stable Carbon Isotopes and Prehistoric Diets in the South-western Cape Province, South Africa*, Oxford, Brit Archaeol Rep S293

Shackleton J & Elderfield H 1990, 'Strontium isotope dating of the source of Neolithic European Spondylus shell artefacts', *Antiquity* 64 312–15

Shackley M L 1982, *Environmental Archaeology*, London, Allen Unwin

Shanks M 1991, *Experiencing the Past: On the character of archaeology*, London, Routledge

Shanks M & Tilley C 1987, *Social Theory and Archaeology*, Cambridge, Polity Press

Shanks M & Tilley C 1992, *Reconstructing Archaeology: Theory and practice*, 2nd ed, London, Routledge

Sharples N M 1991, *Maiden Castle*, London, Batsford

Shennan I & Donoghue D 1992, 'Remote sensing in archaeological research', in Pollard A M, *New Developments in Archaeological Science*, Oxford, Clarendon 223–32

Shennan S 1985, *Experiments in the Collection and Analysis of Archaeological Survey Data: The east Hampshire survey*, Sheffield, Univ of Archaeol

Shennan S 1988, *Quantifying Archaeology,* Edinburgh Univ Press

Sherratt A 1980, *The Cambridge Encyclopedia of Archaeology*, Cambridge Univ Press

Simmons I G 1989, *Changing the Face of the Earth: Culture, environment and history*, Oxford, Basil Blackwell

Sklenar K 1983, *Archaeology in Central Europe: The first 500 years*, Leicester Univ Press

Smith C 1992, *Late Stone Age Hunters of the British Isles,*

London, Routledge

Smith R A 1920, *A Guide to the Antiquities of the Bronze Age*, 2nd ed, London, British Museum

South S 1977, *Method and Theory in Historical Archaeology*, New York, Academic Press

Spencer F 1990, *Piltdown: A scientific forgery*, London, Natural Hist Mus Spindler K 1994, *The Man in the Ice*, London, Weidenfeld and Nicolson

Spoerry P (ed) 1992, *Geoprospection in the Archaeological Landscape*, Oxford, Oxbow Monog 18

Stead I M 1991, 'The Snettisham Treasure: excavations in 1990', *Antiquity* 65 447–65

Stead I M *et al* (ed) 1986, *Lindow Man: The body in the bog*, London, British Museum

Stein J K (ed) 1992, *Deciphering a Shell Midden*, London, Academic Press

Stove G C & Addyman P V 1989, 'Ground probing impulse radar: an experiment in archaeological remote sensing at York', *Antiquity* 63 337–42

Stringer C B 1986, 'Direct dates for the fossil hominid record', in Gowlett J & Hedges R, *Archaeological Results from Accelerator Dating*, Oxford, Oxford Univ Committee Archaeol Monog 11 45–50

Stuart J & Revett N 1762-1830, *The Antiquities of Athens*, 5 vols 1762, 1787, 1794, 1816, 1830

Stuiver M Long A & Kra R (eds) 1993, *Calibration 1993,* = *Radiocarbon 35.1*, Tucson, Univ of Arizona

Taylor R E (ed) 1976, *Advances in Obsidian Glass Studies: Archae ological and geochemical perpectives*, Park Ridge NJ, Noyes Press

Taylor R E 1987, *Radiocarbon Dating: An archaeological perspective*, London, Acad Press

Taylor R E Long A & Kra R S (eds) 1992, *Radiocarbon after Four Decades: An interdisciplinary per spective*, California Conf, 1990, Berlin, Springer

Thompson M W 1977, *General Pitt-Rivers: Evolution and archaeology in the nineteenth century,* Bradford-on-Avon, Moonraker

Tilley A 1992, 'Three men to a room – a completely different trireme', *Antiquity* 66 599–610

Tite M S 1991, 'Archaeological science – past achievements and future prospects', *Archaeometry* 32.3 139–51

Tite M S 1992, 'The impact of electron microscopy on ceramic studies', in Pollard A M, *New Developments in Archaeological Science,* Oxford, Clarendon 111–31

Trigger B G 1980, *Gordon Childe: Revolutions in archaeology,* London, Thames and Hudson

Trigger B G 1989, *A History of Archaeological Thought*, Cambridge Univ Press

Tylecote R F & Gilmour B J J 1986, *The Metallography of Early Ferrous Edge Tools and Edged Weapons,* Oxford, Brit Archaeol Rep 155

Van der Merwe N J 1992, 'Light stable isotopes and the reconstruction of prehistoric diets', in Pollard A M, *New Developments in Archaeological Science*, Oxford, Clarendon 247–64

Veen M van der 1992, *Crop Husbandry Regimes: An archaeobotanical study of farming in northern England 1000 BC–AD 500*, Collis, Sheffield Archaeol Monog 3

Wacher J S 1974, *The Towns of Roman Britain*, London, Batsford

Wagstaff J M (ed) 1987, *Landscape and Culture: Geographical and archaeological perspectives*, Oxford, Blackwell

Walker S 1984, 'Marble origins by isotopic analysis', *World Archaeol-ogy* 16.2 204–21

Weiss R 1969, *The Renaissance Discovery of Classical Antiquity*, Oxford, Blackwell (new ed 1988)

Welsh F 1988, *Building the Trireme*, London, Constable

Wheeler A & Jones A 1989, *Fishes*, Cambridge Univ Press

Wheeler R E M 1923, *Segontium and the Roman Occupation of Wales*, London, Hon Soc Cymmrodorion

Wheeler R E M 1954, *The Stanwick Fortifications*, Oxford, Rep Res Comm Soc Antiq London 17

Wheeler R E M 1954, *Archaeology from the Earth*, Harmondsworth, Penguin

Wheeler R E M 1955, *Still Digging*, London, Michael Joseph

Wheeler R E M & Wheeler T V 1936, *Verulamium: A Belgic and two Roman cities*, Oxford, Res Rep Soc Antiq London 11

Whimster R 1989, *The Emerging Past: Air photography and the buried landscape*, London, RCHME

Wigley T M L *et al* (ed) 1981, *Climate and History*, Cambridge Univ Press

Willey G R & Sabloff J A 1980, A History of *American Archaeology*, 2nd ed, San Francisco, Freeman

Willey P 1992, *Prehistoric Warfare on the Great Plains: Skeletal analysis of the Crow Creek massacre victims*, Hamden CT, Garland

Williams S 1991, *Fantastic Archaeology: The wild side of North American prehistory*, Washington, Smithsonian Institute Press

Williams-Thorpe O & Thorpe R S 1992, 'Geochemistry, sources and transport of the Stonehenge bluestones', in Pollard A M, *New Developments in Archaeological Science*, Oxford, Clarendon 133–61

Wilson D M 1989, *The British Museum: Purpose and politics,*

London, British Museum

Wilson D R 1982, *Air Photo Interpretation for Archaeologists*, London, Batsford

Wood J T 1877, *Discoveries at Ephesus*, London, Longman Green

Woolley L 1907, 'Corstopitum: provisional report on the excavations in 1906', *Archaeologia Aeliana* 3 161–86

Woolley Sir L 1953, *Spadework*, London, Lutterworth Press

Worsaae J J A (trans W J Thomas) 1849, *Primeval Antiquities of Denmark*, London, Parker

Yoffee N & Sherratt A (eds) 1993, *Archaeological Theory: Who sets the agenda?*, Cambridge Univ Press

Zeuner F E 1946, *Dating the Past: An introduction to geochronology*, London, Methuen

Zimmerman L J 1989, 'Made radical by my own: an archaeologist learns to accept reburial', in Layton R, *Conflict in the Archaeology of Living Traditions*, London, Unwin Hyman, One World Archaeology 8 60–7

Zivanovic S 1982, *Ancient Diseases: The elements of palaeopathology*, London, Routledge

Index